Aristocrats and Statehood in Western Iberia, 300–600 C.E.

EMPIRE AND AFTER

Series Editor: Clifford Ando

A complete list of books in the series is available from the publisher.

ARISTOCRATS AND STATEHOOD IN WESTERN IBERIA, 300–600 C.E.

DAMIÁN FERNÁNDEZ

PENN

UNIVERSITY OF PENNSYLVANIA PRESS

PHILADELPHIA

Published by
University of Pennsylvania Press
Philadelphia, Pennsylvania 19104-4112
www.upenn.edu/pennpress

Printed in the United States of America on acid-free paper
10 9 8 7 6 5 4 3 2 1

Library of Congress Cataloging-in-Publication Data

Names: Fernández, Damián, author.
Title: Aristocrats and statehood in Western Iberia, 300–600
    C.E. / Damián Fernández.
Other titles: Empire and after.
Description: 1st edition. | Philadelphia : University of
    Pennsylvania Press, [2017] | Series: Empire and after |
    Includes bibliographical references and index.
Identifiers: LCCN 2017009403 | ISBN 978-0-8122-4946-0
    (hardcover : alk. paper)
Subjects: LCSH: Aristocracy (Social class)—Iberian
    Peninsula—History—To 1500. | Iberian Peninsula—
    Politics and government—History—To 1500. | Power
    (Social sciences)—Iberian Peninsula—History—To 1500.
    | Iberian Peninsula—History—To 1500.
Classification: LCC HT653.I24 F47 2017 | DDC
    305.5/209366—dc23
LC record available at https://lccn.loc.gov/2017009403

Para Alfredo, Isaac, Jane y Maruja

CONTENTS

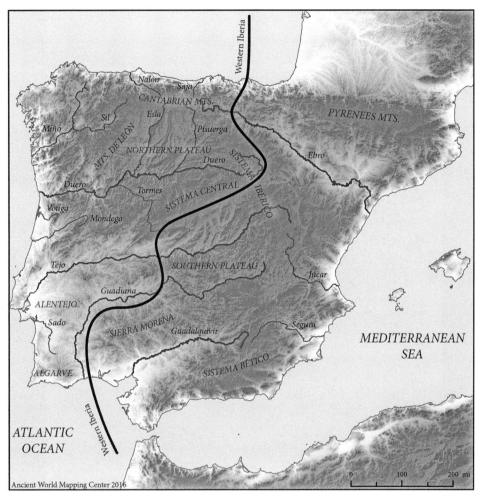

Map 1. Terrain and regions of the Iberian Peninsula.

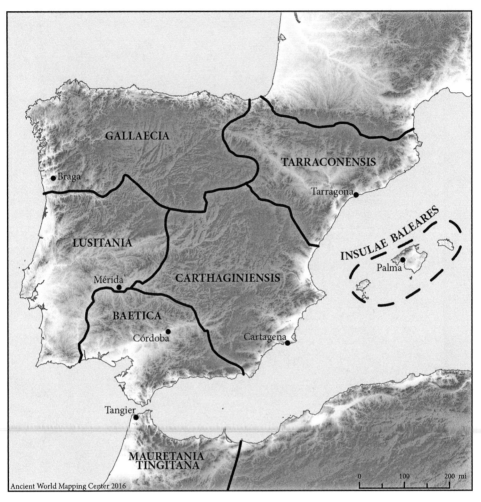

GALLAECIA

TARRACONENSIS

Braga

Tarragona

LUSITANIA

INSULAE BALEARES

CARTHAGINIENSIS

Mérida

Palma

BAETICA

Córdoba

Cartagena

Tangier

MAURETANIA
TINGITANA

0   100   200 mi

Ancient World Mapping Center 2016

Map 2. Approximate late Roman provincial boundaries.

Map 3. The Iberian Peninsula in the sixth century.

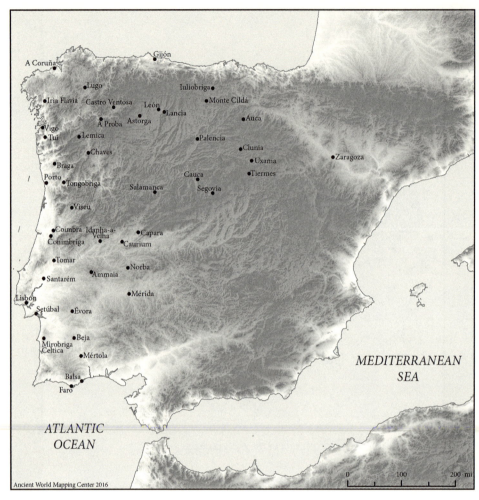

Map 4. Cities and minor towns mentioned in the book.

Map 5. Hilltops and rural sites mentioned in the book.

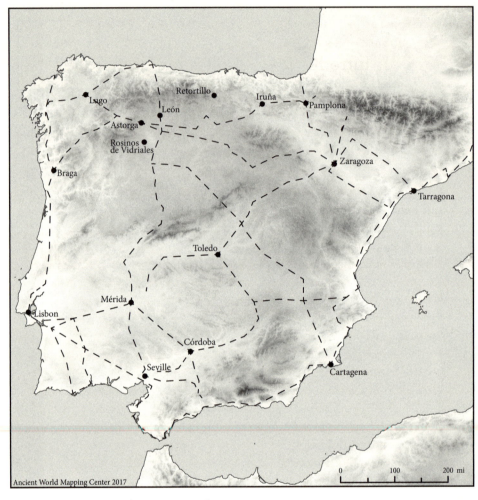

Map 6. Main late antique roads.

Introduction: An Invisible Class
in a Silent Land

This book is about statehood in the westernmost corner of the late antique world. It is neither about late antique state institutions nor about state ideology in late antiquity. Both institutions and ideology play an important role in this book, but its focus lies elsewhere. In the following chapters I will describe the enactment of social power in late antique Western Iberia. I will explain how a class of men (and occasionally women) created, embodied, and reproduced state-sanctioned power in Western Iberia. Simply put, this book will study aristocracy and aristocrats.

I will trace the history of Western Iberian aristocracies in late antiquity, covering the period between the reign of the Roman emperor Diocletian (284–305) and the rule of the Visigoth Reccared (586–601). This book will show how being part of the social elite consisted in enacting statehood at the local level and, hence, pursuing state-sanctioned power. Likewise, conspicuous aristocratic consumption and personal tastes were more than the product of independent cultural developments. Rather, they bespoke efforts to manifest membership in the ruling class of a polity and reveal the competition for power within this class. The ebb and flow of state projects in this remote corner of the late antique world did not result only from events outside of the region. They also, and perhaps predominantly, flowed from the efforts of local individuals to assert their social dominance. Thus this book will emphasize aristocratic agency in the reproduction of state power.

The dramatic dearth of textual evidence poses a serious challenge to the historical reconstruction of Iberian aristocracies. From this perspective, late antique aristocrats in the Iberian Peninsula were an invisible class. Only in a handful of documents do we hear echoes of voices from the dominant social group during the three centuries covered in this book. Not only are aristocracies difficult to trace; the reconstruction of almost every aspect of the social,

cultural, and political life of the peninsula relies on the same handful of scattered texts, making this land between the third and the sixth century a silent
one. Fortunately for this generation of historians, we can now rely on the pa-
tient and uncelebrated feats of Iberian archaeologists over the past three decades. It would be an understatement to say that archaeology has changed our
ability to approach late antique Iberian history. Field surveys, excavations, and
other archaeology-based studies have brought to life a period that was almost
completely in darkness two generations ago. The boom of late antique and
early medieval archaeology has benefited other areas of the Mediterranean
world, but few of these regions needed to fill the gaps of a silent textual record as desperately as the Iberian Peninsula. To put it plainly, this book would
have been impossible thirty years ago.

Through the study of settlement archaeology, daily-life material culture,
and the extant written sources, I will reconstruct the history of late and post-
Roman aristocracies in Western Iberia. The main argument of the book will
be one of concomitant continuity and change. The material record in Western Iberia presents a striking change between the turn of the fourth century
and the end of the sixth century. Cities, monumental buildings in the countryside, nonelite rural settlements, and table wares were markedly different in
the year 300 than they were three centuries later. Although the process of
change was gradual in many cases, there is no doubt that the fifth century
represents a crucial moment of transformation: the Roman administration
vanished from the peninsula. And yet the sudden transformation of material
culture seems not to match the slower paced changes affecting other spheres
of social life. I will argue that the drastic changes in material culture must be
understood as the way individuals with claims to power showed that they participated in governing their communities and sometimes beyond. They expressed tastes, behaviors, and consumption styles associated with the social
distinction of ruling classes. Rather than remain passive historical subjects,
aristocrats actively pursued strategies to secure their social standing. Through
changing strategies they adapted to and embraced different state projects to
maintain their supremacy as a class.

Western Iberia: Connectivity and Microdiversity

My analysis will be restricted to the region I call Western Iberia (or Atlantic
Iberia). By this I refer to the territories of the Douro (or Duero) River Basin

(including most of the Cantabrian Mountains), northwestern Iberia, the lower and middle Tejo- (or Tajo) River Basin, and the Guadiana River Basin. In late Roman times, Western Iberia was organized into two provinces, Lusitania and Gallaecia.[1] In terms of modern political divisions, Western Iberia includes all of Portugal, the Spanish regions of Extremadura and Castilla-León, (and small sections of Castilla–La Mancha, Galicia), Asturias, and Cantabria. Occasionally, I will draw on examples from nearby regions (the rest of Castilla–La Mancha, La Rioja, Euskadi [Basque country], Navarra, and parts of Aragón) for comparative purposes, since modern (and ancient) political boundaries do not always do justice to the similarities between natural and social landscapes.

While late antique Iberia has usually been treated as a unit, there is nothing natural about this choice beyond its peninsular character and the existence of a specific geographical term in Roman times—Hispania. Yet even the way in which Romans referred to Iberia was certainly more complex, since the peninsula was also perceived as a group of regions, of various Hispaniae.[2] In the late antique political map of the western Mediterranean region, the peninsula was part of larger political-administrative territories, including northern Morocco until the fifth century and different regions of southern Gaul thereafter. Furthermore, the peninsula was divided politically between the fifth and the early seventh century. Northwestern and, later, southeastern Hispania were part of different polities, Suevic and Byzantine, respectively.

My criterion to define Western Iberia is based on connectivity infrastructure, which not only facilitated human contacts but also structured social interaction and aristocratic strategies beyond highly localized environments.[3] As in other parts of the empire, the geographical setting of river valleys favored the most direct and regular form of supralocal elite interaction.[4] While the social horizons of individuals with claims to political ascendancy forced them to look beyond the regional and microregional levels, elite competition and emulation depended on continuous interactions with one's peers in the proximate regional context. Connectivity created discrete aristocratic worlds where most aristocrats' social experience unfolded.

While the Iberian Peninsula was part of the broader pan-Mediterranean world, the region studied in this book was further removed from the networks provided by the Mediterranean Sea. Supralocal connectivity was achieved primarily through land routes and supplemented with seasonal navigation in the Atlantic Ocean.[5] Western Iberia, as understood here, included most of the territories in the peninsula that belonged to river systems (and valleys) flowing into the Atlantic Ocean. The most prominent of these rivers are the

Guadiana, Tejo (or Tajo), Douro (or Duero), and Miño-Sil.[6] Smaller, lesser-known rivers such as the Mondego, Sado, Vouga, Nalón, or Saja supplemented the main hydrographic basins. The place of these rivers in the natural infrastructure of connectivity was not due to their navigability. In fact, large vessels with deep draft could rarely navigate these rivers beyond their lower courses. They presented seasonal and intraseasonal variations in terms of flow, which made navigation, even when it was possible, unpredictable—although less so than in rivers flowing to the Mediterranean.[7] Occasionally, the middle and upper courses of rivers flowing to the Atlantic could be navigated with smaller vessels.[8] The valleys formed by these rivers facilitated land routes in an intricate landscape. The Roman road system partially relied on the natural (lowlands) and human (cities) infrastructure along these basins—especially along east–west axes.[9]

While the Atlantic Ocean was a nexus between the Mediterranean Sea and Western Iberian river valleys, oceanic navigation presented its own challenges, and sea connectivity was less intense than in the Mediterranean world.[10] One exception was the Guadalquivir River Valley, a region I excluded from the scope of this book, even though the river flows into the Atlantic. The mouth of the Guadalquivir forms part of a very specific microregion, the so-called Circle of the Straits.[11] This area had been a zone of intense contact with the Mediterranean Sea since the beginning of the Iron Age or even earlier.[12] One should consider the Circle of the Straits a frontier zone between the Atlantic and the Mediterranean. The region of Andalucía had close commercial, cultural, and even climatic ties with the Mediterranean world. The Guadalquivir valley was part of a continuum of coastal regions in southern and eastern Iberia, which also included modern Valencia and Catalunya, as well as the inland areas of Murcia, Aragón, and, to a certain extent, Castilla–La Mancha. Throughout this work, I will refer to all these regions as Mediterranean Iberia.

The umbrella denomination "Western Iberia" does not do justice to the rich diversity of landscapes and climatic conditions in this half of the peninsula. For the sake of simplicity, I will divide Atlantic Iberia into three regions: central and southern Lusitania, northwestern Iberia, and the northern plateau. The first of these regions includes most of Portugal south of the Mondego River and Spanish Extremadura. Central and southern Lusitania was in many aspects a continuation of the Mediterranean world. Temperatures and rainfall made this region of the peninsula particularly suited to the traditional Greco-Roman crops—olive trees, wheat, and vineyards. On the coasts, the natural conditions and the wealth of oceanic resources encouraged the production of fish sauce and salted fish conserves during the Roman period. Despite the unity suggested by the Roman province of Lusitania, this region included varied and diverse microregions. The most uniform area was the interior of modern Portuguese Alentejo and Spanish Extremadura. The fertile plains enjoyed relatively mild winters and dry, hot summers. The inland region was connected to the coast by the main vectors of transportation in the ancient world—the river valleys. Two large rivers, the Guadiana and the Tejo, as well other minor rivers, linked the interior plains with the Atlantic coast. The northern fringes were more fragmented in terms of geography as the region became mountainous. The southernmost part of Lusitania, modern Algarve, was a microregion in itself, with close links to the Guadalquivir Valley. The mouths of the Guadiana and, especially, the Tejo were major route nodes going back to the exchange networks of the Bronze Age. These were points of intense Mediterranean–Atlantic interaction.

In the interior of the peninsula, we find the central plateau (or meseta). Here, the mountains of the Sistema Central create a split between the northern and the southern part of the meseta. I will focus on the northern part of the plateau, which had closer links to the Atlantic world in late antiquity. The northern meseta is almost completely surrounded by mountains of different heights, a circumstance that gives the area its continental climate, with arid, hot summers and cold winters. The structuring axis of this region is the Duero River, which receives its waters from a series of secondary rivers coming down the slopes of the Cantabrian Mountains in the north and the fringes of the Sistema Central in the south. The general flatness of the terrain is interrupted by pronounced hills, the top of which have commanding views over the nearby territory. During late antiquity, human interaction among communities in individual valley lowlands and hills created specific microregions in the plateau. The fertility of the land and the relatively flat terrain favored dry agriculture, including the Mediterranean triad complemented by extensive husbandry. By the late third century, most of the northern plateau became part of the province of Gallaecia. A dense road network crisscrossed the plateau and connected it with main administrative centers and routes. To the west, the road system linked the western frontier of the meseta, Astorga, with the area of Braga and the Atlantic routes. Astorga was an important node in the Vía de la Plata, a road (or road system) that linked northern Iberia with Baetica through the city of Mérida. To the east, the road system connected the plateau with the upper Ebro River Valley. Through this connection, the northern meseta reached communities with more immediate access to the

Mediterranean and southern Gaul. Land roads also connected the plateau with the Atlantic Ocean and the Bay of Biscay through the Cantabrian Mountains, reaching the small city-ports that dotted the northern coast of the peninsula.

The third region is northwestern Iberia, a land that roughly includes northern Portugal and Galicia, but extends to the west into the fringes of the meseta. This region has an Atlantic climate, which means considerable rainfall and more moderate variations in temperature between winter and summer than the other two regions. An intricate terrain of hills, mountains, and valleys extend from the fringes of the plateau to the coast. Agriculture and husbandry was widely practiced in the area, but with certain differences when compared to Lusitania and the plateau. Rye adapted better to the colder temperatures than wheat, although traditionally both cereals were cultivated in the region. Additionally, with the exception of specific pockets in northern Portugal and areas bordering the meseta, vineyards and olive trees did not grow here. The thick temperate forest included fruit trees that were an essential part of the traditional economy of northwestern Iberia. The terrain and vegetation, however, favored animal farming, which was more important for the local economy than in the other regions of Atlantic Iberia. Northwestern Iberia was also rich in minerals, which were extracted throughout antiquity. Due to its intricate landscape, northwestern Iberia was a highly fragmented region. However, there was connectivity between its microregions in ancient and medieval times. The Roman administration developed road networks that linked the two main Roman cities (Braga and Lugo) with Lusitania in the south and the plateau to the east through the city of Astorga. It is therefore hardly surprising that settlement choices traditionally favored hilltop sites, even though the preference for lowland settlement increased after the second century CE. Hilltop sites and the few lowland towns were situated along communication axes. The Duero and Miño Rivers and a considerable number of other minor rivers provided the natural scaffolding for the route network. Navigation along the oceanic coast linked a myriad of estuaries (known as *rías*) that sheltered a considerable number of minor settlements.

In this book, I will analyze the Cantabrian basin as an extension of either northwestern Iberia or the northern meseta, depending on the period and the specific layer of analysis. However, from the point of view of both landscape and climate, the Cantabrian basin shared more with the former than the latter, including an Atlantic climate and an intricate mountainous landscape with river valleys streaming to the Bay of Biscay. A substantial difference is the average height of the mountains, which are somewhat higher than in northwestern Iberia. Agriculture is possible in this region, although usually concentrated in the pockets created by valleys among the high mountains. Pastoralism was better adapted to the environment and had been a central economic activity since before the Roman conquest. The Cantabrian basin seems to have been far less, or at least less densely, populated than other areas of Iberia. Small towns dotted the coast and served as commercial nodes between the inland valleys and the Mediterranean–Atlantic network. In the interior, a handful of small-sized cities and a larger, though never impressive, number of hilltop sites served as centers for economic and, presumably, administrative life. While the intricate terrain was a barrier to smooth communication, the region was never cut off from the surrounding areas. Cabotage navigation linked the coast to major ports in the Atlantic façade and a well-developed network of Roman roads linked the coast to the interior plateau throughout imperial times and most likely later.

Western Iberia as defined in the previous paragraphs was never an isolated region. Moreover, border microregions such as the upper Tejo or upper Ebro Valleys shared several structural and social features with Western Iberia, which will allow me to draw on them to illustrate historical developments in Atlantic Iberia. There is, however, an important reason to limit the geographical scope of my analysis to the regions I described in the previous paragraphs. As this book stresses, state projects were key to defining aristocratic strategies. As a result, the impact of Roman provincial organization at the beginning of the period cannot be underestimated. As I indicated earlier, all the regions analyzed in this book were part of two late Roman provinces (Gallaecia and Lusitania) by the late third century. While elite sociability was not limited by provincial boundaries, provincial capitals and administrative structures created a powerful geographical ordering for most people in the region, as later chapters will show. Although the institutional framework changed throughout the course of late antiquity, it provides a solid starting point for the study of aristocracies and their enactment of state projects.

Late Antique State Projects: Late Roman, Post-Roman, and Visigothic

Three main moments of state redefinition punctuated the history of late antique Western Iberia. The first moment took place in the late third and early fourth centuries, marking the beginning of the late Roman period. A series of political and military reforms associated with Diocletian and his immediate successors transformed the way in which the imperial administration had dealt with local communities during the early empire. A more hands-on, centralized bureaucracy brought the imperial administration into the region. The new supraprovincial capital of Mérida in Lusitania now oversaw Roman government in the peninsula and northern Morocco while the new province of Gallaecia was created to encompass the most militarized region of Iberia— the northern plateau and northwestern Iberia. The imperial administration took a firmer grip on key aspects of infrastructural statehood such as tax collection, appointments of civic magistrates, and the use of city lands. Symbolic proximity to the emperor as well as participation in the administration of his mandates became even more crucial for social and political competition at the local level than in the early empire.[13]

The rapid dissolution of the late Roman state program during the first half of the fifth century put an end to uniform aristocratic strategies in Western Iberia. In traditional narratives, this period inaugurated a long-term process of state building that would culminate in the Visigothic kingdom of Toledo, which spanned the mid-sixth to the early eighth century. There is some truth to this picture, as seventh-century Iberia inherited patterns of social and political interaction that were crafted during the fifth and early sixth centuries. However, this narrative tends to assume the incomplete statehood of post-Roman times, portraying it as a period in which a state had to be very slowly rebuilt from the splinters left by the failing Roman state in the peninsula. A closer look at the evidence, however, shows that statehood was rapidly recreated within two generations between the 410s and the 450s. Individuals with claims to social prominence dealt rapidly with the power crisis created by the withdrawal of the imperial administration. In part they continued to use strategies deployed when there was a Roman imperial project in the peninsula, but they also embarked upon new practices that resulted from their interaction with the so-called barbarian armies and leadership.[14] By the second half of the fifth century, Suevic kings had successfully claimed overlordship in most of northwestern Iberia, while the Visigothic rulers considered the rest of the peninsula part of their kingdom.

The late sixth century would mark the beginning of a new unification process. Between the reigns of Reccared (r. 586–601) and Chindaswinth (r. 642–653), a new state project was crafted in the peninsula. The Visigothic kings built on the military conquests of Leovigild (r. 568–586) but only succeeded in cementing this new state project after the conversion of his son and successor, Reccared, to Nicene Christianity in 587. Between Reccared's reign and the mid-seventh century, a central administration in Toledo attempted to establish a more uniform government and administration of justice, with various degrees of success.[15] An elaborate ceremonial was developed around the king and his capital following Byzantine models.[16] The royal government sought ecclesiastical sanction of the king's rule through council decisions.[17] Visigothic monarchs would eventually receive the Christian Church's anointment at their coronation. The idea of a Christian polity led by the king of the Goths slowly developed, according to which the king was responsible not only for the material but also the spiritual welfare of his subjects.[18] Christian ideologues placed the Gothic monarchy within God's providential designs to defend orthodoxy.[19] Armies were raised on completely different grounds than two centuries earlier, and taxation, while it continued to exist, had a significantly smaller impact on state income.[20] Although rebellions became an endemic problem in the seventh century, the basis of the state project was never challenged. Pretenders did not use different languages of legitimacy; rather, they fought to appropriate the sources of legitimacy that emanated from the court in Toledo.[21] I will call this period "Visigothic" because it is precisely at this moment that the idea of a monarchy under the special government of a God-sanctioned Gothic king spread throughout the Iberian Peninsula and parts of southern Gaul.

This book will mostly cover the late and post-Roman periods. However, I will occasionally mention developments occurring in the later Visigothic period, from the late sixth to the seventh century. The aristocratic trends of the Visigothic period evolved from the structural changes that took place during the post-Roman century and a half, and I will use Visigothic-period sources to reconstruct post-Roman developments. The formation of the Visigothic kingdom of Toledo, however, altered the basis of political domination and the ideological assumptions of state power to the extent that the state no longer resembled what it had been in the late and post-Roman worlds (although it bore striking parallels to the contemporary Roman state—the Byzantine empire). I will call the first two periods, then, the late antique moment in Western Iberia, while in my view the Visigothic period belongs to the early medieval world. I am aware of the problems created by stark periodization, but to counter some of them, I also propose a chronology in which extended formative periods (late third century, 410s to 450s, and late sixth to mid-seventh century) serve as transitions to a century or so of relative stability.

Local Powers, States, and the World of Late Antiquity

I mentioned earlier that the advancement of Iberian archaeology has been critical to the writing of a book such as this. It would be unfair to leave historiographical developments out of the acknowledgments. There is a rich tradition of studying late antique elites in the Iberian Peninsula. Although I will depart somewhat from current approaches to the history of aristocracies, it is important to insist on the extent to which this book relies on previous scholarly work. Perhaps the most powerful narrative in modern Iberian scholarship on the late antique state and aristocracies focuses on the interaction between central and local powers. Not all historians adopt the terminology, but this conceptual model has permeated the most innovative work on late and post-Roman studies in the past three decades. These studies reacted against traditional narratives of late antique statehood based on formal criteria for defining ruling elites in Iberian polities (e.g., birth, office, status). Contrary to this tradition, an exciting branch of scholarship has been more interested in analyzing the power dynamics between central and local elites, understood respectively as the ruling class based in central administrative structures (the Roman Empire and successor kingdoms), and wealthy and locally influential individuals, usually landowners, based in their local towns and the countryside.

Almost half a century ago, Claudio Sánchez Albornoz had already argued that the fourth century was a moment of emancipation, during which landowning elites extricated themselves from formal structures of power. Sánchez Albornoz located these structures in the civic communities, which were no longer necessary to secure the power of the local *potentes*, prominent individuals who could wield power due to their wealth and social influence. These withdrew to the countryside and the safety of their estates and became the de facto local powers, with almost no intermediate political framework between them and the distant (and paradoxically) absolutist state.[22] The idea of power devolution to a rural milieu has since been rejected, as has the idea of a generalized urban crisis, but the interpretative framework of local-central powers has not. The late Roman period is usually described as a moment of power redefinition between local (curial) and imperial (senatorial, *honorati*) aristocracies. According to this view, the fourth century was a moment of crisis for traditional local powers. A new leading class, a so-called senatorial aristocracy, took over local ascendancy owing to their personal ties to the state.

Conversely, current scholarly work on late antique aristocracies sees the post-Roman world as the moment in which locally rooted powers emerged in a context of weakened central authority. Often, these powers are seen as the heirs or survivors of the senatorial aristocracy. Landowners used their social ascendancy to face the newly formed barbarian monarchies, which slowly created central states as the Roman administration vanished.[23] The Roman senatorial aristocracies would have survived most frequently in the ranks of the episcopate. Ecclesiastical office turned into one of the few available career paths in which to assert status and carry on the intellectual pursuits of late Roman literati.[24] The Christian Church became an institution through which local powers channeled their demands vis-à-vis the state.[25] The rise of local powers in the fifth century would eventually establish a new dynamic of central-local power under Leovigild (r. 568–586) and his successors through royal coercion and cooptation.[26] Although in the past decade some scholars have called for further study of what may have been more intense relationships between local and central authorities in the post-Roman world, the operating framework remains one of conceptually separated powers.[27] Central and local powers collaborated, but they maintained distinct interests, and, ultimately, the central authority relied on locally based power figures to govern.

In studies on late antique Iberian elites, the main distinction between central and local aristocracies lies in the former's putative immediate access to state power. While both classes tend to be presented as economically powerful and socially influential, the political primacy of central powers creates an intra-aristocratic heuristic distinction that has repercussions on the assessment of the relative strength of late antique states. It is not difficult to realize how the potent narrative of state strength and weakness serves as the bedrock for the scholarly tradition I have succinctly described. The late Roman state is usually perceived as a powerful entity governing the peninsula (and the rest of the Mediterranean world). It seems a natural consequence that so-called imperial aristocrats dominated over local elites because of their direct access to the institutional and economic benefits associated with imperial power. The opposite would have been the case after the fifth century. Post-Roman states are traditionally described as weak and unable to tame local forces—at least until the late sixth century.[28] Thus, post-Roman men of power at the local level would have been in a much better position to distribute influence and prestige to central aristocrats (namely, kings' representatives and other court officials).

The historiography of local powers has been fundamental to revitalizing the study of late antique elites after generations of scholarly work focusing on the institutional dimensions of state authority.[29] Above all, the study of so-called local powers helped conceptualize the link between economic, social, and political power. This book would have been unthinkable without the conceptual and casuistic contributions achieved by this line of inquiry. In my view, however, the distinction between local and central powers deserves reconsideration. There is an implicit and sometimes explicit risk of considering so-called central powers as the locus of state authority while putatively local powers would consist in an early version of what the modern era would call civil society. In other words, we may be in the presence of a modernizing narrative of late antique Iberia, one that operates on a stark distinction between state and society. It is not surprising that this narrative would be favored in the context of post-Franco Spain and also the realities of autonomist and even separatist movements in various parts of the country.

In this book, I propose to approach aristocracies (both local and central) from a point of view that has been somewhat underplayed in earlier scholarship. Aristocrats could only exist as a social group because they mobilized symbolic, institutional, and economic resources within the context of a state framework. From the point of view of state construction, there was no structural difference between local and central powers. State power existed because local men and women with claims to political authority and social standing enacted it. Conversely, these individuals could claim social and political ascendancy as long as they embraced the practices, rituals, and institutional framework that existed beyond the limits of their localities. Internal hierarchies within aristocracies did matter because of the importance of public competition to assert social standing. Aristocrats at all levels, however, became part of a larger ideological and political project that asserted their social standing while creating class solidarity and competition with aristocrats from other localities. Thus, when historical circumstances brought state projects into crisis, they had to adopt new or reshaped practices of political domination. It does not follow that individual members of the local dominating groups did not suffer from these moments of transition. The competitive nature of aristocratic politics and the conflicting projects of political domination inevitably led to the rise and fall of individuals and families. As a class, however, aristocrats maintained their ascendancy owing to their proactive approach toward state building. At every point in late antique history, local aristocrats in Western Iberia eagerly attempted to become central powers—and most of the time, successfully so.

Fortunately, I can rely on other scholars' groundbreaking work on either late or post-Roman Iberian aristocracies. For the late Roman period, the indispensable studies of archaeologists such as Kim Bowes and Alexandra Chavarría on elite housing, tastes, religious practices, and the overall cultural landscape have contributed to relating Iberian elites to Mediterranean aristocracies but have also stressed regional specificities.[30] With regard to the post-Roman world, archaeologists have also contributed to our understanding of aristocratic identity. The archaeology of hilltop sites and fortifications in various areas of the peninsula, for instance, has quite simply rendered post-Roman elites visible. Historians have also approached aristocracies with renewed interest. A prolific school of scholarship has devoted particular attention to the economic foundations of aristocratic power. The work of historians such as Pablo Díaz and Iñaki Martín Viso has completely undermined the idea of a rentier landowning elite without much involvement in the economic sphere.[31] Above all, they and other scholars have reminded us that the collapse of the Roman administration did not necessarily bring to life nonstate, tribal-like social structures. Post-Roman Iberia (at least most of it) remained a world of aristocracies. Moreover, studies on ethnicity have approached, though tangentially, the question of aristocracies after the fifth century. The Iberian Peninsula is still waiting for a monographic study on what Visigothic identity signified in the late sixth and seventh centuries, after the last few decades' revolution in ethnogenesis studies. To mention just a few scholars focusing on different areas in this buoyant field, Gisela Ripoll, Jamie Wood, and Manuel Koch have created the possibility of a deeper understanding of the meaning of ethnic identity and the complexities of elite self-portrayal after the withdrawal of the imperial administration.[32]

This book will also depart from previous scholarship in another important respect. To my knowledge, this is the first monographic study on late antique aristocracies in Iberia that pays equal attention to both the late and post-Roman periods. By adopting this framework, we can dissociate aristocracies from one specific state or state project and draw overarching conclusions on the nature of elite power in the region. Moreover, this work will situate Western Iberia within the late antique moment of ancient Mediterranean history into the sixth century, as I shall presently explain. This book comes at a moment when scholarship on late antique Iberian aristocracies has begun to bridge the late and post-Roman periods, albeit partially. For instance, two erudite articles by Leonard Curchin cover the fourth to the sixth and even the seventh century, although their focus lies on office holding, legal status, and the institutional roles of civic magistrates.[33] Collective volumes have also contributed to connecting Roman and post-Roman contexts.[34] Except for these individual efforts, however, scholarship on late antique aristocracies operates within the assumption of a marked fifth-century hiatus.

While the third-to-sixth-century periodization represents a novelty in the study of Iberian aristocracies, this chronological framework is certainly not my own invention. It relies on the realization by this generation of scholars that the turmoil of the fifth century had less disruptive effects than was previously thought—a realization that Javier Arce synthesized in his *Bárbaros y Romanos en Hispania, 400–507 A.D.*[35] A series of studies combining archaeological and documentary evidence insists on the late (and even early) Roman roots of the post-Roman world. Michael Kulikowski's *Late Roman Spain and Its Cities* brought the benefits of such a chronology to the full attention of the scholarly world and firmly bridged the late and post-Roman periods as an era worth studying as a unit.[36] Kulikowski's book exposed the continuity of the relationship between city and countryside between the third and the sixth century, despite the changing morphology of urban sites. Likewise, Alexandra Chavarría Arnau's *El final de las* villae *en* Hispania *(siglos IV–VII d.C.)* revealed a process of settlement transformation at odds with a stark political hiatus of the fifth century.[37] She demonstrated how post-Roman patterns of elite housing abandonment were rooted in the world of the late empire. Similarly, Alexis Oepen's *Villa und christlicher Kult auf der Iberischen Halbinsel in Spätantike und Westgotenzeit* began to bridge the differences between the fourth and the seventh century in the archaeology of rural Christianity.[38] In *Hispania and the Late Roman Mediterranean, AD 100–700: Ceramics and Trade*, Paul Reynolds synthesized in a single volume decades of scholarship on ceramics (including his own). The book established a solid foundation for the view that during late antiquity the peninsula's integration into the Roman Mediterranean continued without interruption but followed evolving patterns.[39] Other archaeological publications have also adopted an overarching chronology and the footnotes in my later chapters will give ample evidence of it.

This book follows the chronology proposed by this scholarship and looks at the period between the late third and the late sixth century as the period when early Roman patterns changed in the peninsula. Late and post-Roman periods have much in common, even though the fifth century marks a significant moment of transformation. Since the 2000s, important scholarship has restored the fifth-century hiatus in the history of the Western Mediterranean.[40] We must take this hiatus seriously. Indeed, this book's divide between late and post-Roman periods acknowledges the importance of the break. Monumental architecture was not the only archaeologically visible remains that changed considerably in the fifth century. If the recent reassessment of rural necropoleis by Alfonso Vigil-Escalera proves correct, the first decades of the fifth century may have also brought significant transformations in funerary practices and the internal organization of rural communities.[41] As mentioned earlier, new forms of statehood developed as a result of the military events of the early fifth century. As in other areas of late antique history, however, the impact of state change has to be balanced with significant continuities into the sixth century. As I will argue in this book, post-Roman aristocratic strategies were deeply rooted in the late Roman past. From the early fifth through the late sixth century, Western Iberian aristocrats enacted different state projects that maintained certain basic features of the late Roman world while adapting them to the new circumstances. Even the Visigothic kingdom of Toledo maintained earlier practices, although in this case the new state project relied on significantly different economic, political, and ideological grounds than the late Roman states. The reign of Reccared can be considered the beginning of the end of late antique Iberia and, for the purposes of this book, a turning point in the history of aristocracies and statehood in Western Iberia.

On State and Aristocracy

I believe it is necessary to make explicit how I will use the concepts of "state" and "aristocracy" throughout the book, assuming the risks posed by any theoretical definition. I am aware I will be dealing with concepts that are problematic in both the social sciences and historiography. A comprehensive summary of the theoretical debates could take up this entire introduction, or indeed a whole separate book. I am content to offer working concepts based on specific theoretical contributions, which I believe allow us to look at late antique aristocracies from a renewed perspective.

Despite their disagreements, both Weberian and Marxist traditions perceive the state as a set of institutions that act upon individuals in order to reach a certain end (primarily, to exert sovereignty or to secure class domination).[42] While in both traditions legitimacy is crucial, the ideological aspects of the state tend to be presented as a by-product of the real state—that is, legal, administrative, ceremonial, and coercive institutions. Ideology (or culture) guarantees or resists the state, but it is not in itself the state—except as part of an institutional complex (e.g., school, academia, religion).[43] The state remains a specific entity that is mainly embodied in an institutional form, and, more important, it acts upon society as a distinct entity.

While this understanding of the state is still entrenched in modern historiography on the ancient world, social theory has been challenging it for the past four decades or so. Some challenges have adopted extreme positions, denying even the institutional specificity and agency of the state. In a famous paper by Philip Abrams, written in 1977 but published posthumously in 1988, he questioned both academic sociology (i.e., functionalism) and Marxist approaches toward the state, arguing that they ultimately assumed its real existence and agency.[44] In reality, he argued, the state was no more than an idea—an idea that, in his opinion, hides domination. Abrams did not locate the state at the political level but placed it in the ideological arena, as a purely ideological mode of domination intended to mask both political (institutional structures, a state-system) and economic (class) subjection.[45] Abrams's conclusions were radical: he proposed to abandon the study of the state as an object and rather focus academic research on the state as an idea.

Without necessarily reaching the extreme conclusions of Abrams, other models call for a deeper understanding of the non institutional dimensions of the state. In the early 1990s, Pierre Bourdieu delivered a series of lectures at the Collège de France to consider this question.[46] Although he maintained in those lectures some of the assumptions about the state advanced by traditional theories, he departed from them in his understanding of the origins of the state (by which he meant the modern state).[47] Instead of looking at the emergence of the state as a process of institutional or coercive construction, Bourdieu located it in the accumulation of symbolic capital. This form of capital is the means through which social agents know and recognize other forms of capital (e.g., social, cultural, economic), which indeed states require. While departing from classical Marxist notions of ideology, Bourdieu called attention to the primacy of cognitive structures, which in his view partly constitute the state itself. All members of society regardless of their social class have the state, as it were, in their minds—even though everybody does not always agree on what the state is. Through the accumulation of symbolic capital, the state develops the formidable power to produce an organized social universe without necessarily giving orders. The state produces, in Bourdieu's words, "a social world" which experiences itself as self-evident.

Even if we accept the state as an institutional entity, its boundaries are far less clear than traditional analyses suggest. A myriad of social agents in civil society take over fundamental areas of statehood in daily life. In a 1984 article on the autonomous power of the state, Michael Mann bridged the gap between state and civil society in an alternate way.[48] On the one hand, Mann kept the essential premises of classical state definitions, such as a set of institutions with a particular function and the existence of a conceptual separation between state (state elite) and a civil society. On the other hand, he differentiated between despotic and infrastructural state power. The former is the power of a state elite over society, and the latter consists in the ability of the state to implement its political decisions within society. This distinction is particularly relevant since, as Mann recognized, the techniques of infrastructural power are not specific to states. Other social groups, especially those with greater economic, social, and ideological resources than the rest of the population, are able to provide infrastructural power when despotic institutions face limitations. It follows that the state, however one defines it, goes beyond the narrow set of centrally appointed officials.

These theoretical contributions do not necessarily render obsolete Weberian or Marxist approaches toward the state but pose a real challenge in terms of their assumptions. We cannot approach the question of the state without concepts such as sovereignty (or political domination) and class ascendancy, but the actual dimensions of the state may have exceeded the institutional constraints of classical theories. In late antique studies, A. H. M. Jones's notion of the Roman and, to a certain extent, post-Roman state has cast a long shadow over subsequent historiography. The most acute studies on the late antique state since then have focused on the permeability of the Jonesian state to private interests, its infrastructural limitations or reactive nature, and the mechanisms of communication and collaboration between local elites and the state.[49] The field is now ripe for a redefinition of late antique statehood that reassesses the distinction between state and (civil) society still in operation. While the purpose of this book is not to provide such a redefinition, I hope it will contribute to that end.

In an extremely insightful study of peasant communities in the later Roman Empire, Cam Grey noticed that rural communities rarely differentiated between the state on the one hand and municipal aristocrats and landowners on the other. However, ancient writers and members of the imperial elite in general did distinguish between the state and society in general.[50] I believe Grey's remark touches upon a crucial issue of statehood. Late antique states (and probably premodern states in general) were not distinct from the individuals who asserted political domination at the local level—the so-called local aristocracies. The distinction between state and civil society blurs when we are dealing with enactors of political power, even though they may have had different tasks and relative authority within the state administration (or no formal role at all). As Grey's observation suggests, the aristocracy believed in the separation between themselves and an ideological construct of the state, even when (like many in the nonelite population) they embraced the symbolic project of the state.

Throughout this book, I will occasionally rely on classic understandings of the state as a set of institutions exerting authority over society. However, following Abrams, I believe this type of state belongs to a broader category of political domination of which both state officials and specific local individuals, which I will call aristocrats, were a manifestation. By political domination I mean the effective organization of hierarchical communities within a specific territory. The distinction provided by Mann between despotic and infrastructural power is particularly relevant here as it opens the "state" sphere (i.e., political domination) to actors other than state-appointed office holders. This infrastructural power of local elites offered both a powerful constraint on the autonomy and enormous potential benefits to the reproduction of ancient tributary states.[51] It is through the fulfillment of this possibility that statehood was enacted on a daily basis.

Following some of the contributions of social theorists such as Abrams and Bourdieu, I will consider the state above all as a project that organizes and legitimizes (or legitimizes while organizing) a particular social order. Those with successful claims to decision-making power over economic, administrative, and symbolic aspects of political domination embodied the idea of the state. While central administrations generated a series of symbols and practices aimed at securing political domination, the holders of formal or informal political power at the local level embraced these symbols and enacted them in daily practices, even when their idea of the state was somewhat different from centralized unifying programs. In most cases, these individuals had access to economic, cultural, and social resources that the idea of the state (Bourdieu's symbolic capital) could turn into political domination. In other words, a few individuals controlled the infrastructural dimensions of power that did not differ significantly from the prerequisites to the exercise of state despotic power. The focus of this book is precisely how a group of individuals in late antique Western Iberia enacted the idea of the state as a path to gain social ascendancy.

A fully satisfactory definition of aristocracy seems quite impossible.[52] Perhaps we must rely on etymology as a starting point: the idea of (sociopolitical) power (*kratos*) and the idea that claims to that power belong to a group defined by social distinction (*aristoi*). The problem with the etymological approach is that we may fall into the trap of elite self-perception. The etymological meaning presupposes a theoretical social distinction that exists before the exercise of political authority and makes a particular *aristos* worthy of *kratos*. Certainly, late antique aristocrats claimed to have independent merits to receive social and political recognition, even when they acknowledged that a superior authority (e.g., emperor, king, civic community) was a source of political rewards. This was undoubtedly the case in late antiquity and, perhaps, in most premodern societies. Yet, as I have just argued, only the symbolic categories (or symbolic capital) associated with state power could make personal claims of social distinction effective. Thus, their social ascendancy ultimately depended upon their ability to enact despotic or infrastructural state power, or both.

In order to secure claims to higher status, late antique aristocracies worked to live up to the social expectations of other members of their group and society in general. This contributed to the state's ideological project insofar as it defined the discrete boundaries of a ruling class. Expectations included patterns of social behavior and interaction. More important for the purposes of this book, they also involved socially acceptable forms of conspicuous consumption and mobilization of resources. Wealth was crucial for aristocratic status inasmuch as it provided the resources to satisfy these social needs, which underlaid claims of personal distinction. The importance of wealth for one's social standing can be seen in the many instances in which rulers "created" an aristocrat or enhanced his status. They did so not only by granting titles and honors but also through economic gifts (lands, salaries, tax exemptions), as was appropriate for high status.

Therefore, I do not see a major impediment to presenting Western Iberian aristocrats as a class since they relied on economic exploitation for the reproduction of their social status. It does not follow that all individuals who appropriated surplus produced by others were members of the aristocracy. A free farmer who owned a small plot of land and had a slave or occasionally made use of hired labor during the harvest was far from being an aristocrat as defined here. There was also a grey area of subelite power brokers who left almost no traces in the archaeological and written evidence—lower imperial officers, village leaders and subcurial landowners, rural priests and charismatic monks, minor warrior leaders, for example. Unfortunately, we only hear about them when they climbed to the upper echelons of the social hierarchy. From a strictly economic (i.e., exploitative) point of view, a transregional late Roman senator and the hypothetical small farmer I just described were both members of those classes. In many ways, however, the small farmer shared the majority's daily experience of subjugation and may have had social bonds with landless tenants, even of servile status.

My approach to aristocracy as a class acknowledges the importance of economic resources in maintaining social and political standing. Standing had to be constantly reproduced, largely because others with similar claims subjected it to review and policed its borders.[53] Definitions of aristocracy based solely on legal status or other "objective" criteria (for instance, birth) tend to neglect the extremely competitive nature of aristocratic power. Aristocrats sought wealth because they depended on it to fulfill their social needs. Although my interpretation seems at first glance to lean toward a more primitivist understanding of the ancient economy, this book will also show that aristocrats and the administrators of their lands actively pursued maximizing income from their properties and adapted to changing economic circumstances through shifting managerial strategies. Both in the political and economic spheres, Western Iberian aristocracies were anything but passive actors. This book will show an active class in pursuit of social standing.

The Structure and Argument of This Book

This book is organized into two parts that follow parallel structures. Part I focuses on the late Roman period while Part II covers the post-Roman world. Both sections contain three chapters, each of which is paired with one chapter from the other section. The first chapter in each section presents the main characteristics of urban and rural settlements, particularly in their monumental aspects. The second chapters consider aristocratic identity and elite participation in wider political and cultural horizons. The third chapters discuss aristocratic sources of wealth (mainly stemming from landownership) and the wider socioeconomic conditions that facilitated landowning managerial practices.

I will make two overarching but interrelated arguments. My first claim will provide a model for understanding the dynamics of regional aristocratic power. The social elites of late antique Western Iberia actively sought to participate in different state projects that had secured political domination in the region—as their own social ascendancy depended on the existence of a state able to render their status self-evident. Claims of proximity to the symbolic center of state projects were crucial for the reproduction of social standing. In order to successfully make those claims, aristocrats became agents of political domination within their own region. While negotiation and conflict between centralized institutions and local aristocrats existed, they never acted in long-term structural opposition, such as *curiales*/senators or Romans/barbarians. The nature of aristocratic power demanded that they also engage in social practices that stressed an independent claim to the power they wielded through political domination—a pre-existing worthiness that materialized in their state-granted power. Wealth was thus crucial to their political aspirations, as it allowed social elites to perform actions that revealed to everyone's eyes, but especially to those of fellow aristocrats, that they belonged to the group of those deserving to enact state power.

My second overarching argument, which is related to my first, pertains to the material culture of late antique Western Iberia. I will argue that the changes in settlement patterns, monumental architecture, and other aspects of the archaeological record reveal the agency of local elites in adapting to social, economic, and ideological circumstances created by different state projects. The material record does not reveal the rise and fall of different aristocratic groups, although individual families certainly must have waxed and waned. Rather, it indicates the perseverance of aristocracies as a social class not only through the use of inherited practices but also through a flexible approach to changing sociopolitical environments. In the late Roman period, one relatively homogeneous project prevailed over the peninsula, although there was sporadic regional diversity. In the post-Roman period, a multitude of state projects competed with each other and generated regional differences in material culture and power practices. Many of these practices, however, were rooted in the late Roman past, allowing me to consider the period between roughly 300 and 600 as a relatively congruent unit.

*   *   *

Chapter 1 analyzes cities and the countryside in late Roman Western Iberia. The period witnessed an intensification of certain aspects of monumentality in comparison to other regions in Hispania. Defensive walls surrounded the main cities and even some smaller towns. Aristocrats in cities and imperial authorities devoted resources to the maintenance of public buildings in urban centers, especially those with prominent roles within the imperial administrative hierarchy. Indeed, these latter cities developed most if not all the main features of late Roman monumental urbanism. City life did not decay, contrary to a belief that was widely held not long ago, although by the fourth century fewer cities concentrated the main symbols of settlement status. In the countryside, monumental villas built along major roads became one of the most striking features of the region—and of the Mediterranean world in general. This combination of urban and rural monumentality was almost unique in the empire, with the exception of Aquitaine and specific microregions. I associate this peculiarity of Western Iberia to the more intense presence of the imperial administration after the late third century, when Mérida became the capital of the vicariate, military garrisons and (perhaps) temporarily billeted troops were stationed in the region, and pan-Atlantic communications with Trier became more important than Mediterranean connections with Rome. Western Iberia became more central to the newly organized empire than it had been before.

Chapter 2 focuses on the main actors behind this dramatic transformation: Western Iberian aristocrats and high-ranking imperial administrators. Political leadership was cemented in legally sanctioned statuses. I leave aside the common distinction between imperial (senatorial, *honorati*, and other) aristocracies and local (*curialis*) aristocracies, and argue that all groups followed similar practices of state enactment at the local level—within the spheres granted by their rank. There was no such thing as a state aristocracy in contrast to a local elite. Rather, both groups were part of the state's ruling class, offering political service and claiming symbolic proximity to the emperor as the main markers of social standing. They also shared ways of displaying status and social distinction. The archaeological record allows us to reconstruct aristocratic strategies of identity and competition. Western Iberian elites primarily chose the traditional civilian values associated with early imperial Roman elites to express their social distinction. They also adopted some specifically late Roman fashions, which showed their awareness of trends in other parts of the empire. Overall, we are dealing with an aristocracy whose identity was defined by strategies of belonging to what was perceived to be the imperial ruling class. Western Iberian aristocracies were not provincial elites, but a group that saw itself as partaking in a shared imperial project together with other worthy aristocrats, a project at whose symbolic center was a providential emperor.

Chapter 3 looks at the economic strategies of Western Iberian aristocracies during the late empire. As far as archaeology allows us to reconstruct it, the late Roman period witnessed a moderate bump in investments in production and storage infrastructure associated with large estates. The internal structure of these estates is impossible to re-create, but there is no evidence of property concentration (which may have happened). It is more likely that landowners seized the opportunities generated by the new tax system to strengthen their ascendancy in the countryside. As tax collectors and buyers of small farm production, some landowners were able to benefit from the concentration of production at centralized facilities associated with their estates. Commercial networks, boosted by the tax system, created the infrastructural requirement for this type of strategy to succeed. Exchange networks are well attested through ceramic and other archaeological evidence. Although pan-Mediterranean trade played a significant role in Western Iberia, the bulk of commercialized commodities, and perhaps taxes, were distributed and consumed at the regional level within the peninsula.

In Chapter 4, I describe urban and rural settlements in the post-Roman period. Settlement evolution after the fifth century combines a marked continuity in site occupation with drastic change in the expression of settlement status through monumental architecture. Aristocracies became invisible at the archaeological level, as Roman-style houses were abandoned or reused. Public buildings lost their original use. Only city walls remained as silent testimonials to the late Roman traditions of settlement status. By the end of the fifth century, rural and urban churches timidly emerged in the archaeological record. Post-Roman monumentality reveals a world in which community status was expressed through buildings that denoted spiritual and physical protection. This coincides with the self-portrayal of barbarian monarchies, in which kings were powerful figures who offered protection and showed reverence to the saints. While a similar language of settlement status existed throughout

Western Iberia, its impact varied from region to region. Both urban and rural settlements in central and southern Lusitania, the northern plateau, and northwestern Iberia followed different trajectories after the fifth century.

Chapter 5 offers an explanation for this regional divergence in terms of the ways in which statehood was reconstructed in the fifth century. In central and southern Lusitania, civic governments in the late Roman style (closer to the so-called government by notables) remained in place. The provincial structure with Mérida at its center seems to have continued unaltered after the fifth century. Landowners, civic officers, and, perhaps, the clergy governed their communities in the acknowledgment that the Visigothic king (and perhaps the Suevic king in the early fifth century) was a powerful protector—through the presence of royally appointed officers. In northwestern Iberia, by contrast, the Suevic settlement established contractual relationships with individual communities in a fragmented landscape. The Suevi directly controlled the microregion near Braga and perhaps Lugo. In the rest of their kingdom, the local leadership enacted statehood by granting security, collecting tribute, and enforcing order in small territorial units, at whose center there was usually a small fortified town. Various forms of leadership coexisted, their only point in common being their enactment of agreements with the Suevic king and army. Eventually, the Christian Church would provide a common language to unite all these types of local authority by the mid-sixth century. In the third region, the northern plateau, aristocratic power followed patterns similar to those of northwestern Iberia but with a markedly militarized tone. The reason for this transformation can be found in the events of the early fifth century, when the region became a battlefield and frontier area between different armies (imperial, Suevic, Gothic, and other barbarian groups). It never lost its quasifrontier character until Leovigild's conquest of the Suevic kingdom. In the post-Roman period, aristocrats clung to the few existing cities where civic government was re-created. Most of them, however, asserted their authority from newly occupied fortified hilltops, in the absence of an inherited developed urban network. Their participation in local polities was less structured than in government by notables, yet they offered stable territorial control in the century and a half that followed the dissolution of the Roman imperial project. In sum, each region followed its own path based on its inherited characteristics, the impact of the events of the early fifth century, and their incorporation into a wider post-Roman polity (Suevic and Visigothic).

Finally, Chapter 6 analyzes the sources of wealth of post-Roman aristocrats. Overall, the economy of Western Iberia changed less drastically than the architectural expression of aristocratic identity. There are few signs of elite impoverishment or a peasant golden age. Perhaps the two most noteworthy changes are a reduction of investment in centralized facilities and the declining importance of regional distribution networks in favor of more local exchange patterns. Both processes, however, were very slow paced, and it is only in the late sixth and seventh centuries that they became truly noticeable—that is, during the Visigothic period. The reasons for these changes are myriad, and not all of them can be reconstructed through the extant evidence. The increasingly fragmented political landscape and the declining proportion of tax revenue within state income, however, must have played a very important role. Great landownership prevailed in the countryside as it had done in the late Roman period. The evidence shows a proactive landowning class, interested in adapting the management of their estates to the changing circumstances. Wealth was as fundamental to elite promotion and competition as it had been when Roman emperors ruled over the peninsula in the fourth century.

PART I

WESTERN IBERIAN ARISTOCRACIES IN THE LATE ROMAN EMPIRE

CHAPTER I

In the Shadow of Empire: Settlement and Society in the Late Roman Period

In 406–407, a young boy named Hydatius, from the city of Lemica in modern Galicia, traveled on a pilgrimage to Jerusalem where he met the Christian ascetic Jerome. Hydatius would return to his native land and, in 428, become the bishop of Chaves (in northern Portugal). As a bishop and a writer, he continued Jerome's *Chronicle*, which would become one of the most important surviving sources to study the agitated decades of fifth-century Atlantic Iberia.[1] Hydatius was not the first pilgrim from Gallaecia to make that journey. More than two decades earlier, Egeria, an aristocratic lady from his very province, had visited Sinai, Jerusalem, and other Christian sites in the Holy Land, and thus Hydatius might have been following a well-established route. During his trip to the Holy Land, he might have traveled through the provincial capital Braga or perhaps through the supraprovincial vicariate capital, Mérida. Once on the shores of the Mediterranean, did he stop in a major city such as Carthage, Rome, or Ravenna? Did he visit Constantinople before reaching the Levant, as Egeria had done after her trip in the Holy Land? We do not know any of the answers, but the landscapes he must have seen were certainly different from his small hometown in the Galician hills. Imperial and provincial capitals would have impressed the young Hydatius. The newly built monumental areas of Constantinople or the still standing ceremonial centers of Rome must have made Hydatius's town look like a small village. Even villages in the eastern Mediterranean may have seemed like large cities to a seven-year-old Lemican.[2]

Despite their strangeness, all the cities and rural areas he visited formed part of a landscape that was readable by any person who lived in the Roman

Empire. The relative uniformity that the empire brought to its territories (mixing Greek, Italian, and other local traditions) helped Hydatius and other travelers place settlements and their buildings within a mental landscape based on daily experience. Some cities Hydatius saw may have been bigger and more lavish than his own Lemica. But they were all Roman cities still—and the same Roman model applied, to a lesser extent, to the countryside. What is more, this landscape was not only Roman but also late Roman. By the time the Suevi settled in Gallaecia and Hydatius began writing his *Chronicle*, urban and rural settlements had developed in the sociopolitical context of a Roman imperial state, with a late Roman twist. This settlement landscape and especially some features of its morphology in Atlantic Iberia are the topic of this chapter.

In order to study aristocratic social strategies, I will reconstruct the urban and rural landscape of Atlantic Iberia based predominantly on the most visible aspects of settlement archaeology, that is, the monumental architecture: city walls, ceremonial and entertainment buildings, and elite houses. These buildings were intimately related to the ways in which local aristocrats marked social distinction, since they were, together with imperial authorities, the main social and economic force behind the construction. In general, various trends are noticeable in Atlantic Iberia during late antiquity: defensive walls were built in several cities, ceremonial and entertainment buildings were predominantly maintained and even expanded in cities with special status within the imperial administration, a minimum of pleasurable life was secured in most cities through infrastructural works, and traditional elite houses continued being used in cities and were lavishly expanded in the countryside—just to mention the main transformations. Individually, these changes were not particular to Atlantic Iberia or the peninsula in general. There are instances of similar phenomena throughout the empire, and they characterized most of the urban and rural landscape of the late Roman world. However, the combination of all of them was almost unique. Understanding what this unique combination meant is at the core of this chapter and the next.

In this chapter, I will argue that the settlement evolution during the late Roman period in Atlantic Iberia mirrors the impact of new administrative structures and the triumph of a settlement language characteristic of the late Roman Empire. Western Iberia, which admittedly had fewer early imperial Roman settlement status markers than other parts of the peninsula and the Mediterranean world, caught up with them in the late third and fourth centuries. The transformation at the settlement level went hand in hand with the increasing importance of Atlantic Iberia within the political geography of the empire—when the vicariate capital was established in Mérida and the new province of Gallaecia rearranged the landscape of northern Iberia. Expressions of settlement status became archetypically *late* Roman within a context of intensified state presence. Therefore, monumental architecture and settlement evolution in general ought to be read in terms of regional integration and the impact of the late Roman state on this remote region of the empire. Monumentality in Atlantic Iberia reflects the formation of a provincial landscape with intensified presence of late Roman traditions of settlement morphology.

In general, local aristocrats engaged in a relatively uniform set of strategies to express settlement status. Contrary to the post-Roman period, the late Roman universe of prestige architecture in Atlantic Iberia was homogeneous across the various lands of Atlantic Iberia. Yet this chapter also wants acknowledge diversity. The intervention of local elites and state representatives cannot be followed in every single city or rural territory through the type of monumental architecture typical of the late Roman period. What is remarkable is that diversity can only be traced by invisibility of monumental architecture at the archaeological level rather than through monumentalized alternatives. This means that those who opted out of the system of wealth display in monumental architecture left no trace in the archaeological record. Yet archaeological invisibility does not mean an absence of elites. Rather, the empire-wide language of settlement status may have overshadowed other alternatives, which relied on perishable materials or other forms of wealth display outside of the world of the late Roman landscape of monumental architecture. These alternatives, therefore, became invisible in the late Roman period.

Cities and Monumentality in Late Roman Atlantic Iberia

A quick glance at a map of Atlantic Iberian cities shows an underurbanized world, not only in comparison to the clusters of cities that dominated the landscape of Asia Minor, Italy, or southern Gaul, but also in terms of the Iberian Peninsula itself. The "world of the cities" had always been southern and eastern Hispania. In these areas, Phoenician and Greek colonies together with predominantly ethnic Iberian towns organized the settlement hierarchy after the Roman conquest from the second century BCE onward. Latin migrations and veteran settlement contributed to the formation of a typically Roman melting pot.[3] In Atlantic Iberia, the Roman conquest imposed a territorial organization based on civic communities, but, in most cases, cities had to be created *ex novo*. A network of newly created colonies and *municipia* of diverse status dotted the region by the time of Augustus, when the military conquest of the peninsula ended after the defeat of the last independent chiefdoms in northern Iberia. The granting of Latin right to the whole of Hispania by the Flavian emperors cemented the municipalization of the peninsula by the 70s CE.[4] As a consequence, the Roman administration imposed new mental maps on the conquered population centered on the city–territory framework and the provincial hierarchy of administrative centers.[5]

By the end of the first century CE, most of the towns in Atlantic Iberia had developed several of the features associated with Roman urbanism, including monumental architecture and urban amenities.[6] Cities could range from large and populated towns with splendid monumental centers that imitated Rome's public areas (such as Mérida) to sites with no more than a few Roman-type buildings operating as a political focal point for a dispersed rural population (as in the case of Hydatius's Lemica).[7] To be sure, this does not mean that Atlantic Iberia was less "Romanized" than other parts of the empire. Rather, the local communities, and in particular the local elites, participated in the definition of what being Roman was on their own terms.[8]

Although not all the cities had the same legal status vis-à-vis Rome, these legal differences disappeared in the course of the third century.[9] In every case, the new political organization of the territory led to the formation of local groups who would assume the daily government of their communities and the mediation between these communities and Rome. They did so chiefly through local councils (*curiae*), whose membership was determined by several factors including birth, reputation, service, and, above all, wealth. Two or three centuries of Roman presence had placed the local elites of town councilmen, the *curiales*, in a path-dependent situation in which their status (and wealth) relied on their collaboration with the imperial administration.[10]

The political havoc in the empire between 235 and 284 used to be credited with altering socioeconomic conditions and eventually leading to urban decline, among other calamities. The barbarian raids in the third quarter of the third century added to this climate of crisis. Modern historiography has persuasively rejected past interpretations of crisis in city life or among the urban ruling elites. Cities continued to be firmly governed by their town councilors.[11]

If there was a crisis, it did not affect Roman urbanism significantly. Nor did it alter the basic idea that local leading men ruled their local societies with an authority grounded in urban institutions. On the other hand, the reign of Diocletian and his immediate successors in the late third and early fourth centuries represented a more important moment of transformation in the settlement topography of Atlantic Iberia. In the following pages, I will describe this transformation as much as it can be reconstructed from the archaeological evidence. In order to wholly grasp the impulse behind urban changes, we must frame them within the larger context of administrative reform undertaken by Diocletian and his successors and the way this affected the Iberian Peninsula.

This administrative restructuring resulted in a reorganization of provincial boundaries and administrative hierarchies. The Iberian Peninsula was divided into five (later six) provinces from the initial three provinces that existed during the early imperial period. On top of this provincial organization was placed an administrator of the vicariate of the *Hispaniae*, which also included Mauretania Tingitana (northern Morocco). In this new administrative world, Atlantic Iberia roughly coincided with two provinces, Lusitania and Gallaecia. Two provincial capitals, Mérida and Braga, now dominated the region rather than the previous sole capital of Mérida (northwestern Iberia was part of early imperial Tarraconensis, with its capital in Tarragona). Moreover, Mérida also became the residence of the supraprovincial administrator, *vicarius Hispaniarum*, who oversaw provincial governors, the justice administration, and tax collection.[12] The vicariate of the peninsula and northern Morocco was placed under the supervision of a prefect in Trier.[13] Thus in the late empire, the administrative and tributary links to the peninsula became more detached from Rome (or the other Italian capitals) and more closely mingled with Gaul and Germany.

It is within this political context of growing centrality of Atlantic Iberia that we must place the transformations of city landscapes. In the following pages, I will trace the main characteristics of late Roman urbanism in the region, including constructions of defensive walls, an urban topography centered in the forum, the maintenance of certain public buildings, and the presence of aristocratic residences in towns. Not all of these characteristics applied to every city, and we will see the significance of variations at the microregional level. But they represent the markers of high urbanism in the late empire. By the end of the section, I will argue that there is a correlation between this type of urban monumental architecture and the impact of the late Roman state in Atlantic Iberia.

*   *   *

Let us begin with what was perhaps the most obvious change in the topography of several cities: walled defenses. Massive and impressive walls encircled most of the largest Western Iberian cities by the year 450, whereas most of them were not walled in 250. Unfortunately, chronologies are not as precise as we would wish. Whereas previous scholarship has tended to attribute the construction of walls to a tetrarchic program in the late third and early fourth centuries, a careful reading of the available excavations demonstrates that the process of walling cities more likely happened between the late third and the early fifth century.[14] In the few cases of cities with early imperial walls, the walls remained in decent condition and were even, at some point in the late Roman period, repaired.[15]

The encircling of cities with defensive walls was not unique to this region. Between the end of the third century and the beginning of the fourth century, a considerable number of towns in the Roman world, and especially in the west, were surrounded by stone walls.[16] But the building of city walls was never a uniform process. Whereas certain cities in northern Italy and northern Gaul had these fortifications built in the late Roman period, Mediterranean Iberia and North Africa in general did not.[17] In the Iberian Peninsula, there are two noteworthy characteristics in the geographic distribution of newly built or repaired walls. First, most of the new walls in the peninsula were built precisely in Atlantic Iberia. Second, the geographical location of late Roman walls in Atlantic Iberia reveals that these fortifications protected cities close to the provincial capitals (Mérida and Braga) or along chief roads. It has been argued that this geographical pattern responded to the requirements of the Roman tax collection system. According to this hypothesis, the walled cities were along the "*annona* route," which supplied the imperial army in the Rhine with the resources collected in the Iberian Peninsula.[18] This hypothesis presupposes the simultaneity of wall construction in the years that followed the tributary reforms of Diocletian. As we saw earlier, it is not entirely clear that these walls were built predominantly in the decades around the year 300. I thus prefer to be cautious about associating wall construction with tax collection and transportation.

In terms of the more general meaning of these walls, existing research offers two different, though not necessarily competing, interpretations. While some historians have insisted on insecurity as the reason for this phenomenon, others place greater emphasis on the pursuit of urban prestige associated with walled towns.[19] We must take these walls seriously for what they were: constructions meant to protect (as well as markers of boundaries between town and countryside). Even in the cases of small towns, such as Gijón, these walls had clear defensive functions. On this site, walls based on *opus caementicium* were no rudimentary constructions. More than four meters in breadth, their height must have greatly surpassed the three meters that remain on the site. Twelve semicircular towers have been detected so far, with two rectangular towers at the entry of the site.[20] Walls such as Gijón's do not cast doubts on the defensive nature of the constructions. Yet the fact that these walls had a clear defensive nature does not necessarily mean that they responded to a real security threat. Like in modern countries, feelings of insecurity are very often dissociated from actual peril. But other factors, such as endemic rural unrest expressed in banditry or even the historical memory of earlier barbarian raids, may have bolstered the conviction that defenses were necessary.

Undeniably, there must have been a correlation between state involvement and walled cities. This is easier to affirm in the case of towns with military garrisons, such as León. But in settlements without military roles, state intervention may also have been essential. Many of these walls protected modest-sized towns with limited resources, a feature that hints at the imperial administration taking part in their construction.[21] State intervention could range from total financing and direction of the work to granting permission for a task, which would then be completed by the city on its own. We can imagine that most cases fell somewhere between these two extremes. The imperial state could provide partial assistance by remitting taxes, providing soldiers as laborers, and authorizing the destruction of other public buildings in order to reuse their materials.[22] Walling cities entailed making decisions on the use of urban space, decisions that imperial agents and city governments had to negotiate based on their own interests.[23] As stone fortifications reduced the city's size, the layout of a wall must have been a concern of local inhabitants whose houses would be destroyed or remained outside the walls. The impact of new walled circuits is evident in various cities. For instance, large areas in the southwestern parts of early imperial Lugo were left out of the boundaries of the walled city and became necropoleis.[24] Likewise, the walls

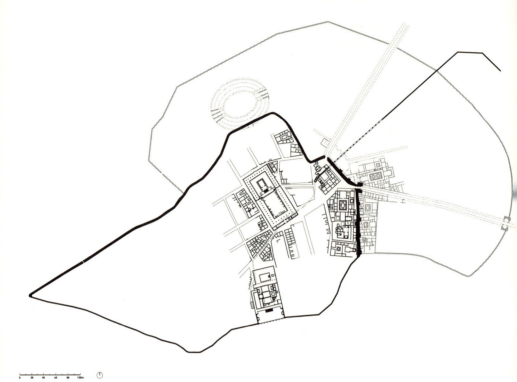

Figure 1. Late Roman Conimbriga. From Virgílio Hipólito Correia and Pedro
Alarcão, *Conimbriga: Um ensaio de topografia histórica.* Conimbriga XLVII
(2008): 31–46, est. XI ©DGPC/Museu Monográfico de Conimbriga.

in Conimbriga cut the amphitheater in two parts and also forced the abandonment of several residences that were left outside the fortress (Figure 1).[25]
Therefore, each fortification must have been the subject of numerous concerns
and interests and cannot be explained by a single cause.

Yet the meaning of these constructions was also associated with settlement
status. We must not forget that the late third century witnessed the construction
of the Aurelian wall in Rome, meant to signify both security to the Roman
dwellers and the embracing of a renewed imperial power in the city.[26] Cities in
other parts of the peninsula (and the Mediterranean world) did have early imperial walls, which had more prestige than defensive meaning.[27] It is as if some
cities in Atlantic Iberia were catching up with the rest of the empire, in a very
late Roman way (that is, by building *defensive* walls). If so, one should not rule
out competition among cities within the region itself. Once a few urban centers
built their walls in the tetrarchic period, other cities may have followed suit dur-

ing the fourth and early fifth centuries. The local population, and particularly its elites, may have encouraged these constructions since the walls would both grant protection and enhance the status of their city vis-à-vis nearby towns.[28] Therefore, a multiplicity of motivations and actors lay behind the construction of urban walls. What they all had in common was the symbolic association between settlement and the urban ideal that prevailed in the late Roman world, as walls became the essence of post–third-century urbanism.[29]

*   *   *

What happened within these walls in terms of settlement morphology and monumentality? In most cases, it seems that city surface decreased from the early Roman city. Less surface area does not necessarily mean fewer people. The little we know about the cities in the area indicates that they might have grown in population density.[30] In the few cases where we have clear archaeological information about urban housing, we know that private residences grew either horizontally, through occupying public spaces (mostly streets), or vertically, with the construction of more stories over existing houses. Mérida, one of the best-excavated cities in the region, shows both types of expansion.[31] Similarly, domestic structures occupied public baths in Lugo by the end of the fourth century; the baths and theater of Lisbon were reused as residential structures by the late fourth or early fifth century; and an aristocratic house was built over part of the early imperial forum in Uxama.[32] Small towns seem to have undergone a similar process. Private houses in Tongobriga, a small city near Braga, occupied public streets during the late Roman period.[33] Simple constructions, perhaps less affluent houses, occupied the cryptoportico of Ammaia's forum (Marvão, Portugal) at some point in the fourth or perhaps fifth century.[34] Overall, in comparison with early Roman urban centers, the late Roman cities in Western Iberia appear to be more densely occupied but, in some cases, within a smaller area.

The monumental areas of early Roman towns were altered to a certain extent, but also here we must be cautious in assessing the evidence.[35] The average early Roman town included a forum with a few public and religious buildings and, in most cases, other urban public entertainment infrastructure. Variations in dimensions and activity existed. Mérida boasted an impressive forum beginning with the early empire (Figure 2). A large complex dedicated to the imperial cult built during the reign of Tiberius and a forum probably monumentalized during Augustus's reign functioned as symbolic and political

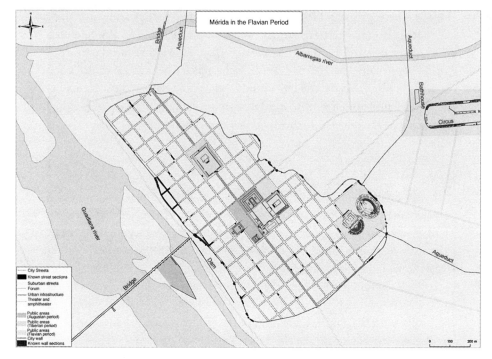

Figure 2. Roman Mérida. Courtesy of Pedro Mateos Cruz.

centers of the city.[36] The Augustan forum was renovated and expanded during the Flavian period into a four-hectare monumental complex of several
buildings, porticoes, and open spaces. Archaeologists have recently argued that
they have possibly identified the *curia* and a court basilica. Added to the other
monumental buildings of the city (imperial cult complex, theater and amphitheater), at least nine out of seventy hectares of the city were dedicated to ceremonial, administrative, and leisure buildings.[37] Most of this forum remained
in use throughout the fourth and perhaps early fifth centuries, depending on
the building.[38] Less important cities also maintained early imperial fora.
Conimbriga, for instance, kept its forum areas with a few interventions, whose
dating is generally ascribed to the fourth century (although not conclusively).[39]
Tomar (ancient Sellium) in Portugal maintained a functional forum until the
mid-fifth century when burials occupied former public areas.[40] Less frequent
is the abandonment of the forum area, although there are examples of this
evolution, such as the city of Iuliobriga (Retortillo, Cantabria) in the *conven-*

tus Cluniensis. This city's forum was perhaps abandoned by the mid-third century, although a military garrison was most likely located not far from the city in the early fifth century.[41]

After the late third century, Atlantic Iberian cities display an uneven landscape in terms of the evolution of public buildings. In some cases, public monumentality associated with traditional Roman cities continued and even expanded during the late empire. In Mérida, public buildings (including a theater, an amphitheater, and a circus) continued in use, and there is even epigraphic evidence for some state intervention in repairs (a unique case for Iberia in the fourth century).[42] In the capital of the diocese, imperial or local intervention did not only involve the maintenance of basic infrastructure. It is very likely that a wide reception hall for high-status attendants organized along three naves was built in the city's theater at some time during the fourth century.[43] On a minor scale, the other large administrative center in Atlantic Iberia, Braga, underwent a similar process of renewed public buildings to match its new political status.[44] Lisbon can also be included in this group. It is very likely that a circus was built or expanded in the city at some point between the late third and early fourth century.[45] At least one public bathhouse, restored in 336, existed in the city.[46]

Contrary to the expansion and renewal in the capital of the vicariate, the average town did not boast new monuments to celebrate the political community of citizens, its gods, or the emperor. The state of the different buildings and open spaces, however, are difficult to determine. Some buildings were maintained, while others were slowly abandoned or reused. The fate of the so-called pagan temples may be symptomatic. It is very likely that the end of traditional cults did not imply the destruction of temples in which their rituals were held, at least during the late Roman period. Occasional attacks on temples may have occurred, but our few literary texts do not mention any. The picture for the whole of the Iberian Peninsula indicates the continuous presence of temples in the central areas of the cities until the fifth century, even when they show abandonment at earlier stages. One of the laws in the *Theodosian Code* addressed to the diocese's governor demonstrates that imperial authorities had an interest in the upkeep of traditional temples—an imperial interest that may also point to local neglect.[47] Very likely the enemies of Roman temples were not the Christians but late antique entrepreneurs in the construction sector seeking cheap building materials. In many cases, temples became a quarry for stone and marble at a time when the large-scale exploitation of natural quarries had ceased.[48]

Christianity does not seem to have had a significant impact on urban topography during this period. Many cities in Atlantic Iberia had Christian communities, some dating from the beginning of the third century if not earlier. During the fourth century, episcopal sees existed in Mérida, Braga, Lisbon, Astorga, León, Faro, and Évora, which could imply the existence of at least one cultic house.[49] Whereas archaeologists have unearthed basilicas that they labeled paleo-Christian, we do not know the precise chronologies of these buildings, except in the case of Mérida. In this city, we know of an extramural *martyrium* and a still unexcavated episcopal church within its walls.[50] Future excavations in Braga, Astorga, Faro, and perhaps Conimbriga and Idanha-a-Velha, may provide other examples.[51] But the Western Iberian evidence of cultic buildings in urban environments pales in comparison to the much better attested presence of Christian basilicas in Mediterranean cities.[52]

In general, with the exception of city walls and, in a very limited number of cases, Christian churches, construction of the last wave of public buildings took place no later than the first half of the fourth century (with the possible exception of provincial capitals). In the average town, the late Roman period inaugurated an era marked by a dearth of monumental public constructions. Yet the lack of new large-scale programs did not always mean inattention or decay. We should not underestimate the sheer cost of maintaining public baths, urban amenities, and the continuing use of traditional spaces. The upkeep of public buildings took as many economic resources as the construction of new ones.[53] Provincial capitals could afford lavish constructions thanks to imperial or local patronage, but other cities could well content themselves with less splendid interventions. Some modest public works, besides the construction of the wall, can be detected in Astorga, where signs of street planning and repairing are evident, or in Lugo and Cauca where repairs were made to street drainage.[54] Even smaller towns, such as A Proba (perhaps the ancient Forum Gigurrorum), in Ourense, continued to use their sewers into the late Roman period.[55] In other instances, unpretentious public buildings made of wood and other perishable materials could become a good substitute for costly stone structures, as was the case of Mirobriga's circus.[56] In several cities endowed with public baths, excavations indicate that resident citizens enjoyed the use of these facilities until at least the late fourth century.[57] As in early imperial Italy, interventions in public spaces show that cities' interest may have shifted from monuments that celebrated Romanness and the triumph of the imperial ideology in the Iberian Peninsula to amenities that guaranteed the local political community some of the pleasures of a comfortable life.[58] In the minds of western aristocrats, late Roman cities still remained places of comfort (*amoenitas*) into the early fifth century.[59]

The economic force behind the construction and, above all, the maintenance of many public buildings came from the imperial administration and, especially outside the capitals, from the local aristocracies.[60] Local men of power did not abandon the fatherland, their *patria*. We lack the body of early imperial honorary inscriptions that bespeaks the proud language of urban benefactions.[61] Like in other areas of the Roman Empire, inscriptions were increasingly focused on the role of the emperor and his functionaries in the repairing and construction of public buildings.[62] The few epigraphic documents recording these activities are consistent with this trend. The above-mentioned repairing of the public baths in Lisbon are credited to Numerius Albanus, governor (*praeses*) of Lusitania. Similarly the constructions in the circus of Mérida are attributed to the intervention of the vicariate's administrator (*comes Hispaniarum*) Tiberius Flavius Laetus and the provincial governor (*praeses Lusitaniae*) Iulius Saturninus.[63] Two other surviving votive inscriptions confirm this trend: an inscription from Astorga by Fabius Aconius Catullinus, governor of Gallaecia, dedicated to Jupiter Optimus Maximus in the 330s and the inscription of (probably) a statue of emperor Gratian by Octavius Clarus, vicarius of the Hispaniae, from Mérida between 369 and 383.[64] Although local elites were no longer celebrated in inscriptions, comparative evidence from other parts of the Mediterranean world advocates for a continuous "euergetic habit" in Atlantic Iberia as well.[65] Monumental architecture of late Roman cities indicates that the basic characteristics of urban ceremonial life remained intact in certain cities, while in other towns traditional public buildings were slowly abandoned. A minimum of urban infrastructure was maintained thanks to the agency of local aristocracies. They might not have been celebrated in inscriptions, as two centuries earlier they would have been. Yet their silent management of public affairs can be recovered from the piecemeal archaeological data.

*   *   *

Did these aristocrats live in the cities of which they were so proud? The bit-by-bit reconstruction based on (mostly partial) excavations suggests they did. The traditional elite house of the early empire consisted of a single-story building with a central courtyard. In some cities, there are clear signs of continuous occupation of wealthy residences. In the La Morería area of Mérida, elite houses expanded horizontally and vertically during the late Roman period, occupying former street areas and building new stories. Some houses added bath areas and apsed halls, typical of Roman elite houses during the period.[66] Other areas in the city show signs of aristocratic residences, although excavations have not yet been as complete as in La Morería. Aristocratic houses in urban sites have been detected in almost every large or medium-sized city excavated in Atlantic Iberia.[67]

In most cities, and especially small ones, typical Roman aristocratic houses are harder to find, although this invisibility does not mean that elites fled to the countryside. If we are to find aristocrats in cities, we must read the fragmentary archaeological evidence carefully. First, early Roman houses must have had some degree of continuous occupation, even if the absence of new constructions inside the houses renders them archaeologically invisible. In the site of Corral Gil del Fuentes, in Palencia, an urban aristocratic house was occupied until at least the fifth century but built as late as the last quarter of the third century.[68] Second, other aristocratic families may have decided to abandon certain traditions of urban housing in favor of urban residences that may not look very different, when excavated, from those of less well-off citizens. I have already mentioned the more compact settlement of late Roman cities. New buildings would have adapted to this new reality by altering housing traditions. One such change was the development of two-story houses, with the seignorial rooms (reception and dining areas) on the second floor, much as they developed in Italy after the fifth century.[69] Large sections of these houses thus disappear from the immediate archaeological record, which is limited to the ground plan and a few sections of the ground floor. Finally, local aristocrats could remain attached to their cities and city dwellings without necessarily connecting status with a particular type of construction, relying instead on archaeologically invisible materials.

We can corroborate this last supposition by examining the urban topography of cities without previous early imperial pedigree. The monumentality of Gijón, a small town in coastal Asturias, seems to appear out of the blue in the late Roman period. A powerful wall encircled this town, and imported materials show intense economic exchanges. No monumental center has been found so far, but the local population could enjoy thermal baths in the city. A rich countryside with intensified economic activity during this period testifies to a buoyant local society. And yet no traces of urban mansions in the traditional Roman style have been discovered so far (although suburban villas have been found). If the local gentry resided in the city, which we may reasonably believe, they did so in houses built with perishable materials that left no traces or that have not yet been excavated.[70]

Taken as a whole, aristocratic urban housing in Western Iberia during the late empire silently altered previous Roman patterns without completely breaking with them. Traditional urban elite houses continued to be in use in some cities, while in others the traditions of urban dwelling may have shifted to other types of residence. The reasons behind this change could vary from town to town and from family to family. Economic considerations may have played a role, although there are no signs of overall impoverishment. Changes in urban settlement, especially a reduced urban area, might have raised property prices and hence redefined construction strategies. Social factors may have played an important role as well. Urban housing could have lost competitive relevance as a status marker owing to alternatives in rural construction or other markers of elite status. Above all, the evolution of urban housing could reflect the changing tastes of local aristocrats. Some would have opted for the more traditional, "early imperial" type of house, while others would have preferred two-story houses or residences largely built with perishable materials. If we can extrapolate from the extant evidence, it seems that traditional elite housing remained a preferred option in cities in which other aspects of late Roman monumentality were present, while other options were followed in cities with less active construction activity.

*   *   *

Based on this evidence, we can now place the evolution of settlements within the broader political landscape of the peninsula and the empire in general. It is worth insisting that Atlantic Iberia offered a less dense urban network in comparison to some areas of the Roman world. Yet this was a provincial landscape in which cities had the same political authority as in the rest of the empire. The vast majority of cities did not interrupt occupation during the late Roman period. Only a handful of small towns evince a drastic reduction in occupation or abandonment altogether, and even in those cases further excavations may reverse this picture. Overall, the "commonwealth of cities" is also characteristic of late Roman Western Iberia. We must not underestimate the weight of the late Roman state. *Civitates*, regardless of their monumentality, were foci of administrative acts (e.g., tax collection, justice) to an extent that other types of settlements were not. They also hosted most of the public ceremonies associated with the rituals of public life. Nothing indicates the end of city institutions during the period, nor does the urban topography underscore new or alternative power structures. If we judge from the persistence of earlier Roman patterns of urban layout and building, the imperial authorities, and more often local aristocrats, continued to be involved in the maintenance and administration of these cities. In particular, there is no indication that the church became a real alternative to traditional forms of urban patronage, even in the few cities with possibly large Christian communities.

In the previous pages, I have described the ideal type of a city, but we must keep in mind that diversity existed and was, in some cases, very marked. Some cities developed late Roman prestige urbanism, while others did not. The former group included first the two provincial capitals, Mérida and Braga. But for all the impressiveness of these two cities, we should not forget that several other cities of average political importance could also boast, to some extent, a potent late Roman urbanism. In this group, we could include such cities as Conimbriga, Astorga, Clunia, Lugo, and Lisbon. Other towns provide fewer cases of monumental architecture that renders late Roman cities visible at the archaeological level. This does not mean that they were not political centers of their territory or that they were in crisis. On the contrary, cities like Chaves or Salamanca were to maintain their central status even after the withdrawal of the Roman administration. In other words, their political standing cannot be doubted, but the material evidence they left differs significantly from that of other cities in the region. Admittedly, this might be due to the lack of extensive excavations. Be that as it may, monumentalized markers of settlement status show significant variations at odds with the fact that all cities shared a similar political and legal status.

Top-tier cities (in terms of monumentality) were unevenly distributed within the different regions of Atlantic Iberia. Lusitania (and especially its central part) offers the largest number of first-tier towns, such as Mérida, Évora, Beja, Lisbon, and Conimbriga. In northwestern Iberia, we can only count Braga and Lugo within this group. Astorga and León, on the western side of the plateau, and Clunia, Tiermes, and perhaps Uxama on the eastern side demonstrate relatively vibrant late Roman urbanism. Future excavations may add other cities to the different regions, but they will not alter the overall panorama.

Certain elements of prestige material culture, such as walls, aristocratic housing, and public buildings, tended to be concentrated in the main administrative centers (Mérida and Braga), as well as in other noncapitals such as

Beja, Lugo, Astorga, and Clunia. The latter cities had been centers where provincial governors imparted justice during their circuit of the province—the *conventus*. Although *conventus* disappeared during the late empire, bureaucratic inertia led to cities keeping some functions associated with their former status. The other *conventus* capital, Santarém, may have been replaced in its local importance by Lisbon, with easier access to Atlantic sea-lanes. To these cities we must add León, the see of the only permanent legion in the peninsula. Finally, the importance of Lisbon, Faro, and Gijón probably derived from their access to the Atlantic Ocean in southern, central, and northern Iberia. These cities were trade nodes, but they could also have been key ports in the transportation of goods for the army (the *annona* route thesis works better for these cities, I believe, than for the others). Thus, the archaeological visibility depends, to a considerable extent, on the importance of a city within the imperial administration.[71] It might then not be a coincidence that the only public inscriptions by imperial governors that survive outside of Mérida or Braga come from Astorga and Lisbon—cities that were crucial communication nodes within the road and sea-based systems.

The relevance of state priorities is even clearer in smaller towns that for strategic purposes, developed some of the features of late Roman urbanism without much of a previous tradition in this area. I have already mentioned the case of Gijón, to which we can add Castro Ventosa (León). This town, very likely the ancient Bergidum, was a hilltop settlement occupied during the late Roman period. The fortified center dominated the communication between modern Galicia and the northern plateau (in the modern Bierzo). No sign of elaborate urbanism has been discovered so far, but the erection of walls during the late third century corroborates the enhanced status of the site.[72] These towns may have been closer to the concerns of imperial authorities (and hence closer to direct imperial intervention in urban infrastructure) than their unimpressive administrative pedigree implies. As we will see in the next section of this chapter, clusters of monumental rural buildings were also articulated from the skeleton provided by major roads.

We must be careful not to reduce a city's archaeological visibility only to its possible placement within the state hierarchy, as the examples of Conimbriga, Évora, or Uxama attest. Competition for civic prestige, the particular wealth of their aristocracies, or another factor that escapes our knowledge may have played a role in contributing to a "high" late Roman urbanism in these cities. Other civic communities may not have been able to keep up with them or may not have been able to successfully persuade the Roman authorities to support (in any way) their demands for prestige urbanism. Additionally, local elites may not have wanted to compete, just as certain aristocrats may not have wanted to live in a traditional wealthy urban *domus*—thus choosing to opt out from an expensive race. But the overall picture shows that the shape and instances of late Roman monumentality were more often than not related to the ideology and priorities of the Roman state and the aristocratic pursuit of those same values. Through defensive walls, traditional aristocratic residences, and the maintenance of urban amenities and ceremonial life, we hear a local ruling group whose identity was attached to the renewed impetus of the Roman state after Diocletian—a topic I will develop further in the next chapter.

To close this section, I should point out that Western Iberian cities during late antiquity followed very similar trajectories in terms of the evolution of their topography and material culture. The differences between the top cities and the rest depended on the intensified presence of certain aspects of material culture associated with imperial or elite interests in the former cities and the less intense presence of them in the latter ones. But the difference is, in most cases, one of degree. The constructions analyzed in this chapter gave homogeneity to the urban landscape, giving a distinctive *late* Roman tone to a substratum of earlier Roman civic culture. A similar phenomenon occurred in the Western Iberian countryside from the late third to the early fifth century.

Rural Settlement and an Intensified Roman Landscape

The Roman conquest not only altered the urban landscape of the Iberian Peninsula, but its impact was also felt in the countryside. Change was not always drastic and varied from region to region. In general, by the second century, a pattern of lowland, dispersed rural settlement prevailed in Atlantic Iberia with a few exceptions in the Cantabrian Basin and northwestern Iberia.[73] Aristocratic presence in rural areas can only be traced by the occasional presence of residential villas. For instance, the phase two sections (late first and second centuries CE) of the villa of Torre de Palma (Monforte, Portalegre) consist of a rural house organized around a small atrium. While the complex included a bathhouse, none of the rooms had sophisticated decorations that can be traced in the excavations (mosaics or wall paintings). A colonnaded court connected the house to production quarters around the eastern court of the villa, while in a later construction phase a western court was added to the complex. At the southwestern corner of this latter court, another small complex known as the portico house served as a storage space and perhaps a residential area.[74] Yet in comparison to other areas of the western empire, including Mediterranean Iberia, the villa phenomenon was relatively limited in both extension and monumentality. The prevailing settlement structure consisted of dispersed sites throughout the countryside with occasional agglomerations providing services to nearby populations.

As in the case of late Roman urban structures, a combination of a relatively stable Roman settlement, with intensified monumentalization, and specific regional variations also characterized the late Roman countryside. By the third century, dispersed rural settlement prevailed in the countryside of Atlantic Iberia and continued throughout the late Roman period. In terms of monumental architecture, the most visible transformation was the construction of lavish aristocratic rural residences (villas) following the fashion of other areas of the western half of the empire. As in the case of cities, the Atlantic Iberian countryside shows that monumentalization followed *late* Roman patterns. And this phenomenon was particularly marked in Atlantic Iberia in comparison to the Mediterranean half of the peninsula and the Roman west in general.

Archaeological findings consistently show that the most striking and visible feature of rural settlement during the late Roman period in Atlantic Iberia is the generalized construction of lavish villas as (very likely part-time) residences of local aristocracies.[75] Examples abound and the typology of the building varies, although their monumentality cannot be doubted.[76] The overall size, décor, and functionality of these villas surpassed the average early imperial villa in the region. To mention one of the best-known cases, the villa of São Cucufate (Vidigueira, Beja) had a two-story residential section (one hundred meters long and twenty-five meters wide) and presented itself to the viewer with a long, uncovered forty-meter-long platform that served as the greeting area. This platform was flanked by two vaulted spaces behind which another covered platform led the visitor to the internal patio and the reception rooms. The use of marble and lavish decorations, the mosaic floors, a large bathhouse, and even a family mausoleum reveal the ostentation with which certain aristocrats made their presence felt in rural settlements.[77]

São Cucufate was not an isolated case, neither in Iberia nor in the western empire as a whole. Lavish rural residences existed elsewhere in the empire (especially in the west), but the impact of these houses and their chronology varied according to the region. In northern Gaul or southeastern Britain, monumentalized villas were built in the late Roman period, but, in most cases, they had been abandoned or reused by the mid-fourth century.[78] Southern Italy and Mediterranean Iberia had examples of lavish aristocratic houses in the countryside into the fifth century but within a context of abandonment and reuse of most early imperial sites.[79] Southwestern Gaul went through a period of intensified villa monumentalization on preexisting, early imperial villas between the mid-fourth and early fifth century.[80] This latter pattern also characterized most of the regions of Atlantic Iberia. Early imperial villas were occasionally abandoned but not as frequently as, for instance, in Mediterranean Iberia. On the contrary, the late Roman empire was, in Atlantic Iberia, an age of rapid and widespread monumentalization of aristocratic houses.

Interpreting the dramatic change in elite residential habits in the countryside has proven more difficult than documenting it. This marked increase in monumentality has sometimes been related to a putative mounting affluence among the imperial elites: larger houses mean wealthier owners. This thesis follows on the idea of a growing wealth gap between rich and poor throughout the late Roman period—especially between imperial and local aristocracies.[81] A variation of this interpretation sees the abandonment of some early imperial villas and the monumentalization of others as the result of land concentration.[82] Although the existence of increasingly regressive income distribution might be true (though it has not been proven so far), this interpretation does not account for the specific geographic distribution of late Roman villas, unless we assume that some provincial elites were wealthier than others. Moreover, the meaning of lavishly built villas may not indicate amounts of wealth but rather particular preferences of conspicuous consumption.

The villa phenomenon is sometimes related to power relationships in the countryside. A landowner's residence was meant to affirm the power of the *dominus* over his slaves, *coloni*, clients, or the rural population in general.[83] Certainly, rural mansions made obvious the economic and social chasm between nonelite individuals and the house owners, even if the former had no direct access to the residence. If we accept this reading, however, we must continue to puzzle over the same riddle of the particular geographic distribution of late Roman villas. Moreover, similar relationships of dominance also existed during the early empire, without leading to the same degree of late Roman villa monumentalization.[84]

A third way of looking at these villas emphasizes the late imperial context of elite culture, the evolution of tastes, and class identity. The display of wealth and certain power practices at villa sites were not addressed to the local population of rustics but to fellow aristocrats. Villas were spaces of elite exhibitionism in the form of sophisticated décor (e.g., mosaics, statuary), reception and dining areas, amenities such as baths, and even funerary spaces.[85] This explanation inserts villas within an empirewide culture that gave meaning to practices, settings, and objects in these rural mansions. Social practices may have included the reception of clienteles and the collection of rents. But more important, they encompassed a series of traditions tied to the elite culture of the empire. The infrastructure of the late Roman villa provided a conducive environment to hunting activities, dining parties, bathing, and other markers of aristocratic behavior everywhere in the western empire.[86] This interpretation allows us to explain why Atlantic Iberia was particularly influenced by the phenomenon of late Roman rural mansions. Part of the argument will be developed in the next chapter. In the following pages, I will focus on the extent to which villas dominated the rural landscape in Atlantic Iberia and their relative impact within the broader rural settlement pattern. The picture that emerges is consistent with aristocratic residences intensifying their monumentality while the overall settlement structure of the countryside remained unaltered from early imperial times.

*   *   *

If we were to base our conclusions on the late Roman countryside in Lusitania (especially its central and southern regions) solely on its archaeologically visible housing patterns, we would conclude that only wealthy aristocrats lived in rural areas. Monumental residential villas in the countryside provide us with the only widespread type of rural house. The late third and early fourth centuries witnessed the beginning of a wave of villa constructions in the countryside, which continued into the second half of the fourth century, as the chronologies of sites such as Quinta das Longas (Elvas, Portalegre) and Torre Águila (Barbaño, Badajoz) attest.[87] The impressive number of newly built aristocratic houses and their no less impressive size and monumentality amaze us, as the next chapter will illustrate. But we must not forget that as field surveys and site excavations confirm, the location of these newly renovated centers coincides in many cases with sites of less monumental aristocratic houses during the early empire.[88] We should not be misled, then, by the sheer monumentality of these sites into believing that the late Roman period altered traditional rural settlement patterns in Lusitania.

Although villas became the most widespread type of rural residence, their location was not haphazard. The available information reveals a close association between villa concentration and cities or, at least, relatively easy access to urban centers. Some of these mansions were located on the outskirts of the main cities—the so-called suburban villas.[89] In most cases, rural aristocratic houses were located on main communication axes, the routes that linked the various cities of the region (the most "urbanized" of the three regions, as we saw in the previous section). In particular, the Mérida–Lisbon axis and the north–south roads that connected central Lusitania with major cities in northern Iberia offer a rich landscape of rural villas.[90]

The predominance of lavishly monumentalized villas at the archaeological level should not mislead us into believing that no other settlements existed or that these villas existed everywhere. Less monumental rural residences have been documented and could have been the norm. Further, rural agglomerations can be found, but their archaeological presence pales in comparison to the monumentalization of aristocratic residences. The region of Alange, in Extremadura, is illustrative in this regard. The area was surveyed before it was flooded as part of an irrigation plan by the Spanish authorities. The village of Alange was probably a minor rural Roman and Visigothic town (Aquae) about which we know very little, located in the territory of Mérida. Settlement in Alange seems to have been steady through the early and late Roman periods, without any sign of intensification. Villas with modest monumentality, on the contrary, appear to have developed after the second century or later.[91] This village-cum-farms type of settlement could have been the norm in specific microregional contexts.

On the whole, luxurious rural mansions dotted the late Roman countryside in Lusitania—a process that began in the late third century and, in most cases, shows continuity with previous, less monumentalized villas. Geographically speaking, however, this pattern of distribution shows that villas were built in clusters throughout specific areas. Proximity to primary cities was one criterion, as was access to major roads that connected rural backwaters with major urban centers. Connectivity to the sociopolitical foci of Roman life in the province remained an essential criterion when it came to deciding on the monumentalization of a rural center.

*   *   *

The geographical distribution of settlements is also revealing in the northern plateau. The northern meseta's villas are concentrated in three areas: the modern province of León (especially near Astorga and León), the river valleys of

Palencia province, and the countryside of the northeastern part of the plateau. In general, these villas confirm the tendency to concentrate settlements on fertile lands near watercourses. Rural mansions in the northern meseta were also located along major communication axes: the roads that connected Astorga with two provincial capitals, Bordeaux in Gaul and Tarragona in eastern Iberia. The chronology of settlements varies according to the microregion. In most cases, and especially in the central and eastern parts of the northern plateau, excavations took place before the second half of the twentieth century. The use of less developed methodologies and the focus on the artistic and architectonic aspects of villas have hindered the understanding of rural evolution in the area. However, the excavations supported by more recent interventions seem to indicate that the villa network did not appear in rural landscapes without early instances of this type of residence. For instance, the villa of Navatejera (Villaquilambre, León) experienced three phases of construction. The first two phases are easier to reconstruct in the villa's bathhouses: one in the first century CE and another one in the late third or early fourth century. The third phase of the villa (mid-fourth century to fifth century) represents its peak both in terms of residential and leisure structures and in evidence for productive activities.[92] The countryside of the northern plateau did indeed experience an early imperial wave of villa construction. In general, however, these were less lavishly decorated and less monumentalized than their late Roman successors.

In the central part of the northern plateau, in modern Palencia and northern Valladolid, the intensity of monumentalization of rural residences overshadowed that of any other microregion of the peninsula, with the probable exception of the Tejo Basin. Early imperial villas existed in this area of small towns. From the third century onward, construction in rural centers gained momentum, reaching a peak during the fourth century, especially during its second half. Luxurious villas covering areas of almost ten hectares (such as the villa of Los Casares in Armuña, Segovia) coexisted with less monumental rural centers.[93] In some cases, their chronology tends to be later than those of Lusitania but similar to other microregions of the plateau. The paradigmatic example of a monumental villa in the area is La Olmeda (Pedrosa de la Vega, Palencia), first excavated in the 1960s and 1970s. This early imperial villa was lavishly monumentalized in the late Roman period. A peristyle villa with large reception rooms, it was built on a square plan with an impressive portico flanked by two towers.[94] The most recent excavations show a wave of construction in the bath area around the mid-fourth century, which may be indicative of the chronology of the rest of the site.[95] Another paradigmatic case, the villa of Almenara-Puras (Almenara de Adaja, Valladolid), presents a similar chronology. In this case, however, a late third-century to early fourth-century building preceded the last villa, although archaeologists have only been able to find production quarters and remains of a bathhouse.[96]

Overall, these three microregions (León, Palencia–Northern Valladolid, and the eastern sections of the meseta) suggest that the wave of monumental villa construction occurred in the middle decades of the fourth century and later (with a handful of earlier examples). Their location followed patterns similar to those in Lusitania. However, these villas flourished against the background of a less dense urban network and an even weaker "top-tier city" context. In this situation, villas clustered close to the few main cities in the region (Astorga, León, Clunia, Tiermes) and along the major axis that crossed the plateau—the road from Braga to Astorga-Zaragoza. Monumental rural houses existed elsewhere in the meseta, but the density of the villa network decreases toward the south and approaching the Sistema Central, the mountains that separate the northern and southern plateaus.[97] As in the case of Lusitania, the road system worked as an attraction pole for villa clusters.

This road system was not like any other within the political landscape of the peninsula. It was the backbone of the military administration as it can be reconstructed from a snapshot of army commands in the late fourth and early fifth centuries.[98] The reconstruction of military organization in Hispania depends almost exclusively on the *Notitia Dignitatum*—a list of civil and military commands throughout the empire compiled at some point (or some points) in the years around 400.[99] Although it is impossible to reconstruct the presence of field armies (*comitatenses*) based solely on the information provided in the document, there are some grounds to take the information about permanent garrisons (*limitanei*) more seriously. According to the *Notitia*, garrisons existed at Lugo, Rosino de Vidriales (Zamora), León, Retortillo (Cantabria), Iruña (Álava), and the otherwise unknown location of *Ad cohertem Gallicam*.[100] The road between Braga and Zaragoza was thus the main axis that connected the permanent military organization within the peninsula. The disproportionate number of late antique milestones near Braga compared to other areas of the peninsula suggests the interest of the imperial administration in maintaining a strong "Western" communication axis.[101] While army presence seems not to have militarized elite culture, it nevertheless intensified the presence of the late Roman administration to an extent that was not repeated elsewhere in the peninsula.

*   *   *

Northwestern Iberia and the Cantabrian Basin provide a different villa landscape when compared to both Lusitania and the northern plateau. Contrary to these two cases, the region had a relatively weak presence of early imperial villas. Iron Age–type hilltop settlements (known as *castros* in Iberian scholarship) survived the first and sometimes second centuries CE, perhaps in relation to Roman military recruitment.[102] Early imperial villas were not unknown but very limited in number. Thus villa construction emerged as a visible transformation of the rural landscape during the fourth century.[103] In other words, the region not only caught up with the rest of the peninsula in terms of the monumentalization of rural residences but also in terms of the very existence of villas in rural areas.

This process, however, was extremely focalized. Wealthy houses are documented in the city of Braga, which may indicate a preference on the part of the local aristocracy for urban settings rather than rural areas.[104] Yet, on a modest scale, the area around Braga and the nearby coastal areas offer some examples of late Roman villas, such as the suburban villa of Dume (Braga) or the coastal residence of Toralla (Oia, Pontevedra).[105] Indeed, the location near the sea of many late Roman villas may be indicating that like in Lusitania and the northern plateau, villa owners privileged easy access to major communication routes—in this case, seaborne. Isolated examples of large monumental villas also existed in the territories of coastal enclaves, such as Gijón. The early imperial villa of Veranes (Gijón, Asturias), which was of modest dimensions, was monumentalized into a one-hectare villa in three successive phases in the fourth and fifth centuries.[106] Surrounded by the Cantabrian Mountains, this villa reveals the reach of imperial aristocratic housing traditions in the remotest corners of the late Roman world.

The case of northwestern Iberia is a healthy reminder that there was diversity in monumental patterns in the late Roman countryside. Villa construction existed, and it paralleled the more intense presence of imperial administration in the region. However, fewer members of the local elite invested resources in the building of these rural houses than they did in other parts of Western Iberia. The paucity of rural villas throughout the region was not unique to northwestern Iberia and was a common phenomenon in other parts of the empire. For reasons unknown (economic, social, and even geographical), local elites did not pursue the same large-scale strategies of rural monumentalization as their peers in Lusitania and the plateau. However, when they did want to leave their mark on the countryside, they followed the same traditions as landowners in the other two regions. It is as if the northwestern Iberian aristocracy spoke the same language of settlement prestige but in a softer voice. As far as archaeology allows us to reconstruct it, rural settlement status could only be expressed in one way.

*   *   *

In all three regions (Lusitania, the northern meseta, and northwestern Iberia), rural mansions did not exist within a settlement void. Other types of rural settlements may have been less impressive, but they sheltered the vast majority of men and women living in the region as a whole. Tracing where these people lived, however, is not always an easy task. Some of them dwelled in sites that could resemble, to a certain extent, small towns. So-called secondary settlements, that is, agglomerated sites with less density than cities and without the legal status of *civitas* (head of territory), were in many cases the most immediate source of services to the nearby rural areas, including housing for local populations working in primary activities. Legally speaking, they were subordinated to a *civitas*. Written sources refer to them as *mansiones, vici, castella,* or *pagi.* These terms mask highly heterogeneous types of settlements that could range from a twenty-hectare site with some monumental buildings (especially baths) to small villages of rural workers with a few houses and no central buildings.[107]

Some "rustics" may have lived within the villa center itself, in workers' quarters, but these areas are not easy to identify archaeologically. Moreover, workers' quarters are difficult to distinguish from production facilities. A series of small rooms in the northeastern section of the Algarvian villa of Milreu (Estoi, Faro) may have been the residence of estate workers based on its proximity to other production facilities. However, they may well have been spaces dedicated to production or storage.[108] Other workers, probably the majority, did not live near villa centers. But villas could certainly exercise symbolic attraction on the nearby peasant population (which was likely a dependent peasantry). More than a hundred rural workers were buried seven hundred meters north of the villa of La Olmeda (the so-called northern necropolis) between the fourth and the second half of the fifth century.[109] On a less impressive scale, an excavation five hundred meters north of the villa of El Vergel (San Pedro del Arroyo, Ávila) has produced eleven burials with simple funerary depositions—including labor tools.[110] In the Asturian valleys, at least thirty-six burials in Paredes (Siero, Asturias) were likely associated with an unexcavated site (identified as a possible villa) four hundred meters south.[111] Villages or villagelike sites existed in the period but had a relatively limited impact at the settlement level. More likely, a large but undetermined number of rural workers lived scattered throughout the countryside in isolated houses or small hamlets. The exception seems to have been in northwestern Iberia and the Cantabrian Basin. In spite of the limited impact of villas on the countryside of these two areas, the rural landscape did alter during the late Roman period. The agents of transformation were not the mansions of local aristocrats but more modest settlements, usually located on hilltops. Small sites (in some cases with Iron Age settlement and abandonment after the Roman conquest) were occupied or reoccupied during the late Roman period.[112]

The hilltop site of Viladonga (Castro de Rei, Lugo) can help us understand what may have been a wider settlement phenomenon in northern Iberia. This *castrum* near the Roman city of Lugo shows signs of occupation from the decades around the turn of the era. Its occupation was suddenly interrupted during the first century CE, but excavations have shown a renewed occupation from the third to the fifth century or later. A series of walls and ditches protected this settlement, but we can certainly doubt that these defenses during the late Roman period had a military purpose. At most, they could offer some protection against brigands or they were used to protect animals, since bone studies indicate intense husbandry. This site presents a structured internal organization, with streets and houses arranged around internal patios. Archaeologists have uncovered the presence of basic artisanal activities, which they mostly deduce from tools or metallic waste. Findings include weights, chisels and picks, a compass, fine wares, weapons, brooches, and nearly 1,500 late Roman coins. Part of the material culture may thus indicate the presence of elite groups. But nothing in the organization of the site suggests an internal hierarchy within the settlement.[113] If local aristocracies lived on this site (which is doubtful), they left no traces in terms of housing patterns. More likely, we are in the presence of hilltop villages such as those existing in other corners of northwestern Iberia.[114]

The mountains of northwestern Iberia prevent us from generalizing based on the best-surveyed plains of Lusitania and the plateau, where villas dominate the archaeological record. Yet future excavations in these two regions may eventually alter the current pattern of villa-centered analysis. Some secondary settlements, such as the hilltop of Monte da Nora (Elvas, Portalegre), remind us that dispersed settlement was not the only possibility in the late Roman Lusitanian countryside.[115] However, even in the case of northwestern Iberia, the phenomenon of hilltop occupation should not be exaggerated. The chronologies of late antique sites are still uncertain in most cases and more precise excavations are needed to specify different sequences, which could range from the third to the sixth century or later (as is the case in Viladonga).

Thus, dispersed, lowland rural settlement seems to have been the norm in the late Roman countryside in the whole of Atlantic Iberia, with focal points in cities and secondary settlements and small towns. These dispersed settlements included peasant huts or hamlets, farms, and centralized production facilities often in association with rural mansions (a topic to be developed in Chapter 3). Against this landscape background, pockets of villa clusters flourished during the fourth century according to the regional lines described above.

*　　*　　*

This overview of the late Roman countryside in Atlantic Iberia indicates that the basic features of traditional Roman settlement structures remained in place after the third century. Generally speaking, there was no drastic difference in terms of types of settlement. Rather, the countryside experienced specific intensifications in some of its constituent parts. In particular, aristocrats built monumental rural houses, which surpassed in size, decoration, and functionality early imperial villas. Just like monumentalized cities, lavish villas in the countryside followed a peculiar geographical distribution, clustered in specific microregions. First, a large number of archaeologically visible aristocratic residences were concentrated in central Lusitania, especially along the Mérdia–Béja–Lisbon corridor and, to a lesser extent, in the Algarve area of southern Portugal. They were also concentrated on the northern parts of the Duero Basin in the plateau region, that is, along the Astorga–Clunia axis, on the road that connected Braga and Astorga to Zaragoza and the Mediterranean. Finally, there was a small group of villas near Braga and the coasts of Galicia. Although this latter group cannot compete in terms of its dimensions and intensity, it certainly brought a marked change in comparison to the early Roman period. It is important to stress that not all aristocrats built monumentalized rural residences, just as strategies of urban housing varied significantly from city to city and within cities. Monumentality could range from the impressive La Olmeda to the more modest villas of the Alange region. We must acknowledge the existence of an invisible elite living in cities or on rural farms, whose residential structures resemble "peasant" sites in field surveys.

The construction of luxurious villas only corroborates the tendency we saw in urban settlements: that is, Atlantic Iberian settlement matches the sudden centrality of the region within the political landscape of the late empire in comparison to the relative isolation of the early imperial period. Villas were built near "top-tier" cities or along major routes linking these cities (central Lusitania, the northern part of the northern meseta, and coastal enclaves, including the territory of Braga). As in the fourth-century Danube-Balkan region, villas clustered in areas with intensified state presence, such as centers of administrative power and important communication axes.[116] Thus, in Atlantic Iberia, there seems to be a correlation among markers of urban status in the late Roman sense, the presence of the Roman state, and the expansion and monumentalization of rural aristocratic houses. The construction of urban and rural buildings reflecting the social and political values of the local elites intensified simultaneously with, rather than in opposition to, the more intensified symbolic and material presence of the Roman imperial administration.

But there may be other reasons behind the location of villa clusters. In this sense, a comparison to urban elite housing can be useful. I believe that the spatial distribution of rural and urban aristocratic houses is in itself revealing of status consciousness. As in other parts of the Mediterranean world, elite urban houses were clustered in specific neighborhoods. The best-documented case is Mérida, thanks to the excavations at La Morería. In this quarter next to the urban wall, thirteen houses have been identified. At least six of them have apsed rooms and private baths—and the number could be larger if further areas are excavated.[117] This was not a feature unique to Atlantic Iberia. Aristocracies throughout the empire developed a sense of identity through living in specific quarters within late Roman cities, as the case of Bordeaux illustrates.[118]

We can extend this argument to elite houses in the countryside, usually concentrated near major cities and important communication axes. This distribution reproduced a Roman ideal of spatial organization according to which territories were organized from the cities and the roads that united them. Rather than seeking isolation, these villas were discretely located at the center of the mental maps of men and women in the Roman world. As in the case of urban housing, we can interpret the location of rural mansions from the perspective of strategies of class distinction. Building lavish rural residences in specific areas was a way of expressing class identity by demonstrating the ability to follow aristocratic tastes in choice of location and type of residence, as the next chapter will argue.

What is more remarkable for the purpose of this chapter, perhaps, is that villa clusters were located along lines of communication and in the proximity of areas with intense imperial presence. As I have argued above, location next to major roads had not only a practical purpose of accessibility but also the symbolic charge associated with centrality within the human landscape of the

empire. Furthermore, each road must be read within its specific political context. The road from Astorga to Zaragoza was symbolically close to the center
of imperial administration in the sense that it linked the major permanent
military garrisons in the peninsula; it could also have been a central communication route of imperial mandates. Villas on the roads reaching Mérida were
obviously tied to a charged locus of imperial administration. To a certain extent, maritime villas along the Galician coasts were also attached to the communication axes reaching both governmental centers and military garrisons.

To be sure, this is a general picture and exceptions are frequent. Further,
rural monumentalization of the type we find in Atlantic Iberia also existed in
the Mediterranean regions of the peninsula, although the phenomenon may
have been less marked. These cases, however, do not deny the impetus with
which Roman aristocrats left their mark on the Atlantic Iberian countryside
after the late third century, especially in comparison to the early Roman period.
This monumentalization occurred in the form of clusters of villas in areas particularly attached to the renewed state presence of the post-Diocletianic world.

Western Iberia and the Late Roman Empire

Perhaps I should begin my conclusion to this chapter by stating the obvious: the
late Roman landscape and settlement patterns of Western Iberia were *Roman*.
Settlement structure and morphology, albeit with local specificities, were culturally readable by any person living within the boundaries of the empire, such as
the young Hydatius and his fellow travelers. Despite the transformations in the
wake of the Diocletianic reforms, Western Iberia did not alter the previous settlement traditions. But this Romanness was particularly *late* Roman in its monumental features—that is, in terms of buildings denoting settlement status and the
involvement of aristocrats and state agents. The impressive defensive walls (as
opposed to earlier imperial "prestige" walls), which were common in other areas
of the empire, developed in the region after the third century. Investment in urban amenities continued into the late fourth century, although, as in other parts
of the empire, specific public spectacles were steadily abandoned, especially in
cities without higher administrative status. Yet local elites never renounced their
aspiration of the basic pleasures of Roman genteel life within the towns. Aristocratic *domus* in urban environments tell us the story of a resilient class for whom
place of residence mattered. The same applies to the countryside. Several areas of
Western Iberia joined other parts of the empire in a wave of luxurious mansion

construction. Thus, the late Roman settlement landscape represents the stone-and-marble incarnation of the involvement of the late Roman imperial state and its aristocracies in the definition of prestige architecture.

Monumentality also reveals some peculiarities of the region. If we compare Atlantic Iberia to other areas in the west, we find a curious combination: cities with newly built walls, relatively vibrant late Roman urbanism within a thin urban network, and a boom of villa construction in the countryside into the late fourth century, if not later, without major abandonment of early imperial villas. This combination is almost unique, with the possible exception of Aquitaine and specific microregions in the western empire—predominantly in the Prefecture of the Gauls centered in Trier, the administrative unit to which Hispania belonged. I have suggested throughout this chapter that this peculiar combination of settlement patterns and the sudden and marked centrality of the Roman state in the region in comparison to the early empire are not coincidental. Both cities and countryside reveal a high monumentality in terms of late Roman standards, which suggests that the region caught up with what had become the language of settlement prestige after the late third century. The combination of walled cities, maintenance of certain urban amenities, the expansion of aristocratic houses in towns and the boom of rural villas make this region almost unique within the empire. It is as if Atlantic Iberian cities and rural areas suddenly unfolded all the items that individually denoted settlement status in the late Roman Empire (especially in the west).

There is no single explanation for this phenomenon, but one cannot help but notice the sudden growth of the region within the administrative and political landscape of the empire in relation to the first three centuries of the era. The administrative reforms of Diocletian and his immediate successors assigned a prominent role to Mérida (and, therefore, its surrounding area). By the late third century, the city was not only the capital of a province but also the capital of the diocese that supervised all the other provinces of Iberia (and Tingitana in North Africa). Similarly, with the split of Hispania Citerior into three (and later four) new provinces, northwestern Iberia now had its one provincial capital, Braga, at the head of the large territorial unit that included the Duero Valley. The impact of Braga being a provincial capital was certainly less marked than the impact on Mérida of being the diocese capital. But rural settlement material culture timidly intensifies near the provincial capital and in towns with possible administrative or military roles. The interior of the province included the potent communication axis with Bordeaux and Trier and the presence of permanent military garrisons, unlike in other parts of the peninsula.

Most signs of monumentalization are located in the main cities (some of which had early imperial administrative pedigree) along the Astorga–Zaragoza road. This focus on the road system may reflect the reorientation of the peninsula as a whole. The tetrarchic reforms forced Iberia to direct its administrative and political focus toward Gaul and the Rhine frontier rather than toward Rome and Milan. In that sense, not only the northern plateau but also the whole Atlantic arch gained centrality in the political geography of the empire.

I have summarized what seems to be the overall picture in terms of settlement morphology, but we must be aware that tension between uniformity and diversity always existed. The late Roman landscape in all Atlantic Iberian regions was relatively uniform in the sense that the archaeologically visible settlements, and especially those elements associated with imperial, civic, or aristocratic prestige, were common to all areas. To be sure, variations existed in terms of their relative density and geographical location, but there were even more significant microregional variations, which I have alluded to throughout this chapter. These differences, however, should not be understood in terms of a greater or lesser degree of Romanization. Rather, the presence of certain settlement features intensified when, for various reasons, local elites interacted with the state and empirewide values. These interactions rendered certain aristocrats or some of their practices visible. But aristocratic choices depended on several factors, some of which remain unknown to us. Elites near Braga preferred to spend more resources on urban houses than on rural mansions, but their peers in Mérida poured resources both into their rural villas and into urban environments. Aristocrats from modern Palencia preferred the former to the latter. Nevertheless, none of these groups departed from existing Roman traditions of settlement. Variations existed within a cultural umbrella that set the parameters for housing and settlement strategies.

This last observation leads us to the question of the agents behind monumental remains. In the previous pages, I have stressed the geographic coincidence between foci of state presence and buildings denoting settlement status. I have put aside the question of who these elites were, how they expressed their identity, and to what extent we can relate certain types of monumental buildings to the practices that marked social distinction. These are the questions I will address in the following chapter.

CHAPTER 2

An Unprovincial Aristocracy: Aristocratic Identity in a Renewed Empire

In the last decades of the fourth century, Ammianus Marcellinus, a former staff officer from Syria, wrote the most detailed description of post-Constantinian Roman politics that has survived. The extant books of his *Histories* cover the period from 353 (during the reign of Constantius II) until 378, when emperor Valens died at the battle of Adrianople. Ammianus's view of events was, of course, not always exempt from personal interpretation.[1] He saw intrigues at court as one of the main problems that affected the empire at his time and particularly during Constantius's reign.[2] The emperor and his intimate advisers were the targets of his diatribes against the reliance on secrecy, denunciation, betrayal, and slander. Ammianus criticized courtiers persuading women to accuse their husbands of treason, even if they were innocent. Mere comments at provincial dinner parties were used to pursue charges of treason against the heads of the households in which these comments were uttered. In Aquitaine, an "old man," a guest of a luxurious and refined banquet, wore the purple cloth used to cover couches and tables to imitate the imperial robe; this joke, lamented Ammianus, brought ruin to the estate. Similarly, in Hispania, a member of the secret service (*agens in rebus*) attending a dinner heard slaves repeating "may we prevail" (*vincamus*), a traditional formula, as they lighted candles. The imperial officer acrimoniously interpreted this expression as a sign of conspiracy and destroyed that aristocratic (*nobilis*) house.[3]

We need to take these anecdotes with a grain of salt. Ammianus probably heard them secondhand, and they were intended to present the reign and court of Constantius II in the worst possible light. But if Ammianus had

Aquitanian and Iberian readers (and he may have had some), they would have recognized the social landscape of elite interaction and sociability in aristocratic houses as well as a world in which local aristocrats shared social spaces with imperial authorities, when they were not one and the same. We do not know the social rank of these dinners' hosts, if they ever existed. Ammianus calls one of them *nobilis*, from which we may suspect, though not confirm, senatorial status.[4] Iberian and Aquitanian readers would have taken the aristocratic identity of these characters for granted owing to the social context of the events.

This chapter will explain how that identification was possible. Contrary to the tendency to treat imperial and provincial aristocracies separately, I will argue that all members of local elites defined their identity in similar terms. In other words, the legal divide between senatorial and *curialis* aristocracies, the divide between different aristocratic ranks, was less crucial than other factors in shaping the identity of the upper strata of Atlantic Iberia. Participation in the administration of the empire and membership in an empire-wide community of taste were crucial strategies for defining social standing, regardless of the particular legal rank of the actor involved. The parameters of social distinction were defined by prominent membership in the imperial project as a political and sociocultural enterprise, a project that local aristocracies embraced wholeheartedly. These strategies did not blur the boundaries between different aristocratic orders, but they created a sense of common aristocratic identity. This identity reveals that we are dealing with a very "unprovincial" aristocracy in terms of its markers of social distinction.

This chapter will tackle two sets of evidence, each of which has survived in a very fragmentary state. First, I will focus on the few extant literary sources dealing with senators, decurions, or aristocrats of undefined rank from Atlantic Iberia. These documents present such aristocrats as enactors of Roman government in various capacities: administrators of imperial mandates, participants in the politics of intercession (that is, petitioning imperial authorities), and even as involved in military defense. Second, I will analyze part of the material record, predominantly housing spaces and decoration, to show to what extent they were used to define social taste associated with an empire-wide elite. Funerary practices, house decoration, private thermal baths, and villa layouts do not intrinsically indicate belonging to a particular elite order, nor were they meant to express aristocratic dominance over subaltern groups. Rather, these items show the enthusiasm of aristocratic groups of different rank for embracing tastes associated with empire-wide elites, tastes that could be read by one's fellow aristocrats. Through their social performance of peer-reviewed taste, local elites affirmed their social identity.

Rank, Local Aristocracy, and State Power

In the Introduction, I contended that wealth was not the sole criterion to define "aristocracy," even though all aristocrats were above the middling line in terms of wealth or had access to considerable income (through salaries). The chief criterion to determine aristocratic status was the exercise of state-sanctioned power. In late Roman Atlantic Iberia as much as in the rest of the empire, social rank determined the possibility of exercising this type of authority, at least at its higher levels. Social mobility existed but access to positions of legitimate authority entailed either the possession of high rank or the immediate acquisition of it. In the minds of late Romans, imperial power was enacted by legally privileged groups. The main three orders into which privileged groups were divided encompassed the senatorial, the equestrian, and the curial orders. The first two categories were related to imperial office (including honorific positions in Rome), while the curial order included the members of local town councils throughout the empire.[5]

This pyramid of rank is, of course, a simplified version of a much more complex reality. Yet the senatorial–curial contrast remained the crucial distinction, in concrete and symbolic terms, among different privileged social actors. Other high-ranking groups existed (for instance, bishops after the reign of Constantine and his successors), but their social standing was defined in relation to the privileges that other groups received.[6] The equestrian order slowly disappeared by the second half of the fourth century, although it became de facto merged with the senatorial aristocracy.[7] Various internal gradations divided both the senatorial and curial orders—gradations that changed throughout the late Roman period. Yet these internal hierarchies were not strong enough to undermine the legal rift between the two broad categories. Thus, there are good reasons to insist on the important divide between the curial and the noncurial (mainly senatorial) aristocracies. From the imperial administration's point of view, privileged groups were broadly divided among people whose rank was attached to high military and administrative positions at the imperial level or magistracies in Rome (and, very often, both) and members of the local town councils, who were formally in charge of the day-to-day administration of the empire's cities and their territories.

This division between imperial and local aristocracies has shaped scholarship on late Roman Iberia and the empire in general. A common trend in both historical and archaeological studies of late Roman Iberia stresses the development of a powerful and wealthy imperial aristocracy, usually of senatorial status, while the local curial elite is perceived as a group battling to fend off political attacks on their privileges—and not succeeding in this battle. However, as I will argue in this chapter, curial and noncurial elites shared strategies of social differentiation and intraelite competition. Both imperial service and symbolic proximity to the emperor were crucial to develop an aristocratic persona, regardless of rank. I will start by reviewing the evidence of senatorial and curial elites from Atlantic Iberia. After presenting both groups separately, I will turn to the practices that made them part of the same self-assertive elite in the late Roman period.

*   *   *

There were two paths toward senatorial status: service in the imperial administration and career paths related to the civic (highly honorific) offices in Rome and, later, Constantinople.[8] The imperial senators entered the order through service in high-ranking imperial administrative offices (governorships, certain military commands, and top administrative positions at court). Success in this career path depended on various factors, including skill (literary or military), economic resources, luck, and, predominantly, connections.[9] Resident senators joined the order through a career of largely honorific civic magistracies (such as quaestorships, praetorships, and consulships), traditionally senatorial governorships, and the prefecture of the city of Rome.[10] This group encompassed the scions of the traditional aristocratic families of Rome and Italy, who had social and economic ties with Sicily and North Africa. The name of "resident," though conventional, is misleading since the requisite residence in Rome could be circumvented and eventually was removed.[11]

In spite of these different tracks, imperial and resident senatorial groups were less differentiated than this presentation suggests.[12] Civic and imperial service often overlapped in senatorial careers. Furthermore, a sense of belonging to a privileged order, common markers of social status, intermarriage, and shared cultural values frequently bridged the gap between different origins. As recent scholarship has shown, claims of imperial service became a sought-after symbol of social prestige by resident (Roman) senators after the reign of Constantine and their main avenue to accruing social capital.[13] Imperial support was crucial to reproducing senatorial status, and its quest was marked with anxiety for an aristocracy not determined by birth. Those who were born within senatorial families had higher chances of obtaining this status but also experienced more social pressure to reproduce the parental standing.[14]

In Hispania, there is little evidence of families without previous senatorial status being promoted to local elites through imperial service. The case of Flavius Eucherius may be one example of promotion through imperial patronage.[15] We first hear about him when he was *comes sacrarum largitionum*, one of the highest positions within the imperial administration, granting membership to the imperial inner council (or *consistorium*).[16] He was probably a native of the northern plateau, near Cauca, as was his brother, Flavius Theodosius, the father of emperor Theodosius I. Flavius Eucherius reached ordinary consulship in 381, after his nephew was proclaimed Augustus in 379 in an attempt by Theodosius to assert the prestige of a newly founded dynasty.[17] Eucherius became *comes* no later than 377, when the future emperor still lived in a discreet retirement in Iberia after his father's fall from grace and execution in 375.[18] We do not know much of his previous positions, but it is likely that it involved a literary education since his career path was within the civil administration. Based on his trajectory in this branch of the imperial administration, it has been suggested that this literary training may indicate a *curialis* origin.[19] If this were confirmed, Eucherius's career would embody upward social mobility within the imperial administration, leading to senatorial status from more modest origins.[20]

Atlantic Iberia may also have boasted a few senators who obtained their status through traditional senatorial careers in Rome, such as Acilius Severus. Consul in 323 and prefect of the city in 325, he was a prominent Christian who corresponded with Lactantius.[21] His son, also named Acilius Severus, had an outstanding career in the imperial administration (which shows the blurring boundaries between the resident and imperial paths). We know of the younger Severus thanks to an inscription that commemorates his restoration of the theater of Mérida sometime between 333 and 337, when he was *comes Hispaniarum*. Perhaps he also followed his father's learned interests, as he is usually associated with another Acilius Severus, a Christian writer mentioned by Jerome in *De viris illustribus*.[22] His patronage over Mérida suggests he was of Lusitanian origin, although this cannot be confidently asserted based only on the inscription.

A Meridan origin of greater certainty can be traced in the life of Valerius Fortunatus, a young candidate who joined the Roman senate through the holding of a quaestorship in 377. The son of a senator himself, he was expected to imitate his father's career.[23] We know of him thanks to a speech of Symmachus supporting his candidacy to a quaestorship without the requirement of paying for public games from one's own purse.[24] Previously, his widowed mother had called for the release of her son from the senatorial order since he could not afford the *munera* associated with the quaestorship. We know that Mérida was Valerius Fortunatus's hometown because the city council wanted him to assume his curial duties, claiming that he had lost his senatorial status. After the case was settled in favor of Valerius, Symmachus requested that the Senate admit him and subsidize his games.

The number of Atlantic Iberian senators was probably not large. The region had supplied the elites of the empire with few senators in the early empire in comparison to Mediterranean Iberia. If we extrapolate from the third-century evidence, few of the senatorial families from the Iberian Peninsula came from Atlantic Iberia (most of them came Évora and Mérida).[25] Likewise, scholars have rejected the earlier theory that the rise of the Theodosian dynasty implied a mass promotion of Iberian men in the imperial administration, especially men from the plateau—the *patria* of Theodosius.[26] If imperial promotion of this type existed, it is more likely to have existed, as it were, via administrative channels in the capital of the vicariate—Mérida.[27] There were probably at least three thousand members of the senatorial order at any time during the late Roman empire.[28] This number was not evenly distributed throughout the provinces. Rome (and Italy in general), Constantinople, and other cities with imperial courts, as well as the traditional senatorial provinces (including Baetica in Hispania) must have concentrated a larger number of senatorial families than other regions. We might expect to find a significant number of persons with senatorial status in or around Mérida since many of the former imperial administrators might have seized the opportunity to live in the province after serving in Lusitania. Further, direct access to imperial authorities in the city may have provided an advantage to local elites seeking social promotion through imperial patronage. All these factors considered, we could hypothesize that local senatorial families in Atlantic Iberia may have numbered between a few dozen and a hundred at any given time. Yet members of the senatorial order who had fulfilled their duties as office holders in Rome could reside in the provinces and become involved in the government of their cities. These are the *honorati* described by late Roman sources. While they did not have to carry the *munera* associated with civic government, they were invested in the government of their cities.[29] They were crucial in bridging senatorial and nonsenatorial elites at the most local level.

* * *

Together with the *honorati*, *curiales* (or decurions) composed the vast majority of locally rooted persons of power. They were the towns' rulers and the men in charge of administering local affairs. At its origins, the members of the *curia* were predominantly former local magistrates, although various criteria of membership existed (including birth and wealth). These assemblies gathered the most influential men of the city, usually landowners. During the early empire and with the increasing municipalization of Iberia, each urban community could boast a well-established *ordo decurionum*.[30] By the late Roman period, every city with a status of *civitas* (that is, the administrative center of the surrounding territory) possessed a *curia* of different size, ranging from thirty to over a hundred decurions.[31] Most of the Atlantic Iberian cities were probably closer to the lower end of this range, with the exception of provincial capitals and other special cases. In the course of the third century, membership in the local *curia* also guaranteed a minimum of legal privilege from which other Roman citizens became excluded.[32]

During the late empire, membership in the *ordo* became hereditary, while imperial authorities often intervened in the appointment of high magistracies within the cities.[33] To secure the fulfillment of tax payments and ensure the maintenance of local infrastructure, emperors intervened in city institutional life in various ways, including a tighter control over city finances and the appointment of decurions—a practice presented in late Roman literature as an imperial benefaction.[34] This policy, more intrusive than those of what had been until then a relatively hands-off administration, aimed at advancing the imperial goal of supervising provinces more tightly. *Curiales* were responsible for securing the collection of taxes, and they were held personally liable if the amount requested was not met.[35] Unlike senators, who were expected to perform euergetic practices in Rome and Constantinople, *curiales* were required to perform these civic rituals in their hometown.[36] At the same time, decurions lost some control in the assessment of tributes at the hands of imperially appointed officials.[37] However, despite the more limited role of local assemblies in the administration of the empire, membership in a local *curia* was a source of prestige and a potential platform of promotion to senatorial rank.[38]

Atlantic Iberia's *curiales* are elusive in the textual evidence. In part, this may be due to the relatively small number of *civitates* in the region. Moreover, as the previous chapter has shown, the nature of the epigraphic evidence, a major source of information about *curiales* in the early empire, drastically dwindled after the third century—a silence that is common to other areas of the empire.[39] Yet the mere presence of cities indicates the continuity of local councils since the imperial bureaucracy depended on this order to rule over cities and territories. In 396, the central administration instructed Petronius, the vicar of the *Hispaniae*, on the role of decurions in witnessing documents of the *gesta municipalia*—the tax and land registry kept by each city.[40] We find hints of the decurions' continued role through scattered mentions of urban magistrates, who were chosen from among the members of the *curia* or granted membership in the *ordo* thereafter. The early fourth-century council of Elvira, which gathered bishops from the whole peninsula (though predominantly from southern Iberia) took for granted the existence of chief urban magistracies (*duoviri*) and civic priesthoods, usually monopolized by decurions.[41] We know of one *duovir*, a certain Caius Lepidus, who left his name on a set of baked mud tablets from Astorga at some point during the second half of the third century. The inscription (known as *itinerario de barro*) describes a series of itineraries throughout Atlantic Iberia.[42] More than a century later, Hydatius complained about the rapaciousness of another urban magistrate, the *exactor*, who collected taxes in the middle of what were, in Hydatius's view, the calamities produced by the presence of barbarian armies in the early fifth century.[43]

The *ordo decurionum* was not a uniform body. A more common division between the majority of its members and a group of its most prominent figures, known as *principales* (*proteuontes* in the Greek East), created a hierarchy within city councils.[44] Among this latter group, we might encounter current and former office holders, such as the *duoviri* mentioned in the council of Elvira. The *principales* had a leading role within the city, which included more direct interaction with imperial authorities. A Latin text inscribed on a bronze *modius*, probably used to weigh taxes in kind, reveals the existence of this hierarchy in a remote corner of northwestern Iberia. The inscription found near A Coruña dates from 369–370: "The legal weight of a *modius* according to the sacred command of our lords Valentinian, Valens, and Gratian, unconquered emperors, by the order of Marius Artemius, of senatorial rank, in charge of the vicariate [of the *Hispaniae*]. Undertaken by the *principales* Potamius and Quentianus."[45] These two otherwise unknown characters enacted the prefecture's regulations on the weight of a grain *modius*, presumably for taxation purposes.

The increasing scarcity of inscriptions celebrating decurions' benefactions to their cities does not mean that euergetic activities ceased in late antique cities.[46] *Curiales* were responsible not only for the poll tax collected on the land but also for the maintenance of certain infrastructures.[47] The above-mentioned *itinerario de barro* is suggestive of the role of local magistrates in handling information about public roads. In general, the state of the road system itself reveals that urban institutional life functioned, since cities were responsible for the maintenance of roads and the *cursus publicus*.[48] Likewise, public bathhouses reveal the presence of decurions, who were responsible for their maintenance according to imperial legislation.[49] As we saw in Chapter 1, bathhouses were one of the few infrastructural works that remained in most Western Iberian cities throughout the fourth century. Moreover, if the construction of walls in several urban centers of Atlantic Iberia bespeaks a language of city prestige and inter-city competitiveness (as I also argued in Chapter 1), we may hypothesize the active role of the local notables in procuring imperial authorization and, perhaps, funds to build these defenses. Local councils took their duties of urban upkeep seriously and made sure every member contributed to this end. That is why the *curia* of Mérida sued Valerius Fortunatus, whose senatorial status was lost owing to poverty, for his reluctance to join the *ordo decurionum* and, hence, its responsibilities. The preservation of urban infrastructure should not be read only as a burden on councilmen. Such an interpretation, focused on the language of extant legal texts and legal disputes, leaves aside the prestige that euergetic practices still carried in the late empire as well as the interest of local elites in marking their social status by performing liturgies from which nonelite members of the urban community were excluded.[50] Whether decurions engaged in these activities by imperial mandate or by their own initiative (or, as is more likely, a mixture of both), early imperial models of euergetic activity still permeated the social persona of town councilors.

*　*　*

The Western Iberian elite landscape included a persistent number of local councilmen and a few members of the senatorial order. The small number of non-*curialis* aristocrats could not afford to detach themselves from the rest of those with claims to high status. The daily practices of social distinction were locally rooted. The above-mentioned Acilius Severus, although a supraprovincial governor with senatorial status and pedigree, thought there was no better way to advertise his affection to his *patria* (or perhaps province) than the restoration of a theater.[51] This is not to say that aristocrats were not aware of social orders or that belonging to each group was not manifested in concrete differences. Those who attended the theater of Mérida, for instance, would have immediately recognized membership in different orders based on seating arrangements.[52] Perhaps the most onerous of these burdens was personal liability in the process of tax collection since members of the *curia* were expected to meet the tributary demands over a city territory out of their own pocket if necessary.[53] These and other benefits associated with senatorial status offered incentives to abandon the late Roman aristocratic lower ranks of local town councilors.[54]

A great deal of legislation aimed at preventing decurions from acquiring the privileges of the senatorial order.[55] However, it is not clear that all *curiales* sought to become members of this order. For one thing, becoming a senator could be an onerous affair. It involved career choices that not every decurion was willing to make. The admission fees to enter and later pursue honorific careers in the Roman and Constantinopolitan senates, in the form of public benefactions, could discourage impoverished candidates, as the episode of Valerius Fortunatus reminds us.[56] Proximity to the emperor was a source of prestige, but it could also lead to rapid downfalls. The elder Theodosius's proximity to Valentinian I may have secured his command in Africa against the rebel Firmus. Yet that proximity (and his success in the campaign, making him a potential contender to the throne) may have cost him his life after Valentinian's sudden death in 375.[57] Certain members of the senatorial order were also subject to an increasing erosion of their prestige. By the fifth century, most of the economic benefits of senatorial status became concentrated in the top echelon of the order—the *illustres*.[58] Furthermore, *curiales* could dodge imperial burdens if they were able to successfully mobilize social and economic resources. The mere manipulation of the fiscal system could bring considerable benefits.[59]

There were other ways in which senatorial and *curialis* elites could find a common ground of aristocratic identity. The structures of imperial administration allowed both senators and decurions to materialize their social standing by advertising their participation in the empire's public life. In a way, Atlantic Iberian aristocracies could mark their standing as enactors of imperial government. Aristocratic identity relied less, in a sense, on belonging to a specific rank than on the materialization of the political consequences of that particular rank. Scattered references in surviving texts allow us to glimpse different ways in which aristocrats assumed political roles. These roles were enactments at the local level of the functions over which the Roman state as an ideological enterprise claimed monopoly, control, or oversight. They involved, for instance, the supervision of the fiscal system, channeling local demands and controversies to the highest imperial authorities, and even the eventual use of military force.

Late imperial legislation reminds us that *curiales* were essential in the process of tax collection (a topic to be developed in Chapter 3). Certainly, they were collectively responsible for the submission of the city's dues. Yet reducing their role to victims of an imperial *dirigisme* fails to acknowledge the other side of the coin. Imperial authorities relied on decurions for the smooth operation of the tax system.[60] Their role in the process of tax collection could be seen as a burden but also as a manifestation of authority. We can thus read the above-mentioned inscription on a *modius* from A Coruña as a sign of the state burden of local aristocracies—the weight of the late Roman state forcing the *principales* to implement its policies.[61] Understanding the inscription as an indication of imperial absolutism, however, assigns too much importance to a language that replicated imperial legislation. Since it is likely that Potamius and Quentianus were in charge of drafting the language of the inscription, it is possible that they used it to publicize their status within their own community through their role as enactors of imperial mandates between the praetorian prefecture and their local *patria*.[62]

Local aristocrats could use their influence to gain access and obtain concrete benefits from imperial administrators and courts—a habit that is usually swept under the generic carpet of patronage. These were not private actions; rather, emperors and aides encouraged these very public appearances since petitioning at court gave the central administration an opportunity to control appointed officials. Above all, these practices were part of the social persona of any aristocrat.[63] The late empire may have witnessed an increasing monetization of access to imperial officials, but personal relationships and the politics of intercession still played a significant (if not the most significant) role.[64] We can sense the influence of lobbying power in one of the most prominent religious controversies in the region, that surrounding Priscillian and his followers. In their fight against Priscillian, Lusitanian bishops (especially Hydatius of Mérida and Ithacius of Faro), mobilized networks of contacts that reached the imperial court to solve locally rooted problems with possible empire-wide implications.[65] Priscillian and his backers, who enjoyed exten-sive sympathy from the Iberian aristocracy, would eventually win the support of the court in Milan and of the provincial governor Volventius against much of the ecclesiastical establishment.[66] Ithacius continued his own lobbying cam-paign, obtaining the support of Gregory, the praetorian prefect of the Gauls in Trier, after which he was able to bring the case against the Priscillianist bishops to the emperor. Priscillian and his allies (Iberian, but also perhaps Aquitanian, aristocrats) managed to maintain a stalemate for a period. Ac-cording to Sulpicius Severus, the emperor did not follow the advice of Gregory because "all things were on sale [in the court] through the wanton-ness and power of a few."[67] Rather, the case was sent back to the vicar of *Hispaniae*, probably to find a negotiated solution at the provincial level.[68] Yet the revolt and usurpation of Maximus in 383 offered a new opportunity to Ithacius—who found a more sympathetic reception at the newly estab-lished court at Trier.[69]

The previous description of events is based on Sulpicius Severus's *Chron-icle*, which is admittedly hostile toward Priscillian and his followers.[70] Thus, it should come as no surprise that he framed the actions of the Priscillianists within a language of venality as opposed to the language of persuasion em-ployed to outline the activities of the "orthodox" Ithacius and his followers. Yet we might expect that both factions used the same lobbying strategies to approach imperial agents—perhaps including a combination of venality and personal influence. Both parties could rely on the political gymnastics of lo-cal elites, who were well trained in approaching imperial officials. Collective actions, such as the city embassies to imperial courts sent by local *curiae*, were a common feature of the late Roman world, and they are well attested in Med-iterranean Hispania.[71]

The politics of intercession were part of the behavior expected of every powerful figure. Idealized images of aristocratic life insisted on the moral qual-ities of those who offered brokerage on behalf of "friends" who were supposed to be one's equals. In a highly stylized description of the younger Theodo-sius's retreat in Iberia before he was recalled to public service, the panegyrist Pacatus praised the emperor for his care of his friends' affairs (*negotia amico-rum*) through his "attention, advice, and material means" and his protection of absent friends' interests.[72] While one must be careful with information provided in panegyrics, it is clear that Pacatus expected this brokerage to be the proper behavior of a powerful figure in a provincial setting.[73] A person with connections at court through his uncle as well as on the local level, the younger Theodosius could discreetly intervene as a local player in the arena of political and social networks on which the imperial administration was based. Moreover, the language of *amicitia* often hid relationships of patronage by members of local elites over nonelite individuals. Political and judicial intercession transcended the boundaries between senatorial and nonsenatorial aristocrats at the local level, even though one can assume that the former held a structural advantage.[74]

Local aristocrats were not only able to mobilize networks of contacts and relationships. The economic muscle of local elites allowed them to dispose of material resources to participate in the imperial political arena. During the reign of Theodosius's son Honorius (r. 395–423), when barbarian armies were active in Gaul and the usurper Constantine III was attempting to gain control over the western provinces, an army was raised in Hispania to face him.[75] The leaders of this mobilization were two aristocratic youths and wealthy landowners (*iuvenes nobiles et locupletes*), Didymus and Verinianus.[76] According to Zosimus and Sozomen, they were relatives of Honorius.[77] It is possible that they first mobilized the Roman troops stationed in cities (the *burgarii*) and, later, armed slaves and peasants from their own domains. Didymus and Verinianus's failure (they would eventually be captured and executed on the order of Constantine III) must not prevent us from noticing that the leadership they assumed was based on claims of state-sanctioned power—in this case, defending the legitimate imperial authority. Late Roman military authorities and even emperors relied on arming slaves and other noncombatant populations in extreme cases.[78] As far as we can reconstruct Didymus and Verinianus's actions, they seem to have acted based on their claims to a personal relationship with the emperor, as members of his family. The court in Ravenna probably agreed to their rise to military leadership, although nothing in the extant sources indicates an official position.[79] In any event, this confrontation ought not to be seen as an expression of local powers resisting imperial authorities in the same way that city walls were not expressions of isolation and retreat to one's local territory. Rather, they show the extent to which local elites mobilized resources to express their loyalty to what was, in their view, the legitimate imperial court.

In these vignettes, we meet decurions, senators, and notables of unknown status intervening alike in essential areas of late imperial statehood. In all these cases, we encounter people with claims of upper social status engaging in public activities in different ways. As performers of administrative decisions, as lobbying agents before imperial authorities, or as military leaders in the face of armed invasions, local elites of various ranks performed political actions whose control the imperial state zealously aimed at regulating. Participation in the administrative and political life of the empire signaled the status of local elites and granted them a common identity at a more fundamental level than the holding of a specific rank. Or, rather, they materialized the political power associated with that specific rank. Again, I do not want to underplay the role of rank in the self-portrayal of aristocrats, but I do want to insist on the essential role that participation in the imperial political arena played in the reproduction of social differentiation. This practice permeated different subgroups within the elite, even when the relative impact of each individual's actions could be conditioned by his placement within the late Roman legally sanctioned social ladder.

Moreover, participation in the political life of the empire was part of local social competition. The *principales* Potamius and Quentianus advertised their distinct status within the *ordo* by determining the weight of a *modius* based on imperial mandates. The intervention of advocates in the Priscillianist controversy was to a certain extent related to power struggles within the Christian Church.[80] Other, less well-documented controversies in different areas of social life may have involved similar power competitions and may have involved interventions such as Theodosius's on behalf of this friends. And aristocratic competition could also lie behind the raising of local armed groups in the early fifth century. A civil war gave the opportunity to join either Constantine III's or Honorius's side. In all these cases, aristocratic social rivalry was intimately related to claims of imperial service, proximity to the emperor, and participation in imperial power structures.

Furthermore, the relevance of internal divisions by social rank among the local elites decreased in importance toward the turn of the fifth century. In a process that is ill documented in Hispania but well attested in other parts of the Mediterranean, a so-called government by notables silently replaced the town councils as the primordial administrative institution in cities. This government consisted of more or less formalized assemblies of imperial officials, local members of the senatorial order (*honorati*), and powerful landowners, many of whom originated from the *ordo decurionum*.[81] As Chapter 5 will argue, this was the typical civic government to be found in the main cities during the post-Roman period, but its roots were in the last few decades (or even years) of the fourth century, when prominent decurions were able to join forces with other local notables to monopolize the decision-making process in cities throughout the empire. Unfortunately, the evidence from Hispania makes it impossible to reconstruct this change in the years before 400.

Legally sanctioned statuses were therefore crisscrossed by a myriad of practices that materialized the political power associated with rank. These created a different hierarchy, invisible to us but obviously patent to contemporaries, based on participation in the political and administrative life of the empire. In this way, Atlantic Iberian elites reproduced, at a much simpler level, the attitudes of the upper echelons of the imperial elite, the senatorial aristocracy of Rome, which increasingly stressed direct relationships to the emperor (or the imperial government) as a fundamental status marker.[82] The emperor ultimately symbolized political life, and proximity to him through his representatives gave ideological sanction to status claims. Senators could easily make the claim since their status generally derived from imperial service. Decurions were certainly not excluded from such associations and the late Roman state offered the possibility, at least for some of them, to stand out within their own communities by stressing their roles as enactors of public decisions.

While enactment of statehood materialized legally sanctioned ranks at the local level, participation in the imperial project implied belonging to an elite that superseded local horizons. Inclusion in an imperial elite was cemented through a series of practices that expressed proper elite tastes and modeled the behavior expected of ruling classes elsewhere in the empire—or what was perceived to be the appropriate attitude of an aristocrat. Sadly, Western Iberia did not leave written documents that allow us to reconstruct such ideas among the local elite. But the wealth of archaeological evidence offers a unique opportunity to re-create, albeit partially, how Western Iberian aristocrats saw themselves as members of the empire's ruling class.

Material Culture and Belonging to an Imperial Elite

The hierarchy based on senatorial and curial orders also permeates certain interpretations of archaeological evidence and monumental architecture in particular. The rise and fall of certain buildings are often explained in terms of the supposed divergent fates of senatorial and curial aristocracies. For instance, the multiplication of rural villas is read as a sign of the concentration of wealth in the hands of the senatorial aristocracy and their ascendancy in rural areas.[83] Likewise, the abandonment of certain public buildings in cities is read as an indicator of the social and economic crisis affecting *curiales*. As imperial office had become the main avenue to attain high social standing, it is argued, aristocratic competition through urban benefactions receded as a source of prestige.[84] The economic burden on the *curiales* led them to cease pouring resources into public buildings.

It is not clear, however, that markers of aristocratic status must be associated with the social muscle of the imperial (senatorial) aristocracy while any symptom of decay or crisis is to be ascribed to the local aristocracy. Although the reading of material evidence I just described can hold some truth, there is a risk of too linear an interpretation. A rural mansion's silent remains rarely reveal the social rank of its owner. The assumption that those who built rural mansions were wealthier than those who did not, and that those who were wealthier were also higher on the social ladder than those with less wealth, may work as a rule of thumb. But we cannot take for granted that senators built villas while decurions did not. It is exceedingly difficult to determine the status of a particular family throughout the generations. Intermarriage bridged the gap between different social ranks, as we can extrapolate from well-documented areas such as the Aquitaine of Ausonius and his relatives.[85] Although new men entered the imperial service and reached high positions, recruitment into the senatorial order largely depended on the demographic basis of families of curial rank.[86] A wealthy decurion may have poured wealth into a rural mansion while a neighboring senatorial family may have followed a different housing strategy. Likewise, a city without a theater does not reveal poorer decurions than a city with that amenity. *Curiales* could have decided collectively that their city did not need a theater to express its status, or imperial authorities may have patronized the construction of a theater in a provincial capital, thus forcing its decurions to maintain it.[87] Thus, status, wealth, and material culture cannot be straightforwardly connected in the archaeological evidence.[88]

Material culture has also been used to support the idea of an independent elite whose power depended on their local tyranny. According to this interpretation, lavish constructions (especially rural houses) demonstrated isolation from the state and closer ties to the material basis of social power in the countryside. A now declining historiographical trend explains these houses in terms of elite withdrawal from the public culture of the empire and its cities into their private domains of the countryside.[89] In this splendid isolation, local elites preserved their lifestyle and wealth; kept their slaves, tenants, and clients under firm control; and offered protection against the rapaciousness of the late Roman Empire. The material culture of the late Roman villas in

Atlantic Iberia is thus seen to indicate islands of elite culture in the countryside, reproducing the values of an aristocracy that was autonomous from the state. According to this reading, rural mansions were primarily meant to stress the abyss between the (again, senatorial) elite and the rural masses. Local landlords would have impressed their clients and peasants with lavish reception halls and impressive facades.

Readings of material culture in the past decade have opened the possibility of new interpretations that emphasize the competitive nature of aristocratic material culture—thus giving room to horizontal strategic action and individual action to signify social distinction.[90] What previous authors saw as buildings intended to impress peasants are now increasingly approached from the vantage point of intraelite dynamics. This section of the chapter will draw on the conclusions of this trend in scholarship and relate aristocratic identity to participation in an imperial elite culture firmly rooted in the values and practices of the ruling classes of the Mediterranean world. In other words, objects, spaces, and behaviors were meant to be read by the owner's peers or, rather, those claimed as one's peers. If aristocratic identity was largely intertwined with one's role in the political life of the empire, as the previous section has argued, this role was not the result of a state imposition but the consequence of carefully chosen strategies by those who claimed special social standing. This standing had to be acknowledged not only by the imperial administration but also by others who made similar status claims. In other words, material culture reveals strategies of class competition and solidarity aimed at stressing membership in an empire-wide aristocracy without particular emphasis on a specific legal status, senatorial or curial. I will illustrate this position by looking at four relatively well-documented cases in Atlantic Iberia: funerary practices, bathhouses, house decorations, and domestic spaces of sociability.

*   *   *

Aristocratic funerary practices reveal a status-conscious elite with specific methods of family self-promotion. Monumentalized funerary spaces were built near some residential villas, especially in the fourth century. Rather than continuing with earlier Roman traditions of burial practices on the outskirts of cities, some families brought the commemoration of the dead closer to their rural residences. Some of these family mausolea are identified as Christian burials, thus providing us with the first widespread concrete evidence of

Christian architecture.[91] Yet the presence of Christianity is not clear in all the mausolea, as is illustrated by the case of the villa of La Cocosa (Badajoz). A 77-square-meter mausoleum located 250 meters west of the villa housed a marble sarcophagus containing human remains (unfortunately the burial had already been disturbed at the time of the discovery). The villa itself reproduced most of the characteristics of aristocratic housing (peristyle, rooms decorated with mosaic floors, bathhouse). The entrance to the mausoleum, a rectangular area with two apsed walls on its sides, led to a central space in the shape of a four-apsed room (tetraconch) with a vaulted ceiling. Marble and glass findings reveal the decorative efforts of the builder.[92]

Nothing indicates that La Cocosa's mausoleum was a Christian burial. Since the site became a church in the post-Roman period, it is possible that the previous building was associated with Christianity. It might be more relevant to notice that the construction of monumentalized burials was part of an impetus of aristocratic assertion that led to the construction of sacred, commemorative pagan buildings next to residential villas. In particular, access areas or roads leading to the villas were frequently chosen as sites for these memorial structures.[93] It is thus possible to understand the archaeological record more in terms of what the builders shared with each other (certain preferences for monumental burials) than what they did not (their religious identity). While the number of monumentalized burials in Western Iberian villa contexts are not numerous, future excavations may expand the number of cases, especially in the cases of mausolea located on access roads rather than next to the villas themselves. Whether generalized or not, there are enough examples to suggest that the monumentalized celebration of family memory in rural spaces was part of the language available to express elite self-understanding.[94] Aristocratic families were able to assert their identity by creating a sense of "ancestral lands"—a frequent practice in Gaul.[95] What makes this practice particularly interesting is that it was not a choice made by elites in other areas of the late empire in the fourth century, but a specifically Iberian trend, and predominantly a Western Iberian one.[96] In any event, aristocrats were aware that buildings (in this case, mausolea), their internal arrangement, and their location had the potential to assert elite identity.

* * *

This identity was rooted not only in the commemoration of one's ancestors but also in constant social interactions. One of the central areas of sociability (including nonelite or subelite sociability) throughout the empire was the bathhouse, a recurrent feature in important Atlantic Iberian cities. In the previous chapter, we saw that several urban, public bathhouses continued to function into the late fourth century, when some of them began to show signs of abandonment. By the mid-fifth century, it is probable that all public thermal baths were no longer in use and that these locations were put to other uses.[97] However, Atlantic Iberian elites incorporated bath spaces into their residences in the fourth and fifth centuries, both in urban and rural settings.[98] Thermal baths were not mere attachments to elite residences but an integral part of aristocratic houses. The owner of the villa of La Olmeda could reach a 900-square-meter bath complex through a corridor, which was accessed from the villa's peristyle.[99] Urban houses also reflected this trend. One of the best documented examples is the so-called house of Cantaber in Conimbriga. At some point between the late third and the early fourth century, a 330-square-meter bath complex was built as part of a series of renovations. The new bathhouse had two large cold pools in addition to pentagon- and hexagon-shaped warm pools. Family members and guests could access this bathhouse from one of the residence's two peristyle patios.[100]

These were private baths in the sense that they were part of an individual's property, but not only family members were expected to attend. In the bath area, the owner and his guests could unite leisure with the conviviality proper to elites throughout the empire. Indeed, the architectural features of late Roman bathhouses in the region reveal their increasingly important role as places of aristocratic sociability.[101] In the newly built thermal baths, the *frigidarium*, or cold pool areas, occupied a significantly larger space than the other sections of the baths. Owners invested considerably in the larger areas, including through the construction of mosaic floors.[102] The importance of the changing room and access hall (or *apodyterium*) also grew in this period.[103] The cold piscine was the first and last stage of the bathing ritual and the natural place for sociability and the display of aristocratic taste in decoration and layout. The baths of the villa of Milreu illustrate this point fully. A large *apodyterium* of almost 100 square meters with mosaic floors received the visitors, who would enter into a *frigidarium* of slightly larger dimensions (105 square meters) amid similar decoration and marble constructions.[104] Similarly, visitors to the villa of Veranes would enter the building through a covered corridor at the end of which they would turn left and gain access to the reception hall. Were they to turn right, however, they would reach a distribution area with direct access to a large *frigidarium* and a series of smaller rooms containing other sections of the bathhouse.[105]

Private bathhouse spaces were therefore intended to engage peer sociability and offer an arena in which the house owner could demonstrate his awareness and participation in a broader landscape of shared elite tastes. This conclusion can be extended to the decoration of houses in general. Indeed, decorative elements also aimed at denoting social distinction through association with elite tastes from the Mediterranean world. Unfortunately, crucial decorative features of elite houses, such as wall paintings, textiles, and precious metallic objects, have barely survived in the Western Iberian archaeological record. Other objects, such as statuary, have been preserved only fragmentarily. One of the best examples comes from the villa of Quinta das Longas, where a series of statue fragments belonged to a sophisticated decorative program that included a nympheum. These fragments were very likely part of statuary groups that are now lost and included giants, Muses, a hunting Diana, nymphs, Venus, and Bacchus, among others.[106] The northern plateau offers fewer examples of villa statuary, although this invisibility may be the result of the prior spoliation of sites. The fragmentary evidence suggests that northern plateau house owners followed similar trends to their peers in Lusitania in terms of tastes and use of statues.[107]

Fortunately, we can rely on a large and growing corpus of floor mosaics from luxurious houses to analyze decorative preferences. The mosaics of the villa of Camarzana (Camarzana de Tera, Zamora) present an example of what is usually considered typical of the Western senatorial aristocracy. Although the chronology of the villa is difficult to determine, it probably dates from the mid- to late fourth century. In the *triclinium*, or dining hall, hunting scenes; equestrian imagery (racehorses?) with the names *Germinator*, *F(e)nix*, *(S)aerasimus*, and *Venator*; and depictions of vine trees were combined with a representation of Orpheus taming wild animals. Mosaics with other motifs have been reconstructed in other rooms, including the abduction of Europa and a possible depiction of Ariadne.[108] Hunting scenes were also popular motifs in mosaic floors. The large reception hall in the villa of El Hinojal, near Mérida, offers another example of such motifs. A scene of a hunter about to kill a boar decorates the center of the room, surrounded by personifications of the four seasons. In another room located on the opposite side of the villa's peristyle is a second hunting scene, in which a mounted hunter is killing a panther.[109] Excavations in Mérida show that similar motifs were used to decorate urban elite houses. Allegorical representations of rural life and hunting scenes were part of the interior decoration of two different *domus* of the provincial capital.[110]

All these *topoi* may reveal owners who shared an interest in elite literary culture as well as hunting, the archetypical male aristocratic activity. Here again, earlier readings of these mosaics stressed a putatively aristocratic flight into a rural world escaping from civic burdens.[111] Further, reading these mosaics against the texts of late Roman literati would associate the decoration of late Roman houses in the region with what was expected to be the literary culture of the late Roman aristocracy. In other words, mosaics could represent the literary and social events of an aristocratic private life. However, the fact that certain mosaic motifs were deployed is not conclusive evidence for the owners' behavior or education. Mythical scenes were common enough in late Roman houses, and a few scenes tended to repeat themselves throughout the provinces of the empire. Likewise, the absence of these motifs in the mosaics does not indicate the owner's lack of interest in literary pursuits or hunting. Although a villa owner who decorated his house floors with racehorses may well have been taking pride in his ability to raise circus horses or celebrating his funding of memorable *ludi*, the absence of such motifs does not indicate the contrary, as in Aquitanian villas. The most common type of mosaic decoration remained geometric patterns and did not necessarily indicate the owner's lack of interest in hunting, horse races, or literature. Rather, these mosaics reveal the owner's interest in reproducing themes that were common to other villas in his region and throughout the Mediterranean world and that expressed ideas of order and strength—*virtus*.[112] The mythical motifs in the mosaics of La Olmeda's reception hall (including a scene of Odysseus finding Achilles on Skyros) related the owner to other aristocrats in neighboring regions (such as Noheda in Villar de Domingo García, Cuenca, or Torre de Palma in Lusitania) or in other regions of the empire.[113] The marble statuary from Quinta das Longas had parallels in other Iberian villas (Valdetorres de Jarama, near Madrid), but it also participated in Mediterranean-wide artistic trends under the influence of the so-called circle of Aphrodisias.[114] It is impossible for us to tell whether its owner hunted, attended circus races, enjoyed literature on mythical themes, or was interested in rural activities. But we can see him (or, rarely, her) claiming to possess decorative tastes similar to those of his peers throughout the empire.[115] There was an international aspect to decoration choices in these houses, as has been argued for southwestern Gaul.[116] Thus, tastes were modeled after the fashion that signaled peer-reviewed recognition of belonging to the empire's elite.

It is perhaps in the house layout itself that we can see the efforts to signify aristocratic taste most clearly. Both urban residences and rural villas reveal the owner's efforts to participate in the world of elite sociability. In particular, a broad category of reception and sociability spaces are characterized as public spaces in rural villas and urban *domus*. They were crucial zones, easily accessible from the house halls or through a peristyle patio, unlike other areas of the residences, whose access the owner jealously guarded.[117] In these rooms, dinner parties and other types of social meetings gathered the owner of the villa with other socialites in highly ritualized encounters.[118] We should not see these spaces as areas of egalitarian social life since status differences among the attendees existed. Yet all the participants could claim a shared appreciation for a lifestyle associated with the upper echelons of Roman society. Not just intended to impress social inferiors, the carefully crafted reception areas and dining halls were meant to express the owner's tastes and those of the few who were admitted to dining parties—that is, other aristocrats or subaristocrats.[119]

We can sense the type of effect the owner wanted to create by looking at the villa of Milreu (Figure 3). A wide access area (over two meters in width) connected a covered walkway that wound around the house's large peristyle to the dining spaces. Looking from the entrance door, the visitor saw a massive U-shaped stone platform. Dinner-party guests could enjoy the view of two small water fountains inside the dining hall, on either side of the entrance. The room itself was of impressive size. A hall of over 120 square meters with mosaic floors, pilasters, and, in a later addition, an apsed area, provided the environment for elite sociability in this villa at the westernmost corner of the empire.[120] A similar investment in social spaces is observable in the so-called House of the Marbles (*domus V*) in Mérida (Figure 4). In this urban *domus*, a large vestibule with direct access to the street received visitors of various statuses. Following the vestibule (with access to the late Roman bathhouse built over early imperial public space), a 96-square-meter peristyle courtyard led to a reception hall with an apsed wall. The peristyle was paved with marble floors, and, facing the entrance to the apsed hall, there was an apsed marble space with a water fountain at its center.[121]

Peristyle patios and apsed halls were not the only way in which aristocratic houses articulated social spaces. The villa of Veranes in Asturias followed a different model. Although a central patio structured the house's different spaces, a covered gallery connected reception areas and sociability quarters

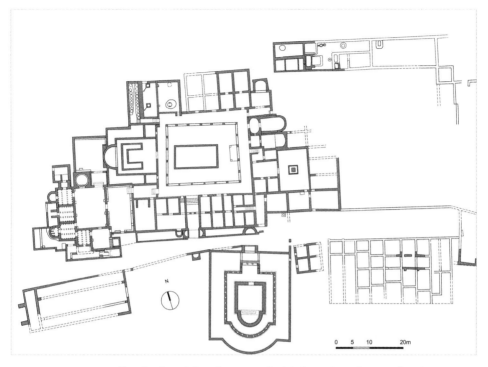

Figure 3. Villa of Milreu (Plan F). From Felix Teichner, *Zwischen Land und Meer: Architektur und Wirtschaftsweise ländlicher Siedlungsplätze im Süden der römischen Provinz Lusitanien (Portugal)*. Mérida: Museo Nacional de Arte Romano, 2008.

without gaining direct access to the open area (indeed, the gallery and the patio were separated by a line of rooms). The gallery directed the visitor to an impressively large rectangular hall (twenty-three meters in length), at the end of which he would find a stair leading to a quadrangular room decorated with geometric mosaics. A previous architectural program in the villa, dated to the late third or early fourth century, had included a large apsed room with mosaic floors right next to the thermal baths.[122] Excavators have not been able to identify the actual meaning of this earlier room, but it shows that apsed halls were not unknown to the owners of the buildings when they engaged in the mid-fourth-century program of monumentalization. For reasons unknown, they decided not to follow that format. Veranes and similar villas indicated alternative architectural forms with a similar purpose of creating spaces for a

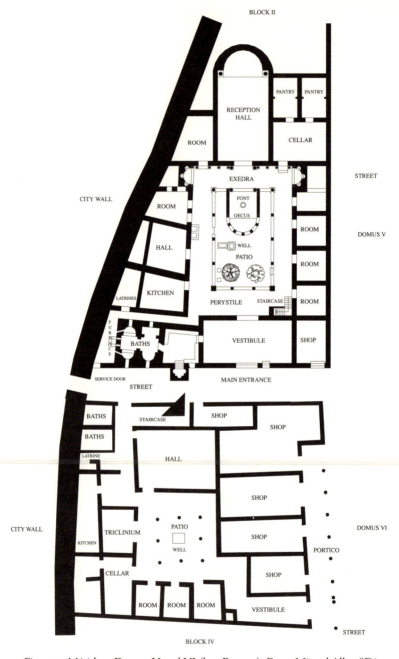

Figure 4. Mérida—Domus V and VI (late Roman). From Miguel Alba, "Diacronía de la vivienda señorial en Emerita (Lusitania, Hispania): desde las *domus* altoimperiales y tardoantiguas a las residencias palaciales omeyas (s. I–IX)." In *Archeologia e società tra tardo antico e alto medioevo*, ed. Gian Pietro Brogiolo and Alexandra Chavarría Arnau, Mantua: SAP, 2007, 163–92.

type of sociability that was shared by other elite houses in the region, even when the builder followed less prevalent architectural models.

The inclusion of sociability spaces and the above-described general spatial organization of aristocratic residences were not unique to Atlantic Iberia. Indeed, they were common features of elite Roman houses, including early imperial ones. The material culture of aristocratic daily life reveals a world in which parameters of social behavior and tastes expressed class identity. These behaviors and tastes placed local elites within the larger context of empire-wide aristocracies. Rather than emphasizing a particular status or hierarchy, the material culture of Atlantic Iberian aristocrats reveals their adherence to the practices of those who claimed special social standing in other parts of the empire. In daily interactions, social status was perceived as a consequence of these practices and not vice versa. What needs to be emphasized is the role of aristocratic agency in this process. To be sure, external models were adopted and incorporated into the symbolic language of material culture. Yet in the process of adoption, they could be resignified to denote participation in a culture of peers throughout the empire. Take, for example, the well-attested phenomenon of apsed rooms in elite housing. These apsed rooms were a recurrent feature of late Roman imperial residences, especially audience halls. Local elites could have adopted these models as a way of reflecting symbolic aspects of imperial monumentality.[123] However, if we give more room to individual and group agency, we also understand the adoption of apsed structures not as a direct transfer from top to bottom but as a social taste associated with elite status.[124] In other words, apsed rooms were not adopted only with the intention of imitating imperial palaces and determining social hierarchies at dinner. Rather, local elites adopted them to express a particular architectural taste that was thought to be proper for an aristocrat anywhere in the late Roman Empire—and especially in southwestern Gaul and Britain.[125] Likewise, local elites did not adopt a "package" but were able to follow their own combination of monumental buildings to denote status, for instance, through regional peculiarities such as rural private mausolea.

*   *   *

Through the survey of funerary practices, private bathhouses, residential decoration, and layout, we can glimpse how aristocrats expressed their elite identity in Atlantic Iberia. The first point to be stressed is that the intended audience of these practices was primarily the aristocrat's own aristocratic group, broadly understood, that included subelite groups. These elements were intended to be read by one's peers and, thus, constituted claims of belonging to a community of elite taste. This does not mean that nonelite groups did not or could not read them. Although we cannot reconstruct how various individuals interpreted these objects and spaces, discursive criticisms against aristocratic lifestyle were common enough among the educated elite that it would be surprising if they did not exist among subaltern groups.[126] Through the cultural and social practices described above, Atlantic Iberian elites could delineate social boundaries. But this delineation was less intended to express the power of the *dominus* over subordinates than it was meant to signify participation in a common life of *domini* throughout the empire. More significantly, this cultural delineation could only work if explicit references to domination were removed and, instead, behavior and taste were emphasized. In a context of fierce late Roman aristocratic competition, the adoption of cultural patterns associated with the ruling class of the western empire (and in particular with the Prefecture of the Gauls) promoted social claims, especially within that vast gray area between the bottom of the curial order and the top of the senatorial aristocracy.[127]

As we have seen, with the exception of funerary monuments, the material culture of elite life in Atlantic Iberia existed elsewhere in the empire. However, this was not the case in all imperial regions, and not even in all regions of the empire's western half. In the case of aristocratic mansions and sociability infrastructure, only elites in Atlantic Iberia (and perhaps northeastern Iberia), southwestern Gaul, and, until the mid-fourth century, southern Britain favored these modalities of elite taste in such a generalized way. The reasons for this are difficult to determine, although in the previous chapter I argued that there was a more intense, renewed state presence in the area at the same time that it suddenly acquired political centrality. However, other models existed and local aristocracies could have opted for those as did, for instance, aristocracies in northern Gaul where material culture became much more militarized. A myriad of individual decisions involving imitation, resignification, and also practical considerations such as cost and availability of labor and materials lay behind regional and subregional peculiarities. But it cannot escape the gaze of the historian that Western Iberian elites shared a language of prestige through housing and private amenities with their peers in other parts of the Prefecture of the Gauls. The imperial project forced them to look, increasingly, to the behavior of aristocrats with a similar focus at the imperial court and its administrative center in Trier.

An Unprovincial Aristocracy

I argued in Chapter 1 that monumental architecture in Atlantic Iberia reveals the renewed presence of the Roman state project—or, more precisely, the presence of a renewed state. The location of newly monumentalized cities (especially through the construction of walls and other urban amenities) and aristocratic houses in both urban and rural areas roughly coincides with the main administrative centers (provincial capitals and former *conventus* centers) and main routes, either over land or waterways. Moreover, the first section of this chapter demonstrated the nexus between elite identity and imperial service. Members of the various legal ranks pursued participation in the political life of the empire as a way of materializing and advertising elite status. Differences in rank (senatorial, curial, and so on) mattered, but they did not prevent those placed at the top of the social ladder from pursuing similar strategies of social differentiation. We have seen three ways in which all groups with high-status claims could express their social standing: through participation in the civic and imperial administration, through the politics of intercession, and through the organization of military defense. We hear of these groups at highly crucial, and sometimes dramatic, moments: the enforcement of tax policies, the threat of a schism in the Church, or civil war. However, comparative evidence (some of it Atlantic Iberian) suggests that there were a myriad of silent instances in which similar practices took place.

The same caveat about the actual impact of legally defined status applies to the ways in which elites used material culture to mark social boundaries. Nothing suggests that senators and *curiales* pursued different strategies. Nor does the material record argue in favor of a crisis of *curiales* and the dominance of senatorial families. This social change may have taken place, and it was certainly the case in many areas of the Mediterranean world by the early fifth century. But the archaeological record in Atlantic Iberia is not proof of that change. Instead, the silent remains of urban and rural houses, mausolea, and mosaics offer valuable information on how aristocrats wanted their social taste to be perceived. These preferences were markedly conservative in character, stressing traditional civilian values of earlier imperial aristocracies. However, within this conservatism, local elites occasionally expressed preferences for certain cultural consumptions, such as apsed rooms or large *frigidaria*, which were more in tune with contemporary building tastes.

Therefore, as far as we can reconstruct Atlantic Iberian social identities, the stark legal division between local-*curialis* and imperial-senatorial does not account for the strategies of social distinction that characterized the late Roman period in this remote corner of the empire. Legal status was the requisite to claim belonging to the Atlantic Iberia elite, but this elite did not only use legal status to express class identity. Indeed, boundaries between the various legally defined groups could be crossed or tactfully forgotten in daily social interaction, just as economic exploitation was never advertised as an elite value, even though it certainly existed.

In sum, late Roman Atlantic Iberian aristocrats defined their identity in terms of participation in the administration of the empire (and in proximity to the emperor) as well as in a commonality of taste shared with other (though not all) imperial elites. Thus, we are dealing with a very unprovincial aristocracy, an aristocratic class whose identity was not expressed through local strategies. Instead, members of the upper echelons of the regional elite relied on strategies of social identity that related them to those they considered their peers, senatorial or *curialis* aristocracies from elsewhere in the empire. The argument is easily made for the senatorial aristocracy, but I would like to stress that the same applies to decurions. For instance, civic office continued to play an important role in the construction of prestige. But the same civic office was progressively conditioned by the imperial administration's decisions and the functions of magistrates were increasingly tied to the requirements and priorities of the late Roman state. In a sense, decurions were increasingly becoming properly imperial functionaries.

Moreover, imperial politics and success in intraelite competition became completely tied to one's role as participant in the political and social life of the empire. Local elites rapidly joined the opportunities that a more intrusive type of state offered to advance their social interests. It would be hard to argue that the more bureaucratized and interventionist state after the later third century harmed Atlantic Iberian aristocracies and, perhaps, aristocracies empire-wide. At the individual level, some members of the local elites could have economically, politically, and socially suffered. Some readjustments were undoubtedly necessary. But the empire still offered plenty of possibilities. In many ways, the fate of local aristocracies of any rank was tied to the success of the imperial project, which defined the arena in which competition was pursued and distinction was obtained. When this imperial project disappeared, local aristocratic groups had to undergo significant readjustments in order to develop a class identity (the topic of Chapter 5).

Atlantic Iberian aristocracies therefore shared relatively uniform strategies of social distinction and competition. These strategies depended on willingness to participate in late Roman statehood and to be recognized by others with similar interests throughout the empire, especially its western half. Local elites took advantage of the social and political opportunities created by the renewed empire. By doing so, they supported the imperial project at the local level. In the next chapter, we will see a similar pattern emerge in relation to the production of wealth, the economic ability that funded all the strategies described in this chapter.

Economic Strategies in a Renewed Empire: Aristocratic Economic Units in the Late Roman Period

At some point during or right after the year 340, the city of Rome's pork butchers guild offered an honorific statue to their *patronus*, Lucius Aradius Valerius Proculus. The explanatory inscription carefully listed the honors and offices he had achieved. The last one in the list was one of the two ordinary consulships, the highest honor in a senatorial public life, which he held in 340. Three years earlier, Proculus had crowned a successful career as imperial administrator with an appointment as the prefect of the city of Rome, the administrative position most sought after by traditional Roman families (an appointment he would repeat in 351). Proculus was a proud pagan in a world of Christian emperors, which did not prevent him from achieving an impressive succession of high-ranking state offices, including the prestigious governorships of Sicily and Africa Proconsularis.[1]

In 321, during his first years as an imperial official, Proculus was sent to the Iberian Peninsula as *peraequator census provinciae Calleciae*, which we could translate as "census leveler of the province of Gallaecia."[2] Put simply, he was in charge of reassessing provincial taxes in northwestern Iberia.[3] In the late Roman empire, reassessing taxes often meant revising the amount of produce that different units of lands had to pay and sometimes distributing unoccupied lands. Although less glamorous than his later appointments, his role in northwestern Iberia was essential to the operation of the same state that would shower him with honors during the following three decades. Later in his career, Proculus would have the opportunity to realize the importance of tax assessment. As governor of various provinces, he would oversee tax collection. As prefect of the city, he would be in charge of distributing those taxes among the people of Rome, in the form of subsidized grain, oil, wine, and other food products.[4]

The work of Valerius Proculus and many others like him in the two Atlantic Iberian provinces, Gallaecia and Lusitania, set decisive parameters for aristocratic economic strategies. The importance of the tax system in aristocratic economic activities cannot be sufficiently stressed since it affected the amount of surplus available to local aristocracies to be used in social status competition. But more important, tributary practices would also provide strong incentives to certain types of economic strategies, including the specialization of production to meet state demands. Thus, one of the arguments of this chapter will be that the economic activities of the landowning class reflect the impact of late Roman taxation, which was implemented in Atlantic Iberia by men like Valerius Proculus between the late third and the early fourth century.

However, no matter how important the taxation system was for the operation of the late Roman state, it did not completely determine the economic strategies of Atlantic Iberian aristocracies. Tax assessment and collection worked against the background of a Mediterranean type of economy centered on the exploitation of large land tracts, which had characterized the region since the first century CE (if not earlier in some microregions). Wealth in the Roman world was, above all, land and the surplus obtained through rural production. The strategies of local economic units could be influenced by state demands. But those very demands rested on the assumption that the economy of the late Roman period was, essentially, a Mediterranean agrarian economy. Large rural estates were the bases of any aristocratic economic strategy in the late empire, as had been the case in the early imperial period.

The study of late Roman Atlantic Iberian rural estates faces a seemingly hopeless challenge. No written records of estate administration or even tax collection have survived. Moreover, the structure of land tenure is a complete mystery—and the list of silences goes on. Historians must respectfully thank archaeologists for having provided us with at least some evidence with which to study the large landowning class's economic practices. In a sense, we are fortunate because late Roman aristocracies in Atlantic Iberia built monumental rural mansions near production facilities. The archaeological visibility of the former helped excavators find the latter and thus document part of Western Iberian aristocracies' economic life.

Based on the surviving archaeological evidence, this chapter will show that the prevailing aristocratic economic strategy manifested itself in the form of economic units that centralized and transformed marketable food staples. These staples included grain, olive oil, wine, and animal products. Other products may have existed, but they are archaeologically invisible. I will trace this strategy through infrastructural investments after the late third century, as well as through material remains and paleobotanical analyses wherever they are available. Unfortunately, because of the nature of the evidence, little more can be said about the workings of the late Roman rural estates in Atlantic Iberia.

These food staples may have originally coincided with state demands made in kind. Hence, the imperial administration had a decisive role in favoring this type of strategy. However, large landowners could use these specialized demands to their own advantage and orient their production and the centralization of produce toward consumption in local and nonlocal markets. Most of the second half of this chapter will tackle the existence of distribution networks hinting at market mechanisms of distribution in late antique Atlantic Iberia. The reach of exchange networks had shifted since the early empire, when the Iberian Peninsula was more deeply immersed in long-distance distribution. The end of large-scale mining in Western Iberia and of the state-sponsored olive oil trade from southern Iberia, and the relative decline of eastern Iberian wine, all reoriented the Iberian economy toward more localized markets. Let us therefore turn our attention to changes and continuities between the early and the late Roman periods.

Late Roman Rural Production Units in
the Western Iberian Countryside

It may sound odd to begin a section on the late Roman economy of Atlantic Iberia by stressing its Mediterranean character. And yet, with the exception of microregions in the northern mountains, the production basis of Western Iberia did not differ significantly from the average local economy of other Mediterranean areas. The so-called Mediterranean triad (wheat, olive trees, and vine trees) was grown wherever climate allowed it. Other cereals such as millet, oats, and rye, more adapted to colder and more humid weather, were also cultivated.[5] Husbandry played an important role in rural production, the most common animals being sheep, goats, cattle, and horses. In coastal areas, fishing and fishing-related activities represented an important share of the local "gross domestic product."

There is nothing odd about this characterization. Mediterranean-type farming had existed in the peninsula since before the Roman conquest. Greek and Phoenician colonies bridged the Iron Age societies of the area with a broader pan-Mediterranean commonwealth. This process was only accelerated by the Roman conquest, sometimes brutally so. Consumption patterns adjusted, as some sectors of the local population began to adopt the traditions of the overlords, while a constant flux of Roman, Italian, and other settlers created a growing demand for Mediterranean-type staples.[6] Taxation, especially in the first two centuries of the era, created a new pressure toward production of commercialized staples, as the local population required cash to pay tributes.[7] But the Roman state also imposed more specific demands. Both the state-run mines in northern Iberia and the large-scale production of olive oil to supply the city of Rome in southern Iberia shaped the economic insertion of the peninsula within the imperial system.

Between the mid-first century and the early third century, Atlantic Iberia had a distinct role in the overall imperial economy. The province of Lusitania and northwestern Iberia were the source of large-scale mining (primarily of gold and tin) from which the imperial administration derived a considerable amount of revenue.[8] The importance of this activity was such that specifically appointed procurators directed it.[9] In northwestern Iberia, it even involved a drastic settlement transformation. A large number of hilltop sites were occupied after the Roman conquest to serve the needs of mining activities in specific microregions of northern Iberia.[10] Furthermore, large-scale metal extraction created an opportunity for local farmers and landowners to direct their production to the population involved in exploiting the mines (including the troops stationed in the area).[11] For a combination of reasons (economic, technical, military, and sociopolitical), large-scale mining ended during the third century.[12]

The other area of direct state intervention in the peninsula during the early empire involved the supply of olive oil to the city of Rome. The heyday of the sale of Baetican oil to Rome was the mid-first century, especially under the Flavian emperors. However, under the Severan dynasty, in the early third century, the imperial state endeavored to develop more direct control over this supply through various mechanisms, including the use of imperial estates in the Guadalquivir Valley. Baetican oil benefited not only Rome but also the army, since the Roman state provided the Rhine frontier with this product.[13]

Baetican oil production continued in late antiquity, although circulation levels dwindled. It was transported after the third century in smaller vessels (Dressel 23 amphorae) that reached various points of the peninsula and the western Mediterranean region. Significantly, two of the largest surviving deposits of this amphora are found in Rome and on the Rhine frontier.[14] Two laws in the *Theodosian Code* from the reign of Constantine show the interest of the Roman administration in regulating the activities of Hispanian shipowners (*navicularii*) involved in state-sponsored transportation of goods to supply the city of Rome.[15] Yet by the mid-third century the importance of Iberian oil in pan-Mediterranean trade had decreased as it was being progressively replaced by African oil.[16]

Thus, by the third century, both large-scale mining and transportation of *annona* olive oil had ended. Neither of these activities disappeared completely. Smaller-scale mines still operated in northern Iberia but became, archaeologically, almost invisible.[17] Southern Iberian olive oil production may have decreased, but it was still an important part of the local economy.[18] It was no longer, however, a state-sponsored activity oriented toward a crucial consumption center. These changes brought to the fore with even more intensity than in previous centuries the economic units on which local aristocratic wealth largely depended—as other archaeologically traceable production faded from the record. In the late Roman period, economic units, which centralized, transformed, and distributed the food staples of the Mediterranean diet, became the only surplus-generating economic sector of unchallenged supremacy at the regional scale, involving new infrastructural investments on visible nonperishable archaeological constructions.

The relative economic uniformity, however, may not necessarily have resulted from an invisible hand directed by consumption markets. The Roman state had a say in the productive standardization. After Diocletian (r. 284–305), the renewed and more intrusive tax system could request pan-Mediterranean products: grains (wheat and barley), olive oil, wine, and animal products.[19] Not only contributions to the army but also the salaries of imperial officials were paid in kind—or, at least, assessed in kind.[20] The evidence for taxes in the Iberian Peninsula is, admittedly, almost nonexistent, and various scholars have made arguments in favor of coin and kind.[21] Yet taxes collected in coin could also have favored standardized production, since taxpayers needed to sell their produce to pay tributes, which would have promoted the production of a few easily commercialized staples. Although by the fifth century the practice of commuting taxes from kind to coin was extended, tributary de-

mands from the late third century onward must have affected the standardization of production. This impact is difficult to assess fully, but it warns us
against approaching the late Roman period as a transition from an early imperial interventionist economy into a market driven one.

The imperial state could make or supplement aristocratic fortunes. Direct transfers of wealth appropriated through taxes or imperial lands were made
available through state salaries and imperial gifts.[22] In Chapter 2, we encountered some Iberians who participated in the upper echelons of the imperial
administration. Although their service may have taken them away from the
peninsula, they kept their personal ties to their homeland and, eventually, returned upon retirement. To be sure, state salaries were not generous, but office granted access to legal fees and less legal extortion, which could supplement
the state payments handsomely.[23] Imperial fiat could also initiate or expand
fortunes through land donations. This may have been the case of the Arian
bishop Potamius of Lisbon who received an imperial property (*fundus fisca-
lis*) from the equally Arian emperor Constantius II. Unfortunately for him,
Potamius died before he even saw his prize, as his Nicene detractor Faustinus
tacitly celebrated.[24]

In addition to imperial largesse and employment, there was a myriad of
nonlanded economic activities from which a person of means could obtain
steady incomes, from renting urban property to financial loans, from corrup-
tion and extortion to semi-industrial production. None of these were perceived
as particularly befitting an aristocrat (with the exception, perhaps, of "gifts"
derived from exploiting positions of power), but we must not underestimate
their impact in the amassing of wealth. In some cases, they could have been
paths toward respectability.[25]

Since we rely almost exclusively on archaeology to reconstruct these nonagricultural incomes, it is worth briefly dwelling on one case to show both
the possibilities and limits of archaeological data in reconstructing this aspect
of aristocratic wealth. Fish sauce and pickled fish, staples of Mediterranean
cuisine, had been produced in the coastal areas of the peninsula since the late
Republican times. Fish factories (*cetariae*) seem to have receded to some extent in the third century but witnessed a renewed expansion after the fourth
century, parallel to the revitalization of Mediterranean exchanges.[26] This expansion included the reconstruction of early infrastructures as well as the use
of new areas for production purposes.[27] Some of the excavated processing
plants reveal the impressive dimensions of this industry, such as the factory
in the secondary settlement of Tróia (near Setúbal, ancient Caetobriga), on

the Sado River estuary. Archaeologists have found several industrial complexes concentrated in this site, and many more are suspected to be underwater at present, which hints at a production site of considerable magnitude.[28]

Documenting fish factories is easier than determining the social status of their owners. Fish industries were one available source of income for the land-owning elites. The investment required was certainly above the means of poor people—but not, for instance, those of a wealthy freedman.[29] In some cases, production units were located in proximity to residential villas. At Tróia, the baths of a residence have been completely excavated, but scholars working on this site have found some evidence of larger residential structures.[30] A facility of over a hundred meters long, facing the Atlantic Ocean at Cerro da Vila (Loulé, Faro), on the Algarvian coast, was part of a larger aristocratic residential complex.[31] The correlation between elite buildings and fish factories is well documented in northwestern Iberia, yet most of the fish-processing factories in the Algarve were not associated with villas (although examples do exist).[32] Still, as I mentioned in the previous chapter, the absence of villas does not equal the absence of aristocrats. Thus, although archaeology does not provide conclusive evidence of aristocratic involvement in all instances, the production of commercialized fish products on an "industrial" scale was an option available to those aristocrats with the resources to undertake such an enterprise.

The paucity of evidence for artisanal or semi-industrial activities linked to local elites might be due to more than just the fate of archaeological evidence. Neither nonagricultural activities nor state transfers were solid bases for long-term aristocratic wealth. In the first case, social taboos limited elite involvement in mercantile, industrial, and financial activities, and aristocrats tended to avoid them (or, very often, to disguise them).[33] In the second case, imperial whims could generate a starting point for a fortune (especially a landed one), but it was not able to secure its maintenance in the long term. The larger part of aristocratic income stemmed from the elites' profits as landowners.

*   *   *

The basic property unit in the late Roman West from the point of view of agricultural production was the *fundus*. The term refers to a large land tract under single ownership. Landowners could have more than one *fundus*, consolidated in a single area or, more commonly, scattered throughout a region or even several regions.[34] In this case, it was frequent to find an administrator (*actor* or *villicus*) in charge of each unit.[35] This latter case was the norm among the wealthiest members of the senatorial aristocracy. The emperor himself possessed several *fundi* empire-wide, including in the Iberian Peninsula, such as the *fundus* that bishop Potamius received near Lisbon. Most aristocrats, however, may not have owned much land beyond the territory of their city—especially those from the decurions' rank.

We can only speculate about the size and structure of these properties. Attempts to reconstruct the rural properties have relied on two methodologies. The first one consists in relating rural property to settlement patterns. Based on this methodology, the late Roman countryside appears completely dominated by large properties with scattered rural workers in small tenancies. Lavish rural villas would have been the settlement expression of large properties and dispersed nonelite settlements the counterpart of peasant tenancies. The increasing monumentality of these villas as well as the disappearance of some early imperial, smaller villas has been read as the settlement marker of larger properties concentrated in fewer hands.[36] This interpretation of settlement archaeology would thus support scholars who argue for a concentration of property throughout the late Roman period, usually in the hands of imperial bureaucrats.[37]

While there might be some truth in the overall model, we cannot take settlement patterns as a direct indicator of property structures. Villas were residential and not property or production units per se, even though *villa* as a term increasingly merged both residential and territorial meanings in late antiquity.[38] The previous chapter showed how rural elite houses resulted from conscious social strategies within a context of intraelite competition. Villas were not primarily conceived as centers of estates, even if they could operate as such in numerous instances. Most of all, they do not tell us about those landowners who decided *not* to build a rural residential house.[39] Furthermore, the size of a villa does not reveal the dimensions of its owner's properties but rather the amount of wealth that the owner and their successors were willing to pour into expressing their status in the rural milieu. Settlement archaeology, in spite of the wealth of information it offers, cannot uncover some fundamental aspects of landholding.

The second attempt to reconstruct property structures consists in applying models developed in other areas of the Roman Empire, for which more written documents are available. This approach, however, is not exempt from risk. Although areas with relatively abundant late Roman documentation, such as the eastern Mediterranean and Italy–North Africa, shared some characteristics with Atlantic Iberia, they may have been very different in terms of property structures and estate economy. For instance, Italy and North Africa were particularly influenced by transregional landownership, especially that held by the Roman senatorial aristocracy and imperial estates.[40] The eastern Mediterranean countryside presented various forms of property structures but with a much stronger presence of village communities and small, free landholdings than the western Mediterranean.[41]

* * *

While settlement archaeology cannot be used to unveil property structures, it could offer an entry point to understanding economic units. Monumental residences help archaeologists find production quarters associated with several of these mansions. These production quarters, and not the villas themselves, were the epicenter of *some* large economic units. They could also act as the economic foci of small peasant holdings and even other small *fundi*.[42] I propose to consider the centralized economic facilities as indicators of direct control of agricultural surplus rather than ownership of specific tracts of land, which are impossible to trace through field surveys and excavations. In other words, settlement archaeology reveals the concentration of certain aspects of the economic process in direct association with residential villas—from which we can confidently assume aristocratic involvement. They show the direct intervention of a landowning class in the economic cycle through the centralization of rural production for transformation and distribution purposes.

Before I embark on the analysis of this strategy, I want to clarify one issue. The evidence does not indicate that this was the only strategy available. More hands-off models may, and probably did, exist. For instance, owners of large properties could easily content themselves with dividing their property into tenancies and collecting rents in cash without almost any other intervention. But excavations and surveys indicate that economic units under more intense managerial control of the landowning class or their representatives were far from isolated. I posit that the typical economic unit in Atlantic Iberia (as in several other places of the Roman world) was committed to the production of the basic food staples of the Mediterranean diet, without much significant diversification. Those in charge of these economic units invested in infrastructural improvements to facilitate this production and increase productivity through the centralization of certain aspects of the economic cycle.

The type of large-scale rural production in Atlantic Iberia described here only continued or, in some cases, accentuated the already existing predominance of mixed Mediterranean agriculture. Cereal cultivation was at the basis of the late Roman agrarian economy. Cereals largely remained the main staple of Roman diet as well as an important part of the state requests in the form of a tax.[43] Where pollen analysis is available in the regions under study, they confirm the importance of these crops.[44] Not all the lands in Atlantic Iberia were adapted to the same cereals. Wheat grew easily in southern Lusitania and the plateau, while other cereals, especially barley, must have played an important role in grain production because of its resistance to dry climates and its use as animal fodder.[45] Comparative studies with other parts of the Roman world (for which we have evidence of cereal growth) suggest that the *fundi* associated with the few excavated production quarters of villas must have produced considerable amounts of cereal for self-consumption, tax payment, and supply to nearby cities. All this is plausible and probably true, but insufficient to determine any trend in cereal production during the late Roman period.[46] Nothing in the extant evidence suggests that late Roman crops surpassed early imperial numbers in a significant way.

Olive oil, another member of the Mediterranean triad, is ubiquitous in rural production quarters. Climatic conditions favored the culture of olive trees in southern and central Lusitania. Our evidence of olive growth in the northern meseta is scantier, but it existed.[47] However, the scale of this region's olive oil production must have been lower than in Lusitania. The Duero River was the northernmost limit of oil cultivation, but even north of the Sistema Central, evidence of large-scale oil production is flimsy—at least in comparison to Lusitanian production units. Oil production was not part of large economic units in northwestern Iberia and the Cantabrian Basin.[48] Production on a considerable scale involved a minimum of infrastructure that is normally found in sites associated with rural mansions, such as the villa of Milreu, in the Algarve. An only partial excavation of its *pars rustica* has unearthed a four-level building with five olive presses that were active at least until the early fifth century.[49] In central Lusitania, the excavations of São Cucufate indicate that olive oil production played an important role within the villa economy.[50] Palynological studies of the Proserpina reservoir near Mérida, however, reveal a decline in the total impact of olive tree cultivation after a peak in the second century.[51] While it is dangerous to extrapolate from this single case to the rest of the region, it is possible to envisage a scenario in which the overall importance of olive oil declined within large economic units, especially in comparison to the heyday of the *annona* oil supply from southern Iberia.

On the contrary, wine production may have gained in importance as a large-scale staple product, corresponding to a decline in wine imports, as we shall presently see. Large-scale wine production appeared in Atlantic Iberia after the Roman conquest, although wine had certainly been produced in significant quantities since the sixth or fifth century BCE in particular sites.[52] Vine trees only grew in specific areas, mostly in Lusitania and, to a lesser extent, the plateau region, although we cannot reject the possibility of wine production in limited pockets north of the Duero, in Gallaecia.[53] We know about wine production through the containers in which grape juice was fermented and stored (*dolia*) and the presses used to transform grapes into juice. Sometimes oil and wine presses are difficult to distinguish from each other, and only a paleobotanical analysis can corroborate the function of an individual press.[54] Nevertheless, a handful of excavated sites seem to suggest that at least in the area of Mérida, wine production increased from the third century onward in association with monumental villas, such as Torre Águila, La Sevillana (Esparragosa de Lares, Badajoz), and, possibly, São Cucufate and Pozo de la Cañada (Guareña, Badajoz).[55] In the Algarve, the villa of Milreu added a new section dedicated to wine production to the already existing olive oil press and storage area.[56] Our evidence in the northern meseta is still fragmentary, but we may witness the appearance of evidence confirming a similar development. Excavations in the villa of Almenara in Valladolid hint at wine production in association with the fourth-century villa.[57] The chemical analysis of *dolia* from Viña de la Iglesia (Sotoserrano, Salamanca) also indicates wine production, although the exact chronology of the site has yet to be determined.[58] A fragment of *dolia* in the rural quarters of the villa of Sahelices El Chico (Salamanca) might point in the same direction.[59] On a more impressionistic note, the mosaics at the villa of Quintanilla de la Cueza (Cervatos de la Cueza, Palencia) depict allegories for the four seasons and feature a bacchant with a chest of grapes for the fall section of the floor.[60]

Animal farming also played a key role in the rural economy of Atlantic Iberia. There is little evidence of large-scale organized transhumance, as would appear in the late medieval and early modern Castilian *mesta*, but it may have existed to a lesser extent.[61] Individual paleobotanical analyses suggest that animals in search of pasture moved within a small area, but more studies are needed to determine whether this was a generalized phenomenon or a microregional trend.[62] In northern Iberia, particularly in Galicia and the Cantabrian Basin, animal products had considerably more importance for daily consumption than in the southern regions. An earlier anecdote by Strabo on the use of butter instead of oil for cooking in this region is corroborated by pollen studies, which show that olive trees rarely grew in this climate.[63] Some towns and secondary settlements in northwestern Iberia specialized in different types of cattle. For instance, excavations at the agglomerated settlement of A Proba de Valdeorras (Ourense) have produced a considerable number of bovine remains against fewer sheep, goat, and swine remains. Oxen and cows were used as traction animals and as a source of dairy products rather than for their meat, as the study of bones from Lugo shows. In that city, cows were sacrificed at an older age than other animals, which indicates the lack of interest in cattle as a source of meat.[64] Even a small rural settlement could specialize in bovines, as in the case of the farm of El Fresno (Bembibre, León).[65]

The centralized economic units associated with villas could well concentrate animals. Hydatius of Chaves certainly took it for granted when he thought of villas and cattle as sharing a common space. He recorded that "lightning set fire to villas and burned flocks of sheep," among other portents that indicated the end of the times.[66] In the last few decades, impressionistic descriptions like this one are corroborated by bone analysis in villas' rural quarters. Sheep bones appear in considerable numbers at the villa of Almenara in the meseta, where they represent the majority of domestic animal remains (followed by bovines).[67] Some of these animals may have been for household consumption. The kitchen of the villa of Noville (Mugardos, A Coruña), on the northern coast of Galicia, shows mostly sheep and goat as part of the center's animal diet (very likely together with fish).[68] But animals could also have been raised for nonhousehold consumption, such as the cattle raised in the villa of Navatejera. They very likely provided the city and military camp of León with fresh meat during the late Roman period, whether in the form of direct sales or taxes (or both).[69] Animal farming is not well attested to in Lusitanian villas, although that does not mean it was not part of the estate economy. But, as in the case of cereal, husbandry leaves fewer imprints on the archaeological record if animals are not butchered and consumed on site.[70]

Therefore, the most archaeologically visible evidence of the Atlantic Iberian economy suggests the presence of economic units that centralized the food staples of the Mediterranean triad as well as animal products, varying according to the climatic characteristics of each region. We can assume large properties behind these units, but the actual structure of these properties is lost to us. Rural estates were not involved only in the production of the Mediterranean triad and animal products: other activities are well attested, including pottery making and textiles, to mention a few.[71] But cereal, wine, oil, and animal products overwhelmingly dominate the archaeological record of economic activities, both in rural mansions' production quarters and in palynological evidence. The economic strategies of the Atlantic Iberian landowning class gain visibility when this group assembled a large concentration of food staples next to their rural residences.

*   *   *

Now, were these elites only involved in the concentration of rural production or did they also intervene in the production cycle itself? The extent to which landowners were directly involved in this production is hard to reconstruct in the absence of written evidence. Scholarship on other parts of the Mediterranean world suggest a variety of possible strategies, from direct control over land and the production process ("demesne") to less hands-on control, in which most of the decisions were left to tenants, who were only responsible for rent payments.[72] We might expect a variety of strategies in this area, as economic units of different size, productive potential, and natural resources would have favored different types of land management.

There is, however, one way of looking at landowners' involvement in production through nonwritten sources. The presence of large-scale infrastructural investments reveals landowners' interest in controlling at least part of the production cycle. In several late Roman sites, excavations trace an intensification of infrastructural investments. This evidence, patchy and elusive as it may be, relates to three areas of the economic cycle: production, storage, and transformation of agricultural products. Through the examples of dams, storage facilities, and presses, we will trace the willingness of some members of the landowning elites to invest in large-scale food staple production.

Water management was crucial for securing steady production in the rural world of southern and central Lusitania, an area with precipitations of less than six hundred millimeters per year and very dry summers. Dams were essential to regulate artificial or natural watercourses. A large number of stone-built dams in southwestern Iberia (more than 70 percent of the known dams in the peninsula) testify to the importance of artificial irrigation in the area. To be sure, irrigation systems could result from communal efforts and not necessarily from the direct involvement of a landowning class. It would be surprising, though, if landowners were not interested in such an improvement to their lands, which could also supply water to their bathhouses.[73] Moreover, dams are usually found in association with villas. Although their precise chronology may range from the second to the fourth century, the few studied cases suggest a late Roman date for most of them.[74]

Storage was also essential for the accumulation of commercialized crops. Evidence of storage facilities in rural areas is limited, not least due to difficulties in finding or lack of interest in excavating nonmonumental spaces. However, the extant evidence suggests that storage was intimately associated with villas and not with peasant family units in the late Roman period (after the fifth century, as we will see, the opposite is true).[75] The association of villas with storage facilities reveals the interest of a landowning class in centralizing production—through the direct exploitation of their own lands or the collection of rents (and taxes) in kind from their tenants. While some of the storage areas were built in the late Roman period, others date back to the early imperial era, although they were maintained during late antiquity. Examples such as the villa of Monroy (Cáceres) in Lusitania, with nine walls of a storage building unearthed so far, or the silos in the villa of Veranes or the villa of Bares, in northwestern Iberia, all indicate investment in an important part of the production cycle related to the accumulation of rural surpluses.[76] The northern plateau offers fewer examples of storage areas, very likely owing to the lesser archaeological visibility of rural quarters in the absence of large-scale wine and olive oil production. But some sites indicate possible late Roman investments in storage as well.[77] It is important to stress that storage facilities associated with residential villas were not just intended to store produce for intrahousehold consumption. Over three hundred square meters of storage area in the villa of São Cucufate indicates surpluses that were very likely for circulation and consumption outside the limited framework of a single rural estate.[78]

Wine and olive oil production required infrastructure that does not appear very impressive but was nonetheless sophisticated—notably presses. At some point during the late third or early fourth century, the villa owner of Torre Águila decided to reorient its commercial production away from a previous focus on olive oil. Although oil was still produced on a modest scale, wine began being produced in "industrial" quantities. During the second third of the fourth century, presses and other infrastructure required for wine production were placed in two (and possibly three) halls, which were also renovated for this purpose.[79] Slowly, excavations in other villas, including previously unknown sites such as Miralrío (Mérida, Badajoz), suggest that investment in oil or wine production and storage intensified in the late Roman period.[80]

These investments may appear to be modest, but the numerous infrastructural expenditures associated with rural mansions suggest that at least some members of the landowning class were involved in the production of commodities such as oil, wine, and cereal. It is important to insist on the fact that landowners could easily have contented themselves with collecting rents in cash, a practice that many of them certainly followed. Well-documented regions like Egypt show a range of managerial strategies, and the same could apply to Atlantic Iberia.[81] Part of the landowning class of Atlantic Iberia, however, found it beneficial to engage in direct management of at least part of the production cycle.[82] These investments allowed them to seize the opportunity to participate in the exchange networks that permeated the Iberian Peninsula. Although this economic practice was not necessarily new in some parts of Atlantic Iberia, it seemed to intensify during the late Roman period, at least in comparison with third-century standards.

The case of northwestern Iberia shows both the impact of this economic model and the problems associated with the type of evidence that reveals it. We saw in Chapter 1 that villas in this region tended to be located along the Atlantic coast, with only a few examples in the interior. Whereas there were only a few instances of agricultural facilities associated with rural villas in the early imperial period, the late Roman countryside witnessed a small and highly localized boom of such units.[83] Likewise, late Roman settlement patterns and radiocarbon analyses in the region reveal the end of nucleated peasant settlement in hilltop sites during the second and third centuries, to be replaced by lowland, dispersed settlement in the late Roman period.[84] This pattern corresponds to what field surveys reveal in the northern plateau and Lusitania. There is a striking correlation between this type of dispersed rural settlement and the more likely type of rural labor described in this chapter (a dispersed rural population working its plots and paying rents in kind or coin). Thus, northwestern Iberia caught up with Lusitania and the plateau, since similar economic units became not only archaeologically visible but also represented an important innovation in an area where large-scale mining (and the settlements associated with it) had prevailed until the third century. Yet in the interior areas, the material remains of centralized economic units such as those described in this chapter are rare to nonexistent. Either these economic units did not exist, or, more likely, they are archaeologically invisible owing to the mountainous areas' lack of the luxurious villas that made the units archaeologically visible in other regions.

*   *   *

In sum, the economic strategies of the Atlantic Iberian landowning class shared several common features. The evidence indicates that economic units with a focus on the concentration and transformation of a few food staples (particularly the Mediterranean triad but also animals and animal products) prevailed as the most dynamic sector in the regional economy associated with local landowning elites. Property structures within these economic units cannot be determined, but infrastructure investments, even modest ones, indicate that landowners were concerned with increasing the productivity of their economic units. This was not a new model. In many ways, the late Roman period was, indeed, Roman.[85] Yet the ubiquitous rural residences that render production quarters archaeologically visible reveal intensification from an earlier period, especially considering the third-century hiatus in most sites. By the late third and early fourth centuries, local aristocrats who built lavish rural residences also invested in infrastructure related to food staple transformation, storage, and circulation.

Why did this model prevail? In part, as I mentioned, the crisis of the early imperial economic specialization forced local agents to partially reorient their economic strategies, which they did swiftly as reorientation may not have involved drastic changes in property management or even production. The culture of the Mediterranean triad and animal farming was nothing new in the area. The novelty was, once again, the intensification of centralized units to gather and transform these products. In order to understand these changes, we must consider the question of how new external demands contributed to this generalization of a particular economic model. In other words, we need to place these economic units within the different types of distribution networks that arose after the third century in the larger Mediterranean context.

Distribution in Late Roman Western Iberia

We should not take the specialization of aristocratic economic units for granted. In fact, most rural producers would not pursue specialization since the practice goes against the logic of peasant economy. Both small landowners and tenants depended on diversification to avoid risking the survival of their family on the bad crop of a single item. In the late Roman Mediterranean world, they micromanaged their economic strategies in order to cope with the threatening demands toward uniformity.[86] They did so against the background of aristocrats specializing in concentrating and transforming a few food staples. Since, as I argued before, this was not a "natural" economic choice, we need to discover the structural conditioning that made this type of strategy preferable to others. In this section, I will contend that state and supralocal exchange networks generated the economic and physical infrastructure that made this strategy their final choice.

The renewed state of Diocletian and his successors established a novel taxation system. Imperial officials were now in charge of assessing and collecting taxes in a much more intrusive way than they had been during the early empire, when that task was predominantly left to the cities and their local administrations. From the reign of Diocletian onward, land and personal units were assessed by specialized officials, such as Lusitania's *censitor quinquennalis* Iunius (?) Batia (or Batianus), known through an inscription from the rural areas of Salamanca.[87] As tributes were now assessed and sometimes collected in kind, state authorities determined, at least in part, what types of items had to be produced. They did not do so arbitrarily; rather they relied on existing productive traditions so as to disrupt production patterns as little as possible. Nevertheless, the imperial administration and especially the army became steady consumers of food staples and other rural products.[88]

Tax collection is archaeologically invisible and, thus, hard to document in Atlantic Iberia. Yet the practice of collecting tributes in kind (or at least part of them) appears to have continued into the fifth century. In his *Chronicle*, Hydatius bemoaned the arrival of barbarian armies in the peninsula in 410, which was accompanied by a series of calamities. Among them, tax collectors "plundered" the "goods stored in cities."[89] Although the apocalyptic narrative of Hydatius turns the actions of state agents into plundering, this was certainly not the perception of the *exactor*.[90] Since, as Chapter 6 will illustrate, later Visigothic documents also make reference to payments of tribute in kind, we can expect rural production in the late Roman period to be at least partly oriented toward these types of payments. We cannot determine, however, how much of the total tributary mass was collected in kind as opposed to coin. Tribute in coin, however, may have had similar centralizing effects. Independent peasants needed to sell their production in order to pay taxes, and the role of landowners as mediators in these market transactions is attested to in other parts of the Roman world.[91]

Taxes had multiple destinations. Administrators and military garrisons were the most immediate recipients of these tributes. As explained in Chapter 1, most of the permanent garrisons in the peninsula were precisely in Atlantic Iberia, especially in Gallaecia. A certain proportion of those taxes may have been directed to the Rhine frontier (and the northwestern African borders). Although the age of the Iberian Peninsula as the main provider of olive oil for the *annona* had come to an end in the second century, Baetican oil amphorae still supplied modest quantities to the Rhine area and the western Mediterranean, including Rome.[92] More likely, the imperial administration oriented tributes in kind toward field armies temporarily stationed in Hispania.[93] Likewise, authorities could buy local surpluses for that purpose, if taxes were paid in coin.

Translating archaeological evidence into the potential demands of the Roman state is not an easy task. It has been suggested that rural villas in Atlantic Iberia were not merely the centers of economic units but also tax collection entities.[94] Landowners acting as tax collectors vis-à-vis their tenants and small peasants were a recurrent feature of the late Roman countryside.[95] Moreover, as we will see in Chapter 6, there is evidence of a similar practice in the Visigothic kingdom, probably as an inheritance of earlier times. I am inclined to accept at least a partial link between landowning and tax collection, but, as I have already pointed out, there are difficulties involved in translating villas into economic or property units.

As seen in Chapter 2, tax collection was part of the aristocratic persona of local landowners. As decurions, they were responsible for their city's taxes, but they were also able to display social status by presenting themselves as enactors of state mandates. There may have been other reasons encouraging landowners to undertake the apparently burdensome task of collecting tributes. If landowners deployed social and economic muscle at the local level, they were able to use the tax system in their favor. It is not clear whether all the decurions were able to profit from this situation or, more likely, a small group within each *curia*, which increasingly concentrated most local influence and wealth.[96] Be that as it may, tax collection may have been a profitable source of income for local landowners. Yet, archaeologically, this strategy remains invisible.

* * *

Perhaps the centralized economic units of Atlantic Iberia reveal the operation of the tax system in a different way. Most of the new investments in production quarters took place between the late third and the early fourth century, precisely at the moment when the workings of the new tax system were established. This system incentivized the private accumulation of certain food staples to pay taxes. Avoiding expensive conversions in cash and judicial penalties must have been incentive enough to organize part of the production around the demands of the imperial state.[97] The state's demands in kind were not very different from the potential demands of local and supralocal urban and rural markets. Standardized production of food staples could thus serve the dual purpose of tax payment and allocation of rural surplus through exchanges. This conjunction could certainly compromise production diversity, as large economic units would have had the incentive to concentrate on a few items to meet both state and market demands. But great landowners could perfectly dispense with diversity.

The problem here is, again, the lack of written evidence. We think that cities *must* have consumed rural produce, yet documents of proof do not exist. We know of rural markets in the Iberian Peninsula only through one entry from the Council of Elvira in the early fourth century, attended predominantly by Baetican bishops, in which rural markets (*nundinae*) are mentioned.[98] In the case of supraregional markets, a few descriptions of Iberian products from other parts of the empire, such as the fourth-century *Expositio Totius Mundi et Gentium*'s praise of oil, fish sauce, textiles, lard, and horses from the peninsula, do not provide us with any information beyond an impressionistic list of regional specialties.[99] Diocletian's Prices Edict regulated the cost of transportation between Lusitania and diocese of Oriens, with an expected cost per day similar to other important seaborne routes. This suggests a commercial route between Western Iberia and the eastern Mediterranean by the turn of the fourth century important enough to catch the attention of imperial authorities, yet the content and intensity of this trade is impossible to establish. Nor does the absence of other routes in the edict indicate a lack of seaborne lanes.[100] Once again, for lack of better sources, we are forced to rely on the archaeological evidence to reconstruct possible market distribution networks. The material record provides two types of relevant evidence. The first consists in containers and other evidence of agricultural production in centralized economic units. The second involves fine wares, some of them produced locally and others produced in other regions of the Roman world. These ceramics are useful indicators of the reach of the distribution networks on which rural production relied. Overall, the evidence shows that the Western Iberian landowning class oriented its production toward local and regional markets when supraregional products that had had considerable weight in the local economy during the early empire became less important.

*   *   *

Let us start with the Mediterranean triad. Wine was widely consumed in late antiquity and not reserved just for the socioeconomic elite. To be sure, there were different qualities and types of wine, and consumption was a subtle way of marking social status.[101] We saw that Atlantic Iberian economic units had the capacity to produce large quantities of wine, especially in Lusitania. Even if Lusitanian wine was commercialized in the Mediterranean Basin, however, we still lack evidence of large, locally produced amphorae to trace its commercial routes. Perhaps, as in other parts of the western empire, wine was transported in skins or wooden barrels impossible to trace in excavations.[102] We know of these barrels from stone replicas in funerary monuments, where they are known as *cupae*. A large number of Lusitanian and central Iberian *cupae* date from the second and third centuries.[103] Although we can explain this archaeological silence by resorting to the possible existence of other containers invisible to the archaeologist, the reason why Lusitania and the northern meseta never "exported" its wine could well be that this production was oriented toward local markets and, perhaps, military units.[104] A possible late Roman Lusitanian wine amphora seems to indicate that it served for short-distance transportation.[105] Moreover, supraregional wine amphorae, which had supplied Iberia with quality wine during the early empire, are almost absent in late Roman strata, both in urban centers (Braga) and rural sites (such as the villa of Povos, near Lisbon).[106] We might be in the presence of, as it were, an import substitution wine industry during the late empire, as more households, including elite ones, were served by locally produced wine.[107]

Like wine, olive oil was a major commercialized item in antiquity—and not only as a food staple but also as a lighting fuel.[108] The evidence for the locally produced olive trade in Atlantic Iberia is even more elusive. Southern Lusitanian economic units probably supplied the commercial networks of Iberian olive oil to some extent, especially those in the Alentejo. Baetican oil amphorae still supplied the Rhine area and the western Mediterranean in modest quantities.[109] The evidence for the continuous production of olive oil in the area illustrates the enduring demand of local and regional markets for this product. As in the case of wine, the lack of a locally produced amphora suggests that a considerable part of the production must have been consumed within the region.[110] The estates of Lusitania and the plateau now faced favorable conditions to distribute their production in local settings. Starting in the third century, Baetican olive oil had a decreased impact Mediterranean-wide and even within the Iberian Peninsula.[111]

Although the production of food staples seems to have been oriented predominantly toward local and regional markets, part of that production may have been directed to Mediterranean- and Atlantic-wide exchanges. The only concrete and large-scale evidence available to trace supraregional distribution comes from fish sauce and conserve amphorae. Fish products did circulate throughout the Roman world. Iberian fish amphorae are found in some coastal cities of the eastern Mediterranean (Alexandria, Caesarea, and Beirut), but it is in the Western Mediterranean and the Atlantic coast that Iberian fish products left a significant mark.[112] As we saw earlier, there is no conclusive evidence linking fish products to large land properties, although there is no conclusive evidence on the other side either. Thus, distribution of fish amphorae does not directly prove that aristocratic land units were oriented toward supraregional markets. Nevertheless, fish amphorae do indicate the existence of a commercial infrastructure that could include nonfish products, even as ancillary commerce. These "international" markets may not have been the primary focus in the allocation of production from aristocratic *fundi*, but they certainly were an opportunity to be considered. The absence of locally produced wine and olive oil in this pan-Roman trade system further suggests that its orientation was primarily local.

Archaeology does not offer much help in terms of what may have been the largest part of rural production: grains and animals. The latter had a clear local orientation, although the state may have requested some forms of animal products for medium-distance consumption. The author of the *Expositio totius mundi* praised the lard and horses from *Spania*, although it is hard to say where they were produced and to what extent they circulated.[113] In the case of grain, we must face an absolute silence of both written and archaeological evidence. Cities in the region, which were occupied continuously during the late Roman period, could and certainly did offer markets for grain products. Perhaps some grain was sold to Mediterranean- or Atlantic-bound cargoes or was even commercialized overland toward eastern Iberia and southern Gaul. Even if this was the case, we face a frustrating documentary silence.

Overall, scanty as it is, the evidence of locally produced food staples also suggests the local consumption of these items. Exceptions existed, notably among them fish products (which were also consumed in the peninsula). Container invisibility might be preventing us from tracing long-distance exchanges, and other products, such as textiles, hides, or metals, might have been part of cargoes directed to overseas markets. The more reduced impact of imports in comparison to the early empire, however, does suggest that local production gained a larger share of local markets after the third century.

Although local products left limited archaeological traces, excavations and surveys do reveal the skeleton of distribution networks. Thanks to ceramics (table and cooking wares in particular), it is possible to reconstruct a distribution infrastructure that included products other than those that survived archaeologically.[114] The spread of ceramic distribution uncovers a world of exchanges that included city and countryside alike. Both supply and cost offer the main explanations to the dimensions and regional distribution of ceramics, showing market mechanisms behind their circulation. As in almost every other region in the empire, different circuits of distribution permeated Atlantic Iberia. I will reconstruct two of these networks through which the production of aristocratic economic units (and others) could journey to local, regional, and supraregional markets. The first one, the maritime network, linked Atlantic Iberia to the Mediterranean Basin and the rest of the Atlantic Basin. The second one, the land network, connected different microregions of inland Iberia with each other. As we will see, these two networks did not oppose each other, but they involved different transportation costs and types of vehicles.

The inland network is mapped upon the distribution areas of a locally produced fine ware, the Terra Sigillata Hispánica Tardía (TSHT).[115] In terms of form and style, the production of late Roman sigillatas evolved from early imperial traditions into the so-called Terra Sigillata Hispánica, produced in the northern meseta and the Guadalquivir Valley in Baetica. While the production of these ceramics never ceased, evolving later into the TSHT, they experienced a severe production decline during the third century. Production of sigillatas reemerged at full strength during the first decades of the fourth century, with the clear influence of African sigillatas. A second wave of TSHT forms appeared during the second half of the fourth century, this time under the increasing influence of Gallic fine wares.[116] The late Roman manufacturing centers of TSHT were located in the northeastern corner of Western Iberia, with two main areas of concentration: the province of Burgos, in the northern plateau, and the upper Ebro Valley and La Rioja.[117] The production of fine wares in the eastern corner of the plateau certainly took advantage of the favorable conditions for commercialization that this location gave them. The Burgos-Rioja microregion was the crux of several routes connecting inland markets: the Lusitanian plains and the northern and southern plateaus to the west and south, as well as the upper and middle Ebro Valley and southern Gaul to the east and north. Land transportation costs acted as de facto tariffs against other kinds of fine wares from coastal areas, and the TSHT wares may have benefited from a state-sponsored road system.

Excavations do not leave room for doubt about the pervasiveness of this type of ceramic, even in areas difficult to access, such as the noncoastal Cantabrian Basin.[118] The frontier of the TSHT commercial influence was the middle Ebro Valley and the city of Zaragoza to the west and the area of Braga to the east.[119] Its distribution followed the lines of the many roads that crisscrossed the northern meseta along the Duero Valley, which may have allowed glass bowls produced in Braga to reach rural villas in Salamanca.[120] In terms of internal distribution, TSHT ceramics reached all types of settlements, from cities such as Astorga or Lugo, to secondary sites such as Iria Flavia (A Coruña) or Castro Ventosa, to rural villas such as Almenara or La Olmeda.[121] In terms of temporal framework, the chronology of the TSHT ranges from the late third century to the mid-fifth century, almost coinciding with the late Roman period. In general, excavations show that the supply of these fine wares ran steadily during the period, even when the workshops changed from the upper Ebro region to the upper Duero Valley.[122]

The circulation of TSHT reveals dynamic distribution networks inland, usually considered less favorable to exchanges owing to transportation costs. Doubtless, land transportation was more expensive than seaborne trade, but distribution networks of sufficient scale could overcome, at least partially, these disadvantages.[123] The reach of the TSHT was more than merely microregional. Braga and Mérida were well supplied with these ceramics, which must have shared their journey with other products. Probably not by chance, Braga and Mérida were located at the end of two major road axes that structured communications in the northern plateau and Lusitania, while the TSHT workshops were located at the other extreme.

This inland network was not the only platform for distribution at the supralocal level. Atlantic Iberia participated in a pan-Mediterranean network, which becomes visible through African table wares (ARS) and, to a lesser extent, amphorae.[124] The axis of this network was the powerful distribution link that united North Africa and Italy (and especially Rome), as the North African countryside became the source of grain and oil for the city of Rome. Whether state driven or market driven, the cargoes that linked Tunisia and Italy undoubtedly represented the main supraregional network of the western Mediterranean.[125] This network, however, was not only limited to the Rome–Carthage axis. Ships transporting African and other regions' goods navigated the waters of the Mediterranean in search of other markets. They would bring African products to the eastern Iberian coast, for instance, as the vast numbers of African amphorae and ARS wares found in excavations show.[126] What these ships brought in exchange is hard to say, although shipwreck evidence suggests that the norm was a mixed cargo of products with different origins. To give just one example, the Sobra shipwreck (near the Croatian coast) had a cargo of African, Lusitanian, and perhaps Italian and Greek products.[127] In other words, there was a well-oiled western Mediterranean commercial network that was also linked to the eastern Mediterranean.[128]

This pan-Mediterranean network, whose archaeological symptom is the presence of African ceramics, extended to the Atlantic shores of the Iberian Peninsula as well. In fact, it included the whole of the Atlantic Basin, from Morocco to Britain and the Rhineland. In the Western Iberian case, the "world of ARS wares" had a considerable coastal imprint. ARS wares are the dominant, and in some cases the sole, late Roman fine wares in many coastal urban centers. In the city of Mirobriga Celtica (Santiago do Cacém), for instance, late Roman ARS (C and D types) make up more than 40 percent of Roman sigillatas, whereas TSHT (the other late Roman fine ware found in the peninsula) represents less than 1 percent of the same group.[129] Almost 25 percent of the fine wares for the whole of the Roman period in the small coastal town of Balsa are late Roman ARS, whereas no fragment of TSHT has appeared so far.[130] ARS wares also dominated the fine-ware landscape of inland cities in Lusitania (Conimbriga) and even in southern Gallaecia (Porto), although the proportion of TSHT grows as we move away from the coast.[131] Findings in rural areas, and especially villas, tend to corroborate this distribution model.[132]

The connection between the ARS commercial zone and the regional markets in Western Iberia developed through specific areas of intensified exchanges. Two important commercial enclaves were the contact area between the Mediterranean cargoes and Western Iberia. The first one is the southern Lusitanian coast, especially the city of Faro. The large number of fish industries in the area can explain its integration into the Mediterranean-wide circuits. The boost that the inland port of Mértola (including its newly built city walls) experienced during the fourth century may be due to its role as commercial *entrepôt* linking the Lusitanian countryside and its dense villa network with the Atlantic–Mediterranean routes. The second enclave linking Lusitanian markets to the core of the Roman world was the combined estuaries of the Tejo and the Sado Rivers. Like the Algarvian coast, this area concentrated a large number of fish industries, as we previously saw. The considerable number of African products even in secondary sites like Tróia tells us about the intense commercial contacts between this microregion and the Mediterranean world.[133] The port of Gijón, on a smaller scale, may have played a similar role in relationship to inland Asturias and the fringes of the northern plateau. From the point of view of ceramic networks, this small (but fortified) town was the meeting point between a Mediterranean–Atlantic network (ARS and Gallic sigillatas) and the Duero Valley (TSHT).[134]

The presence of African fine wares tells us about a regional network that included Lusitania and parts of Gallaecia in which intraregional and local exchanges must have constituted the bulk of the commercial exchange. The Mediterranean "imports" were the icing on the cake, and their presence drastically diminishes as we move away from the coast. The pattern of distribution is anything but linear. Whereas ARS predominate over TSHT in São Cucufate, the opposite is true in the villa of Quinta das Longas.[135] Even in the interior of Extremadura, not far from the southern borders of the northern meseta, ARS wares supplied the demands of the villa of Olivar del Centeno (Millanes de la Mata, Cáceres). The commercial networks linking the coast to these inland sites also brought the African imports—and hence, the products that integrated the Mediterranean-based distribution.[136] The Tejo-Sado area has a large number of TSHT pieces, although it clearly belonged to the ARS world, indicating intense concurrent contact with the Iberian interior.[137]

In sum, the distribution of fine wares in Atlantic Iberia shows a marked distinction between coast and interior and, to a lesser extent, between south and north. The closer a site is to the TSHT production centers and the farther from the Atlantic coast, the more likely that fine wares from La Rioja and the northern meseta would prevail at the archaeological level. Similar patterns of distribution tended to characterize both urban and rural settlements within the same area. The more logical explanations for this distribution are cost and availability of a steady supply. The price of African products may have considerably increased as one moved farther away from the coast and land transportation had to supplement seaborne shipping. The availability of local products may also explain, in part, why TSHT wares reached central Lusitania and western Gallaecia, in spite of the costs of land transportation. The presence of these wares (albeit in small numbers) at Quinta das Longas, in the territory of Mérida, reveals their ability to compete against African imports, which do not show up in the late Roman dump area. Indeed, the owners of the villa had access to other coastal products, such as fish amphorae from the Sado and Tejo estuaries, which constitute the overwhelming number of large containers at the site.[138]

This distribution pattern shows that commercial networks crisscrossed the territory of Western Iberia. These networks were not limited to coastal areas and transregional trade; rather, they included the interior regions, which were supplied by land. Urban and rural areas were perfectly integrated into distribution networks, a connection that is further corroborated by coinage distribution.[139] If ceramics did not travel alone, and they most certainly did not, then the production of rural estates, to a certain extent, must have accompanied these table wares. The existence of this commodity circulation must have reduced the transportation cost of ceramics and justified the scale of production, which solely depended on land haulage. As the Levantine evidence suggests, late antique landowners could rely on independent merchants or their own agents.[140] Such local middlemen or agents are hinted at in the Council of Elvira in Iberia. Clergy were forbidden from attending rural markets; instead, they were reminded that they could send a son, a freedman, a hired worker, or a friend of similar social status to deal with economic transactions.[141]

If what I have argued so far is true, then we can see why a model of economic units specialized in a few Mediterranean items (but never one alone) prevailed. These units were not serving primarily long-distance consumption centers. Nor did they have to compete with large-scale Mediterranean imports (with the exception, perhaps, of coastal areas), as the impact of Baetican oil and Tarraconensian wine drastically declined after the third century. Some local production was transported toward military units on the frontiers but significantly less than during the early empire. Military presence also diminished as some of the legions that had remained in the peninsula in mining districts disappeared after the late third century. Landed units transformed rural production into economic surplus by primarily supplying local markets, both urban and rural, supported in part by the transportation backbone that the empire provided. Perhaps Atlantic Iberia also witnessed a smaller version of the "consumer revolution" that characterized the late Roman North African countryside, although we lack the sources to document it.[142]

To what extent this strategy resulted from maximizing benefits or avoiding risks is impossible to tell. The Iberian evidence lends itself to different interpretations. One can argue that landowners sought to maximize benefits through investments and market orientation. Yet one can also point to the fact that economic units never specialized in a single commercialized crop nor engaged in large-scale, long-distance trade. Perhaps we must limit ourselves to more modest aims and argue that landowners adapted to the changing economic but also political circumstances of the third and fourth centuries in order to secure steady incomes to reproduce their social standing.

New Opportunities in a Traditional Economy

Throughout this chapter, I have reconstructed aristocratic economic strategies based on a desperately silent set of archaeological findings. There are vast areas of economic history of late Roman Atlantic Iberia that are lost to us. Land tenure, labor organization, mechanisms of commercial transactions, tax collection—all these issues, which are crucial to the economic strategies of the large landowning class, cannot be determined. At most, we can draw comparisons with other parts of the empire, a methodology that is not exempt from risks. I used this latter approach sparingly, although it might be the only avenue to know more about rural estates in the future.

I mentioned some caveats that we must keep in mind when dealing with this type of evidence. I want to stress two, which I think are the most important. The economic units of the landowning class became visible thanks to the aristocratic habit of often building rural mansions in association with production facilities. In other words, aristocratic status display allows us to link economic muscle with social standing. There are, however, other possible strategies that remain archaeologically invisible. Further, the circulation of goods is only traceable indirectly, mostly through the circulation of fine wares and amphorae. This means that most locally produced items left no trace, since we lack specific containers that would allow us to find out the different localities they reached.

Keeping these considerations in mind, the economic strategies of local aristocracies were shaped by at least three structural constraints. First, the region inherited productive structures in which land ownership was the main source of economic standing in the long run. Economic strategies had been molded by centuries of relentless incorporation of Mediterranean economic traits in the peninsula region. We should not overemphasize the differences between the early and the late empires. The late Roman economy in the Atlantic was essentially Roman. Local aristocracies who possessed medium-sized or large tracts of lands did not step on uncharted territory when they organized their economic units. They relied on at least two centuries of experience in obtaining economic surplus from the exploitation of land and rural labor. Centralized economic units, in some (but not all) cases associated with residential villas, were not new phenomena either. Moreover, cereal, vine, and olive tree culture together with husbandry had been at the core of rural exploitations since the Roman conquest.

Second, access to markets was crucial for the distribution of food staples. These distribution networks were not necessarily a new feature in the region. But after the third century, the overall role of Atlantic Iberia (and the peninsula in general) within the economy of the empire changed. The decline of large-scale mining in Lusitania and Gallaecia put an end to one of the region's most prominent exports. Likewise, the reduction of the impressive supply of olive oil originating in Baetica (and the parallel decline in the trade of Tarraconensian wine) meant that long-distance trade was less intense in the region. Imports from other parts of the empire did not completely cease after the third century—nor did exports, as fish industries bounced back in the fourth century. But their impact on the local economy dwindled. While this process took place, economic units continued supplying local and regional markets. These economic units showed a remarkable capacity to centralize food staples, without any visible trace of them being shipped overseas. Within this regionalization of markets, large agrarian enterprises prospered. In this chapter, we saw the skeleton of regional distribution through the study of fine-ware ceramics. Little is known about the merchants who fleshed out that skeleton. Most likely, a mix of landowners' deputies, local middlemen, and long-distance traders distributed rural production.

The third structural feature that shaped aristocratic strategies was the late Roman administration, and it did so in various ways. Requests for taxes in kind, at least at the beginning of the late Roman period, can explain economic units specializing in three or four products that coincided with the main state demands, products that could also be commercialized in local and regional markets. It must be more than a coincidence that most of the infrastructural investments in centralized economic units took place between the late third and the early fourth century, precisely when men like Valerius Proculus implemented the late Roman taxation system in the region. Moreover, the role of landowners as primary tax collectors (or taxpayers) only reinforced the tendency toward the centralization of commercialized staples. Whereas the link between archaeological evidence and taxation is not as straightforward as one could wish, the transformation of the late Roman countryside points at a discrete reorientation of the traditional economy at the time when the imperial administration reorganized its tax system and became more intrusive in the rural world.

The Roman imperial administration framed economic strategies in various other ways. Imperial demands and state-sponsored transportation of produce provided the communication backbone to transport items oriented toward private exchanges. TSHT circulation indicates persistent movements along the main roads that connected provincial capitals. Mediterranean–Atlantic routes could be partially linked to the supply of the Rhine frontier since Iberian products still reached military garrisons in the fourth century, albeit in less quantity than in the early empire. Merchants who were required to carry state taxes could also transport private loads in their caravans or on their ships. Changes in state practices can even explain, at least partially, the growing regionalization of economic exchanges. The end of large-scale mining and of the supply of Baetican oil to Rome were, after all, decisions of state authorities. Moreover, imperial salaries and land grants could have favored investments in the production units of those who joined the ranks of the equestrian and senatorial aristocracies. This was, perhaps, the least important of all the imperial state's roles in defining economic strategies, but it was certainly crucial in shaping social and political strategies of local elites. Nevertheless, we must take note of the state's ability to start landed economic fortunes through intervention.

The late Roman evidence, although limited and problematic, therefore suggests that the state reforms of the late third and early fourth centuries shaped aristocratic economic strategies—at least within the limits of ancient economic structures. The economic units from which aristocrats obtained the surplus to perform in social competitions swiftly adapted to changes in state organization. Above all, there seems to be no opposition between a putatively oppressively taxing bureaucracy and the aristocracy. Rather, the latter functioned within the parameters established by the former. All in all, local landowners were anything but stagnant economic agents. They adapted to economic circumstances, such as declining long-distance trade or the redefinition of central administration demands, to pursue profits from their economic units. This income was critical to the social competition and status performance described in the previous chapter. In a sense, the economic strategies of Western Iberian aristocracies show the same "unprovincial" character as their social strategies. Like their peers elsewhere in the empire, local elites seized the opportunities offered by the late Roman state and its economy to reproduce their class preeminence.

PART II

WESTERN IBERIAN ARISTOCRACIES IN THE POST-ROMAN WORLD

CHAPTER 4

Adapting to a New World: Post-Roman Settlement in Western Iberia

In the year 483, Zeno, bishop of Mérida, wrote a poem (or had it written) for an inscription commemorating what he considered to be an act of regeneration of his city. A Visigothic military leader, who probably had some form of political power over the region, had authorized (and possibly funded) repairs to a bridge and the city walls. The inscription, now lost but recorded in an eleventh-century manuscript, celebrated the *dux* Salla, who "thus surpassed, while imitating it, the notable work of the original builder." Zeno did not shy away from mentioning that it was his own zeal that persuaded Salla to embark on such a work. Thus, the poem optimistically continues, "The Augustan city [i.e., Mérida] shall be blessed for many centuries, because the zeal of the dux and the priest have renewed it."[1]

By 483, the political situation of the Iberian Peninsula had drastically changed from the world of the late empire. Bishop Zeno may never have seen a Roman governor ruling from what used to be the former capital of the Spanish diocese. Mérida and Lusitania in general had been the scene of military confrontations between various armies that were only occasionally under nominal Roman imperial command. One generation separated Zeno's inscription from the previous attested presence of a direct representative of the empire in eastern Iberia, the last stronghold of the empire in the peninsula. Moreover, that a Christian bishop would now be considered (at least to all outward appearances) as the natural leader of an urban community was an attitude that would have surprised almost anybody a hundred years earlier.

And yet, the language of the inscription exudes the old Roman tradition of civic benefaction as well as pride in past status. Zeno calls Mérida "the

Augustan city," recalling the traditional name of the Colonia Augusta Emerita. For all the changes that the "ruinous age" may have brought to the region, the settlement language of the Roman Empire carried on as a reminder that cities and territories continued (or ought to continue) as the basic element of the hierarchy and organization of settlements. The author of the *Lives of the Fathers of Mérida*, writing almost two centuries after Zeno's poem, still relied on similar categories. Suspecting that a newly arrived foreigner in Mérida was his nephew, bishop Paul asked him about his origins. The foreigner, who indeed turned out to be his nephew, declared his "fatherland, city, village, and parents."[2]

The persistence of settlement language does not mean that these settlements remained unaltered during the fifth and sixth centuries. The present chapter will describe some of the changes undergone by both urban and rural areas, particularly those associated with late Roman forms of aristocratic and state wealth display. As we will see, important morphological and structural changes took place between approximately 450 and 600. Urban and rural settlements continued to exist and, overall, maintained similar relationships with each other as during the late empire. But their monumentality and their most archaeologically visible aspects had drastically changed.

This chapter will trace three overarching trends in post-Roman Western Iberia. First, the fifth and sixth centuries reveal the persistence of earlier principles of settlement structure. Settlement patterns show little rupture from the late Roman period, and local elites continued being involved in the maintenance of status symbols at the settlement level. Late Roman sites were occasionally abandoned, but in most cases continuity in occupation was the norm. Some of the most fundamental aspects of Roman settlement structure persisted after the disappearance of the imperial administration, especially the city-territory organization. There were a few innovations, notably the occupation of hilltop settlements in northern Iberia and the slow appearance of villages in the central peninsula. But even these new forms of occupation did not necessarily break with previous settlement patterns, nor did they represent a crisis in aristocratic power. Rather, post-Roman innovations show the initiatives of local elites to maintain the basic hierarchy of settlement created by the Roman conquest and assert their ascendancy locally.

Yet settlement occupation, though continuous, was not exempt from transformation. In particular, there was a noticeable change in public and private monumental buildings throughout the region. Post-Roman settlement transformations are most visible through the ways in which wealth was displayed in architectural form. Late imperial public buildings were permanently abandoned while traditional Roman elite houses were no longer built and maintained by the end of the fifth century. The post-Roman period did not only witness the abandonment of earlier traditions of monumentality. Defensive walls remained a standard feature in most cities and even in secondary settlements. Moreover, local communities and their prominent members poured resources into the construction of urban and rural basilicas and other Christian buildings. Rather than a period of decline in monumentality, the post-Roman world was a moment of transformation in the social priorities expressed by prestige buildings.

A third overarching trend encompasses the marked differences between regions in terms of the relative impact of new forms of settlement status display. While similar changes in urban and rural settlement morphology and structure took place in central and southern Lusitania, northwestern Iberia, and the northern plateau, each region shows a specific chronology and was affected differently by these transformations. In terms of the archaeologically available information, Western Iberia was a less uniform world in the sixth century than it was during the fourth century. By the seventh century, however, both urban and rural landscapes were becoming more uniform in parallel to the consolidation of the Visigothic kingdom of Toledo. That process, however, remains outside the chronological framework of this book.

In Chapter 1, we noticed the relationship between the structure and morphology of settlements and the impact of the late Roman Empire's renewed state project. Post-Roman monumentality unveils the social priorities of the mid-fifth through sixth centuries, when that project was no longer available. The instability of the early decades of the post-Roman world made the status of each community a crucial element in negotiating their position within emerging polities. Local elites sought to enhance their *patria*'s bargaining power vis-à-vis barbarian armies with defensive walls that would not only provide security but also assert the status of cities and citylike settlements within the new circumstances. Furthermore, post-Roman settlements show the impact of a subtle cultural change among aristocracies and new discourses on wealth and Christian piety. It would not be until the late sixth and seventh centuries that Iberian aristocracies would collectively pour riches into religious buildings and foundations, but this process began earlier in some regions and microregions of Atlantic Iberia. As in late Roman Western Iberia, monumentality at the settlement level cannot be detached from the state(s) and the way in which aristocrats saw themselves participating in it.

Cities Without Empire

One of the most remarkable contributions of post-Roman urban archaeology in the last decades has been to remind us that cities continued to be occupied after the fifth century.[3] The gathering of this evidence has the aura of a feat, considering the difficulties archaeologists had to face. Post-Roman strata are always difficult to detect because of a simpler material culture in which perishable materials predominated. Moreover, a persistent though declining lack of interest in non-Roman periods and a limited knowledge of post-Roman ceramics have prevented us from acquiring a detailed knowledge of fifth- and sixth-century cities. As Iberian archaeologists have risen to the challenge and overcome these difficulties in the last few decades, the invisibility of post-Roman urbanism has begun a reversal. The notes to this chapter will provide ample evidence of this change.

Yet continuity in urban occupation does not imply unaltered urban landscapes. Cities did change topographically and institutionally. In what follows, I will describe the main characteristics of towns in terms of settlement prestige architecture and trace a handful of well-documented examples of continuity, transformation (abandonment), and innovation (new buildings) in urban contexts. However, the purpose of this section is not to offer a balance sheet of what survived and what did not. Rather, the following pages will describe what "being a city" meant after the withdrawal of the Roman administration. In general, urbanism was defined by the ability to offer protection through defensive walls and the development of ceremonial centers associated with Christian buildings. Other buildings and markers of urbanism may have existed, but they remain archaeologically invisible.

The next chapter will deal with civic institutional and political frameworks in greater depth, but a quick overview of post-Roman city governments will help clarify some of the arguments presented in the following paragraphs. As we saw in Chapter 2, the standard model of urban government in the late Roman period was an institutional order of *curiales*, potentially combined with the presence of members of the senatorial aristocracy and the imperial administration. After the fifth century, urban leadership relied upon less standardized, but not necessarily less effective, categories. Chapter 5 will argue that the government of urban centers was taken over by a collective leadership that included landowners, royal representatives, "strong men" (military leaders), and, eventually, bishops and some clergy—similar to a type of civic administration usually known as government by notables. Political realities varied from town to town, but a combination of some or all of these groups ruled over cities and territories instead of the former imperial and local administration.

In spite of all these institutional transformations, the infrastructure that had supported Roman civic ceremonies and amenities was not completely abandoned. It certainly lost its original raison d'être, and, by 450 or so, most likely all of the games and religious ceremonies associated with ancient cities had ended.[4] But archaeological findings show that after the fifth century, public buildings were reused in three ways.[5] In some cases, private houses were constructed in former ceremonial or entertainment buildings. A good example of residential reuse are the fates of Lisbon's theater and bathhouse, which were occupied by poor houses by the fifth century.[6] Some temples, such as the one dedicated to the imperial cult in Mérida, underwent a similar transformation.[7] In other cases, productive activities replaced ceremonial use in buildings that had once been public. Former public baths in Clunia housed artisanal activities during the fourth century or later, as pottery makers reused the thermal heating infrastructure to produce ceramics.[8] A third form of reuse of public buildings saw them transformed into burial areas, thus altering urban patterns more drastically. Fifth-century graves under the steps of a former temple in Conimbriga (perhaps by then a Christian basilica) are an early example of this practice, which continued into the seventh century and later, as illustrated by graves in the bathhouse of Clunia's forum or the necropolis in the former ceremonial center of Tiermes.[9] Burying the dead within the city limits reveals a radical change in the very conception of urban space. As in other areas of the Mediterranean world, the prohibition on burying the dead within city boundaries was slowly abandoned, although some cities maintained it into the sixth century.[10]

Taken as a whole, these examples may depict a crisis or decline of Roman urbanism. Doubtless, the buildings associated with the benefactions of local aristocracies no longer retained the function for which they had been originally intended. The appearance of cities may have drastically changed in the course of a century. But in most cases, these developments began in the late fourth century, as was discussed in Chapter 1. By the year 450, at least one generation had passed since the last wave of public games and civic ceremonies (with the notable exception, perhaps, of provincial capitals and other isolated examples). The post-Roman evidence shows less decline than uninterrupted urban occupation leading to an efficient use of abandoned spaces.

* * *

The transformation and reuse of traditional monumental infrastructure did not apply to every building in the late Roman city. Urban walls, the *late* Roman monumental feature par excellence in the region, do not show signs of abandonment. Rather, they were maintained and repaired, as the above-mentioned inscription from Mérida proves. Occasionally, forts or other reinforcements could be added to earlier defensive structures.[11] Wall repairs are harder to document from an archaeological point of view. Certain city walls, however, were in good condition in the early Middle Ages, suggesting they had been maintained throughout the post-Roman period. The walls of Braga, for instance, were admired in Arab sources, and excavations near the defensive perimeter have yielded materials from the fifth and sixth centuries.[12]

Defensive walls also became the most prominent settlement feature of a series of newly occupied sites in the plateau and in northwestern Iberia. Starting in the fifth century, but continuing into the Visigothic period, excavations reveal significant hilltop human presence in this relatively underurbanized area.[13] These sites present morphological features that make them resemble small towns more than villages. One such instance is found in the province of Palencia, on the southern slopes of the Cantabrian Basin. In the early fifth century, the population of the Roman settlement at Santa María de Mave moved to the twelve-hectare walled hilltop site of Monte Cildá, two kilometers away. Monte Cildá's walls were constructed within the Roman architectonic tradition, and they may have been built strictly speaking in the late Roman period.[14] Smaller hilltop sites were also fortified following the late Roman architectural tradition to a certain extent. The five-hectare site of Cerro del Castillo at Bernardos, located in the southern part of the Duero Basin, emerged out of the blue in the first half of the fifth century with walls that followed the late antique style of urban defense. Building, including of residential structures, never ceased on this site during the post-Roman and Visigothic periods. This mobilization of resources for construction is accompanied by evidence of a material culture typical of urban centers in the peninsula (post-Roman ceramics, glass, and so forth).[15]

Not all the fortifications were as impressive as Monte Cildá or, to a lesser extent, Cerro del Castillo. The hilltop La Cabeza de Navasangil (Ávila), occupied in the fifth century, was a small settlement of less than two hectares. A combination of a 1.5-meter-wide fence and the site's granite rocks protected most of the site. Only at the entrance was a more sophisticated structure built, including two towers and a small building just outside of the walls, which probably hosted a small guard.[16] Similarly, the first phase of El Cristo de San Esteban at Muelas del Pan (Zamora) presents a simple fortification system protecting a relatively small area of four hectares.[17] These small fortifications also existed in Galicia, although we need proper excavations to confirm what surveys suggest.[18] It is thus difficult to generalize, given that we are dealing with a very complex phenomenon of new settlement occupation in which each site presents unique characteristics. All cases, however, share a hilltop location accompanied by fortifications of some sort. They reveal sometimes potent, sometimes discrete initiatives by local communities and their leadership to assert settlement status through walled sites.

In the second half of the fifth century, walls remained one of the most important symbols of settlement prestige. The Visigothic kingdom of Toledo inherited this symbolism to an extent that the monarchy provided new cities or promoted foundations (that is, existing settlements with newly acquired administrative status) with walls. During the seventh century, a series of hilltop fortifications with a military character appeared in northern Iberia. The best-documented cases come from the area of La Rioja, but similar fortifications may have existed in other areas in the northern plateau.[19] In the upper Iregua Valley (La Rioja), these fortifications may have been created to control mountain passes and, potentially, to fulfill other state functions. They hosted small military garrisons, and their defensive military character prevails over other practical considerations (including water supply). Their relative uniformity and synchronism suggests more centralized planning, probably emanating from the court in Toledo.[20] Not only military settlements, however, were provided with walls. In 578, Leovigild founded the city of Reccopolis (Guadalajara, in the southern plateau), named after his son and future king, Reccared. The city had a clear ceremonial and symbolic status, as indicated by a large two-story building (probably with palatine or military functions) and a church, with all of these buildings organized around a large square.[21] By the second half of the sixth century, walls became part of the language of royal authority at the settlement level. The inscription of Zeno with which I started this chapter suggests that we can trace the ideological framework of this practice back to the early decades of the post-Roman period.

*   *   *

City walls were not a new feature in Western Iberian urbanism, as they had been part of the prestige settlement language since the late third century. The most visible change in urban topography during the post-Roman period was the increasing role of Christian buildings as foci of urban ceremonial life. The institutional history of urban Christianity during this period has been primarily attested to by references to bishops in local councils. The signature of a particular city's bishop would represent *post quem* the moment when a city definitely had an organized and institutionalized religious community. In this light, by the end of the post-Roman period, several of the main cities in Atlantic Iberia had achieved the high status of an independent Christian church. While these cities were usually the first-tier cities of the late Roman period, there were also a few newcomer cities, such as Porto—cities without a late imperial pedigree, which, for reasons that will be explained later, had independent Christian communities.[22]

Yet the existence of episcopal offices hardly reveals the impact of Christianity on the city layout. During the post-Roman period, Christian monumentality accelerated, and by the late sixth century, every episcopal see probably had at least one major church. Post-Roman Christian churches are attested to at Viseu, Mértola, Uxama, and, possibly, Conimbriga—although future excavations might modify some of these buildings' chronology. As such, they joined Mérida, Braga, Idanha-a-Velha, and Astorga, cities with late Roman urban basilicas.[23] Additionally, hints of churches in Lugo, Cauca, and Lisbon await further excavations for confirmation of the presence of these buildings in the sixth century.[24]

Christianity became not only more present in cities but also altered the topography of the Roman urban landscape. A recent reassessment of Idanha-a-Velha's site illustrates this phenomenon (Figure 5). Near a possible late fourth- or early fifth-century baptistery (and perhaps episcopal church), another baptistery was built, very likely adjacent to an episcopal basilica. Between the two baptisteries, under a ninth-century church, another large building has been proposed as the episcopal residence. A two-nave rectangular building to the west of the second baptistery had administrative or storage purposes (*horreum*), which would confirm the increasing roles assumed by the episcopate

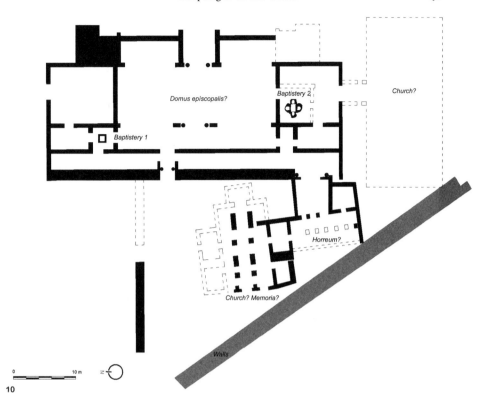

Figure 5. Idanha-a-Velha—Episcopal complex. From Isabel Sánchez Ramos and
Jorge Morín de Pablos, "Nueva lectura arqueológica del conjunto episcopal de
Egitania (Idanha-a-Velha, Portugal)." *Madrider Mitteilungen* 55 (2015): 398–428.

in urban contexts. North of this later building, another building has been identified as a small church or a memoria.[25] While future interventions may modify part of this interpretation, the sheer volume of structural investment
bespeaks a noticeable Christian presence in the urban fabric.

Our best-documented case, Mérida, confirms the cracks in the façade of
late Roman ceremonial and symbolic centers (Figure 6). As the forum lost its
original functions, the local church became immersed in the development of
a suburban religious nucleus which included the church of Saint Eulalia (with
her relics), a monastery, and a hostel for pilgrims—all this within a burial area.
Inside the walls, there were at least three churches (including the episcopal
"palace" with its atrium).[26] To be sure, few cities in the peninsula could compete
with the religious prestige of a pilgrimage center like Mérida. However, the

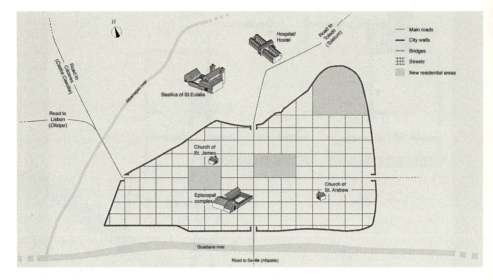

Figure 6. Post-Roman Mérida. Courtesy of Pedro Mateos Cruz.

impact of Christianity on the former capital of the diocese merely represents
a large-scale version of microtransformations in other cities. To take a nearby
example, a three-nave basilica of about nine hundred square meters was built
right outside the city of Mértola in the mid-fifth century. The construction
site coincided with a Roman necropolis that had been active since the first
century CE. The site's use as a burial ground continued with the foundation of
the church. Excavations found a series of sixth-century graves and funerary
inscriptions, some of them belonging to members of the ecclesiastical ladder.[27] As in the case of Mérida, an extramural foundation created alternative
ceremonial centers to the traditional public areas (and the churches within
the walls).

Monumental Christianity altered the geography of Roman towns in two
ways. The first change consisted in bringing graves within the city limits, sometimes seeking inhumation near the relics of a saint or the founding clergy of
the town.[28] The second change involved a destructuring of the ceremonial
spaces associated with Roman civic life through a fragmentation of symbolic
centers. Rather than concentrating religious and civic ceremonies in one focal point, the forum, Christianity dispersed the ritual aspects of urban life in
different parts of the city through the foundation of multiple churches. These
changes were not unique to Atlantic Iberia but common to a broader western

Mediterranean context.[29] Overall, by the late sixth century, the Christian landscape of Atlantic Iberian cities may have extended beyond the presence of an
episcopal basilica within the walls. Not all cities had the lavish religious buildings that Mérida could exhibit. Small towns very likely limited their Christian ceremonial center to one (perhaps modest) church. But the change in the
available vocabulary of monumentality by the year 600 is noteworthy—a
vocabulary that was now supplied by a Christianized ideology.

*　*　*

In spite of all the progress of the past few decades, there are whole areas of
urban archaeology that remain inscrutable. Archaeological focus on the period's few status buildings neglects the possible existence of other constructions, which also belonged to the architecture of power and prestige. For
instance, we know that some form of administration existed in the Suevic
kingdom and in Visigothic Lusitania before the mid-sixth century. Moreover,
the Visigothic kingdom of Leovigild and Reccared counted on an established
hierarchy of counts and dukes based on provincial and city districts. Archaeology has not provided any example of a courthouse or a governor's residence
(similar to the late Roman *praetorium*). Even in well-excavated eastern Mediterranean cities, these buildings are difficult to find. Political authorities of
different types may have continued using late Roman buildings to administrative effect. Holding court did not require a specific building, and even churches
could serve as places to settle disputes.[30] A passage in the *Lives of the Fathers
of Mérida* (which I will discuss in greater detail in the next chapter) mentions
a conflict between the Arian and the Nicene factions of Mérida over the
ownership of basilicas being settled by a council of judges gathered in the
atrium of a church.[31]

Evidence of palaces and ceremonial centers in post-Roman cities (neither
Suevic nor Visigothic) is relatively weak. The Suevi were the only people with
continuous courtly centers in Atlantic Iberia all through the post-Roman period. Suevic kings chose Braga as their residence, though the city might never
have achieved the status of what we would consider a permanent capital. A
possible ceremonial center has been identified in the area of Falperra, although
its chronology is too wide (fifth to sixth centuries) to deduce a precise sense
of its meaning.[32] There also are occasional references to Suevic kings in other
cities, such as Lugo, Mérida, or Porto, yet without much archaeological evidence
supporting their presence.[33] Visigothic political and administrative centers

remained outside of the peninsula, in Aquitaine, until the early sixth century.[34] We know that the Visigothic kings took residence in various Iberian cities after 507, but, as far as sources show, only once in Atlantic Iberia and for a brief period only, between 549 and 554.[35] Yet Mérida never turned into a "courtly" city for prolonged periods. These courts were unstable by comparison to the former Roman governmental staff in the provincial capitals, and we cannot establish the number of courtiers nor their real social standing. They certainly included a minimum of ceremonial rituals, as they absorbed some of the Roman court's activities. Fifth-century sources mention constant embassies and negotiations between kings and local communities at court.[36] Royal courts were also important centers of intense gift distribution and gathering of tributes. Yet no trace of courts can be discerned from an archaeological point of view.[37]

If archaeologists have not yet found traces of kings' and their entourages' residences, they have been equally unsuccessful in finding clear evidence of aristocrats' private residences. Traditional urban aristocratic houses practically fade from the archaeological record in the late Roman period. By the fifth century, the few late Roman urban *domus* excavated so far show rapid transformations. In Mérida, houses were subdivided and occupied by multiple families that shared the former peristyle (now a patio) as a common space (Figure 7).[38] Likewise, large rooms at the so-called Casa del Aqueducto in Tiermes were subdivided by the fifth century.[39] Fortified hilltops in the plateau have offered up evidence of residential spaces that were likely occupied by members of the local elite. Recent excavations at the site of La Cabeza de Navansangil have unearthed two spaces that seem to have been occupied by elite or subelite groups based on their surface area (eighty square meters) and the material culture found. However, nothing in the internal organization suggests a division of spaces in the traditional Roman fashion.[40] The archaeological indicators of aristocratic presence are sometimes weaker than we would wish. For instance, in the above-mentioned house of the former temple in Mérida, archaeologists have found twenty gold *tremisses*, which might point to the comfortable economic situation of the house owners at some point.[41] But even if we optimistically take this hoard as evidence of elite presence, nothing in the layout of the house has yet indicated the will to display social status in residential form. Like in other parts of the western Mediterranean, elites faded in the fifth century at the housing level.[42]

Aristocrats did not disappear from cities, however, as literary sources occasionally mention their urban dwellings. When the Suevic army entered

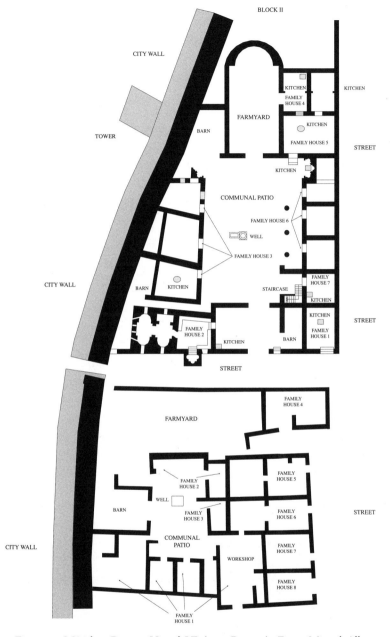

Figure 7. Mérida—Domus V and VI (post-Roman). From Miguel Alba, "Diacronía de la vivienda señorial en Emerita (Lusitania, Hispania): desde las *domus* altoimperiales y tardoantiguas a las residencias palaciales omeyas (s. I–IX)." In *Archeologia e società tra tardo antico e alto medioevo*, ed. Gian Pietro Brogiolo and Alexandra Chavarría Arnau, Mantua: SAP, 2007, 163–92.

the city of Conimbriga, they captured "the family of the noble Cantaber," who presumably lived in the city.[43] According to the *Lives of the Fathers of Mérida*, the *dux* Claudius's house (*domus*) was located close to the basilica where the trial over the ownership of Christian buildings was held.[44] How can we reconcile the aristocracy's literary presence with its archaeological absence? As we saw in Chapter 1, in all likelihood aristocratic urban houses were already changing in the late Roman period. Old-fashioned urban *domus* coexisted with less visible houses, namely, two-story houses and less spacious residences built with perishable materials. If so, changes in housing patterns exemplify less the presence or absence of certain social groups than the shifting strategies of that group to assert distinction in an urban context. The late Roman model of the aristocratic house was no longer a way of marking one's membership in the elite.

*   *   *

By the sixth century, post-Roman cities had turned into rather different places than the Roman towns of the Flavian period. Most of the traditional civic buildings (including those constructed for entertainment) had lost their use as public monuments and had turned into residential quarters, burial areas, or quarries for construction. Local elites still ruled from the city in most cases, but they no longer lived in aristocratic Roman *domus*. Rather they dwelt in new houses whose layout archaeology cannot determine. Within and outside the late antique defensive walls, which now protected these cities, Christian buildings dotted the centers of ceremonial life associated with religious and even nonreligious rituals. As for other prestige buildings, we can only conjecture on their existence based on scanty written documents. Although our archaeological evidence for the period is patchy, it nevertheless shows consistency with developments in other post-Roman western Mediterranean regions.[45]

Important chronological variations hide behind this simplified depiction. We must not think that the year 450 or the decades around it marked an absolute watershed. We are dealing with slow-motion processes, some of them rooted in the late Roman period. Take, for example, the case of abandonment of public entertainment and civic ceremonial buildings. As we saw in Chapter 1, this process began during the second half of the fourth century in some cities. Similarly, excavations attest to changes in aristocratic housing practices in urban areas during the fourth and early fifth centuries. Likewise, the development of monumentalized urban Christianity varied from region to region and from city to city. By the year 500, Mérida's topography reflected the weight of its local church. But it would not be until the sixth century or later that we would find a similar rearrangement in other Iberian cities.[46] Nevertheless, there is a clear tendency toward a shifting expression of social and communal status through monumental architecture. And the central decades of the fifth century seem to have been a turning point, when earlier traditions of urbanism were definitively abandoned while the new trends described here began to gain ground. Why was that the case?

The key to understanding the post-Roman urban world lies in the ways in which urban political centrality was expressed. Cities, wherever they existed, remained foci of political action in post-Roman Iberia, very much as they used to be when the empire ruled over the peninsula.[47] As we will see in this and the next chapter, civic government was such a fundamental feature of post-Roman politics that it had to be re-created at the very local level wherever the late Roman *civitates* structure was weak. In a context of multiple, competing supralocal actors (mostly Suevic, Visigothic, and occasional imperial interventions), as well as intercity competition, the bargaining power of a post-Roman city was largely defined by its ability to offer resistance to immediate threats. Many towns may have envied the fate of the fortified hilltop of Coviacum (presumably Valencia de Don Juan, León), which was able to resist the attacks of a Gothic army in 458.[48] Walls became altogether a fundamental aspect of urban prestige for very practical reasons, perhaps more than in the late Roman period. We tend to see city walls as signs of insecurity, but perhaps we should look at them as exactly the opposite: as markers of the local community's self-assertion. Walls were prestige elements because they could offer protection and hence boost the status of a city in an always-fluctuating political landscape.[49]

However, physical might was not the only language expressing urban prestige. Christianity provided another shared vocabulary, able to show a city's status through its monumental buildings. Churches and other Christian buildings, like city walls, were polysemic structures. We can see them as merely display buildings that embellished urban centers, but we would be missing another meaning on which local communities placed a great deal of importance. In the context of post-Roman politics, churches, their saints, and their clergy were seen as protectors of the town. Christian ideologues publicized the victories that these saints could achieve. When Theoderic reached Mérida in 456–457, which was at that time under Suevic overlordship, Hydatius reported in his *Chronicle* that the Visigothic king avoided plundering the city, "deterred by the prodigies of the holy martyr Eulalia."[50] More than a century later, the same saint appeared to king Leovigild in his dreams, according to the *Lives of the Fathers of Mérida*. She threatened the Arian Leovigild with death if he did not restore the Nicene bishop to his see, which the king promptly did.[51] In the fifth century and later, the power of saints provided a language to explain negotiations between cities and outside powers. The bishops associated with the cult of saints in a particular town could act as effective negotiators with nonlocal powers by mobilizing the symbolic capital attached to their city's religious prestige.[52]

*   *   *

In Chapter 1, we noted the political and social agency of local elites and imperial authorities pursuing the building and maintenance of prestige infrastructure in post-Roman cities. In the post-Roman period, aristocrats and, eventually, monarchs and their representatives played a significant role in the construction of prestige architecture. The inscription of Zeno does not reveal where the funds for these constructions came from, but the *dux* and the bishop were crucial to the process leading to the repairs. For fifth-century and early sixth-century hilltop fortifications, the initiative of local groups may have been more important than any royal intervention (in itself, a late sixth-century and predominantly seventh-century phenomenon).[53] Building, repairing, and maintaining walls were post-Roman acts of power over which local aristocrats and royal administrators kept a social monopoly.

Aristocratic patronage over urban ecclesiastical foundations is likely to have contributed to the development of an urban monumental Christianity.[54] The *Lives of the Fathers of Mérida* provides a myth of origin for the see's wealth: a bequest by a leading citizen of Mérida after the successful intervention of one Paul, a doctor and later a bishop, in the aristocrat's wife's childbirth.[55] Although the story could be pure invention, it illustrates the ecclesiastical writer's ideal donor figure for a city church. Christianity was a widespread urban phenomenon by the early fifth century but hardly a monumentalized one. What changed during the fifth century was the willingness of well-off Christians to pour resources into their local Christian communities. This impulse was eventually expressed in the construction of basilicas and other religious buildings in urban and suburban contexts. Although aristocrats may have donated funds to urban Christian communities to secure the protection of the saints, other concerns were at least equally important. Urban churches are the archaeological expression of a much denser social phenomenon since lands and other forms of wealth supported these churches and their personnel. The so-called patrimony of the Church was acquired in slow motion over several generations. It grew out of discrete donations by the wealthy during the post-Roman period, as the Church focused on this demographic as the quintessential donor while providing new ideas on the correct use of wealth. In other words, urban Christianity became archaeologically visible only when the wealthy were persuaded that donations to the Church supported the social relevance of their riches—and, as a synecdoche, their own crucial role within their communities.[56]

The so-called end of the Roman city in Western Iberia was not a traumatic episode if we look at it from the point of view of settlement continuity. Most cities, indeed, continued to be occupied after the fifth century and were not abandoned by local elites. The main visible transformation was the way settlement status was displayed through monumental architecture. Throughout the period, cities developed a markedly post-Roman urbanism, in which defensive walls and Christian ceremonial buildings became town hallmarks. Not every city adopted these features in the same way and at the same time, but the available language of urbanism clearly changed after the mid-fifth century, setting new parameters to express city prestige. It is hardly surprising, then, that new minor towns on hilltops and later royal foundations adopted some or all of these markers of settlement status. This language was silently crafted throughout the fifth century, when a city's defensive and symbolic power determined its status within the rising barbarian monarchies. Local elites, royal representatives, and monarchs themselves embraced the vocabulary of settlement prestige—a vocabulary that bespeaks, among other things, the regeneration of statehood after the demise of the imperial administration.

The Post-Roman Countryside and the End of Late Roman Monumentality

The post-Roman countryside is, in a way, the "invisible" Atlantic Iberia. The lack of excavations is even more discouraging than in urban areas. The problems that affect study of urban centers—the difficulty of dating artifacts and the fact that research priorities are elsewhere—also apply to the countryside, with the aggravating added factor that dispersion in settlement patterns makes statistically relevant data less available. Thanks to the painstaking efforts of Iberian archaeologists to document even tiny sites and their promptness in undertaking emergency excavations to preempt the damage done by present-day infrastructure projects, we can now appreciate that the post-Roman countryside was certainly a world of change, but not in the sense previous generations believed. Scholars no longer accept theories of regression and crisis in rural areas uncritically, as archaeology begins to identify post-Roman sites in larger numbers than a couple of decades ago.

Indeed, the rural world in the aftermath of empire seems to have undergone a vivid process of reinvention that challenges ideas of rural conservatism. Settlements changed, and they did so in a way that bore meanings other than "decadence" to those agents of change. In this section, I will review three of the most noticeable transformations of rural settlements: the so-called end of the villa, the changes in nonelite rural settlements, and the construction of rural churches. Like changes in urban settlements, the transformation of rural monumentality was associated with the rapid disintegration of the Roman imperial administration and its symbolic project incarnated by local aristocrats. At the same time, the new type of rural settlement reveals certain ideological principles of post-Roman statehood and the active role played by local elites in reshaping the countryside.

* * *

Rural archaeology has demonstrated that Atlantic Iberian settlement morphology changed by the end of the fifth century, at least in terms of its most visible late Roman development—the residential villa. A strikingly simultaneous abandonment of late Roman villas as aristocratic residences took place throughout the fifth century.[57] Local potentates, who had built impressive rural residences during the previous century, no longer invested in new mansions or the maintenance of old ones. More remarkably, archaeologists have failed to find alternatives to aristocratic residences in rural areas in the post-Roman period. Although some residential villas continued to be occupied as aristocratic houses into the sixth century (notably in coastal areas), these exceptions do not change the overall picture.[58] Even Iberian written sources mirror the end of the villas by a displacement in vocabulary. In the second half of the fifth century, *villa* ceased being a synonym for an elite house, and it only survived in fossilized formulae. The term would appear in later centuries but with a different meaning—*village*.[59] Both at the archaeological and literary level, the fifth century marks the end of the villa.

The chronological coincidence between the presence of barbarians and the abandonment of villas was once turned into a causal relationship. The newcomer armies would have destroyed markers of Roman "civilization" in their supposedly destructive raids. But several rural mansions, such as the villa of Almenara, near Cauca, were abandoned during the fifth century without any sign of violence.[60] Occasionally, some villas present signs of destruction, but these are hard to assign to one specific event. Excavations at the villa of Valdanzo (Soria), for instance, have found mosaic-tile rooms destroyed by fires after the fifth century. Blaming barbarian arsonists, however, is rather problematic. The strata associated with the destruction have not produced many materials, which is why archaeologists suggest that the villa had already been abandoned at the time the fires were lit.[61]

Rather than simply being abandoned, most villas were reused for different purposes in the post-Roman period. Former residential houses were used as buildings dedicated to productive activities, such as workshops or storage areas, and residences for working, nonelite populations. Atlantic Iberia does not offer many examples of this type of post-Roman evolution (although it was relatively common in late Roman Mediterranean Iberia).[62] Most of the examples come from Lusitania, such as the villa of Pozo de la Cañada, which was continuously occupied by economic activities into the ninth century, or Cerro da Vila, where basins with probable production purposes were built in one of the corridors of the peristyle villa at an unknown date after the early fifth century.[63] The small number of productive reuses of villa centers might be related to the concurrent continuous use, well into the post-Roman period, of late Roman production quarters, especially in Lusitania, as we will presently see.

Another trajectory of post-Roman villa development, and perhaps the most common one in Western Iberia, consisted of turning the former villa or its immediate surroundings into burial grounds. In the case of La Olmeda, more than five hundred graves were found in the so-called southern necropolis, with burials dating from the fourth through the sixth century, while the villa seems to have been abandoned at some point in the fifth century.[64] La Olmeda is one of the most impressive cases, but similar post-Roman evolutions also occurred on a smaller scale. Excavations at the late Roman villa of Currás (Tomiño, Pontevedra), by the mouth of the Miño River, have found twenty burials dating back to the sixth century, with another twenty that remain unexcavated.[65] The meaning of this transformation is obscure. It is tempting to analyze these burials as evidence that the rural estate's peasant population was using the abandoned villa as a symbolic center, but the archaeological data alone do not offer conclusive evidence. It is possible that some of these necropoleis were associated with new types of rural settlements, either farms or villages. But we lack firm evidence of such agglomerations in the case of burials in (perhaps former) villas.[66]

Another part of the post-Roman evolution of villas was the construction of Christian basilicas in former residential areas or nearby areas. In the villa of Milreu, a large building, which has been (inconclusively) interpreted as a nymphaeum, a mausoleum, and a hall, became at some point between the fifth or the sixth century a Christian basilica. A sixth-century baptistery and a series of burials (together with a small mausoleum) dating from the late fifth to the seventh century signal the transition between the two moments.[67] I will discuss rural basilicas in greater detail presently. As a final example of post-villa evolution, churches in or near former villas remind us that monumentality was not completely lost in these sites, which could be transformed into a new type of status building.

The evolution of villas matches some developments of post-Roman cities, where the abandonment of monumental areas and aristocratic *domus* gave way to uses that were divorced from prestige display (such as nonelite housing, burials, or productive activities). But whereas the presence of aristocrats in urban environments can be traced, even if indirectly, through written documents, tracing aristocratic residence in rural areas is a more challenging task. For instance, seventh century sources make reference to aristocrats and their *villulae*, which by then had become a standardized term of rural settlement. In his *History of Wamba*, Julian of Toledo mentioned that king Recceswinth died in the year 672 near Salamanca in the *villula* of Gerticos.[68] We will encounter other mentions of *villulae* later in this book in relation to their economic activities. As a settlement type, however, they remain a mystery. Were these former villas occupied but now with poorer material structures? *Villulae* could also refer to completely different types of residences, built with materials invisible at the archaeological level. And yet post-Roman archaeology has detected "peasant" houses but not aristocratic ones. In any event, both through the terminology of property structure and *villula*, post-Roman sources declare the presence of aristocrats in the countryside, even though most of their houses remain invisible.[69]

In all likelihood, individual members of local elites did have residences in rural areas. Whether part-time or full-time residences, these houses resemble poorer people's houses at the archaeological level—hence their invisibility.

Thus, rural housing ceased to be a way of displaying status as was done in the late Roman period. For instance, occupation in northwestern Iberian villas continued into the sixth or even seventh century, as ceramics and burials in the coastal villas of Bares (Mañón, A Coruña) or Noville indicate.[70] And yet no monumental constructions took place from the fifth century onward.[71] I argued in Chapter 2 that residential villas were ways of expressing a social status by adhering to an imperial culture that linked local elites to empire-wide aristocracies. The decades around the mid-fifth century marked the moment in which the link between local elites and a sociopolitical system that granted status markers to those elites broke down. These houses were no longer readable as status markers. What might have been interpreted as a simple change of taste was in fact a much deeper phenomenon of shifting language to express social and cultural separation.[72]

Another theory for this settlement transformation is the impoverishment of local aristocracies, who would not have been able to afford building and maintaining Roman-style rural houses after the fifth century. Yet the cost argument only makes sense within this broader context of sociocultural transformations.[73] The events in the fifth century might have affected the income of local aristocracies—although, as we will see in Chapter 6, there is little evidence to support this idea. But even a declining income could sustain villa-like settlements of smaller size if necessary to assert aristocratic status. Late Roman villas were not markers of wealth but markers of social competition through the display of wealth. This means that individual aristocrats and families had the social incentives to allocate resources in these constructions, sometimes at a higher level than what they should have "rationally" spent. Therefore, change in aristocratic rural residences was not so much a question of disposable wealth as an issue of priorities for how this wealth would be spent. Fewer monumentalized houses had existed during the late Roman period: the number of fourth-century villas was significantly smaller than the number of local aristocrats. Once the social incentives for luxurious Roman-style villas disappeared, less lavish houses had the opportunity to become the norm in aristocratic housing.

* * *

In this context of less visible markers of aristocratic status in rural housing, archaeologists have begun to document the presence of rural settlement agglomerations starting in the fifth century. There is a growing consensus to call these sites *villages*, and I do not see a major impediment to using the term (it is certainly much better than calling them, teleologically, "proto-villages"). Agglomeration did not occur everywhere or at the same pace, as we shall momentarily see. But whereas surveys indicate that in the year 300, the typical nonelite settlement was an isolated hut or, at most, a small hamlet of a few houses, by the year 600, larger, agglomerated settlements become more visible. These villages are usually detected indirectly, through hearths, postholes, and burials. The study of necropoleis indicates that these sites might have had a constant population of up to a hundred inhabitants, who lived within ten or fifteen households. Although residential structures do not show any internal hierarchy, buildings and storage spaces might indicate some forms of economic centralization, to which I will return in Chapter 6.[74]

In Western Iberia, village archaeology is still in its infancy. The best post-Roman evidence for this type of settlement comes from the region of Madrid, in the southern rather than the northern plateau. One of these villages, Gózquez, was inhabited between the early sixth and the mid-eighth century. Twelve to fifteen households occupied the site, with each family living in a sunken wooden hut, and the settlement also boasted some buildings with stone foundations. The site has a marked rural character, although there are signs of small-scale artisanal production (pottery). A nearby necropolis with up to five hundred graves attests to its stable occupation throughout the period. It is estimated that a hundred or so people on average lived in Gózquez at any given time.[75] Social horizontality prevails at the settlement level: each household occupied a similar area (including the house and the space for garden crops). Excavations at Gózquez and post-Roman villages have failed to find higher-status buildings such as fortifications, seigniorial housing, or churches.[76]

Excavations in sites like Gózquez and others in the Madrid area match what archaeologists have begun to find in the northern meseta, but less frequently in other regions. Unfortunately, in the northern meseta, we depend mostly on field surveys while we wait for the "northern Gózquez" to appear. Yet surveys seem to corroborate the pattern described in the Toledo area, although we should not overestimate the numeric impact of villages in the fifth and sixth centuries. Future excavations in certain settlements in the Duero Basin may reveal sites of this nature.[77] A process of village formation was very likely under way in northwestern Iberia in the post-Roman period, although the information is still fragmentary.[78]

In spite of that fragmentary nature of the material evidence, it is clear that a process of change occurred in the post-Roman countryside, especially in northern Iberia. In a region with scarce Roman occupation, such as the Alagón Valley in Salamanca, field surveys have found an increasing number of small sites dated to after the fifth century with a typically peasant material culture and with no sign of aristocratic presence.[79] A somewhat similar pattern can be found in the surveys of the Leonese Páramo (between the Esla and Óbrigo Rivers in modern León).[80] Likewise, the southeastern part of the Valladolid province presents some evidence of newly occupied rural sites after the fifth century along with other sites with continuous occupation between the Roman and post-Roman periods.[81] Although the information from these surveys needs to be verified by excavations, it clearly shows that changes in nonelite rural habitat were contemporary with the appearance of villages immediately south of the Sistema Central. In most cases, however, with only a few exceptions, the sites detected by surveys are different from Gózquez.[82] Where proper excavations did take place, such as in El Pelambre (León) or Vega de Duero (Valladolid), the settlement model more frequently involved small farms with one to three families than larger villages as in the Madrid region.[83] Perhaps future excavations will reveal sites similar to La Genestosa (Salamanca), which has been partially excavated (Figure 8). A series of single-family peasant houses in various nuclei are spread over a surface of forty-nine hectares without a marked internal hierarchy or structuration. In one of those nuclei (El Cañaveral), two houses of eighty square meters each have been found, and about eight other possible structures have been identified, though not excavated.[84]

We also need to wonder about the identity of the social agents behind the expansion of farms and villages. In certain cases, villages and farmsteads followed house construction techniques that were, as it were, imported from central Europe.[85] Iberian scholarship is divided between those who believe these houses were the product of an internal, "Roman" evolution and those who put greater emphasis on the effect of an external, "barbarian" influence.[86] The so-called sunken huts, usually built with perishable materials or stone foundations, represent an architectural innovation in the fifth and sixth centuries. While it is not possible to assume ethnic identities directly from housing practices, these new constructions reveal the presence of individuals with technical knowledge of and cultural attachment to these forms. The fact that these houses first appeared in the plateau, where other types of nonlocal traditions of material culture gained visibility during the fifth century, may not be a coincidence, and I will return to these considerations in the next chapter.

More relevant for the purposes of the present argument is the role of aristocrats in the development of villages and settlements with two or three

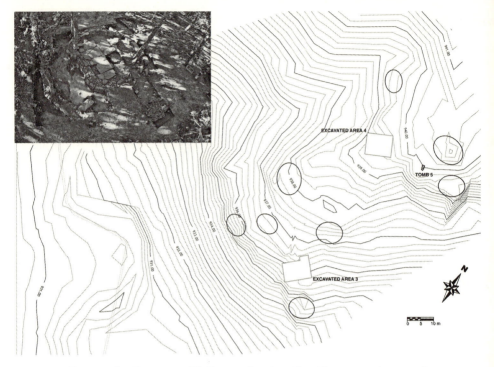

Figure 8. La Genestosa—El Cañaveral and residential structure (excavated
area 3). Courtesy of Iñaki Martín Viso, University of Salamanca.

farmhouses. Opinions vary among scholars, from those who see these sites as
semiautonomous peasant developments to those who argue that rural settlement was related to large landholdings, even though the exact nature of
property structures cannot be determined archaeologically.[87] Based solely on
the archaeological evidence, it is problematic to argue either way. We may assume that peasants enjoyed a certain level of autonomy of choice regarding
the expansion of villages and farmsteads, particularly to provide security and
strengthen bonds of solidarity against potential landowner demands.[88] However, as we will see in the next chapter, aristocracies did not vanish in the meseta after the mid-fifth century. If anything, aristocratic power became more
localized, centered in a handful of cities and predominantly on hilltop settlements. Landowning structures were still powerful forces in the region, and as
far as we can reconstruct economic domination from seventh-century evidence, landowners collected rents and probably taxes from small peasants
and tenants. Therefore, we should expect a minimum level of aristocratic in-

volvement in the changes affecting rural settlements. Parallels from other areas of the post-Roman West show how the formation of villages can perfectly coexist with large and powerful land ownership.[89] I will return to these issues in Chapter 6, but at this point it is important to stress that aristocratic ascendancy limited any possibility of fully autonomous peasant enterprise. While landowning elites may not have taken the initiative to settle rural populations in villages (though nothing indicates the contrary either), peasant settlements cannot have gone unnoticed, and there must have been at least tacit landowner approval. If aristocrats did intervene in the formation of villages, we might be in the presence of a silent process of rural elite identity assertion that differs from the methods typical of the late Roman period.[90] Such a process was not meant to oppress rural workers, who could be exploited through other mechanisms. Rather, organizing, founding, or protecting a village, or the occupation of new lands, may have played a crucial role in defining elite identity vis-à-vis other potential landowners through the marking of boundaries between those who could and those who could not afford such projects. Unfortunately, in the absence of written evidence, the archaeological remains per se do not offer conclusive support to this argument.

There is another reason why we need to be cautious about inferring too much peasant autonomy from post-Roman settlement changes. Although I have referred to villages and farms, the latter clearly predominate over the former in terms of numbers. Villages did develop, and in some areas from the fifth century onward. But we need to wait until the period between the seventh and tenth century to observe a significant number of villages in the peninsula. Most of the peasant habitat was still dominated in the post-Roman period by dispersed houses, as it had been in the late Roman world. Post-Roman peasant houses, however, are archaeologically visible because of the construction techniques involved (sunken cabins with postholes or stone-based structures) and, in some cases, owing to their being grouped in twos, threes, or more. Moreover, after the fifth century, production infrastructure such as silos or mills were built more frequently close to farmhouses, which also facilitates discoveries in surveys and excavations. I shall return to this last point in Chapter 6.

*   *   *

The rural world was not a shabby place full of houses built with perishable materials and semiabandoned villas. Rural Christian buildings partially inherited the tradition of prestige architecture in the countryside. These buildings were not the private *oratoria* and mausolea that had characterized the late Roman Christian countryside. After the fifth century, monumentalized rural Christianity assumed the form of basilicas aimed at providing fundamental spiritual services, such as baptism, eucharist, and burial. The dimensions of these basilicas did not match the size of late Roman villas, yet they were ample enough to receive more attendants than the fourth century's small pious gatherings of aristocratic families and their friends. Larger congregations of local peasants now had a space in which to access the sacred world under the leadership of a local priest.[91] For the standards of the period and the region, rural basilicas were impressive buildings. One hundred meters north of the (former?) residential center of the villa of Torre de Palma, a three-nave basilica (separated by granite columns) with two apses on both ends was in all likelihood erected during the late fifth or early sixth century (Figures 9 and 10). To this building, which was more than four hundred square meters and had marble-decorated gates, was added a two-hundred-square-meter baptistery in the sixth or seventh century. Marble and stucco decorated the walls of both the church and the baptistery.[92] By the seventh century, churches like Torre de Palma had become a common feature of the Western Iberian rural landscape.[93]

The pace of development of rural monumental Christianity did not apply to all regions equally. Lusitania can boast an earlier start. Some rural basilicas date from the fifth century or perhaps earlier, such as the complex at Montinho das Laranjeiras (Alcoutim, Faro).[94] Similarly, the fifth-century church at Torre de Palma may have had a fourth-century predecessor.[95] Monte da Cegonha (Vidigueira, Beja), one of the first rural *oratoria* dated so far in the whole of Hispania, was built in the middle decades of the fourth century.[96] Thus, southern and central Lusitania started the post-Roman period with an experience of rural Christianity. Only in the second half of the fifth century and throughout the sixth century, however, did the construction of Christian buildings gain momentum in the Lusitanian countryside. In some cases, earlier basilicas were adapted to the new demands of an episcopally led Christianity. The *oratorium* at Monte da Cegonha was turned into a church at some point in the late fifth or early sixth century. The ninety-square-meter basilica had had a reliquary and probably an altar in the fourth century. During the fifth century, Monte da Cegonha hosted several burials. By the late sixth century, the three naves of the basilica were divided by new columns, no more burials were done within the building, the basilica was newly repaved, and a

Figure 9. Torre de Palma site plan. Courtesy of Stephanie Maloney, Director, Torre de Palma Project 1983–2000.

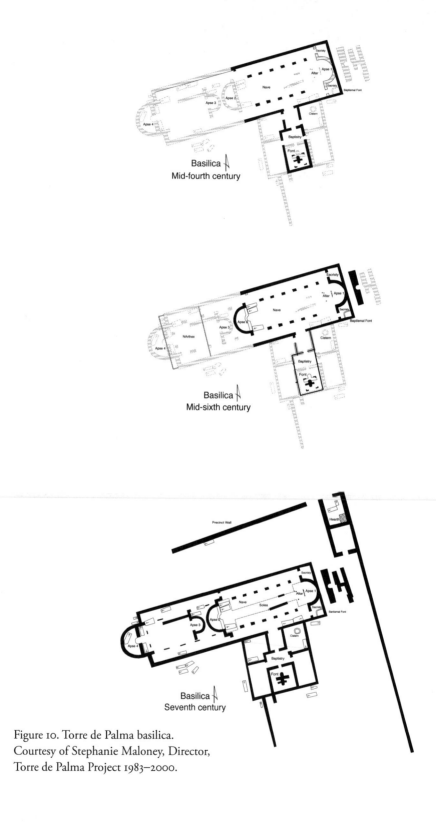

Figure 10. Torre de Palma basilica.
Courtesy of Stephanie Maloney, Director,
Torre de Palma Project 1983–2000.

baptistery was added.[97] In other cases, post-Roman church buildings appeared without an ostensibly Christian construction preceding them. This might be the case of the church associated with the baptistery and the cemetery at Vila Verde de Ficalho (Serpa, Beja).[98] In general, rural Lusitanian basilicas were not built in uncharted monumental territory. Rather, most of the archaeologically documented churches appear in association with former villas. Unlike the other two regions of Western Iberia, the central and southern Lusitanian countryside maintained settlement monumentalization between the late and post-Roman periods, even though the nature of those monuments significantly changed.

In the plateau, a handful of cases, such as Marialba (Villaturiel, León), match the chronology of Lusitanian basilicas, but overall the process of construction became generalized much later, in the sixth and seventh centuries.[99] Epigraphic evidence links the construction process to the monies of local aristocrats, such as the dedication of a church by the children of the *inlustris femina* Anduires and her husband near Uxama, perhaps in the late sixth century.[100] Kings might also have intervened, as in the Christian center of Santa María de Mijangos, not far from the hilltop of Tedeja (Burgos). A surviving inscription indicates that the church may have been dedicated during Reccared's reign, but the site seems to have had a cultic and burial use since at least the mid-fifth century.[101] These are exceptions, however, and monumental rural Christianity remains ubiquitously invisible in the plateau.

In northwestern Iberia, the invisibility of post-Roman rural churches contrasted with a relatively developed ecclesiastical network by the mid-sixth century.[102] Literary evidence suggests that the construction of basilicas was gaining momentum in the second third of the sixth century. The Second Council of Braga gathered in the year 572 considered it necessary to remind bishops that they should not request presents in order to consecrate basilicas.[103] In the Cantabrian Mountains, however, neither written nor archaeological sources offer unambiguous signs of Christianity until much later, perhaps into the high medieval period.[104]

* * *

The construction of rural basilicas is often associated with the phenomenon of so-called private churches.[105] Some of these churches might have belonged to an earlier parishlike structure, in that they were under the direct supervision of the bishop and supported by the metropolitan church.[106] In most cases, however, we are dealing with the local initiatives of propertied elites who donated lands and other resources for the maintenance of these churches. These basilicas were built by landowners within or near their estates and endowed with lands for the support of the clergy. The phenomenon is first attested to in the Iberian Peninsula in the first half of the sixth century, although it may have had its origins in the second half of the fifth century.[107] The term *private churches* does not do justice to the complexity of determining who owned these buildings. Even if the founder and his or her heirs retained a right of oversight of the basilicas, the building belonged to the church itself and the local bishop administered it. Rather than private churches, we are in the presence of privately founded churches over which the founder and the heirs kept a symbolic attachment as well as certain rights to defend the proper use of the endowment. But, unlike in other parts of the post-Roman West, episcopal authority over the management of these churches was rarely challenged as long as bishops respected the wishes of the founder.[108]

The phenomenon of privately founded churches in the Iberian countryside brings to light religious transformations as well as new modes of expressing aristocratic family identity. Christian ideas on gift giving granted a way of coping with the seeming contradiction between riches and Christian life. Churches became loci of family memory, where the founder and his relatives would be buried and receive prayers for their salvation. The growing concern with the fate in the afterlife and the expiation of sins gave the impulse to the construction of these churches. Founding churches or monasteries was a way for aristocratic wealth to be transformed into "wealth of the poor" and allowed generations of wealthy Christians to deal with the constant tension between their riches and the evangelical calls to a life of poverty.[109]

In the case of rural basilicas, we should also remember that these churches were not built within the more communal context of the city. Rather, they were anchored in the reality of land property in the countryside. The proximity to former villa centers is particularly relevant. We saw in Chapter 2 how rural burial practices marked elite attachment to ancestral lands or, at least, the beginning of a tradition that associated family memory with lands. The association between one's family and a basilica is crucial to understand the rise of these buildings. This link between the founder, his family, and the church could be traced in the efforts of later Visigothic councils to regulate the different spheres of influence of both founder(s) and bishop, under whose jurisdiction those churches fell.[110] These efforts were not directed at displacing the patronage of the founding family over a particular basilica; rather, the Church's canons (as well as secular legislation) repeatedly reminded lay and ecclesiastical elites how the revenues associated with the different churches ought to be distributed. We must not forget that the aim of late sixth- and seventh-century legislation of so-called private churches was to prevent, above all, episcopal exploitation rather than abuse by the founder.[111]

Local landowners and men of power in general thought of these buildings as something more than religious attachments to their own (former?) family residence. They were buildings meant to last (hence the land endowments they received) and to stand out from other buildings, including aristocrats' own rural residences. But they were also there to be attended by a community larger than the family of the founder. If the villages in the plateau created a physically agglomerated community, rural basilicas were the spiritual agglomerations of the founder, his or her family, and a larger rural population, many of whom (though not necessarily all of whom) were under some form of direct or indirect control from the founder. If the interpretation of rural villages as the result of aristocratic initiative is correct, we find in rural churches another option for local elites to intervene in the rural landscape at the settlement level.

When rural houses in the Roman style no longer displayed distinction, Christianity became one of the most prominent languages readable by other members of local communities and, more important, by one's peers. Building rural churches was, during the post-Roman period, a way of marking the distance between those who had means (lands) and influence and those who did not. I do not wish to deny the existence of personal piety or profound religious beliefs as the motivation for building these rural basilicas. However, personal religion was expressed through the construction of Christian monuments in and near one's lands, endowed by personal property, and in which the members of the founding family could be buried and prayed for. Thus, as in the case of city walls, we should not read these churches as "instruments of oppression." Oppression did exist, but churches were not directly aimed at controlling the rural masses.

When building or endowing basilicas and other religious centers, aristocrats were not looking downward, but rather sideways and, eventually, upward in the social ladder. The seventh-century Visigothic monarchy would develop models of sacred kingship, including a ceremony of royal anointment, and the king would become the ultimate protector of the Church.[112] The Visigoths' conversion to Nicene Christianity in the late sixth century contributed to this development. But barbarian rulers began to experiment with these ideas in earlier centuries, a process that went almost unnoticed by hostile, non-Arian sources.[113] While Christian piety and elite attempts to mark social status were important forces behind the process of church foundation, rural basilicas also appeared in a context where state power began to be associated with the protection of the Church from a legal and economic standpoint. In the post-Roman West, the construction of churches was slowly becoming an act with clear political meaning. Builders were encouraged to claim that they were acting in the best interests of the kingdom by allowing the entire population to benefit from their generosity.[114] Building, endowing, and protecting churches became, during the fifth and sixth centuries, acts reserved to those with enough economic and social muscle—to the extent that seventh-century conciliar literature only expected the kingdom's most powerful people to found churches.[115]

*   *   *

The post-Roman countryside shows transformations at the settlement level consistent with what we saw happening in cities. Significant continuity in occupation was the norm rather than the exception. It is hard to find signs of a generalized crisis after the fifth century based solely on occupation evidence. To be sure, some sites were abandoned, but, to the same extent, new sites were occupied—or reoccupied after a hiatus during the Roman imperial period. The case of late Roman villas is paradigmatic in this sense. There are few signs of post-450 aristocratic occupation, although in specific instances villas may have been used as elite residences into the sixth century. The end of aristocratic occupation, however, does not entail depopulation. The same villa centers were reused as burial zones, productive spaces, nonelite residences, or spaces for Christian worship by an archaeologically elusive rural population. The language of crisis may only be used to signify transformation rather than decline.

Rural monumentality also changed during the post-Roman period. Whereas rural house traditions in the late Roman countryside united local aristocracies with a Mediterranean-wide Roman elite culture, the fifth century transformed that relationship. Visible differences between aristocratic and non-aristocratic houses disappear from the archaeological record, although we must bear in mind that other, archaeologically invisible markers may have existed. Markers of distinction in decorative items such as metals, textiles, or woodworks escape the eye of the archaeologist. Yet stone, marble, and brick constructions as well as decorative architectural items no longer formed part of the language of social distinction in rural residences, although they partially remained in buildings associated with Christianity. Rural churches express the willingness of their founders to mark the special status of religious buildings. This status was intimately linked to land—former family lands that presumably contributed to the maintenance of the church. But aristocrats who built churches were also looking upward, to the Visigothic (and Suevic) kings. By the second half of the sixth century, church building and endowments (including monastic foundations) were becoming part of the language of power. Therefore, social distinction could still be displayed in the rural milieu by focusing one's wealth on religious foundations and, perhaps, maintaining some form of control over the process of village formation. Be that as it may, the countryside of Western Iberia continued to be an arena for aristocratic intervention. The language of such interventions, however, drastically changed when the imperial administration no longer ruled over the peninsula.

The Regional Turn: Urban and Rural Settlements and the End of Empire

To conclude this chapter, let us review the common characteristics of urban and rural settlements in the post-Roman period. Although barbarian armies may have brought disruption to Western Iberia, the traditional Roman settlement structure did not alter significantly. Settlement morphology did change, but nothing indicates devolution to pre-Roman, indigenous traditions. In most cases, the same Roman settlements continued to be occupied after the fifth century. When change happened, it did so through the occupation of new spaces rather than marked and generalized abandonment. By the year 600, urban and rural settlements may have been very different from their late imperial predecessors, but much of the Roman settlement landscape was still present. The city-territory hierarchy was hardly altered. Rather, in places like the plateau and northwestern Iberia, it was replicated to a certain extent at the local level when a low density of urban settlements was inherited from the post-Roman period.

There are many reasons for this continuity, and some will be explored in later chapters. One structural feature stands out: the persistence of connectivity throughout the post-Roman period. Our knowledge of the post-Roman road system is limited, but it seems that the late Roman road network was maintained to a certain extent into the Visigothic period. Cities may have played an important role in the upkeep of roads, but our evidence is opaque in this area. The location of newly occupied hilltops and necropoleis near late Roman roads suggests the structuring character of earlier communication axes in settlement preferences after the fifth century.[116]

Yet change is undeniable. It may not have affected nonaristocratic buildings (although in some cases it did) nor altered the traditional Roman settlement hierarchy. However, monumental architecture of status display was drastically transformed in the course of the fifth and sixth centuries. The evidence presented in this chapter demonstrates that no matter how much continuity we wish to find, aristocracies drastically changed their strategies of social distinction at the settlement level. The long-term process of change was punctuated by a crucial break in the mid-fifth century. Changes in settlement morphology and monumental architecture did not become generalized until at least a century later. In the central decades of the fifth century, though, these new expressions of settlement status and morphology began to be adopted in very few cities and rural areas. At the same time, some of the most salient features of late Roman monumentality were abandoned (with the exception of city walls). The reason for this change, I contend, is the sudden withdrawal of the Roman administration in the first half of the fifth century. I have related markers of settlement status to the presence of the renewed Roman state of Diocletian and Constantine in the previous chapter. The rapid dissolution of the political structures that sustained that state in the peninsula put an end to the wealth display associated with the prestige granted by that state. The departure of the Roman state and the end of the association between local elites and an empirewide ruling class rendered that state's markers of distinction obsolete and, more important, unreadable. The conditions of the fifth and sixth centuries brought about noticeable changes to the main social concerns addressed by building initiatives. In urban contexts, status architecture expressed the symbolic and physical aspects of protection, security, and bargaining power. It denoted membership in a world in which each community negotiated with one or several supralocal powers. In the countryside, changes to settlements reflected the local elites' increasing interest in building family memory by associating it with landed property. Pouring riches into Christian buildings and walls became a marker of aristocratic distinction. Supralocal powers, namely, monarchies or royal representatives, were also involved in this same process. Founding churches were acts of men and women of power, indicating knowledge of "proper" wealth spending. Likewise, state powers were particularly involved in wall construction, and by the late sixth century, military conquest was symbolized by the construction of fortifications. Therefore, rather than showing insecurity and Christianization, the archaeological record shows there was a strengthening association between aristocratic and state practices. New practices of distinction were only born in parallel to the rise of new projects of statehood (described in Chapter 5) that made them readable by different social groups and, particularly, by different regional aristocracies.

Although a similar language of settlement prestige existed across the regions, the way this language bore concrete effects at the settlement level differed along regional lines. Central and southern Lusitania, northwestern Iberia, and the northern plateau presented different combinations in terms of settlement structure and morphology after the fifth century. In the first region, late Roman settlement patterns persisted into the post-Roman period to a larger extent. Occupation in most late Roman cities is well documented, as is the presence of an important episcopal network. Archaeological Christianity is certainly stronger here than in other parts of Western Iberia. Lusitanian cities seem to have continued investing resources in their walls. Very few secondary settlements developed any of the status symbols of post-Roman cities. The primacy of late Roman cities was not, as it were, challenged—at least from a purely archaeological perspective. Rural areas also show a remarkable degree of continuity in settlement. Villas lost their functionality later in this region than in other parts of the peninsula—in some cases, perhaps as late as the sixth century, but most of them throughout the fifth century. Continuity in occupation is well attested, either through burials or basilicas (and a handful of production reuses). Continuity was also expressed by the absence of alternative settlements. The dearth of villages or other types of rural settlement beyond the former villas suggests the continuing predominance of nonelite dispersed settlements in the countryside. Rural Christianity had a greater impact on this region than on the other two at the monumental level. Central and southern Lusitanian elites rapidly adopted a language of rural monumentality that allowed them to stress family memory, piety, and patrimony. By the early sixth century, the Lusitanian countryside may not have boasted as large a number of monumentalized aristocratic residences as in the fourth century. But despite the changes in the morphology of some settlements, uninterrupted occupation prevailed over abandonment or innovation.

Northwestern Iberia had always had a weak urban presence, which continued after the fifth century. Braga and Lugo (as well as a handful of cities in northern Lusitania) can boast a relatively vivid urban landscape. The hierarchy of settlements based on Braga, Lugo, and a handful of middle-sized towns continued into the post-Roman period, as the political organization of the Suevic kingdom seems to have maintained it. Yet, unlike southern and central Lusitania, minor towns developed certain markers of post-Roman urban status, particularly the presence of an episcopal see (for instance, Tui) and protective walls (for instance, Porto). A dense ecclesiastical network existed in the late sixth century, but the picture of a well-developed episcopal Christianity is at odds with its archaeological paucity. Unlike central and southern Lusitania and the plateau, the monumentalization of the countryside had been relatively weak during the late Roman period. The same relative weakness in monumentalization continued after the fifth century. In particular, few rural churches have been found so far. This absence contrasts with our written sources, which indicate the presence of privately founded basilicas. It seems as if the construction of Christian buildings in rural areas only took off in the second half of the sixth century, if not later. Another remarkable continuity was the uninterrupted process of nonelite hilltop occupation that had begun in the late Roman period.

In the northern plateau and the Cantabrian Basin, late Roman urbanism had also been relatively weak, but a few important cities remained at the head of the settlement hierarchy. In the post-Roman period, continuity in occupation is matched by the weakness of urban status markers. Contrary to Lusitania, monumental Christianity in urban centers is absent in both cities and hilltop sites, with a few exceptions. Unlike the other two regions, the episcopal network was limited to a handful of cities (perhaps no more than five). Urban Christianity at the archaeological level would not achieve significance until the seventh century or later. Yet the post-Roman period was anything but static at the settlement level. Starting in the fifth century, several fortified hilltops began to supplement the relatively weak urban network with settlements possessing some markers of post-Roman urbanism (e.g., walls, stonebuilt houses, some economic complexity). It is as if the newly occupied sites tried to speak the language of settlement prestige symbolized by defensive precincts. Important changes took place in the countryside. On the one hand, monumentality as a marker of aristocratic distinction was almost completely abandoned. Although several villas were continuously occupied, occupations usually took the form of burial grounds or squatter occupation. On the other hand, rural basilicas only appear, timidly, in the late sixth century, and it is not until the seventh century that the countryside of the region noticeably displays Christian buildings. While there is a perceptible lack of status markers at the settlement level, peasant agglomerated settlements may have become, by the sixth century, a frequent aspect of this region's countryside. The role of aristocracies behind this process is not clear, although a minimum of elite involvement must have taken place.

A quick review of the main changes at the local level shows that the three regions shared a common language of settlement structure and monumental architecture but with marked regional variations. This language was not necessarily unique to Atlantic Iberia, but the way in which settlement patterns and prestige architecture were combined was peculiar to each region in the western parts of the peninsula. Understanding what these changes meant in terms of elite identity and statehood is the topic of the next chapter.

CHAPTER 5

Crafting Fragmented Statehood: Aristocratic Identity in the Post-Roman World

In 407, the troops of Britannia proclaimed their commander emperor of the Romans. Known as Constantine III, he succeeded in controlling Britain, Gaul, and Iberia at different moments until 411, when he was captured in Arles and executed in Italy. This relatively brief attempt at usurpation would have momentous consequences for the history of the Iberian Peninsula and Western Iberia in particular. Constantine III reached a tenuous agreement with the "legitimate" emperor, Honorius, two years after his proclamation. However, Constantine's general in Iberia, Gerontius, rebelled against his authority and sought the support of the barbarian troops that had been active in Gaul since 406. In 409, Suevi, Vandals, and Alans crossed the Pyrenees and eliminated the rest of Constantine III's support in the peninsula, while Gerontius appointed a new puppet emperor, Maximus. Gerontius would eventually be defeated and committed suicide in 411. Maximus was only able to maintain his authority briefly and ultimately sought exile among the barbarian troops that had supported him.[1]

By the end of 411, there was just one Roman emperor in the western half of the empire, but the situation in Hispania had drastically changed. The Suevi, the Vandals, and the Alans had taken four provinces: Gallaecia, Lusitania, Carthaginensis, and Baetica.[2] Although the surviving sources are not straightforward about how these armies took the provinces, the most persuasive interpretation so far indicates that they received these provinces probably following an agreement with what they considered the legitimate Roman authority (Gerontius and/or Maximus).[3] This settlement marked the beginning of a historical process leading to the withdrawal of the Roman administration in Western Iberia and eventually on the peninsula in general. The process did not only derive from local events but was also primarily the result of the weakening of the central administration in Italy after a series of military setbacks (including the loss of North Africa and growing pressure by the Huns). By the 450s, the imperial administration no longer controlled Western Iberia, which was predominantly under the influence of armies led by Suevic and Visigothic rulers.

In the previous chapter, we examined the reshaping of both urban and rural settlements during these tumultuous decades—a reshaping that relied on a preexisting settlement structure but also involved a redefinition of prestige architecture. In this chapter, I will address the adaptation of Atlantic Iberian aristocracies to the new situation in the fifth and sixth centuries. There is a tendency in modern scholarship to stress the continuity of late Roman aristocracy after the fifth century, to the extent that the post-Roman world is often assessed in binary terms, depending on the survival or not of the senatorial-Roman aristocracy versus the impact of a newly arrived barbarian aristocracy. I will stay away from this dichotomy. Although these were significant categories, the enactment of state authority and social markers of elite belonging were more important than ethnic identities to the definition of social standing. Roman or barbarian (or, better, Suevic and Visigothic) identities were important insofar as they could be used to advance claims of social status in specific contexts. Yet nothing in the extant evidence suggests that Romans and barbarians pursued different strategies to assert aristocratic claims at the local level.

The end of empire had a tremendous impact in this regard. Until the early fourth century, status claims were cemented by membership in specific ranks (senatorial or curial) with concrete legal privileges. As we saw in Chapter 2, the boundaries between these two ranks were never an impediment to common elite identity, but claiming high social standing outside of these ranks was an arduous path. By the late sixth and seventh centuries, when the legal evidence re-emerges in the Iberian Peninsula, these categories had disappeared. What did not disappear was the language of social status. Written sources repeatedly refer to *nobiliores, honestiores, inlustres*—but contrary to late Roman rank statuses, these categories were never legally defined.[4] Rather those who wanted to be considered as such had to defend their aspirations through a series of concrete actions and symbolic claims. As the main legal divide became the distinction between the free and the unfree, while other legally sanctioned divisions disappeared, Iberian elites had to distance themselves from the non-elite free to claim privileged access to power structures.

During the silent decades of the fifth and sixth centuries, new forms of crafting aristocratic identity were developed in Western Iberia. In this chapter, I will make two interconnected arguments. I will argue that the strategies of social promotion depended on a combination of inherited structural patterns from the late Roman period and the historical events that led to the establishment of new state projects—the Suevic and Visigothic monarchies. In particular, the events of the 410s to the 460s were crucial to determining the parameters through which local elites would relate to newly arrived armies and, eventually, newly formed state projects. New types of institutional arrangements dominated Western Iberia, including civic or civiclike government, territorial communities regulated by pacts with barbarian leadership, and royal and ecclesiastical government. Enactments of statehood were possible through all these channels, while claims to participation in local leadership now relied on a myriad of symbolic and concrete aspects, such as landholding, family, military power, or protection of the Church, to mention a few.

My second argument concerns the regional impact of these processes. In contrast to the relative uniformity of the late Roman period, post-Roman aristocracies pursued regionally specific patterns of social and political identity. Relying on the scanty written sources available but also the archaeological evidence presented in the previous chapter, I will reconstruct elite strategies in central and southern Lusitania, northwestern Iberia, and the northern meseta. While similar strategies of social distinction existed all throughout Western Iberia (and the whole peninsula for that matter), each region presented unique combinations or emphasized one or more of these strategies. The differences arose, as I mentioned earlier, from each region's disparate inheritance from the late Roman world and the particular type of statehood crafted during the fifth century (and especially before the 460s).

Throughout this chapter, I will describe the different political and social strategies of local elites in each region. By combining the scanty written evidence and the archaeological record presented in the previous chapter, I will provide three, as it were, ideal types of post-Roman social strategies in relation to elite identity and statehood. I realize the hypothetical nature of such reconstructions and the risks involved in modeling social strategies based on a frustratingly small amount of material and written evidence. But although we have few pieces of the puzzle, I believe they form a relatively coherent picture. While I will focus on the dominant practices in each region, all the practices I describe existed in all three regions. The impact of some practices, however, may have been less important in some regions or is less visible in the extant documentation. For the sake of simplicity and space, I will avoid repetitions, but the reader must bear in mind that the three regions shared social practices throughout the post-Roman period.

Central and Southern Lusitania: A World of Civic Notables

After the events of 411, Lusitania was granted to the Alans, who also received Carthaginensis. What this occupation meant is not clear, and very likely the Roman administration was still operational up to a certain level when the Gothic army of Wallia, fighting under the Roman banner, crushed the Alans in 418.[5] Hydatius's *Chronicle* records that two years later, a *comes Hispaniarum* (Astirius) waged war in Gallaecia; so we may suppose that Lusitania had returned to Roman control by then.[6] But the defeat of the *magister militum* Castinus and the Gothic auxiliaries at the hands of the Vandals in 422 seems to have left Lusitania to face the Suevi from the north and the Vandals from the south without imperial support.[7] By 429, Lusitania was being plundered by the armies of the Vandal Gaiseric and the Suevi Heremigarius.[8] In all likelihood, the Suevi controlled Lusitania in some form between 429 and 439, since Hydatius recorded Suevic activities both in Gallaecia and Baetica.[9] In that last year, king Rechila entered Mérida and began Lusitania's Suevic experience, which would last until the defeat of the Suevi by Visigothic troops in the 450s.[10]

The available information on the various military operations does not convey an image of either constant disruption or large-scale material destruction. This time, the stability reached in Lusitania was different from the peace that Astirius and the imperial troops may have brought in 420. The 430s witnessed a major break with the previous period that cannot be underestimated. Lusitania and Mérida in particular no longer anchored the head of the imperial administration in the peninsula. The rest of the administration moved to the safer coasts of eastern Iberia, in Tarraconensis, at a time when access to Ravenna was more important than easy communications with Trier. The two decades between the settlement of barbarian armies in the peninsula and the establishment of the "pax Sueva" may have created the conditions for a new, more flexible approach toward alternative centers of power. Very likely, Rechila and his entourage kept Mérida as a main residence, a telling acknowledgment of the city's political centrality.[11] Hydatius did not register any conflict worth mentioning between local communities and the Suevi, in contrast to his analysis of northwestern Iberia. We can envisage a relatively stable agreement between the Suevi on the one hand and the representatives of the local population and the imperial administration on the other. This allowed the Suevi to control Lusitania *in toto* without problems until the mid-450s. Hydatius hinted at this agreement in his brief remarks on the surrender of the *comes* Censurius, an envoy to the Suevi from the imperial government, the year after Rechila entered Mérida. According to the *Chronicle*, Censurius surrendered *in pace*, a term that Hydatius used for agreements between barbarian armies and local groups.[12] If so, a similar arrangement was negotiated in 452–453 between the Suevic court and two imperial *comites*, who were sent to "maintain the [previously] imposed agreements."[13] By then, the situation in Italy and the Suevic expansion into Baetica and Carthaginensis had given the Suevi more room to maneuver beyond the previous pact.

Though short-lived, the Suevic experience in Lusitania deserves more attention than we tend to grant it. If we believe Hydatius, "war and plundering" continued in other parts of the peninsula during the Suevic expansion (Carthaginensis and Baetica) but not, significantly, in Lusitania.[14] By the time the Visigoths began to gain ascendancy in the peninsula in the 450s, one or two generations of Lusitanian aristocrats had experienced two different political eras: one in which barbarian groups fought over the province in the context of a still operating imperial government and armies (411–429) and another in which a barbarian army governed without much direct imperial involvement (429–456). It is hard to say where aristocratic preferences lay or even whether all aristocrats held the same opinion. But the relative stability of the second period of Suevic rule vis-à-vis what Hydatius described as "plundering" by the Alans, Suevi, and Vandals—and imperial troops that included one or more of these groups during the first period—may have contributed to the sense that the barbarian alternative was, at the very least, the lesser of two evils.

Suevic hegemony came to an end in southern and central Lusitania with the invasion of the Goth Theoderic in 456–457, who allegedly acted on an imperial Roman request. From 457 to 468, the region again became a battlefield for Suevic and, this time, Gothic ambitions.[15] We know today that the Visigoths would eventually control the peninsula—but this was far from certain for the local population in the fifth century, when alliances could be built with either side. A certain Lusidius, "a foremost citizen" of Lisbon, led his city's change of allegiance from the Gothic to the Suevic side in 468. From the Visigothic point of view, other Romans backed this betrayal since the Gothic army retaliated against both Suevi and Romans, according to Hydatius.[16] In any event, by the late fifth century, central and southern Lusitania were under Visigothic overlordship. Although Visigothic authority is usually described as weak until the reign of Leovigild in the mid-sixth century, this fragility may be more apparent than real. From very early on, the Visigoths established mechanisms of state legitimacy and administration. These mechanisms operated on the institutional bedrock of the late Roman government by notables and a growing association of monarchical legitimacy, the ability to offer security, and the patronage of Christianity. This type of statehood was somewhat different from what Reccared and his successors would eventually achieve in the late sixth and early seventh centuries, but it successfully met the early fifth-century contingency, which combined the withdrawal of the imperial administration, the existence of a solid network of cities, and the presence of non-Roman but potentially peace-granting barbarian armies and courts.

* * *

Based on what can be reconstructed from the extant evidence, local elites maintained the basic parameters of city-based government, both during the Suevic experience and the Visigothic period. Owing to Lusitania's well-established network of *civitates* during the Roman period and the influence of a regional government in Mérida, it is not unimaginable that the *pax* achieved by the Suevi and later the Visigoths was founded on a catchall agreement with the provincial elites rather than a case-by-case treaty with each community. Such an arrangement would have guaranteed the permanence of the civic government and also likely the preeminence of Mérida at the top of the political edifice of the province (the latter is corroborated by the predominance of the city as the main mint of Lusitania during the Visigothic period).[17] Continuity in the urban government, however, does not mean that the institutional framework remained unaltered. Curial government in the Roman fashion (a distinct *ordo* based on birth or office holding with legally defined privileges and obligations) waned in the second half of the fifth century. What replaced it is difficult to reconstruct because of the nature of the sources—predominantly ecclesiastical and, for the later period, royal in their perspective. One such source for the region is the inscription mentioned in the previous chapter dealing with the repairing of the bridge and walls of Mérida.[18] The complete inscription reads as follows:

> Ruinous old age had caused the ancient walls to crumble
> And the edifice, fallen and broken with feebleness, was swaying.
> The road suspended over the river had lost its use
> And the fallen bridge denied a free journey.
> Today, in the time of the powerful Euric, king of the Goths,
> When he ordered the lands rendered to him to be embellished,
> The generous Salla strove to grow his reputation with deeds
> And added his own (name) to the inscriptions of the ancients.
> For after he renewed the city with remarkable walls,
> He did not fail to accomplish this greater wonder:
> He built arches; he laid foundations in the depths of the waters;
> He thus surpassed, while imitating it, the notable work of the
>   original builder.
> And also the love of the highest priest Zeno for his homeland
> Urged on the construction of so great a defense.
> The Augustan city [Mérida] shall be blessed for many centuries
> Because the zeal of the dux and the priest have renewed it.
> In (the year) 521 of the era [483 CE].[19]

The poem discretely unveils the ideological project of the Visigothic monarchy. Between Theoderic's invasion and the inscription of Mérida, there is almost a generation gap. In that period, not only did Gothic power become more assertive, especially after 475, but local elites also became aware of the ideological needs of newly established monarchies. The inscription not only presents Euric as a Gothic (and non-Roman) ruler, but it also portrays his power as founded on his ability to secure peace and prosperity through his *potentia*. Zeno approached Visigothic powers as benefactors, presenting himself as a patron of his city (*amator patriae*). It seems as if the first generation of Lusitanians to live under Gothic rule adopted mechanisms of persuasion that preserved their distinct non-Gothic institutional identity while legitimizing a newly formed Visigothic kingdom because the latter could grant protection and stability and was open to the demands of local civic leadership. Rather than representing the mere survival of a classical *topos* or a Christianization of euergetism, the language of patronage in the inscription fulfilled the Visigothic monarchy's need for legitimacy during the reign of Euric, who de facto seized entire regions from the withering imperial authority. As in the Roman Empire, inscriptions celebrating the reconstruction of buildings granted legitimacy to the ruler by situating him within the history of the city.[20] Simply put, local elites approached Euric (through Salla) not as a new Roman emperor, but as a Gothic ruler who granted peace and prosperity to civic communities through his or his representatives' munificence.[21]

The inscription presents two of the main characters of political life in post-Roman Lusitanian cities: royal officials and bishops. It is rather difficult to trace the formation of the Visigothic hierarchy of royal officers. The inscription mentions a *dux* (Salla), and this title denotes two not necessarily exclusive statuses in later sources: a high-ranking military official and a supralocal, "provincial" office holder.[22] It is not clear in what capacity Salla ruled over Mérida, although it was probably as both.[23] The most frequent royal official in Visigothic cities was the *comes civitatis*, who had important judicial and administrative roles in the seventh century.[24] This position certainly dates back to the kingdom of Toulouse, although its origins are difficult to trace, and its importance for the Visigothic administration grew as the kingdom expanded in the second half of the fifth century.[25]

The crucial role of bishops in post-Roman cities is a well-attested phenomenon not only in Iberia but also in the post-Roman West in general.[26] The episcopate took over several functions that promoted its role as a civic leader in important spheres such as justice or the care of the poor. Bishops were expected, by the sixth century, to be channels of communication between cities and kings—especially when it came to denouncing abuses by royal officials.[27] A century earlier, their role was also crucial in providing an ideological foundation to rising powers. A vignette from Hydatius's *Chronicle* serves to illustrate this point. In 456, when the armies of Theoderic invaded the peninsula, the king "was preparing to pillage Mérida but was deterred by warnings from the blessed martyr Eulalia," according to the bishop of Chaves.[28] This attitude differs drastically from the stance that Theoderic's army took in Braga in October 456: the city was pillaged and "the basilicas of the saints stormed," among other calamities suffered by clergy and consecrated virgins.[29] In between these two events, Theoderic learned that Marcian's troops had defeated the Vandals and that the Suevi had appointed a new king.[30] The Visigothic ruler needed to secure his position as he was far from his kingdom's capital in Toulouse. Moreover, the Gothic king might have been reminded of the fate of the Suevic king in 429. Heremigarius was punished by God (his army was defeated by the Vandals and he died in the river Guadiana) after pillaging Lusitania and causing *iniuria* to the martyr Eulalia.[31] The persuasion of Eulalia may have been a negotiation crafted between Theoderic, Mérida's establishment, and the city's bishop. Indeed, after the saint persuaded the king not to loot the city, he spent the winter in Mérida without any conflict.[32] The episode not only reveals the emerging episcopal leadership and the role of the local church in brokering agreements with newly formed powers. It also indicates the growing importance of episcopally led practices (such as the cult of saints) and episcopal authority in the formation of ideological instruments of negotiation with individuals and groups that otherwise have dubious claims of legitimacy.

The prominent role of bishops within their cities derived from the increasing authority they secured from the fourth century onward. There may be a distortion, however, produced by the preponderance of ecclesiastical sources in the surviving documents. Owing to this unbalanced evidence, we must be cautious before granting an overwhelming share of political authority to the episcopate in urban leadership, an authority that was certainly developed by the seventh century but whose origins may have been gradual and not exempt from challenges. Actually, the revelation of the Mérida bridge poem also lies in what it does not explicitly mention—the nonepiscopal urban leadership. Since the characters involved in requesting and granting are the bishop and a royal officer (a *dux*), the standard interpretation of this inscription supports the idea of the end of civic government and its replacement by episcopal leadership and royal officials. Zeno is, in this view, taking over the patronage of the city, which had characterized the attitudes of local aristocrats during the late empire. However, there are reasons to believe there were more actors involved in Mérida's government besides the bishop and the *dux*. If we accept the idea that the inscription promotes the bishop's act of patronage, we might as well accept that, as in the Roman Empire, there is an element of competition to such acts of self-promotion. In other words, Zeno and bishops in other cities promoted their role as civic patrons in competition with (and in collaboration with) other potential patrons.[33]

There are other reasons to believe that the local government was not limited to royal and ecclesiastical officials. Although formal city councils faded in the fifth century (a process that saw parallels in the eastern Mediterranean), various individuals with different claims to high status could participate in the decision-making process and enactments of state power at the local level. Modern scholarship calls this type of city-based government a "government by notables"—as we saw in Chapter 2. Some of these actors were entitled to privileged positions through urban and royal offices—*defensores*, city administrators, counts, and dukes, for example. Prominent landowners were also part of this post–fifth century type of urban government throughout the Mediterranean world.[34] As the next chapter will show, *curiales* are attested in seventh-century Visigothic legislation, and we may assume from this that the category remained relevant in post-Roman cities. However, it is not clear that the term denoted an inherited *ordo*. In all probability, *curiales* increasingly signified urban-based landowners with certain fiscal responsibilities (the fifth century is the more likely candidate for this transition). Bishops and clergy perhaps joined this type of institution in the course of the fifth century.[35] Even if other nonelite but free individuals were able to participate, landowners, officials, and clergy could simply use their social and symbolic influence to limit any attempt at extending real influence beyond the limited circle of notables.

Unlike postcurial civic government in the eastern Roman Empire, city-based leadership never became institutionalized in Visigothic legislation. However, continuity in civic government can only be reconstructed through piecemeal information gathered from later Visigothic laws. While the early sixth-century *Breviary of Alaric* preserved some late Roman legislation on city-based government, we need to wait until the second half of the sixth century for new legislation on this issue.[36] Furthermore, there are too many striking coincidences between late Roman and Visigothic civic administration not to suspect a minimum of continuity during the fifth and early sixth centuries. One such example is taxation. In the late sixth century, cities were allowed to choose the officials in charge of tax collection (*numerarii*), a practice that subsisted until the end of the Visigothic kingdom. According to a law from Reccared's reign, the *numerarii* were to be chosen by the bishop and the people (*populus*) of the city—a vague formula that seems to hide the reality of a more reduced number of prominent taxpayers. Together with the *numerarius*, the law of Reccared also mandated that the *populus* choose a *defensor civitatis*. As we saw in Chapter 2, *defensores* were attested since the second half of the fourth century, and their role became particularly crucial around the year 400. *Defensores* are attested in the *Breviary of Alaric*, although only as judicial officers in charge of minor cases, and they remained urban judicial authorities into the seventh century.[37] The same law of Reccared mentions that they had to be chosen (together with the *numerarii*) without interference from royal officers, had to complete their term without being replaced after one year, and should not pay for their office, which suggests it was an attractive position.[38] The post-Roman defensorate thus offered an alternative type of leadership to the episcopal and comital office.[39] The *populus* to which the law refers could include (and might be limited to) the *curiales* and tax-paying landowners mentioned in a mid-seventh-century law of Chindaswinth.[40] The law mandated that land transfers be registered in public documents in order to secure tax payments. These registers also appeared in other pieces of legislation. A law implemented under Sisebut mentioned similar public registers, in which former slaves of Jewish owners had to be listed in order to pay taxes as free people.[41] These city polyptychs bore a close resemblance to Hispania's *gesta municipalia*, which the administration of Honorius regulated in 396.[42] Thus the presence of important landowners in city councils derived not only from their wealth but also from their role as infrastructural state agents in the collection of tribute.

The *Lives of the Fathers of Mérida* also offers some hints at urban council-like institutions. The text mentions a number of wealthy senators in the region in the first half of the sixth century.[43] To be sure, the term *senator* embodied ideas of elite Roman lineage. However, in the context of seventh-century hagiographic texts, it may well refer to a politically influential person, such as someone in charge of decision making in a local landowner assembly or other kinds of leading individuals rather than an ethnically defined Roman elite identity.[44] The other explicit mention of a "senate" in Visigothic literature comes from the *Life of St. Aemilian*, where a "senate of Cantabria" refers to a regional assembly of landowners in the upper Ebro Valley.[45] A second vignette in the *Lives of the Fathers of Mérida* also hints at urban councils of notables. During the reign of Leovigild, a dispute arose between the Arian bishop Sunna and the Nicene bishop Masona over the possession of certain basilicas within the city. Leovigild ordered the Nicene bishop to hand over these basilicas to the Arian congregation. The king did not treat this matter as a church affair to be solved by an ecclesiastical council but as a civic conflict over the property of two institutions. Judges (*iudices*) heard the cases of both bishops. The judicial council, according to the hagiographical text, settled the case in favor of Masona.[46] Since in the Visigothic period the term *iudex* came to denote any person with judicial authority, owing to the matter under discussion it is not unlikely that we are in the presence of a body of prominent men deciding on the property rights of two urban institutions. These two episodes are, admittedly, indirect and from a later period, even though they refer to events taking place in the second half of the sixth century. Yet together with the (also fragmentary) legal sources, they convey echoes of civic government in Lusitanian cities by the end of the sixth century. This type of government did not appear out of thin air. Rather, as in other parts of the Mediterranean, it arose from a historical process starting at the turn of the fifth century.

*　*　*

These practices, which were similar to late Roman urban government by notables, re-created statehood in central and southern Lusitania. Participation in basic acts of government (tax collection, justice, urban administration) became avenues to exhibit social standing. Yet these claims also had to be cemented by practices that would enforce the idea of social distinction. We saw that in the late Roman period, Western Iberian aristocracies displayed behaviors and tastes that tied them to the social attitudes of an empirewide elite. As we saw in the previous chapter, the material culture that expressed this behavior disappeared over the course of the fifth century, although less quickly than in other parts of Western Iberia. Certain aristocratic houses may have maintained their use as elite residences into the fifth and perhaps the early sixth century. These were the exceptions, though, that showed the conservatism of certain members of the local aristocracy rather than the main trend of the period.

In the post-Roman world, "being (elite) Roman" acquired a new connotation. As far as can be reconstructed from the extant evidence, ethnic identity does not seem to have been a decisive marker of aristocratic status. There was nothing like an intrinsic Gothic nobility or a Roman senatorial aristocracy. There is some indication, however, that ethnicity did play a role in the self-portrayal of aristocrats.[47] Admittedly these sources are late (all from the seventh century), but, again, one can suspect they emerged out of older practices. In one rare instance in which ethnic origins are described in a surviving epitaph, the seventh-century funerary inscription of a certain Sinticius from Alcácer do Sal (Setúbal) reminded its readers that he descended from Gothic ancestry, without any other indication of social status.[48] Even in the seventh century, therefore, Gothic identity was a significant factor to emphasize. However, when ethnicity is related to aristocratic standing, we find people of both Roman and Gothic ancestry. In the *Lives of the Fathers of Mérida*, ethnicity was a mechanism used to stress being of good birth, either Roman or Gothic. The partakers in the rebellion of Witteric against Reccared in 587 are described as "respected Goths who were most distinguished by birth and wealth, and not a few whom the king had appointed counts in various cities."[49] The main royal officer who crushed the revolt, the duke Claudius, was a "*vir clarissimus, dux* of the city of Mérida . . . of illustrious birth and Roman stock," according to the text.[50] Thus, the *Lives* stresses the importance of good family origins in its characterization of aristocratic groups—regardless of their ethnic origin.

The strategy of social distinction based on prestigious Gothic or Roman ancestry was particularly curious since intermarriage between Goths and Romans made purely ethnic claims more difficult to assert.[51] Nor was there, by the seventh century or perhaps earlier, any legal separation between Goths and Romans.[52] By the time these sources were produced, legal texts hardly mentioned Goths and Romans as distinct peoples. Indeed, Romans were disappearing in legal texts, and Goths were mostly mentioned as a synecdoche of the kingdom.[53] Moreover, there were no fixed criteria to determine what "good ancestry" meant, whether Roman or Gothic. Office holding could be one such criterion, but the *Lives of the Fathers of Mérida* (and all other sources) is not clear on this point. In the absence of legally defined orders, family status had to be reproduced in each generation. One's family status was fundamental in a context of government by notables, in which peer-reviewed markers of aristocratic identity were crucial to participation in civic politics. Unlike, say, in Vandal Africa, Roman identity in Lusitania was less a way of connecting with fellow Romans elsewhere in the (former) empire and more about asserting all-important good origins, though these were not determined by Roman identity.[54] The same can also be argued about Gothic identity. Thus, Roman and Gothic ancestry both represented ways of placing family status within a recent but not immediate historical context in which both groups were more clearly distinct. In other words, the late sixth and seventh centuries used these categories to claim elite family standing since the central decades of the fifth century and earlier.

Archaeology also provides an indicator of these efforts to assert family status through family memory. As we saw in Chapter 4, of the three regions of Western Iberia, central and southern Lusitania was unique in terms of the earlier development of Christian buildings in the countryside. By the time this phenomenon started in the Suevic kingdom by the second third of the sixth century, Lusitanian aristocrats had three generations of experience in this regard. As we saw in the previous chapter, these basilicas reflected changes in Christian piety but also ways of claiming social standing by performing pious acts reserved to the few and powerful. The close proximity of certain rural churches to (former?) villa centers reveals the efforts to stress elite family identity in a context in which that identity was fluid and needed to be validated by one's peers. All in all, there is a clearer effort in Lusitania than in other parts of Western Iberia to emphasize family status through discrete markers such as origins, piety, and office-holding ancestry.

*   *   *

Based on this information, it is possible to attempt a reconstruction of the strategies available to local aristocrats to claim social standing. Local elites rapidly adapted to the presence of new powers. The Suevic experience must have played a crucial role in shaping their interaction with the Visigothic monarchy. If Lusitania was incorporated into the Suevic sphere of influence as a single political unit (unlike the piecemeal set of pacts in northwestern Iberia), we should not be surprised if a minimum of institutional continuity was carried into the post-Roman period. Not only did civic government remain a basic feature of local societies, but the political and symbolic centrality of Mérida seems unquestionable. Civic government had changed in the fifth century, as government by notables (office-holders, landowners, and, perhaps, clergy) had replaced the curial government and the imperial administration. Bishops probably had a more relevant role than other civic officials but were by no means the only urban authorities. If recent assessments of post-Roman episcopates in Gaul can be extrapolated to Iberia, the episcopate was more often recruited from the families of civic notables than from the supposed remainders of the Roman senatorial aristocracy.[55] All in all, the ruling class of Lusitanian cities participated in the support of state functions in various roles—tax collectors, religious authorities, royal officials, and members of city-based councils, among others.

Although similar strategies would develop in other parts of Western Iberia during the late sixth and seventh centuries, Lusitania may have joined urbanized Mediterranean Iberia in this early development. In a context in which the distinction between orders disappeared, freedom and slavery were becoming the sole remaining social boundaries. Those who wanted to push for aristocratic claims needed to deploy as many strategies as possible to separate themselves from the mass of free, nonelite people. In the absence of well-defined criteria, "good" family origins, office holding, landowning (and tax collection), and other subtle social markers could determine social standing by one's peers in different ways. New forms of Christian piety could also provide techniques to stress social differentiation through the construction of rural basilicas. In a sense, central and southern Lusitanian cities adapted the late Roman model of government by notables to the end of the order-based imperial system and the presence of a presumably peacekeeping barbarian army.

Northwestern Iberia: From a Contractual to a Christian Kingdom

The fate of post-Roman Iberian aristocracies in northwestern Iberia was markedly shaped by the way the Suevi settled and consolidated their power in the first half of the fifth century. In the fragmented landscape of this region, the Suevi established their kingdom through a series of agreements with local communities. With the exception of the main cities in northwestern Iberia, territorially defined communities integrated the Suevic polity one by one on a contractual basis. This situation allowed the formation of authority practices based on leadership over small territories and the enactment of agreements with the Suevic court. This politically fragmented scenario should not be interpreted as a sign of weakness on the part of the Suevic kingdom. Rather, it represents a successful adaptation to the military and political conditions of Suevic settlement and the territorial and administrative situation inherited from the late Roman period. By the second third of the sixth century, however, a process of ideological unification coalesced in the idea of a Christian kingdom in which both the monarchy and the landowning elite would participate in the support of the Church. This unification was disturbed when Leovigild conquered the kingdom in the year 585.

*   *   *

The settlement of the Suevi remains one of the most obscure episodes of post-Roman Iberia. It is estimated that no more than 25,000 Suevi crossed the Pyrenees, which implies the presence of 4,000 to 5,000 soldiers—a relatively small population in numerical terms, although Suevi numbers might have increased with the incorporation of local Roman populations or remnants of other barbarian groups.[56] The Suevi very likely considered the area around Braga, and perhaps Lugo, as their heartland, but not the rest of Gallaecia.[57] From here, as the imperial administration withdrew, they began their advance to other areas of the region. Still in the 430s the Galicians (and not the Roman army) were able to offer effective resistance to the Suevi from their "more secure fortified sites" and were even able to inflict considerable casualties on the Suevic armies.[58] Nevertheless, by the end of the decade, these armies were already established as a local power to be reckoned with in the region. It was the beginning of the Suevic expansion, which would make the Suevi army the de facto power in most of Western Iberia. That situation ended in 456–457 when the Suevi were defeated by Theoderic. Although Hydatius claimed this was the end of the Suevic kingdom, it managed to survive with a more limited geographical reach. From Theoderic's victory until its conquest by Leovigild, the kingdom controlled the Braga and Lugo regions and kept influence over northern Lusitania and the territory of Astorga.[59] The territorial identity of the kingdom was firmly established by the central decades of the sixth century, when *Gallaecia* became synonymous with the former Suevic kingdom rather than the old Roman province.[60]

Based on testimony in the *Chronicle* of Hydatius, we have tended to believe that the Suevi settled in opposition to a native population that supported the imperial government or its proxies (Visigoths). However, the settlement of the Suevi may have been less disruptive than the impression gleaned from Hydatius. While the *Chronicle* seeks to portray the Galician (i.e., Roman) population under constant attack and pillage by the Suevi, Hydatius admitted on several occasions that the Suevi and the Galicians had entered into treaties (*paces*) that may have regulated the conditions of settlement.[61] In the absence of an effective local Roman authority, in 430 the Suevi began to advance outside the territory of Braga into interior Gallaecia, which, in the interpretation of Hydatius, broke the *pax*.[62] It took two embassies of Aetius's legate, the *comes* Censurius, to finally reach an agreement between the Suevi from Braga and the population of the new areas into which the Suevi were expanding. It is important to note that this agreement affected only the new areas, presumably the interior of northwestern Iberia, including the city of Chaves. Hydatius himself recognized that the agreement was reached only with "the section (*pars*) of the people of Gallaecia with whom they had been in conflict."[63] This passage suggests that other *partes* were already in seemingly unproblematic coexistence with the Suevi (Braga area) or had not yet come into conflict with them or fallen under their direct rule (perhaps the *ulteriores regiones* that Rechiarius would invade in 448).[64] When Theoderic supposedly destroyed the Suevic kingdom and entered Braga in 456, an outraged Hydatius mentioned that the Gothic army made hostages of Romans who may have been collaborators, if not straightforward allies, of the Suevic army against the Goths.[65]

The Gothic incursion of 456–457 certainly had a destabilizing effect on the region, and, again, conflicts between the Suevi and local Romans are recorded. But it is not clear whether the conflicts resulted from the Suevi's "usual treachery" (*solita perfidia*), as Hydatius seems to believe; from a brief civil war between Suevic factions; or from conflicts that arose after the negotiation of a new *pax*.[66] Communities may have decided to seize the opportunity to obtain better conditions in their agreements, which may have caused episodes of political violence.[67] It is unclear, however, whether local men of power acted independently from the Gothic army or not, but the Goths were an active force in Gallaecia during the period from 456 to 463. Hydatius himself was taken prisoner in 460 by the Suevi, who were helped by three otherwise unknown informers (and possibly urban notables), Dictynus, Spinio, and Ascanius. These three characters betrayed the Goths who were leading an incursion into Gallaecia at the time. While Hydatius did not mention that he supported the Goths, the fact that he was taken prisoner in that context reveals at least a tacit approval of their presence.[68] This situation changed with the ascension of Remismund as the only king of the Suevi in 464–465. The event not only put an end to the divisions within the Suevic armies, but Gallaecia seems to have reached considerable stability afterward, in spite of Hydatius's dislike of the new status quo. This stability was also secured by agreements with local groups, such as the *pax* with the Aunonenses.[69]

To be sure, some members of the local landowning elite may have regretted their settlement with the Suevic army, especially those who lost lands or even relatives at the hands of the newcomers. Moreover, picking the wrong side during a war or civil conflict could be fatal for men with leadership roles. Hydatius mentioned that a Suevic group killed a leading figure (*rector*) of Lugo, a member of the local aristocracy (*honesto natu*), and certain Romans on Easter in 460.[70] Yet the presence of a local army may not have been bad news for everyone. For those who embraced the new situation with enthusiasm, the Suevic expansion of the 440s and early 450s may have turned into an opportunity for unexpected wealth. More important, if used appropriately, a Suevic army could also secure peace. The post-Roman countryside in Gallaecia could be a dangerous place, as it was notably after the defeat of the Suevi by Theoderic, when bandits pillaged the region near Braga.[71] Coastal communities were vulnerable to sea piracy, which intensified after the disappearance of the Roman fleet in the Atlantic. Hydatius mentioned four hundred Heruli on Lugo's coast in 455, but this episode was not the only instance of sea-based banditry. Vandal piracy was also reported on the shores of Gallaecia not far from Tui in the same year. And again in 459, Heruli seaborne armies raided the region according to Hydatius.[72] The fact that Hydatius was so specific about these episodes may not necessarily be only due to his Galician focus. Rather, he sought to remind his readers of the Suevi's failure to meet the expectations of these communities and agreement partners. This was, in short, a direct attack on the Suevic claim to legitimacy. Military protection must have been an essential component of the agreements between the Suevi and local societies.

* * *

Based on the support the Suevi received from some local aristocrats, it is clear they began to be perceived as an attractive alternative to communities who faced the end of the late Roman imperial monopoly of violence. Coercive power, once jealously reserved to a specialized branch of the imperial administration, became a local matter, and it seems as though it rapidly became a defining element of local power. The connection between local military and political powers is tangentially attested by later sources. In the year 576, Leovigild conquered a small region of *montes Aregenses*, probably in eastern Ourense. Although the Aregensi territory is traditionally thought of as an independent polity at the border between the Suevic and the Visigothic kingdoms, there are reasons to believe, as I will argue presently, that it was indeed part of the Suevic kingdom or area of influence.[73] A certain Aspidius was at the head of this unknown subpolity. John of Biclarum referred to him as a "prominent person of the region" (*senior loci*). After Leovigild's conquest, he was taken prisoner with his family, his wealth was confiscated, and the *locum* under his command was subjected to Leovigild's power.[74] Aspidius was not a tribal chief but a man who possessed enough wealth to merit confiscation. The relatively mild treatment he received (he was taken prisoner, perhaps as a hostage) separates him from a regular bandit or a so-called primitive rebel. He was also able to raise an army large enough to force a king to campaign against him.

Military leadership was not the only way in which local men of standing could perform acts of statehood, such as tax collection and even minting coins.[75] Moreover, the incipient Suevic administration offered a channel to consolidate local standing through royal office or, at least, service to the king. One case documented by Hydatius reveals the use of these opportunities early in the post-Roman period. The above-mentioned Lusidius, the leader from

Lisbon who reached an agreement with the Suevi and changed his city's allegiance from Gothic to Suevic, approached the Roman emperor (Anthemius or Leo) at the head of a Suevi delegation.[76] As during the Roman imperial period, embassies were crucial acts of community status negotiation— particularly after the fifth century in the context of constant negotiations between barbarian armies (and eventually kingdoms) and the declining but still relevant imperial power.[77] Hydatius himself undertook at least one such embassy to Aetius in 431 after the Suevi began to expand their ambitions beyond western Gallaecia and sought to impose new agreements with local communities under their influence.[78] In both cases, embassies were undertaken by influential persons whose leadership was city based—such as Lusidius, the foremost citizen of Lisbon, and Hydatius, the bishop of Chaves.

Overall, the fragmentary evidence suggests that social standing was deeply rooted in local circumstances, focalized in cities and small (fortified) towns. Military, tributary, and perhaps judicial governance were founded on agreements between local communities and the Suevic leadership in the first half of the fifth century. At least during its first century, the Suevic polity must have resembled a contractual community of smaller geographical units throughout the intricate mountainous landscape of northwestern Iberia. Large cities may have been governed by notables, although there is no mention of royal officials in the extant sources. As late as the second half of the sixth century, administrative practices varied from city to city, which indicates distinct civic governments. The First Council of Braga mentions different regulations on burials within city walls, which varied in each *civitas*.[79] In smaller places, men with enough economic or social clout could and did embrace the opportunities that these agreements afforded to exert social preeminence by enforcing the system of pacts that gave stability to the Suevic kingdom. This was the world of *rectores*, *seniores*, and other generic titles, in charge of public affairs in cities, small towns, and hidden valleys with their hilltop centers. They incarnated the security and legal sanction brought by a kingdom built on agreements in the central decades of the fifth century.

*   *   *

It is worth noticing that these types of leaders did not adopt a Suevic identity— especially outside of the Suevic heartland of Braga and its microregion.[80] The elements of "barbarian" material culture (i.e., from the northern and central European Roman frontier) are rather limited (at least by comparison to the

northern plateau) and very likely associated with a military rather than supposedly Suevic identity.[81] The episode of Aspidius and the way it is related by
John of Biclarum is particularly revealing. The chronicler did not mention that
this territory was part of the Suevic kingdom, but the probable location of
the locum of the Aregensi in eastern Ourense (and the other *loca* under Aspidius's command) suggests otherwise. The following year, Leovigild would
launch a campaign against the "lands of the Suevi," by which he probably meant
the region of Braga-Porto, thus making Ourense a reasonable bet for the location of the Aregensi.[82] The use of a geographical term to designate Aspidius
and his *loca* may have originated from the Aregensi themselves, whose political identity was less attached to Suevic ethnicity and more to the political
agreement that defined their local membership in the Suevic kingdom. The
enigmatic Sappos, the inhabitants of Sabaria who might have been based in
the former *mansio* of Sibarim, may provide a similar illustration. The location
of this area is unknown, although it was probably in or near the modern province of Zamora.[83] We only know of it through a short entry in John of Biclarum's *Chronicle* describing the conquest of the region in Leovigild in 572. As
in the case of the Aregensi, the Sappos seemed to have adopted a markedly
geographical identity—but neither a political (*civitas*) nor an ethnic one.[84]

Both in the case of the Aregensi and the Sappos, their regional rather than
political denomination in the extant sources stressed common identities that
did not necessarily emerge out of a tribal or so-called gentilic revival in the
absence of the state.[85] Quite the opposite: we may here be witnessing the manifestation of a statehood tied to a contractual relationship between these frontier communities and the Suevic monarchy. I do not wish to underestimate
the role of Suevic ethnicity in the definition of certain actors' elite status. What
is important to note, however, is that it does not seem to have been the only
way to express social identity. State roles assumed by local potentates did not
force adscription to a particular ethnic category. Political unity may not have
coalesced into an ethnic redefinition of northwestern Iberia by the mid-sixth
century, but it does not follow that this state was weaker than other post-
Roman kingdoms.

While a Suevic identity may not have taken root everywhere in the kingdom, the cultural markers associated with late Roman elite culture rapidly
vanished in the course of the fifth century. As we saw in the previous chapter,
some villas were occupied into the fifth and sixth centuries, but no new villas
can be dated after the fourth; and even in cases of continuous occupation, we
do not know whether the type of occupation was aristocratic or not. Traditional

ceremonial buildings were abandoned, and so were bathhouses and other visible late Roman monumental features. Elite and civic monumentality, however, was never particularly strong in northwestern Iberia, with the exception of defensive walls. Indeed, this latter feature endured the withdrawal of the imperial administration in cities and smaller towns (including hilltops). These walls, the result of local initiatives, bespeak the importance of defense at the very local level in the imagination of local communities. The militarization of settlement identity was not reserved to the main cities (as in Lusitania) but also extended to local communities in the intricate landscape of Galicia and nearby regions.

*   *   *

In place of a Suevic identity, Christianity increasingly provided a shared idiom for social and political prestige by the second third of the sixth century. By the mid-sixth century, a dense network of episcopal sees had developed in the Suevic heartland, as can be reconstructed from the so-called *Parochiale Suevum*—a list of episcopal sees and dependent churches in the Suevic kingdom.[86] Bishops are not only attested in long-established important cities, like Braga or Lugo, but also in formerly secondary settlements, such as Tui, Iria Flavia, Dume, and Porto. Various reasons may lie behind these promotions. Porto was occasionally the residence of Suevic kings and a strategic fortress at the mouth of the Duero.[87] Dume hosted a prestigious monastic community founded by Martin of Braga.[88] In any case, thanks to the *Parochiale Suevum*, we know that the dioceses between the Miño and the Duero controlled a dense network of subordinated churches.[89] In the silent decades of the early sixth century, the western fringes of northwestern Iberia (that is, the region closest to the center of Suevic power) developed an institutional Christianity that emulated the relatively strong Lusitanian episcopal network. While the episcopate and clergy offered avenues to influential careers, this was not the main choice of most prominent landowners. Rather, as had happened in Lusitania three generations earlier, religious foundations in the form of churches or monasteries—pious acts reserved for those with enough economic muscle—provided the northwestern Iberian elites with the main mechanism through which they marked social distinction.

The process of church building is, however, fragmentary at best in the archaeological record. As we saw in Chapter 4, Christian buildings are only sparsely attested and tended to be concentrated in cities and probably some minor towns.[90] Conciliar documents, however, suggest that landowners were building churches by the mid-sixth century, either in towns or in rural areas. The process caught the attention of the bishops gathered in the second council of Braga because they expected that such donations would be accompanied by the necessary resources (presumably lands) to maintain each new church's personnel.[91] Behind their complaints about these, as it were, incomplete donations, the fathers gathered in the second council of Braga conceived of a world in which wealthy donors left their imprint on the kingdom's territory through lavish gifts to the Church.

The process of church building was not dissociated from the Suevic monarchy. We know with certainty that at least by 572, Suevic kings had embraced Nicene Christianity, but it is possible that the Suevic monarchy had been intermittently Nicene since the second half of the fifth century.[92] As in the Vandal kingdom, Arian kings could also take their religious agenda seriously, especially at times in which religious identity was crucial for political reasons.[93] In 464, Remismund rose as king of the Suevi and began to reverse the chaotic situation that Theoderic's invasion and the ensuing Suevic civil war had created. He signed a peace treaty with the Visigothic king and began an exchange of gifts and hostages.[94] It is most likely that the kingdom was at the time a client or a polity subordinated to the Visigoths. Within a year or two, a certain Ajax, a leading Arian from the East who lived in the Gothic kingdom, obtained a leading position (an episcopate?) under the patronage of the Suevic king.[95] Hydatius did not offer much information, but his concern with events in the local Arian Church in this particular case is indicative since his narrative otherwise ignores Arian initiatives. The convergence of Remismund's ascension, his efforts to consolidate Suevic power, and the ecclesiastical organization of the Arian Church cannot be coincidental.

As in other post-Roman kingdoms, church building and general protection of the church was increasingly associated with royal authority and could be used by those with claims to social and political standing to demonstrate their commanding positions in a Christian polity. It is, therefore, very likely that the involvement of aristocracies in patronizing religious foundations coincided with the growing interest of the monarchy in the same process no earlier than the first half of the sixth century. By 561, the Suevic monarchy supported the religious initiatives of Catholic bishops to regulate and bring uniformity to the kingdom's Christian life.[96] An inscription found forty kilometers south of Braga, in Vairão, celebrates the construction of a church by the consecrated virgin Marsipalla during the reign of an otherwise unknown "most serene king Veremundus."[97] The inscription presents several chronological problems, but a new assessment of it has suggested that it must be dated to 535.[98] We cannot determine the religious affiliation, whether Nicene or Arian, of both the donor and the king. However, this is our earliest evidence of a pious (aristocratic) donation in the Suevic kingdom, which is placed under the reign of a praiseworthy ("most serene") king. Another otherwise unknown king, Chararic, is mentioned by Gregory of Tours as the builder of a church in honor of Saint Martin of Tours during the episcopate of Martin of Dume/Braga (556–579/580). Although Gregory is not always a reliable authority on events outside of the Frankish kingdom, this reference combined with Marsipalla's inscription and the canon of the second council of Braga insinuate the growing visibility of the phenomenon of church building in the Suevic kingdom—particularly in the Suevic heartland near Braga.[99]

At the same time, the Church provided grammars of government that could unite the king and the various *seniores* throughout the realm. One such attempt survives in Martin of Braga's tractate *Rule for an Honest Life* addressed to king Miro and probably written in the years after 570. Martin knew that he could not expect Miro to be a king-monk, subject to the demands of an ascetic Christian life—unlike those he called "the few outstanding worshippers of God."[100] Rather, he offered a catalogue of moral virtues (*prudentia, magnanimitas, continentia,* and *iustitia*) based on Stoic philosophy, which provided the king and other enactors of state power throughout the kingdom with a language to describe the proper behavior of rulers. Justice (*iustitia*) was based on a simple idea. "First fear God and love God . . . You will love God if you imitate Him in desiring to do good to everyone and harm to no one; then everybody will call you a just man, and will follow, revere, and approve you."[101] Such principles were aimed at stressing proper behavior rather than proper policy and would have been expected from any person of power who claimed to lead an honorable life. Martin and the Suevic episcopate did not assume that the *seniores* of the kingdom would become perfect (ascetic) Christians. Rather he offered those with claims to ruling others a pathway to good government, in which violent excesses would be avoided through the acceptance of basic guidance by the Christian leadership.

By the time of the Visigothic conquest, a program of state reorganization under a new ideological aegis was under way. Men (and occasionally women) of power were embracing a language of authority based not only on their prominent military and political positions at the head of small communities throughout the kingdom but also on their partaking in the moral enterprise of the Suevic monarchs. Ideas of good government could potentially become a common language of power shared by kings and leading subjects under the ideological guidance of the Church. In order to share in this endeavor, *rectores* and *seniores* had to possess enough wealth to found and maintain a church or a monastic foundation in addition to marshaling soldiers and imparting justice. As a result of canonical legislation, gifts without the resources to secure the operation of a foundation would not receive ecclesiastical sanction. "High" piety was progressively limited to fewer people, and this restriction would eventually provide a language of aristocratic self-definition throughout the kingdom for the first time since the withdrawal of the imperial administration. It does not follow that all aristocrats accepted these premises, but they were increasingly exposed to ideas and practices that made other alternatives less viable.

*   *   *

Landowners and other preeminent figures in northwestern Iberia rapidly seized the opportunities brought by the inescapable presence of foreign rulers in the region in the early fifth century. By the second half of the fifth century, a status quo had been achieved, based on the arrangements undertaken during the Suevic settlement and expansion. These arrangements were subject to repeated negotiations in the first decades of Suevic rule, which could potentially lead to violent conflicts. In general, however, less traumatic solutions may have been the norm. The presence of a local military leadership and, eventually, a more formalized kingship allowed those who could mobilize people and symbolic and economic resources to join the Suevic project through the performance of local state functions and, occasionally, direct service at court. Suevic leadership at the local level was articulated on the previous Roman landscape of cities and increasingly on the secondary settlements of the intricate mountainous landscape surrounding river valleys. This fragmented geography probably favored territorial rather than ethnic or civic forms of identity. Symbolic attachment to Roman elite culture seems to have faded rapidly, although, as we saw, it had not been particularly remarkable in terms of monumental architecture. Still, Suevic ethnic identity did not function as a catalyzer of the kingdom's unity. Rather, political agreements that secured a minimum of stability became the foci of adherence to the polity of the Suevi. By the second third of the sixth century, however, Christianity began to occupy part of that space. This Christianity was not the elite monasticism of the late empire, which may have subsisted intermittently among the clergy. It was instead a new type of Christian discourse in which power meant power within the guidance of the Church—including the use of wealth and influence to establish religious foundations. In a sense, the Suevic kingdom was becoming more centralized than it had been a century earlier, contrary to common assumptions on the inexorable fragmentation of post-Roman kingdoms. Had the Visigothic conquest not happened in 585, this new ideological unity would have been achieved within one or two generations. Instead, northwestern Iberia joined the rest of the peninsula in the formation of a Visigothic Christian polity.

The Northern Meseta: Filling in the Gaps of the State

The transition between the imperial period and the post-Roman world had its own characteristics in the northern plateau and (as far as we can reconstruct it) in the Cantabrian Mountains. We saw in Chapter 1 that imperial military presence was stronger in this region that in other parts of the peninsula, at least in the late fourth century, although this presence did not translate into a militarization of elite culture. Owing to its location, the plateau became in the first half of the fifth century something of a frontier zone between territories under the control of barbarian armies and the remnant of the imperial administration in Tarraconensis. At the same time, it was a contested territory between different armies into the late 450s. Moreover, the plateau entered the fifth century with a sparse urban network compared to Lusitania but with a more self-assertive landowning aristocracy (and perhaps a wealthier one) in comparison to northwestern Iberia. These historical circumstances and structural characteristics would define the parameters of aristocratic strategies in the fifth and sixth centuries. The plateau's leading groups developed a more marked military identity than in other areas of Western Iberia while they embraced, to the extent possible, political constructions that tried to reproduce civic-like government in a very localized context. In the absence of a strong network of Roman *civitates*, they opted for fortified hilltop settlements to pursue avenues of social distinction through the enactment of (post-Roman) statehood. Therefore, while it retained its own peculiarities, the plateau presents a combination of social strategies that existed in Lusitania and northwestern Iberia.

* * *

The first impact of the civil war between Constantine III and Honorius was felt in the meseta in 408–409. In his *History against the Pagans*, Orosius depicted the illegitimate (in his mind) troops of Gerontius ransacking the fields near Palencia, although the wording of his description of the requisitions ("*almost as if* in price of victory") can also be interpreted in a way that suggests regular tribute.[102] In the 410s, a group of Vandals took the northern plateau as their territory, if the above-mentioned interpretation of Hydatius's description of barbarian settlements is correct.[103] Other armies had joined the Vandals in their settlement in Gallaecia by 418.[104] War between the Vandals and the Suevi soon broke out, and, under the pressure of imperial troops, the Vandals abandoned Gallaecia and made their way to Baetica.[105] By 429, the Vandals (or at least a large part of them) sailed to Africa while the Suevi were advancing in "central Gallaecia," by which Hydatius may mean the territories between Braga and the plateau. Local populations resisted the Suevi in fortified settlements, which suggests that the plateau was under nominal imperial control but also that local communities had begun to see these fortified settlements as the best response to the unstable situation.[106] In 433, the Suevi reached a settlement agreement with Aetius regarding "the Gallaecians," a term Hydatius may have meant to also include the plateau communities.[107] In the 440s, events in the periphery of the plateau may have increased the barbarian and Roman military presence in the region. Hydatius mentioned that the *dux utriusque militiae* Asturius was fighting peasant revolts (*bacaudae*) in nearby Tarraconensis in 441 while his son-in-law, Merobaudes, conducted a similar campaign near Pamplona.[108] Still in 449, *bacaudae* were active in the upper Ebro Valley, attacking *foederati* troops, while the Suevic king Rechiarius waged war in Vasconia.[109] Thus, the plateau differs from Lusitania in that it transitioned into the post-Roman period within a much more conflictive situation—or at least under its constant threat. At the same time, the disarticulation of the Roman military axis along the Braga-Zaragoza road and the lack of a powerful urban administrative structure created the conditions for a more drastic political and social reorganization. Local communities, however, seem to have reached a stable point between 433 and 456. The only Gallaecian events worth mentioning in Hydatius's *Chronicle* for those years included the presence of Manichaeans, natural prodigies and portents, and an incursion of Rechiarius into northwestern Galicia.[110]

After Theoderic's invasion in 456, most of the northern plateau came under the Visigothic sphere of influence. Astorga and its territory remained under Suevic control. It is harder to reconstruct what happened in the highland territories surrounding the plateau. In the Cantabrian north, the situation may have been similar to the plateau's, although with a less articulated royal administrative presence.[111] Both Suevic and Visigothic kings fought intermittently against different Basque and Cantabrian groups. The organization of local societies seems to have followed the same patterns as parts of northwestern Iberia, that is, nonurban hilltop sites. In the middle of the seventh century, Wamba is said to have attacked the Basques in their fortifications (*castra*). Local leaders or members of prominent families were possibly taken as hostages after the peace reached in the campaign.[112] This could also be the case of the *Rucones* or *Ruccones*, who seemed to have occupied the northern slopes of the Cantabrian Mountains (and perhaps eastern Asturias). This group was fought both by the late Suevic kings and the Visigoths until their final conquest by king Suinthila in 629.[113]

As a consequence of the events that took place in the early decades of the imperial authority's disintegration, the northern plateau rapidly developed frontierlike characteristics.[114] With the possible exception of the Suevic-Visigothic border from the late fifth century onward, a formal frontier in the proper Roman sense never existed.[115] Rather, the northern meseta region was vulnerable to military incursions by different armies. The plateau occupied a strategic military position both before and after 507, when the Visigoths lost Aquitaine. The threat of the Basques and other groups in the Cantabrian Mountains continued into the seventh century, although it never posed a major threat to the Visigothic monarchy.[116] The fertile fields of the meseta were also open to the potential attacks of semiautonomous buffer polities in the meseta's western fringes. Frankish incursions into the Ebro Valley region could easily reach the meseta and, therefore, gain direct access to the rest of the kingdom. As a result, the region's local elites deployed unique strategies of social standing that relied on more flexible approaches toward territorial administration.

*   *   *

The extent to which Visigothic administration replaced Roman government is difficult to reconstruct, but it is very likely that some form of territorial (or even provincial) oversight existed, at least by the sixth century if not earlier. It is remarkable that the region did not have to be reconquered by Leovigild (unlike other parts of his kingdom) in the second half of the sixth century. The fringes of the meseta (parts of Zamora or northern Burgos) were the exception.[117] But it seems that the northern meseta was already, in its own way, an integrated part of the Gothic polity. Little is known about the region's type of administration and the basis of local elites claiming ruling positions. A controversy between the Christian community of Palencia and the metropolitan see of Toledo over the consecration of churches reveals the silent presence of royal authorities in the first half of the sixth century. In a letter written in 531, the bishop of Toledo, Montanus, disapproved the Palencia Christian community's practice of having their churches consecrated by bishops from other jurisdictions. Presumably, the Palencians invited the bishop of Astorga (formally in the Suevic kingdom) rather than the bishop of Toledo or other bishops from the newly formed ecclesiastical province of Carpetania and Celtiberia.[118] Montanus addressed a certain Toribius, a religious leader (perhaps an ascetic Christian or a priest) but not yet a bishop, who seems to have been a leading figure of the church of Palencia. Montanus warned Toribius that if the Palencians did not end this practice, "it will be necessary to bring this [situation] to the attention of our lord [king Amalaric] and to inform our son Erganus; and, thus, the commands of his majesty and the judge's sentence will severely punish this presumptuous act."[119] Montanus could therefore threaten Toribius and his congregation with the intervention of the (Arian) king to settle affairs within the Church through the agency of a local official, the *iudex* Erganus. We do not know in what capacity Erganus was an *iudex*— *comes*, *dux*, and so forth. Yet the letter leaves no doubt that a royal administration existed in the plateau to the extent that it was believable its agents could enforce ecclesiastical rulings. Even Toribius himself could have been a former royal official since Montanus mentioned he had had a flourishing secular career before his ecclesiastical vocation.[120]

In addition to some form of Visigothic administration (and Suevic government in the western parts of the plateau), it is very likely that cities kept civic institutions. A few cities maintained their central status and had bishoprics established. Traditional episcopal sees such as Segovia and Salamanca may have at some point been governed by notables—including a bishop and royal officials.[121] Similarly, Palencia was probably an administrative center with an episcopal see.[122] Other cities in the plateau, such as Osma, also had episcopal sees at some point during the late sixth and seventh centuries, although we do not know if the same applies to earlier periods. To these cities, we need to add Astorga and León from the Suevic area.

The low-density urban network, however, forced local elites to pursue a different strategy to deal with the peculiar political and military situation of the region. Local populations and their leadership rallied around smaller settlements, such as the hilltop sites I discussed in the previous chapter. The political and social centrality of these sites continued during the Visigothic period as they were likely centers of tax collection and large estate administration, as the next chapter will discuss. If we extrapolate from the practices of the nearby upper Ebro Valley (a region with similar structural characteristics), more or less formalized assemblies of landowners ruled over local communities.[123] In other words, in the absence of a large number of cities with a tradition of urban government, local elites tried to re-create small *civitates*-like communities in these hilltop sites. Their features included markers of "high" late Roman urbanism (defensive walls) and, probably, political institutions similar to those of government by notables—predominantly landowners, without officers such as counts or bishops. Rather than isolation, these hilltops bespeak the willingness to accommodate preexisting social structures to the new realities of the post-Roman world in the plateau. They did not undermine the urban model of administration. Rather, like hilltop sites in late antique southern Thrace and Macedonia, they were "urbanizing" communities—regardless of whether they succeeded in this endeavor.[124] In other words, local power was not built in belligerence against a central state but rather as an attempt to join that state from the historical and structural conditions of the region.

While *civitates* jealously protected their political rights, microregional landowning elites could strive for institutional recognition. The town of Auca, near Burgos, became an episcopal see by the second half of the sixth century, if not earlier. The actual location of the town is not known, although it is conventionally taken to be Villafranca Montes de Oca in the province of Burgos. Whereas the creation of this episcopal see might have coincided with Leovigild's campaigns in Cantabria, the appearance of an episcopal see cannot be dissociated from the extant political importance of landowners' more or less formalized institutions in the microregion.[125]

Auca was, nevertheless, an exception. Most of the newly formed hilltop settlements could not achieve institutional enhancement as *civitates*. Since civic institutions could be imitated but not reproduced in these smaller settlements, militarized leadership may have been crucial to define aristocratic status. Still, we must be cautious because little is known of the military organization of the Visigothic kingdom until the second half of the seventh century. Indeed, the hilltop fortifications that emerged in the fifth century do not seem to have formed part of a centralized military strategy. Rather, they were diverse and highly localized initiatives, aiming at providing a minimum of security at the microregional level but also emphasizing the presence of some form of monopoly of coercion and a basic political organization. As I argued in Chapter 4, each of these hilltop fortified sites followed distinct chronological and topographic trajectories and seem therefore to have resulted from highly localized initiatives—likely aristocratic enterprises. In this environment, where central and civic institutions were a distant presence, statehood resulted from local impresarios' ability to mobilize wealth and, more important, people. Since social status and political leadership were not guaranteed by belonging to a particular order, membership in the community of men of power could be marked by the mobilization of military clienteles.

A famous episode narrated by Procopius in his *Wars* hints at the type of militarized environment that might have prevailed in the plateau. He mentioned that Theudis married a woman from a wealthy Hispanian house (*ex oikias tōn tinos epichōriōn eudaimonos*). From the estate owned by his wife, he took two thousand men to serve as his personal guard of lancers (*doruphorōn dunamis*).[126] This is a very large personal retinue but hardly surprising for a king. Nothing indicates that this army was raised in the northern plateau, even though there are some hints suggesting that Theudis had a power base in the northern or southern meseta.[127] In any event, it would not take a big leap of imagination to guess that on smaller scale, local landowners could also raise personal retinues from among their rural workers of different status.[128] This practice was not necessarily a Visigothic innovation since it was rooted in attested late Roman practices that continued during the kingdom of Toulouse.[129] Some of these retinues may have been garrisoned on small hilltops, such as the site of La Cabeza de Navansangil, which I described in the previous chapter. Different types of weapons (cavalry as well as infantry weapons) were recovered from this small settlement.[130] Rather than private armies, we may be dealing with local militias that provided a minimum of security in the tumultuous fifth century and could enforce the decisions of a community of landowners with enough wealth to mobilize them.[131] If a recent reassessment of the cemeteries in the northern and southern plateaus is correct and we should date them (or most of them) to the fifth century, it is possible to reconsider accessories (belt brooches) and nonspecialized weapons (axes, spears, and perhaps knives) with which some peasants were buried in this light.[132] While certain members of the local elites could pursue avenues of social distinction through civic, royal, and ecclesiastical office in one of the plateau's few cities, the majority of landowners were left to claim status in the less institutionalized world of hilltop sites. The ability to separate free men of means (i.e., with an armed retinue) from other free men was essential to mark boundaries between the elite and nonelite. Overall, the northern plateau was not a military region with a formal frontier but rather a militarized area with frontierlike characteristics. The distinction may be subtle, but it is important to understand the potential continuities with and departures from the late Roman period.

*   *   *

This frontierlike character also relates to distinct traits of material culture departing from previous late Roman precedents by the turn of the sixth century. Chapter 4 has already described certain types of nonelite houses built with construction techniques that were not common in the peninsula during the Roman period. I was cautious then to ascribe too much ethnic significance to these houses since they were frequent in other parts of the empire during the fourth century. Funerary archaeology has also provided modern researchers with some of the most intriguing and controversial material from the post-Roman period, raising questions about ethnic identities in the northern plateau. A series of late fifth and early sixth-century cemeteries have produced a number of female adornments (belt buckles, combs, and brooches) associated with the material culture of fourth-century cemeteries on the Danube frontier.[133] While most of the burials in peninsular cemeteries did not include any type of adornment, the presence of artifacts associated with a region where the Visigoths were active in the fourth century must be considered seriously.

Debates about these cemeteries arose from a controversy over the relationship between literary evidence, material culture, and ethnic identity. Two curt entries in the so-called *Consularia Caesaraugustana* mention Goths entering Hispania in 494 and "taking *sedes*" in 496.[134] Minimalist interpretations of Visigothic presence in Iberia support the idea that Visigothic groups only began to intervene in the peninsula in the late fifth century, and then mostly to carry out military campaigns rather than take lands to settle. In this interpretation, the cemeteries do not reflect the presence of a Visigothic settlement.[135] However, other scholars have characterized these cemeteries as "Visigothic" owing to the presence of adornments originating from central Europe.[136] According to this perspective, these cemeteries are explained by earlier settlements resulting from land divisions between Goths and Romans in the form of *tertiae*—a possibility supported by the marked rural character of these burials.[137]

In the absence of other evidence, it is hard to assess the ethnic origins of the people who were buried in these necropoleis.[138] Adopting such personal adornments was a practice undeniably imported at some point in the fifth century. In general, these cemeteries show the impact of adornments that were typical of the Danubian frontier in the fourth century. Even if it is not possible to relate ethnic origins to materials such as belt buckles or brooches in a straightforward way, the presence of such items reveals a regional break with the late Roman period that cannot go unnoticed. Newcomers most likely introduced this fashion—whether Vandals, Suevi, Goths, or Romans (or a combination of these groups). It is thus tempting to associate these cemeteries with a particular military culture, although only indirectly, since we must bear in mind that most of the prestige items were worn by women. We may also be in the presence of a more flexible approach toward performative ethnicity through the use of certain adornments.[139] The drastic change in material culture is symptomatic of a process of changing identity, an identity that was neither barbarian nor Roman but intensely post-Roman.[140] We can treat these objects as pure fashion statements, but we would need to explain why this fashion did not spread to other regions of Western (and eastern) Iberia until the late sixth century. Whether those adopting the adornments claimed to be Romans or barbarians, they certainly embraced the display of symbols that were unique to the plateau context by the turn of the sixth century. It is also remarkable that most of the burials do not show markers of elite status through wealth display. Jewelry and adornments are limited to a small number. Moreover, nothing indicates social stratification beyond the presence of female adornments in some graves.[141] It might thus be tempting to believe that performative ethnicity mattered more in the plateau than in the other areas of Western Iberia, although there does not seem to be any reason why this should be the case.[142]

Christianity played a limited role in the social distinction strategies of these elites until the seventh century or perhaps the late sixth century. As we saw in the previous chapter, the process of church building was not particularly intense in the post-Roman plateau. This does not mean that the region was under-Christianized or that a supposed Arian Visigothic presence attempted to stem the expansion of Christian construction. Aristocrats may have supported religious initiatives but not necessarily in the form of privately

founded churches. Again one must face a frustrating silence in the sources. In
the absence of a well-developed episcopal network, it is possible that Christianity evolved in distinctive ways in the region—for instance, as a more individual type of piety. Charismatic asceticism or similar forms of Christian piety
may be what Hydatius denounced as Manichaeism in Astorga, but it is difficult to generalize from this fragmentary testimony.[143] In post-Roman Cantabria (upper Ebro Valley), the "senator" Honorius provided support for saint
Aemilian's hermitage, which received numerous visitors, according to his ha-
giographer Braulio of Zaragoza.[144] Charismatic ascetics offered people like
Honorius models of behavior that fit the new realities of power, very much
like Martin of Braga's contemporary efforts in the Suevic heartland. As Aemilian preached to the *senatus* of Cantabria (whose members listened "with
reverence"), men of power had to avoid crimes such as "murder, theft, pollu-
tion, and aggression."[145] We do not have evidence for the plateau during the
fifth and sixth centuries, but in the seventh century, the western fringes of
the meseta hosted monastic communities and individual ascetic enterprises.[146]
Like the foundation of churches, the support of ascetic enterprises and monastic communities was an activity in which kings were involved. If we are to
believe the *Lives of the Fathers of Mérida*, Leovigild himself supported the monastic enterprise of a Nicene émigré monk named Nanctus in the territory of
Lusitania.[147] Be that as it may, the evidence of aristocratic foundations in the
plateau seems rather slim for the post-Roman period and tends to be concentrated toward the second half of the sixth century, if not later.

*   *   *

The northern meseta moved into the post-Roman world in somewhat different
conditions than the other areas of Western Iberia. The region had a marked
frontier tone from at least the mid-fifth century onward. The Suevic and Visigothic areas of influence, and eventually kingdoms, were not alone in having
interests in the plateau and nearby microregions. The Cantabrian north, and
perhaps certain areas of Zamora and León, also became somewhat autonomous, though not necessarily independent, from either polity. This situation
encouraged the slightly more marked military character of material culture
at the settlement level but also, to a certain extent, elite identity. It would be
surprising if local elites themselves did not adopt military leadership as a
distinct marker of status in the competitive career toward high status in a
context in which the ability to mobilize men became crucial to keeping the

peace—as is attested in other post-Roman contexts such as the Middle Rhine.[148] Here more than in any other region of Western Iberia, Roman civilian elite culture—including housing tastes—may have been abandoned more rapidly.

Like in northwestern Iberia, the practice of power became a more localized affair, although this localization had less to do with the terrain and barbarian settlement conditions than with the low density of the urban network. As in Lusitania, a state administration seems to have operated through a network of *iudices* and other royal officials in a few *civitates*, but this situation did not prevent the emergence of alternative centers, especially during the tumultuous decades around the mid-fifth century. Local aristocracies adapted institutional practices to territorial realities and defensive imperatives. Landowning elites participated in the administration and military life of the Suevic and Visigothic kingdoms from urban and urbanlike sites that retained the main features of late Roman urbanism—especially defensive walls. But it would be a mistake to read these rapid changes as signs of a deeper crisis than that experienced by, say, Lusitania, where continuity in civic government and the urban network suggests the perseverance of certain late Roman institutions. Rather, I would argue, the northern plateau experience demonstrates the success of practices that evolved during the post-Roman period, such as the ability of local landowners to enact state power at the local level. Moreover, statehood in the meseta was re-created rather rapidly, within one generation. The material incarnation of the state may have looked different than its late Roman predecessor, but, unsurprisingly, it maintained structural features of that world on a smaller scale.

Aristocracies and the Construction of Post-Roman Statehood

This chapter offers three different regional models to explain the re-creation of statehood after the crisis of the late Roman imperial project. That project failed not as a result of an intrinsic weakness but as a consequence of military and political events that cut Western Iberia loose from the rest of the empire. Depending on the region, the imperial project was no longer available to local elites within a generation or two of the arrival of barbarian armies. Individual members of local elites certainly suffered from this situation, especially when their interests or convictions induced them to join the wrong side of a conflict between different armies. Yet as a class, local aristocracies rapidly adapted to the new situation, especially after they realized that barbarian armies could offer the social and political stability that the imperial administrations in Arles, Ravenna, or Constantinople were no longer able to provide. By the time Theoderic invaded Hispania in 456, the events that had unfolded in Western Iberia during the previous forty-five years had created new avenues to social standing, detached from loyalty to a symbolically and politically distant emperor.

While the three regions followed somewhat divergent trajectories, they also shared common experiences. I have emphasized the differences for analytical purposes, but I do not wish to create the impression they were mutually exclusive. To take one example, *civitates* and collective bodies of notables dominated the political landscape of central and southern Lusitania. They also very likely characterized cities such as Lugo, Astorga, or Segovia. These three cases, however, may have been the exception rather than the norm within their own region. Likewise, certain members of the Lusitanian aristocracy secured their social standing through the performance of military duties. Yet they did so in a less markedly militarized elite culture than in the northern plateau. While the available vocabulary of aristocratic identity was similar, aristocracies phrased that identity differently according to regional circumstances.

Two features shaped the regionally specific strategies of aristocratic distinction in the post-Roman period. First, the structural patterns inherited from the late Roman world were fundamental in defining the social and territorial platform of post-Roman aristocracies. Late Roman civic government had turned into an informal government-by-notables type of administration by the turn of the fifth century, and this was maintained into the post-Roman period wherever cities were able to preserve their institutional power. Participation in the enactment of state functions at the local level remained a constitutive part of the aristocratic persona. Traditions of private and public buildings to denote status at the settlement level were carried on into the post-Roman world.

Second, negotiations with barbarian armies and their settlement conditions between 411 and the 460s created different regional realities in terms of the institutional arrangements that could be used as platforms for aristocratic power. The historical contingencies of the earlier decades of the fifth century would also contribute to shaping the particular regional evolution of aristocracies. It was during this period that local elites and newcomer powers crafted post-Roman statehood on the premises of existing structures and new circumstantial demands. The withdrawal of the central imperial administration may have created a power vacuum, but the social physics of aristocratic power rapidly filled it with new forms of social and political authority. In the post-Roman period as much as in the late Roman period, there was never an intrinsic opposition between local and regional or supraregional aristocracy. In both cases, social standing largely depended on the ability to enact state mandates and public authority at the local level.

There is, however, a significant difference between the late and the post-Roman periods. A marked hierarchy of social orders based on legal privileges had characterized the late Roman Empire. *Curiales* and senators were legally different from other free people, not to mention the nonfree. This distinction vanished in the fifth and sixth centuries, as the legal and political apparatus that had given force to such distinctions disappeared from Western Iberia by the 450s, if not earlier. In order to claim social ascendancy, privileged groups as well as certain members of the newly arrived armies had to pursue other avenues of social distinction. Wealth and landownership in particular remained a crucial way of defining aristocratic status and the political participation attached to that status. As the next chapter will show, taxation remained connected to landowning structures and therefore landowners were fundamental agents of infrastructural statehood. Moreover, wealth could be deployed in different ways to make status claims. While in the late Roman period, those claims were made through symbolic participation in an empire-wide community of elite taste, the post-Roman world forced more localized strategies. I have traced three of them in this chapter: gifts to the church (especially through the foundation and endowment of rural basilicas), the construction of walled settlements, and the support of private militias. And there were certainly many other reminders of aristocratic distinction that cannot be reconstructed from the surviving material and written documents. In all cases, wealth defined the aristocratic class as long as it was used in the service of ideological principles supporting statehood.

CHAPTER 6

Preserving Wealth in a Changing World: Post-Roman Aristocratic Economic Strategies

The anonymous *Life of Fructuosus* tells the story of the seventh-century monk-bishop of Braga who preached an ascetic Christianity to his fellow aristocrats at the height of the Visigothic kingdom. When Fructuosus was a boy, according to his hagiography, he visited the mountains of El Bierzo with his father, a high commander (*dux*) of the Visigothic army. On that occasion, his father asked shepherds for accounts (*rationes*) of their flocks.[1] This passage has been highly controversial in modern historiography. The father's activities support different theories on taxation, state, and landownership in the centuries that followed the end of the imperial administration. One interpretation argues that Fructuosus's father was collecting revenue from land he had received in exchange for military service—a sign of the proto-feudalization of the kingdom.[2] Another interpretation maintains that he was acting as a landowner, collecting rents from subordinate peasants.[3] Finally, others argue that Fructuosus's father was collecting taxes from landowners.[4] The debate itself is revealing. By the seventh century, taxation was a less ubiquitous and uniform practice than it had been three centuries earlier, when Valerius Proculus, whom we encountered in Chapter 3, visited Gallaecia to assess provincial taxes.

As we also saw in Chapter 3, environmental conditions, access to markets, and the taxation system set limits on landowners' economic strategies while giving them opportunities to take advantage of state infrastructure. The same parameters applied to the post-Roman world. There was, however, an important difference. After the fifth century, taxes represented a decreasing part of state-appropriated surplus, while landowners, especially those with large estates, were obligated, at least in theory, to allocate more resources to supply the royal armies with soldiers or raise militias to meet local needs. This transformation was slow paced and would not take its final form until the second half of the seventh century, when taxes represented just a small part of state financing. The post-Roman period was a world in which taxes were still collected and the central administration devoted legislative and political efforts to keeping the system afloat.

In this chapter, we will see how local landowners adapted to the changing situation of the fifth and sixth centuries without necessarily abandoning many of the late Roman patterns. The agrarian economy based on Mediterranean products and animal farming did not undergo any major changes. Large properties with scattered tenancies worked by a rural population of varying statuses continued to be the norm after the fifth century. Central forms of management are attested and large properties still collected taxes, even though the impact of taxation was declining. Yet throughout the post-Roman period, the large-scale investment in production and storage infrastructure that had characterized several late Roman economic units receded. When production infrastructure becomes archaeologically visible, it does so through small silos or mills associated with peasant farms or unstructured villages. These dwelling units, as discussed in Chapter 4, were not necessarily independent from aristocratic influence. Rather, as I will argue presently, they illustrated large estates adapting to changes in the reach of markets and attempting to exploit the resources available within their property.

Indeed, the reach of post-Roman distribution networks shows a marked downsizing after the fifth century. By the seventh century, exchanges became predominantly local with only a few signs of supraregional networks. Pan-Mediterranean and medium-distance inland regional exchanges faded, as far as they can be reconstructed from ceramics. Instead, local exchanges become more noticeable, and, by the seventh century, they largely predominated over other type of markets. As in the case of ancient taxation, the transformation of exchanges from regional to local was slow paced. There was a myriad of intermediary situations during the fifth and the sixth centuries. The transformation did not affect regions equally, with the coastal areas remaining in contact with supraregional markets for a longer time. It is only in the seventh century that the patterns of ceramic distribution become unambiguously local.

Slow-motion change determined the economic strategies of local aristoc-racies after the fifth century. The withdrawal of the imperial administration had less of an impact on elite economic developments than on status display or political organization. Change is certainly visible during the seventh century, however, as a result of two centuries of incremental transformations. These small and highly localized changes show the determination of landowning elites to maintain their economic muscle in order to support their social and political claims to high status. Above all, this chapter will show the engagement of landowning elites in preserving their wealth and steady income through-out a period of social transformation.

Taxation and Landownership in the Post-Roman World

In Chapter 3, I argued that the economic strategies of Western Iberian elites were shaped by the Mediterranean agrarian economy and the demands of the late Roman state, which encouraged the centralization and distribution of food staples by large economic units. In order to evaluate elite economic strategies in the post-Roman world, it is necessary to assess to what extent this condi-tioning subsisted after the withdrawal of the Roman administration, in par-ticular the role of the tax system in encouraging specific strategies. But before I reconstruct tax practices in the post-Roman period, I must briefly address the question of co-called barbarian settlements. A well-known historiograph-ical debate continues to discuss the early arrangements between barbarian armies and the imperial administration in the western empire throughout the fifth century. While this is a complex controversy with many nuances, it ranges between two extreme positions. At one end of the debate are those who argue that barbarian armies received tax shares from the lands on which they settled. At the other end are those who maintain that barbarians received a portion of land that usually became tax exempt in exchange for military service.[5] This issue is particularly relevant for the purposes of this chapter because the crux of the problem is to what extent the late Roman tax system was maintained after the imperial administration withdrew from the peninsula.

Our knowledge of the first barbarian settlements is rather limited, and we must rely on the vague descriptions of Hydatius. The Alans, Suevi, and Van-dals divided four provinces either as an agreement among themselves or as a result of negotiations with the imperial authorities for whom they probably fought.[6] Based on Hydatius's account, it is hard to tell if they took land, taxes, or a combination of both.[7] The *Chronicle* remarks that in 411 the Suevi and other armies distributed the lands by lot *ad inhabitandum*.[8] Although there have been arguments in favor of taking this term as a technical expression denoting (land-sharing) settlement, it is far from clear that Hydatius uses it in that sense.[9] As I discussed in Chapter 5, Orosius's description of the troops of Gerontius ransacking the fields near Palencia, "almost as if in price of victory," may be an indication of tribute collection. In the long run, the Suevi became landowners, although we cannot determine whether they received lands in exchange for military service or not. While Hydatius referred to *paces* between Suevi and Romans, the content of these treaties remains unknown. The agreements likely varied from community to community, and the association of the area around Braga with the main political center of the kingdom may suggest that they took more lands in that region than elsewhere.[10] What we cannot tell is whether Suevi became landowners as a result of a two-thirds to one-third division of (some) lands or as a consequence of expropriations of those who opposed them (or a mix of both).

As for the Visigoths, by the time of Theoderic's intervention in 456, they had developed a practice of land distribution in Aquitaine. Regardless of whether Visigoths received lands or tax shares in 418, it is certain that Gothic kings followed a policy of distributing land to their followers four decades later.[11] Visigothic legislation referred to potential Goth-Roman conflicts over land, and so it is highly likely that some mechanism of distribution was in place at some point in the fifth century.[12] While Euric's legislation may have addressed a predominantly Gallic concern, the survival of similar legislation in later Visigothic codifications suggests that similar legal issues may have had to be addressed in Iberia. In any event, when the Goths began to intervene more actively in the Iberian Peninsula, at least some of them were landowners in Aquitaine.

The impact of Visigothic settlement and landownership within the peninsula and in Western Iberia in particular is hard to assess. I have already mentioned the difficulties related to the obscure passages from the *Consularia Caesaraugustana* and the Goths taking *sedes* in Hispania in 497. As in the case of the Suevi, it is difficult to determine whether this passage means that they received lands or just settled in cities or military garrisons. As seen in the previous chapter, it is possible that the northern plateau became an area of intense settlement, but there is not much evidence to support this argument beyond the interpretation of material culture along ethnic lines, which is very problematic. The settlement of Goths after the mid-fifth century or the early sixth century must have occurred with marked regional and microregional variations, but these variations cannot be reconstructed. It is remarkable, however, that Gothic settlement, if it existed on a large scale, left no trace of conflict or resistance. The relative ease of the process may be due to the fact that by the time the Visigoths intervened in Western Iberia, the region had already come to an accommodation with the Suevi. Perhaps the Goths simply replaced the Suevi in their arrangements with local communities, with the addition of the lands they took from "Romans" who sided with the Suevi.[13] This may explain the reference to the *sedes* that the Goths took in Tarraconensis according to the *Consularia*. This was the only province that was not under the power of the Suevi before the 450s and maintained some degree of autonomy into the late fifth century. Individual Goths very likely became landowners between the mid-fifth and the mid-sixth century, but how this happened is hard to tell with certainty.

In the end, there is no blanket formula to determine the settlement of barbarian armies in the peninsula throughout the fifth century. Settlement and land acquisition may have been a piecemeal process. Conditions in the 410s were very different from the situation in the 450s.[14] The first barbarians settled when the imperial administration still existed in the peninsula and very likely had bargaining power with the four different armies. Four decades later, that power was much reduced. From the 450s through the 500s (when Visigothic settlement supposedly took place), Gothic courts and armies dominated much of the peninsula, but their relative strength varied from region to region and from decade to decade. Division of land and payment of taxes were some of the possible ways in which settlements could be negotiated, and I am inclined to believe that there was a combination of both. As I mentioned earlier, we have evidence of both land-based taxation and potential conflicts resulting from earlier land division in the late sixth century. Yet barbarian landownership had more than a single origin. By the sixth century, marriages, political expropriations, and the redistribution of land probably became a much more frequent avenue toward (large) landownership than presumed partitions between Romans and barbarians. With these considerations in mind, we will now look at what taxation may have looked like in the fifth and sixth centuries.

*   *   *

There are two questions on post-Roman taxation that are usually discussed together but that, in reality, ought to be treated separately. On the one hand, there is the question of whether taxes were collected and, if so, how. The answer is clear: taxes were collected in post-Roman Iberia and they were collected through a series of procedures involving central administration and local communities, landowners in particular. On the other hand, there is the problem of the relative impact of taxation within state income. In other words, how much income did the administrations of the various post-Roman states derive from taxes and how much did they obtain through other mechanisms (chiefly personal services and royal lands).

The second question is more difficult to answer, not least because of the absence of documents containing reliable statistical information. One way of approaching the issue is to assess how military needs were met—whether the Suevi and the Visigoths relied on paid armies or land-based soldiery and income from royal properties. Sadly, we know few details about military organization in the Suevic and Visigothic kingdoms until the second half of the seventh century, when military laws addressed the question in depth. By then, free men, and especially free men of means, owed unpaid military service.[15] These laws probably represent a reform compared to previous practices of recruitment after Visigothic monarchs faced serious threats (especially rebellions), which may have put earlier recruitment practices under stress.[16] Pre-seventh-century military organization may have combined landed and paid armies. It is also possible that in the late seventh century some military ventures were still funded by the royal government through taxes. As we saw in Chapter 4, there were military initiatives in the northern plateau that may have involved centralized planning and state financing. In general, it is very likely that both Suevic and Visigothic military demands were met through a combination of taxes and rents throughout the fifth and sixth centuries, with rents having a growing impact.[17] Seventh-century legislation includes norms dating back to the sixth century that regulate the collection and distribution of rations for the army (*annona*) in cities and fortified settlements.[18]

Taxation never completely disappeared, and later Visigothic monarchs took the payment of tributes seriously. How much land was subject to taxation by then is unclear, but the fiscal pressure was real enough to make tax evasion desirable. By the seventh century, it is possible that certain lands were subject to taxes while others were exempt. The *LV* V.4.19 issued by Chindaswinth (r. 642–653) ordered that when a landowner transferred part or all of his property, the purchaser or beneficiary of such a transfer should pay the taxes associated with that particular land. While the wording of the law is not completely clear, it seems that certain landowners were responsible for paying specific tributes, perhaps associated with former civic *munera* (*curiales* and *privati*, "who are customarily required to provide horses and pay duties to the public treasury").[19] The transfer of land was an occasion for purchasers of such lands to avoid paying these tributes, perhaps because they or their other lands (or both) were exempt from such fiscal duties.[20] Land transfers could thus potentially lead to a reduction of tax revenue—hence the royal command to register such lands as tax-paying properties after a sale. In the seventh century, if not earlier, the Iberian Peninsula was probably an archipelago of islands of taxation, as has also recently been argued about Ostrogothic Italy.[21] By the end of the century, the nontributary sea level may have risen to cover even more land.[22] The existence of islands of taxation implies both the reduced impact of taxes within the overall structure of the state and the continuous collection of taxes. Even as late as the 693, kings issued legislation to secure the payments of taxes owed to the crown.[23] Taxes remained an important, albeit declining, source of income for the Visigothic monarchy into the seventh century. Therefore, we should not underestimate their role in state financing during the fifth and sixth centuries.

As for the first question, whether a centralized tax system existed and how it functioned, the available evidence also appears late in our period (in the late sixth and seventh centuries). A letter collected in Cassiodorus's *Variae* and dated to sometime between 523 and 526 describes tax-collecting institutions and practices in the peninsula during the Ostrogothic protectorate, such as city polyptychs, land tax and other tributes, tax-collecting officers, and coin minting.[24] The purpose of Theoderic's letter was to prevent abuses by tax collectors, although we do not know whether the letter addressed a generalized problem, as the text claims, or specific complaints, as is more likely from the list of complaints, some of which are unrelated to taxation.[25] Be that as it may, taxes continued to be collected in the early sixth century. We know that by the reign of Reccared, tax collection was the duty of officers known as *numerarii*, who were appointed by a court official with the title of *comes patrimonii*, a simplified version of the late Roman tributary bureaucracy.[26] Taxes were assessed in kind but could be paid in coin at an official exchange rate—a mechanism that had existed during the late empire (known as *adaeratio*). Also similar to the late empire, taxation was controlled by the central government, although local communities may have had ways of preventing abuses. In addition to centrally appointed officials, civic authorities were set in place to oversee some aspects of tax collection. In order to prevent these abuses, Reccared reminded his subjects that cities appointed the *numerarii* and the *defensores*—legislation that we encountered in the previous chapter.[27] One such *numerarius* is attested as late as the 690s in Mérida.[28] Bishops also played a role in the tributary machinery as overseers of royal functionaries and protectors of local taxpayers against abuses, which would fit with their role in civic structures of government by notables.[29]

There are pros and cons to taking the tax practices of Reccared's reign as the norm for the whole post-Roman period. Late sixth-century taxation could have resulted from the centralizing effects of Leovigild's policies and conquests—and, hence, the growing number of documents dealing with taxation from his son's reign. Moreover, Leovigild and Reccared embarked on a construction program on a scale that the Iberian Peninsula had not witnessed since the walling of cities in the late third and fourth centuries.[30] Thus, we should be cautious at projecting back in time the tax administration of the late sixth century. Yet certain late Roman practices (such as taxation in kind, *adaeratio* mechanisms, and a centralized bureaucracy in charge of tax collection) suggest uninterrupted tributary practices throughout the post-Roman period. During the Ostrogothic protectorate in the 510s and 520s, Theudis is said to have regularly sent taxes to Ravenna, whose collection could have followed late Roman parameters.[31] In 523, the Ostrogothic court attempted to organize the peninsular administration, including the fiscal apparatus.[32]

Coinage also supports the hypothesis of an uninterrupted tax system, despite changes in the amount, frequency, and type of taxes that may have been collected. In addition to the continuous circulation of imperial coins, both Suevic and Visigothic kings issued gold coinage, first as imitations of the imperial issues and, from Leovigild onward, as original pieces under the name of the reigning monarch.[33] Post-Roman kings primarily issued gold coins (*tremisses*, fractions of late Roman *solidi*), which were used for large transactions (tax and penalty payments and royal expenses).[34] This was not a commercial coinage intended for everyday transactions, although it could be used for those purposes—especially for supraregional trade and elite consumption.[35] The constant issuing of gold coins and the relative stability of its metallic content indicates (as imperial *solidi* still circulated) the presence of a state in need of paying large sums of money and the corresponding collection of revenue in gold by that same state.

In sum, taxation did not disappear in the Iberian Peninsula after the withdrawal of the imperial administration. The amounts paid in taxes, the number of lands subject to tax, and the types of payment may have varied once the unifying presence of the late Roman Empire disappeared. The piecemeal and regional or even local agreements between barbarian armies and Western Iberian communities could have undermined the earlier tendency toward relative uniformity. But behind these variations we encounter fiscal islands that operated on similar structural principles to those of the late empire. Taxes were assessed over lands and in kind, they could be commuted to coin, and there was an administrative infrastructure in charge of tax collection, whose basic unit was found at the city level. The proportion of taxes in state income declined over time, but that process may have been slow, with occasional peaks of taxation such as during the late sixth century.

*   *   *

If a tax system continued during the post-Roman period, we may wonder if there was a relationship between the collection of taxes and landowning structures—that is, if landowners were responsible for the collection of the taxes of their tenants and other small landholders close to their estates. Information for the post-Roman period is scantier than for the late Roman period—largely owing to the thinner archaeological evidence. However, late sixth- and seventh-century documents offer a view from the end point. If analyzed cautiously, this information can be used to reconstruct the silent fifth and early sixth centuries, given that I have argued for a minimum level of continuity between the post-Roman and the Visigothic periods in terms of tax collection administration.

The Visigothic slates offer some support to the idea of large properties as centers of tax collection, although the reconstruction of this practice is somewhat indirect. A considerable number of these sixth- and seventh-century documents contains lists of products or quantities of grain. Some slates are plainly lists of people and dry measures.[36] In other cases, the actual product that is received or paid is not even mentioned. A slate from seventh-century Pelayos (Salamanca) refers to the reception of goods from different hilltop sites (*castra*).[37] Others describe payments from what are presumably land units (*cussus*).[38] When the product is mentioned, the slates also list products other than grain or dry measures. One surviving slate lists a series of textiles, very likely payments of some sort, and another slate lists what seems to be a distribution of cheese (as a result of centralized production with milk contributed by different households?).³⁹ There is an even more mysterious set of slates that only lists numbers, which likely indicates an unknown accounting practice (payments, distribution, and so on).⁴⁰

These documents have received various interpretations, sometimes being treated as estate accounts (primarily listing rent payments), sometimes as tax registers.⁴¹ Both interpretations are based on contextual evidence since the internal information does not lend absolute support to either theory (although there are some slates that make reference to taxes).⁴² Perhaps the apparent tensions between taxes and rent in the Visigothic slates would be resolved if we placed them within long-term managerial traditions, under which large estates collected rents and also taxes. The *PV 5*, a slate that could date from the sixth or seventh century, offers perhaps the sole example in which this late Roman tradition is documented. This slate, from an unknown archaeological context in Paralejos de Solís (Salamanca), lists a series of names and, mostly, numbers of dry measures (in *modii* and *sestarii, sc. sextarii*). The names can be grouped in three categories: those in the nominative, who seem to be paying; those in the dative, to whom payments seem to be made; and one person, a certain John, who handled the largest amounts of *modii*:

[—] six s(extaria)
[—] and Simplicius, one modius
[—] Masetus, six sextaria
[—] gave ropes for one modius
[—] and Sigerius and Iustina, one modius
[—] Precurasor, three modii
[—] (. . .)deo, eight modii
[—] John [—(took?)] sixty modii for the services (*in angarias*)
[—]ota twelve (modii?)
[—]
[—] adds for Sigerius to the modii from Lebaia
sixteen modii of sowing seeds, [—] modii of wheat
To Flascinus, two modii; to Flaina, six sextaria with [—]
her co-freedwomen. Flaina, one sextarium, Maxima, four sextaria
Manno, one modius, Procula, three sextaria, Bonus and Flamnus
and Nonnus the elder and Patricius, one modius
John took (or paid?) for the horses (*ad kaballos*)
thirty-three modii. Masetius two modii
In (?) Bodenecas, three modii⁴³

According to the reconstruction of the slate, John uses important amounts of grain for two purposes—to pay certain contributions (*in angarias*) and to buy or provide horses (*ad kaballos*). Although John might have been in charge of large purchases for the estate, it is more likely that he used those *modii* to pay taxes. Both *angariae* and *caballi* appear in Visigothic legal texts in reference to tributes demanded by the state. *Angariae* were compulsory services according to late Roman and Carolingian uses of the term.[44] *Caballi* could refer to dues for the maintenance of the road system (*cursus publicus*) or another type of tribute (perhaps a military tax). In the Visigothic Code, payment of *caballi* is associated with *curiales*, and, as seen in Chapter 2, *curiales* were in charge of the maintenance of the road system in their city's territory.[45] In the slate, the relationship between these two concepts and tax payments is further reinforced by the fact they represent by far the larger amount of grain in circulation, undertaken by the same person.

I believe there is reasonable support to understand the lines about John as a description of tax payments from an estate (with John acting in a managerial position) or to an estate (with John being a landowner who is paying his taxes through the estate). But this odd list of "payments to" and "payments from" does not resemble a tax register. For instance, why would small payments to other people be registered? Or why would a tax collector annotate small payments to various characters? Moreover, an unknown character is registered as not only paying grain but also sowing seeds (*semertura*, sc. *sementura*), which more likely refers to the repayment of a seed loan rather than the payment of a tax demand. Furthermore, the *sextaria* may refer to the payment of olive oil rather than grain.[46] We can solve these problems if we look at this slate as an accounting sheet from an estate in which rents are collected, expenses documented, and taxes paid. The document is silent on the identity of payers of smaller amounts of grain: these could be tenants paying rent or submitting taxes to a landowner so that he can, in turn, pay their taxes; or both. Be that as it may, the more likely reconstruction of this register lies in an account of the grain that enters and exits the estate's granaries. We can thus reconcile the tax and rent theories pertaining to the Visigothic slates: in the late sixth- or seventh-century territory of Salamanca, tax and rent were part of the same managerial world.

It should come as no surprise, then, that royal estates' overseers (*vilici*) were among those whom Reccared warned against collecting taxes for their own benefit.[47] The role of estate manager facilitated abuses in the tributary arena, as it might have been normal for a sixth-century peasant to pay his or her dues through a landowner or his or her representative. Landowners could manipulate the demands from the state in their own benefit as long as they could control, at the local level, the process of tax collection. The institutional framework described in the previous chapter (civic government of officeholders and landowners, landowners' assemblies, and other types of local leadership) had not only social but also fundamental economic consequences—such as oversight of the tax collection process. The reigns of Leovigild and Reccared did not represent a departure in the fundamental structures of taxation but rather a reordering of previous practices. Like in the late Roman period, taxation and private landownership were not in conflict but overlapped in the interests of both state administration and landowners' ascendancy in the countryside.

It is less likely, however, that taxation had the same impact on the economic strategies of the landowning elite as it did during the late empire. The less uniform tax system of the post-Roman world encouraged multiple economic strategies as opposed to the relatively uniform impact of the late Roman state demands in the fourth century. The adaptation of rural production and the maintenance or abandonment (partial or total) of late Roman models of economic units near residential villas could reflect an adaptation to the changing supralocal demands. In a context of uncertainty and rapidly changing statehood in the post-Roman period, landowners could show more flexibility in their managerial conduct without risking an economic reprisal from the state. Let us then turn our attention to the economic and managerial developments of the post-Roman world.

Production, Labor, and Management in Post-Roman Large Properties

Wealth remained, in the post-Roman period, landed wealth. Imperial salaries disappeared during the first half of the fifth century as a potential source of income. Barbarian royal patronage may have provided other sources of income. Kings granted gifts, but whenever these are mentioned in documents, they tend to be landed gifts, such as the *locum fisci* given by Leovigild to the abbot Nanctus in the second half of the sixth century.[48] By the late sixth century, royal officials received some kind of payment. Reccared's law prohibiting illegal tax demands reminded royal officials and administrators of royal properties that the king provided them with "income from our fiscal resources" (*nostra largitate . . . compendia ministramus*).[49] We cannot determine whether the practice was new. The law prohibited officials from demanding taxes for their own benefit, which suggests that at least some of them did so. It is not hard to imagine that in the spirit of administrative reform adopted during the reign of Reccared, the king was trying to reorganize an earlier practice of royal officials receiving salaries or rewards based on tax income. However, as was the case during the late Roman period, state-granted income and lands only constituted a portion of aristocratic wealth, which otherwise remained profoundly landed wealth.

Within *fundi* and other rural exploitations, the prevailing economic activities did not differ from the late Roman period. Mediterranean-type agriculture and animal farming persisted during the fifth and sixth centuries. There is little evidence of drastic changes, such as a putative increasing weight of husbandry vis-à-vis agriculture. Archaeological findings reveal minute differences that become noticeable at the microregional level and reflect a wide range of production practices. In northern Galicia, almost halfway between inland Lugo and the coastal villa of Bares, the microregion of the interior Galician plateau fostered a mixed agricultural and pastoral economy. The study of the soils of As Pontes (Abadín, A Coruña) indicates that intensive cereal cultivation shaped the rural landscape between the fifth and the eighth century and would dominate the area until modern times.[50] In another area with comparable characteristics, the lower Bierzo, a similar process of agricultural expansion took place in a typically pastoral area.[51] In the Avilan Sierra de Gredos, the pine forest withdrew while olive trees expanded between the sixth and seventh century.[52] Pollen analysis from the area of La Armuña (Salamanca) shows a marked deforestation that unfolded in the post-Roman period, after the relative stability of the vegetation landscape during imperial times. These new lands became pasture areas although agricultural activity remained at its late Roman levels.[53] Also in Salamanca, a similar pattern of husbandry intensification after the fifth century was detected in La Genestosa.[54] Deforestation also occurred in central Lusitania, near Mérida. The pollen analysis of the Proserpina reservoir (built in Roman times to supply the Roman colony with water) indicates that deforestation occurred between the years 500 and 900. Although this forest withdrawal may have been related to the lower temperatures of the early Middle Ages (and therefore, a greater consumption of wood for combustion), the clearance of new lands may also imply a process similar to that which occurred in the post-Roman Salamanca area—that is, expansion of cattle raising.[55] Animal farming may have also intensified in small valleys in Asturias, although this conclusion is based on hilltop occupation. But Roman-period cultivation of walnut and chestnut trees expanded.[56] In general, the post-Roman period was not characterized by a regression to a pastoral economy. If anything, various strategies developed to adapt to highly localized circumstances. The development of different microregional economic trends (rather than one specific trajectory for the whole of Atlantic Iberia) distinguishes the post-Roman economy in the region.

*   *   *

There were different types of labor relationships in the countryside. The overall picture reveals a rural world of rent-paying tenancies worked by laborers of different social statuses and with varying contractual arrangements but similar economic conditions. Whether this situation was new to the post-Roman period or represents a carryover from late (or even early) imperial times is impossible to confirm. Yet it is consistent with other trends in the post-Roman West, including areas in which large properties are well attested to.[57]

The social status of these laborers was never uniform, ranging from free to slave. Slight differences in fifth-century funerary deposits may indicate status distinctions within peasant communities, although it is impossible to attach material culture to specific social statuses.[58] There is an almost obsessive insistence on slavery in legal documents from the seventh century. Slaves and freedmen are ubiquitous in Visigothic legislation, while free peasants and the late Roman category of *colonus* are never mentioned (other than under the generic category of free people).[59] The overwhelming presence of slaves in legislation is sometimes seen as an indicator of slavery becoming the dominant rural relationship into the Middle Ages.[60] However, royal edicts may have been more concerned with marking a clear social line than describing rural workers' status. The previous chapter noted that in the absence of legally sanctioned social orders, as there was during the late empire, freedom and the lack thereof became the main legal social markers. The emphasis on slavery in legal codes may have been a response to shifting social representations in the post-Roman period rather than a growing importance of slavery for the Iberian population.

What disappeared from legislation was not necessarily free peasantry but its tributary denomination as *coloni*. This deletion is not surprising, given how little Visigothic laws concerned themselves with taxation in comparison with the imperial codes. Post-Roman mentions of *coloni* appear in the so-called *Testament of Vincent* and a Visigothic formulary. The first document, an early sixth-century donation from a deacon to a monastery of Asán in the upper Ebro Valley, refers to properties, which included *coloni* and slaves, as clearly distinct social categories.[61] In the same document, Vincent mentioned a landed holding as a *colonica*, which was worked by a slave whom he manumitted.[62] It is likely that the term made reference to a tenant with some form of attachment to the land but who was certainly of free status. This impression is reinforced by the second document that refers to this category, a seventh-century Visigothic *formula*, which records a model lease contract in which the tenant agrees to pay an annual rent "as it is customary with *coloni*."[63] The term, in the post-Roman context, maintains the idea of a free rural, rent-paying worker, with some association with a particular land, as was the case with some categories of late Roman *coloni*. However, the relationship between *coloni* and taxes vanishes in post-Roman sources.

In the management of large estates, landowners may have had a more status-blind attitude than the stark language of the *Leges Visigothorum* portrays. Indeed, Visigothic laws offer profuse evidence of slaves with their own *peculium* (goods possessed by a slave), which could include land or goods related to rural production.[64] By the time the code was assembled under Recceswinth and Chindaswinth in the mid-seventh century, slaves with *peculium* may have hardly differed from tenant holders in economic terms, although they clearly did in terms of status.[65] Perhaps their situation did not significantly differ from the freedmen's, whose obligations to their former owners were also inherited by their descendants.[66] In practical terms, a world of ambiguous servility may have taken contractual forms, as suggested by the study of a sixth- or seventh-century Visigothic *formula*, in which a person voluntarily surrendered his status to a *dominus* in exchange for an amount of money and other unspecified benefits, but without necessarily becoming a slave.[67] Both free, allodial peasantry and chattel slavery probably existed, but in between these two categories there were myriad legal and informal arrangements. Free peasants subordinated through tenancies and patronage relationships coexisted with slaves who were treated almost like independent tenants. Varying restrictions on individual freedom operated in labor relationships to create a situation of generalized servility, though not generalized slavery.[68] Landowners did not limit their labor force to one single legal or economic category. Small variations from property to property are likely to have characterized the post-Roman countryside.[69]

*   *   *

These variations can also be found in the way in which *fundi* were managed. In the late Roman world, we noticed the archaeological prevalence of one particular mode of land exploitation: the production unit with centralized facilities for storage and distribution. We also saw that wine and olive oil production were associated with estate centers and implied a significant level of investment. Storage areas and other production activities were also part of centralized estate infrastructure. Rent-paying tenants of different legal status were likely responsible for production, although there may have been a certain level of direct management for specific crops (most likely for wine). This was not the only managerial model in the late Roman period, but it was an important one, as far as can be reconstructed from the always-problematic archaeological evidence. After the early fifth century, this pattern seems to break down, and various types of managerial models become visible in both archaeological and written evidence.

Direct exploitation and the centralization of resources continued in certain cases. Occasionally, production quarters in some former villas remained in use after the fifth century. There were marked regional variations, however. In the plateau, where late Roman infrastructure investments are less visible than in Lusitania, new investments in facilities became even rarer after 450. The rural quarters of late Roman villas may have continued to be active in some cases, such as the production areas of the villa of Navatejera. A fifth-century reform in the *pars rustica*, involving the construction of a brick oven, may bear witness to the tenacity of late Roman models after the fifth century in very specific contexts.[70] The excavated houses at the hilltop site of La Cabeza de Navansangil very likely hosted granaries.[71] Written sources corroborate the persistence of central management and accounting in the plateau. A sixth- or seventh-century slate from Diego Álvaro, near Ávila, records a list of payments by a certain Simplicius. Among other payments, Simplicius gave a cow to one Matratius.[72] The animal was said to have calved in the *curtis* of Simplicius's lord, Valentinus, a possible reference to central buildings within a large estate.[73] Further north, on the western edge of the plateau, the father of (the future saint) Fructuosus requested accounts of his flocks from his shepherds.[74] These records may have looked like a sixth- or seventh-century slate from Diego Álvaro in the meseta, in which horses and bovines are listed.[75] Although no centralized infrastructure is mentioned, both documents show the interest of the landed elite in managing animal farming.

The region of central and southern Lusitania also presents a mixed panorama of abandonment and continuity of late Roman economic strategies. While some centralized facilities in this region witnessed a rapid transformation, others continued with their production activities almost unaltered during the fifth and sixth centuries. Wine production in São Cucufate ceased by the mid-fifth century in parallel to other transformations affecting the residential villa.[76] But wine production at Torre Águila may have continued throughout the Visigothic period.[77] The fish factory of Cerro da Vila may have continued production throughout the fifth and sixth centuries, although the end date of that facility is not completely clear.[78] Olive oil production is attested or suggested at individual villa sites, such as Milreu or La Cocosa, into the sixth century.[79] A slate found in El Barrado (Cáceres) dating from the late sixth or early seventh century, mentions two individuals concerned with the collection and storage of olives, which was, apparently, a delicate issue: "Faustinus to lord Paulus: I greet your [dignity?] and beg you, lord, that you gather the olives yourself as it is customary. You must make sure that the slaves collect [the olives] under oath so that they do not commit fraud against you. Collect the barrels, the pieces of bark, and seal [the barrels] with your ring. Also check that the covers, which have been fastened with a buckle, [are] just as I put them down."[80] Excavations in coastal villas of northwestern Iberia show a similar continuity, although there are fewer *partes rusticae* excavated in this region and continuity is assumed based on residential occupation of mansions, such as the coastal villa of Viveiro (Lugo).[81] Some fish industries survived to the fifth and even sixth century.[82] Other facilities, such as the salt-decanting pools of Toralla, may not have outlived the mid-fifth century.[83] But, as Chapter 3 argued, there are fewer signs here, at least archaeologically, of the model of estate management with centralized storage and distribution facilities than in the rest of Western Iberia. This model remained an option during the fifth and sixth centuries, and certain landowners followed it. Overall, in terms of managerial patterns, the three regions show a mix of continuity and abandonment compared to the late Roman period.

Other managerial practices, however, become more visible after the fifth century. Post-Roman villages and farms are particularly interesting because they open a window onto the world of peasant production in individual households.

At Gózquez (in the southern plateau), for instance, only one building with a complex layout may have had centralized functions, especially because it housed a press, possibly an oil press. Even in this case, it is not clear whether the house belonged to an administrator of the village or a family of higher status and wealth, or both. Moreover, the dimensions and material structures of the press are humble in comparison to the oil facilities of fourth-century Lusitanian units.[84] A small settlement of El Cuquero (Salamanca) was newly occupied in the sixth century. It offers evidence of olive oil production similar to sites in that microregion.[85] But we should not take this, as it were, devolution of olive oil production to small units as a sign of autonomous production. A fragment of slate from Ávila dating from the first half of the seventh century shows that olives as well as wheat were used as a means of payment, very likely for rents.[86]

Post-Roman villages and peasant farms show modest storage infrastructure. At the site of Vega de Duego (Valladolid), two holes (silos?) were excavated in what seems to be a marginal zone comprising residential areas but without any sign of monumentalization. The site has been dated to the second half of the fifth century.[87] Excavations in Galicia show similar family storage structures in villages and farms. Most of these sites date to the high Middle Ages, although it is increasingly accepted that in many cases they originated in the fifth or sixth century.[88] Although silos may have had considerable capacity, they never matched the late Roman storage infrastructure associated with rural villas.[89]

The post-Roman evidence therefore shows signs of other alternatives, in which production, storage, and perhaps distribution were dispersed among peasant households. This model did not conflict with the existence of large properties: it was particularly suited to rent-paying tenancies. The recently discovered numeral slates at the site of La Genestosa, in a clearly peasant context, seem to indicate a connection between peasant units and great landholding structures.[90] Moreover, the model presented here did exist during the late Roman period, although it was archaeologically visible in only a few settlements. In the post-Roman period, this trend gains archaeological visibility thanks to new construction techniques in peasant housing and changes in burial practices. For instance, farmyards at La Dehesa del Cañal (Pelayos, Salamanca) only became visible thanks to the peasant structures associated with the site.[91] The common wall for protection of animals at La Mata del Palomar (Segovia) was found in association with twenty-two sunken structures, some of them with postholes.[92] The archaeological visibility pattern of post-Roman farms and villages may distort the importance of post-Roman peasant household production in the same way that the proximity of production quarters to late Roman villas increases the visibility of a strategy that might have otherwise gone unnoticed. While both strategies existed in both periods, however, I believe there is a noticeable shift in their relative importance after the fifth century. The archaeological information merely (but meaningfully) reveals change in the material culture associated with economic strategies of large landownership in a context of shifting regional and supraregional trends. In some cases, landowners may have contented themselves with collecting rents in cash or kind. The centralization of cereal and animals continued in the post-Roman period (and later) while cash crops such as wine and oil became increasingly less associated with large infrastructural units. In other cases, the late Roman managerial model remained unaltered for decades but with fewer investments. Finally, in yet other cases, more interventionist measures were implemented, but they involved a greater interest in smaller-scale and less monumentalized settlements. The devolution of production to smaller-scale units (for instance, smaller oil installations) may indicate microspecializations within large properties. For instance, the different farmyards associated with each peasant household at La Dehesa del Cañal may be a sign of a small peasant agglomeration microspecializing in animal farming to take advantage of nearby pastures.[93] We must not forget the fragmented nature of large properties. In landscapes such as the northern plateau or northwestern Iberia, each *fundus* had access to lands with different productive capacities. If the information from the Ebro Valley can be extrapolated to the rest of northern Iberia, large properties were divided into smaller, noncontiguous units with access to different ecological niches.[94] Large-scale specialization made less economic sense in a context of declining tributary and state-sponsored transportation infrastructure. In purely economic terms, diversifying production or cash rents were more suitable to the post-Roman context.

The evidence of post-Roman production and management shows a combination of relative continuity with the late Roman period and very localized changes. This description is consistent with the evolution of taxation and landowning structures I described in the first part of this chapter, where a mix of continuity and minor change can be traced (or, in some cases, hypothesized). The slow dissolution of late Roman tax structures encouraged the development of different managerial strategies after the fifth century. Yet precisely because of the slow pace at which the tax system faded, the transformation of estate administration is only visible in the long run—by the seventh century, when most centralized facilities were no longer in use. Before addressing these changes in full, we must pay attention to changes in distribution patterns, which seem to indicate very similar trends.

Localized Exchanges and Post-Roman Distribution Networks

Chapter 3 argued that Mediterranean-wide exchanges, as evinced mainly by African fine wares and amphorae, were an important aspect of commercial life in late Roman Western Iberia. However, I also posited that the impact of long-distance trade was less marked than it had been during the early empire. In the post-Roman period, foreign merchants still engaged in commerce with the Atlantic Iberian regions. The *Lives of the Fathers of Mérida* mentions Greek merchants during the episcopate of bishop Paul (around the mid-sixth century) in an episode meant to legitimate the choice of his successor, Fidelis. Paul, being "a Greek," received a group of traders from his own region in the Eastern Mediterrnean. These traders sent a present to the bishop in the hands of a boy they had hired. The youth, Fidelis by name, turned out to be Paul's nephew and would later become his successor in the see of Mérida.[95] Regardless of the veracity of the story, the seventh-century writer of the *Lives* assumed a certain familiarity by his readers with eastern Mediterranean merchants. While this vignette may suggest long-distance trade between central Lusitania and the Mediterranean world, only archaeology has been able to flesh out the evolution, intensity, and reach of these commercial exchanges. As the anecdote in the *Lives* implies, regional and supraregional markets did not disappear during the fifth century. The existence of these networks experienced changes that involved, in some cases, a drastic reduction of their volume and reach, at least in terms of archaeologically visible items. Meanwhile, other regional networks emerged at full strength during the fifth century. Overall, however, if we judge from pottery evidence, regional and supraregional networks receded in intensity in post-Roman Atlantic Iberia.

The first significant trend is the disappearance of the Terra Sigillata Hispanica Tardía distribution network by the end of the fifth century, if not earlier.[96] Chapter 3 showed that the distribution patterns of these ceramics reveal regional and supraregional exchanges in the interior areas of the peninsula during the late Roman period. It is difficult to determine whether circulation ceased as a result of declining production or vice versa. Pinpointing the end date of TSHT production is extremely difficult (possible dates range from the mid-fifth century to the turn of the sixth century).[97] Be that as it may, regional distribution of TSHT declined in the course of the fifth century in Atlantic Iberia, even though, according to the standard chronology, production in Riojan kilns may have lasted until the early sixth century.[98] The northern meseta and the Cantabrian Basin, however, did not remain isolated from regional exchanges. Since the early decades of the fifth century, a new, pan-Atlantic commercial network became noticeable through fine wares produced in southern Gaul known as *dérivée de sigillée paléochrétienne grise* (DSP). In particular, the lands of Atlantic Iberia received fine wares from Aquitainian workshops (the so-called Atlantic productions).[99] Its distribution followed a Bay of Biscay circuit that comprised Aquitaine, the upper Ebro Valley, and the Cantabrian Basin. Like the TSHT findings, DSP findings indicate that these Gallic wares reached cities, secondary settlements, and rural areas. Fragments of DSP were widely distributed not only along Cantabrian ports, such as Gijón or Cape Higuer (Guipúzcoa), but also in the interior of the peninsula, in cities like Clunia or villages like El Cañal de Las Hoyas (Pelayos, Salamanca).[100] A few fragments are even attested in southern Lusitanian cities.[101] Yet DSP wares never matched the impressive number of TSHT wares. The few findings in northwestern Iberia and the meseta in general contrast with the large number of DSP findings in eastern Iberia, which may cast doubt on the intensity of the Bay of Biscay circuit during the post-Roman period.[102]

The pan-Mediterranean network, which had supplied coastal Iberia in the late Roman period with imported wares and amphorae (predominantly African), continued to do so after the fifth century but with some significant changes. Mediterranean imports still reached coastal Lusitania and some specific enclaves in Gallaecia during the fifth and sixth centuries. Although African goods, and especially African Red Slip wares, never ceased flowing into the Iberian ports, their number steadily dwindled after the end of the fifth century. Conversely, Levantine wine amphorae and sigillatas from the Aegean region appeared in increasing quantities during the late fifth century and into the early seventh century. Atlantic Iberia received and exchanged these products in the same ports of entry that had sheltered cargoes containing African and other Mediterranean products during the late Roman period. Eastern amphorae and fine wares become visible in fifth- and sixth-century strata in such cities as Braga, Lisbon, and Gijón.[103] Eastern ceramics and containers occasionally reached inland rural sites, although in very limited quantities.[104]

The relative replacement of African products by eastern ones does not imply two different commercial networks. On the contrary, the presence of African and eastern goods reveals that the ancient Mediterranean commercial routes still connected Western Iberia to the core of the Greco-Roman world. Mixed cargoes of African and eastern products very likely reached coastal Lusitania and Gallaecia in ways similar to those found in the Loire region and the British Isles.[105] Yet, as in the case of the Bay of Biscay network, the number and variety of Mediterranean products drastically declined after the fifth century, even when we consider a possible sixth-century revival. The number of these products never matched those of fourth- and fifth-century African origin, and their distribution remained ever more limited to the coastal areas. If we were to judge only from the ceramic evidence, Mediterranean commerce saw a steady decline into the seventh century, in the same way that regional and supraregional networks lessened in northern Iberia.

The "end of the empire" cannot by itself explain the evolution of the commercial relationships between Atlantic Iberia and the Mediterranean world. A comparison between Atlantic and Mediterranean Iberia shows that the latter witnessed a considerable intensification of the commerce of African products after the mid-fifth century, coinciding with the Vandal conquest of Africa.[106] The increase in commercial exchanges with Africa was probably the result of the liberation of surpluses previously destined for the commercial and tributary distribution between Carthage and Rome. Once the Vandals took over the fertile lands of North Africa, the surplus generated within that territory was able to circulate independently from the requests of the Roman state.[107] In any event, these products never reached Atlantic Iberia with the same intensity as they did the Mediterranean ports of the peninsula.

* * *

We must not think that the fading of supraregional networks means a reversion to a natural economy without exchanges. The evidence from the Visigothic slates, to mention one example, convinces us to the contrary. Local markets, including rural markets and secondary settlements, were the natural places to sell production in order to meet rent or tax demands whenever it had to be paid in coin, as in the payments recorded in a slate from Diego Álvaro.[108] There is increasing evidence for means of transaction (coinage) that could support local markets, as we have become aware of the different kinds of coins used in the post-Roman period. The fifth- and sixth-century Iberian economy was not demonetized. In addition to the uninterrupted use of late imperial coins, cities like Conimbriga and Clunia, or even rural sites like La Olmeda, have provided evidence of post-Roman imitations of late Roman coins. Mérida may have issued its own bronze coinage before the seventh century in the same way as several cities did in Mediterranean Iberia.[109] Credit may have taken new forms, including loans from the local churches. Bishop Masona of Mérida is said to have established a fund of two thousand *solidi* to support the poor, although we do not know what these loans were used for.[110]

Iberian archaeology is on its way to providing us with a more refined analysis of common wares, an invaluable source of information of local exchange networks. These ceramics, of more local distribution, have been particularly useful to trace the distribution network and reach of local exchanges. As in the case of fine wares, it is assumed that other goods were transported with common wares, hence their importance to detect local markets. Common wares were used for transportation within relatively short distances, as with the vessels bishop Masona used to distribute wine, oil, and honey after crushing the smaller containers (*vasa parvula*) with which the poor came to ask for food alms.[111]

Common wares differed from fine wares in various aspects, chiefly among them their production techniques, including lower cooking temperatures and less sophisticated kiln ventilation.[112] Stylistically speaking, there were two typical common wares after the fifth century. The most refined of these ceramics, sometimes referred to as "imitation of sigillatas", may have been produced in specialized workshops. While their production techniques were not as sophisticated as those used in the Roman fine wares, they maintained a certain degree of quality, scale of production, and similarity in forms that assimilated them to their more glorious predecessors (and certain fifth-century contemporary productions).[113] The second common ware tradition was also rooted in the Roman past and included cooking and kitchen wares produced with less refined techniques. Different ceramic styles coexisted during the post-Roman period. For instance, in the Mérida region, two types of common wares circulated and were of a different quality and degree of standardization.[114] Throughout the peninsula, however, different ceramic traditions had merged by the end of the sixth century and the beginning of the seventh century into what some scholars have called the Visigothic ceramic tradition.[115]

Common wares were not a novelty in the post-Roman period. Their presence in the late Roman period is somewhat overshadowed by the scholarly interest in fine wares. However, even elite residential mansions could have predominantly relied on common vessels on their dining tables.[116] There was no abrupt break between late and post-Roman traditions of common ceramics but rather gradual and piecemeal changes in style and functionality into the seventh century. What marks the difference between late and post-Roman common wares is the relative importance that the latter attained in the reconstruction of distribution networks.

The distribution of common wares, particularly those of sigillata imitations, shows that their circulation was limited to the territory of a city or a secondary (usually hilltop) settlement. If we can generalize the processes in the province of Segovia to the rest of the region, ceramics in the plateau followed this pattern of central production. The local imitations of TSHT are found almost exclusively in cities and *castra*, although the kilns have not yet been found. A sample of grey ceramics from Astorga imitating contemporary Gallic wares may have been produced in the city or within the region but not in supraregional centers.[117] The reach of local productions could also be quite narrow. The case of Asturian imitation ceramics shows highly diversified types of wares produced within a small territory, as the ceramics from Gijón differed from those found about thirty kilometers south in the nearby area of modern Oviedo.[118]

The distribution of common ceramics reached cities and rural areas alike. The integration of ceramic distribution in city and country would slowly fade away in some areas, but not until the seventh century.[119] In some cases, cities could have been the epicenter of common ware distribution owing to the urban character of ceramic production. In northwestern Iberia, Braga and Lugo produced imitations of DSP starting in the fifth century, and the same clays were used in the production of common wares of lower quality.[120] Conimbriga also had its own particular evolution of locally produced common wares, with a similar pattern.[121] In the case of the plateau, however, there is no clear evidence concerning where common ceramics were produced in cities, since there is little evidence of kilns so far. Where we do have firm evidence of ceramic production, kilns are found in markedly rural settlements, such as the site of La Carrera II (Soto de Cerrato, Palencia).[122] But the uniformity of distribution of certain common ceramics reveals the integration of rural areas with cities and hilltop fortified sites. Thus, although the horizons of distribution networks shrank after the fifth century, common wares offer evidence of the infrastructure of exchange networks at the local level during the post-Roman period.

*   *   *

The transition from regional and supraregional networks evinced by fine wares to local circuits of exchanges verified by common wares was not always sudden. The post-Roman ceramic traditions show that the transition between a combination of regional and local networks to a predominantly local distribution had many regional variations. Chronology within the post-Roman world indicates that this transition happened in two steps. During the fifth century, certain common wares circulated in networks that surpassed the local level. Formal similarities and, more important, shared production techniques of certain imitation ceramics make us wonder to what extent these networks demonstrated the presence of commercial ties between different localities. The burnished common wares from the meseta are a good example of this fifth-century development. While the larger number of sites and pieces of this production has been found in the province of Segovia, it was widely distributed in other sites of the meseta, mostly in its western localities. Surprisingly, these burnished common wares may have reached the coasts and valleys of Asturias in significant quantities as well as specific sites in the southern meseta and a handful of northern Lusitanian cities.[123] Imitation ceramics in the upper Ebro Valley also show a striking resemblance to those of Segovia and the western plateau.[124] Other common wares that imitated late Roman sigillatas tend to corroborate the idea of locally produced imitation wares but with possible supralocal distribution, even when their classification remains problematic.[125]

The sixth century, and especially its second half, witnessed a considerable retraction of supralocal networks. This regression mirrors in its chronology the fading presence of extraregional fine wares, whether of African, eastern Mediterranean, or Gallic origins. In part, the end of sigillata imitations resulted from changes in the production sphere, with an increasing presence of domestically manufactured ceramics. At the same time, the overall evolution of post-Roman ceramics tended toward the merging of cooking wares, table wares, and storage ceramics, which simplified previously compartmentalized ceramics, a process well documented in the northern plateau.[126] Whereas domestic production may indicate a retraction to a household economy (which nevertheless existed during the late Roman period), archaeologists have been able to identify different types of ceramics, some of which followed better production techniques. These ceramics still incorporated a minimum of standardization and the use of skilled labor, indicating an orientation toward exchanges.[127]

A natural economy exempt from exchanges did not replace the commercial networks of the late Roman period. Rather, surpluses were commercialized more locally. What undermined the late Roman model of economic units with infrastructural investments in centralized facilities was not therefore a change from a market-oriented economy to a natural, intra-household consumption economy. Both coexisted during the late and post-Roman periods. Rather, the more localized demand encouraged a less marked specialization in a few food staples. The buoyant countryside of the fifth and sixth centuries strengthens this argument, as local economies went through different reorientations to adapt to the new circumstances. The archaeological fading of late Roman economic strategies not only mirrors more localized (and slowly declining) tributary practices but also shrinking distribution networks. We have seen that this shrinkage had begun in the late Roman period, as regional networks prevailed over supraregional distribution patterns (especially in comparison to the early empire). The post-Roman period witnessed a further downsizing of these commercial horizons from the regional to the local. The downsizing was never abrupt and varied considerably from region to region—but it did happen.

It is hard to pin down a single cause for this downsizing. It can most likely be attributed to a multiplicity of factors. Political instability may have played a role, since producing for distant markets (even regional ones) posed serious risks in the fifth century. Taxation revenue was now being consumed more locally than in the late Roman period. The more local consumption of taxes deprived market exchanges of the powerful infrastructural support on which the late imperial movement of tributes relied. The end of Roman military garrisons along the Braga–Zaragoza axis can explain why the distribution of TSHT faded during the fifth century. Lacking a military supply route along which it could be distributed, the transaction costs involved in its circulation increased, and thus other alternatives (imitations) became more attractive. Furthermore, the declining impact of taxation may have taken part of the agricultural production out of the commercial networks from where taxpayers could obtain cash to pay taxes. All these factors must have contributed to the growing importance and archaeological visibility of local exchanges. Be that as it may, the evidence supports not so much the idea of a reversion to a natural economy as the growing importance of local exchanges and the distribution of rural production. As in the case of taxation and changes in managerial strategies, the transformation was not abrupt, and it is only visible over the course of several decades, and even centuries.

The Slow Withdrawal of the Tax World

The structure of the post-Roman rural economy did not change significantly compared to the late Roman period. Its production basis also remained similar to that of the late empire. Although in specific instances there may have been an expansion in husbandry, there were also microregions in which agriculture expanded after the fifth century. Microregions differed in the relative weight of different types of production without there necessarily being an overarching trend. There was no norm, unless it was highly localized variation itself. Western Iberia did not become a pastoral economy. Nor did it show signs of rural stagnation or decline. Quite to the contrary, the post-Roman countryside was a buoyant world where social actors were noticeable through discrete microinterventions, such as by clearing land, terracing buildings, occupying new spaces, and, to be sure, abandoning previously occupied areas. Material culture did change, but, again, the change unfolded over the course of two or three centuries. Some of the transformations we observe had actually begun in the late Roman period, such as peasant occupation of hilltops in northwestern Iberia or the declining impact of supraregional exchanges. Nevertheless, it is possible there may have been a simplification or an impoverishment of the economy, or an economic contraction, although this cannot be deduced with certainty from the information collected in the previous pages. It would also be challenging to find a single specific moment to blame for this process of change. The economic basis for rural production moved at a slow tempo as a result of a myriad of secular and natural trends impossible to reconstruct with the extant evidence.

The barbarian settlement did have an impact on Western Iberia, and we saw ample evidence of this in Chapter 5. However, it is less clear that it had an immediate bearing on the economic strategies of landowning elites. Perhaps the scale of exchanges decreased more quickly because of the more localized consumption of taxes. The gradual decline of supraregional and regional exchanges actually supports the idea that the overall impact of taxation decreased in the long run, but the process did not immediately result from barbarian settlement. Nor does the evidence suggest a massive destruction in rural production as a result of barbarian presence, contrary to the impression conveyed by late antique writers. Instead, the landowning aristocracy actively pursued its economic benefit by adapting to circumstances that varied from region to region, and even from microregion to microregion. We may assume that an indeterminate number of barbarians became landowners. They would have joined the ranks of the landowning aristocracy and adopted their managerial practices, and thus they would not have left any distinct archaeological signs of differentiated strategies.

More diverse and flexible managerial practices became visible after the fifth century. While centralized production, storage, and distribution facilities produced the main archaeological evidence before the fifth century, peasant economic units grew in visibility thereafter. There were different types of land management in both the late and the post-Roman periods. In this sense, we are not dealing with the introduction of new types of practices after the fifth century. But the changes in the material culture must mean something, even though we cannot draw quantitative conclusions based on the rather impressionistic picture conveyed by the evidence. The meaning of this change relates to the declining impact of taxation throughout the period. The centralization of production during the late Roman period was favored by the role of large properties in the tax collection process, a role that at least some of them retained into the seventh century. Fourth-century landowners had incentives to invest in relatively large-scale centralized infrastructure because they could also collect their tenants' and small holders' tax payments or become the ultimate buyers of small properties' production to allow their owners to pay their taxes. Moreover, the late Roman administration organized large-scale transportation infrastructure that could accommodate the distribution of private products. These conditions gradually disappeared in the fifth and sixth centuries. The declining amount of taxes and/or the declining number of lands subject to taxation reduced the incentives for landowners to maintain similar managerial practices.

We see relatively few signs of the peasantry's growing independence. The archaeological evidence regarding rural workers, especially in villages and farms, could be interpreted as indicating a self-assertive peasant population vis-à-vis the landowning aristocracy, but, as I argue in this chapter, it may also reflect the new economic strategies of large properties. Indeed, written sources convey an impression of peasantry dependence, within various degrees of servility. Landowners seem to have followed very flexible strategies in relation to rural workers, but the overall picture suggests similar economic forms of dependence and various legal statuses, such as slave, freedmen, or free status, or contractually defined servility. Overall, the Western Iberian evidence was not a golden age of the peasantry. This is not surprising since, as we saw in the previous chapter, landowning elites rapidly reconstructed state power at the local level during the fifth century. A power vacuum that would have encouraged a more economically independent peasantry never existed or, at most, was short-lived (with the possible exception of in the Cantabrian north). The evidence does not indicate a worsening of rural workers' conditions either. The social status of laborers may have changed, although we do not have firm evidence in that regard. But even so, a change in status would not necessarily entail a change in the peasant family's economic conditions.

Flexibility also characterized managerial strategies. At one extreme of the spectrum, there was some continuity within centralized facilities for the production, storage, and distribution of marketable products. This strategy is perhaps most noticeable in Lusitania in the fifth and, to a certain extent, the sixth centuries. At the other extreme, a pattern of rent-paying tenancies with minimum infrastructural intervention may have also existed (as it probably did in the late Roman period). In between, a mix of centralized administration and scattered family units with microspecializations could have been the norm. This type of management was better adapted to landscapes like the northern plateau or northwestern Iberia. The fragmentation of large properties created *fundi* with small units in different ecological niches—valleys, hills, mountains. With the decline of the incentives to centralize the production of a handful of food staples, large properties were able to rely on self-subsistent family units better able to exploit their ecological niches. This peasant economy existed within the context of large properties that still collected rents and, occasionally, taxes. At the same time, at least some owners of large properties were expected to participate in royal military enterprises or local self-defense initiatives with their own resources (including, in some cases, their own soldier-peasants).

In sum, change did occur after the fifth century. Yet rather than experiencing a drastic economic decay or productive reorientation, the evidence suggests that Western Iberian landowners adapted to the changing conditions while maintaining the basic parameters of the economic structure in terms of landholding. By the seventh century, the accumulated effects of two hundred years of discrete changes and experimentation brought about new economic strategies, with large properties following different managerial practices but generally oriented toward local markets. As in other areas of social life, the economy of large properties shows that Western Iberian aristocrats did not live the end of empire passively. Rather, they were active social agents who fought to preserve their position in a changing world. Judging from the evidence presented in this chapter, they did so successfully as a class.

Conclusion

I started this book by stating that its central theme would be statehood in late antique Western Iberia. While I touched upon aspects of institutional organization and state-sponsored ideological frameworks, my focus has been on how statehood operated in day-to-day social practices. I argued that it did so through the agency of a social class that I have called aristocracy. These individuals enacted an otherwise abstract state power through practices that entailed political domination over a particular territory within larger polities—the Roman Empire and the successor kingdoms, Suevic and Visigothic. The distinction between central and local powers is, therefore, more analytical than conceptual. Both central agents and local aristocracies enacted the same type of state power.

Indeed, one of the arguments I developed in the previous chapters insisted on the importance of state enactment for cementing elite social status. Aristocratic standing was not independent from the state, which was the case in two interrelated ways. First, aristocrats depended on the legal and coercive sanction that state institutions could provide to enforce their position—as classical theories of state emphasize. But aristocrats also depended on being perceived as the local face of the state to claim social standing. Their participation in crucial positions of power materialized their assertions of social status. Both in the late and post-Roman periods, individuals of power legitimized their standing based on various criteria (birth, rank, wealth), which could only be fully expressed once they achieved political preeminence. This was because state projects emphasized that the leading roles of political dominance belonged to those who fulfilled specific criteria of social distinction. The language of state-sanctioned discourse insisted that political authority belonged to the illustrious, prominent, most renowned, or distinguished, to mention a few epithets. Enacting state power rendered other forms of social power concrete. In other words, aristocrats could not exist as such outside of the state sphere while the state could not exist without individuals able to enact it. Thus, the distinction between central and local powers meets its limits as a hermeneutical tool.

The intimate relationship between aristocracy and statehood provides the social context to understand the changes in material culture. The archaeological record in general and monumental architecture in particular reveal two moments of change—one in the late third and early fourth centuries, the other in the central decades of the fifth century. While change was certainly slow and encompassed several regional variations, these two moments undeniably underwent a faster tempo of change. These transformations, I have argued, relate to the symbolic and political priorities of Atlantic Iberian aristocrats, who funded, commanded, or negotiated the construction of different types of buildings denoting settlement status. These buildings marked the ideological priorities of authoritative individuals as members of larger state projects— civic pride, elite sociability, family memory, military potency, Christian piety, among others. With the ebb and flow of state projects, those priorities shifted and were expressed in the different ways I explained. Perhaps the most important trend was the formation of uniform strategies of status display during the late Roman period and the more regionally fragmented practices of the post-Roman world. The late Roman state brought relative uniformity to dissimilar regions such as Lusitania, northwestern Iberia, and the northern plateau. The political and military circumstances of the fifth century allowed for more regionally distinct elite strategies.

Membership in aristocratic groups implied specific forms of consumption. The ability to gain access to such forms of consumption depended to a large extent on landed properties and, secondarily, on direct state income (salaries, gifts). Western Iberian aristocracies were a leading political group as much as they were a social class in economic terms. In the same way that these elites adapted culturally and politically to different state projects, landed aristocrats also took advantage of the different opportunities that state frameworks offered to pursue economic gain. Far from being a *rentier* class without interest in maximizing benefits from their economic units, landowners and, more likely, their estate managers adapted to the changing economic circumstances. The main two trends to which they adapted were, as I pointed out in this book, the varying impact of the tax system and the shift toward more regional and even local exchange networks. While both developments were related to each other, we must not underestimate the secular trends toward new distribution networks regardless of changes in the tax system.

In sum, this book shows the agency of aristocrats in the political, social, and economic spheres. I sought to provide internal explanations for change rather than merely seeing the region as a passive recipient of events beyond its reach. Late Roman elites adhered to the post-Diocletianic state project, but they did it with their own tone—carefully choosing which practices of other imperial elites to adopt, which resulted in an almost unique combination. Likewise, the transformations of the post-Roman world resulted less from the still-to-be-proven destructions of the fifth century or a barbarization of the Roman world than from the rapid adherence of aristocrats to the new world in the absence of empire.

Finally, I also stressed the extent to which the post-Roman world was rooted in the practices crafted during the late Roman period—in the same way late Roman practices never marked an abrupt rupture from the early Roman period. Structural conditionings (landscape, resources, family and communal traditions, and so on) acted as powerful forces that had to be reckoned with when state projects were implemented in the region. The post-Roman world was not a barbarian era, a moment during which earlier Roman practices were dissolved and replaced by non-Roman traditions. While change did happen, it took the form of an adaptation to new possibilities of state projects based on inherited practices that had proven successful in securing social dominance for generations. I believe this model provides a stronger conceptual framework than narratives in which the Roman world falls, to be followed by the rise of a new, so-called barbarian age in the Iberian Peninsula.

The first half of the seventh century witnessed the consolidation of a new state project under a Gothic monarchy with new religious overtones. This was still, in many ways, a Roman world. Yet it was not Roman because it looked back to a distant Roman past; rather, it was because the Visigothic state carefully watched the still living Roman world of the eastern Romans. To a certain extent, the post-Justinian Byzantine world was the bar against which Romanity was measured. A new notion of Gothic monarchy and the role of the Gothic people in Christian history provided the foundations for new types of legitimacy at a time when, paradoxically, ethnic differences were less clear than they had been a century or two earlier. The seventh century opened up opportunities for new aristocratic strategies, some of which were rooted in the late and post-Roman worlds, but others of which were the product of a new state project, which truly belonged to a new era.

ABBREVIATIONS

AE   *L'Année épigraphique: Revue des publications épigraphiques relatives à l'antiquité romaine.*

Amm. Mar.   [=Ammianus Marcellinus, *Res Gestae*] Seyfarth, Wolfgang. 1978. *Ammiani Marcellini rerum gestarum libri supersunt,* 2 vol. Leipzig: Teubner.

Brev. Al.   [=*Breviarium Alarici*] Haenel, Gustav. 1849. *Lex Romana Visigothorum.* Leipzig: Teubner.

CE   [=*Codex Euricianus*] Zeumer, Karl. 1902. *Leges Visigothorum,* Monumenta Germaniae Historica. Leges, vol. 1. Hanover: Inpensis Bibliopolii Hahniani, 3–27.

Chron.   [=Hydatius Lemicensis, *Chronica*] Burgess, Richard. 1993. *The Chronicle of Hydatius and the Consularia Constantinopolitana.* Oxford: Oxford University Press.

CIIAE   Ramírez Sádaba, José Luis. 2003. *Catálogo de las inscripciones imperiales de Augusta Emerita.* Mérida: Museo Nacional de Arte Romano.

CIL II   *Corpus inscriptionum Latinarum,* vol. 2, Inscriptiones Hispaniae Latinae. 1869. Berlin: G. Reimer.

CIL VI   *Corpus inscriptionum Latinarum,* vol. 6, Inscriptiones Urbis Romae Latinae. 1876. Berlin: G. Reimer.

CIL XVI   *Corpus inscriptionum Latinarum,* vol. 16/1, Miliaria Impreii Romani. Provinciarum Hispaniae et Brittaniae, Miliaria Provinciae Hispaniae Citerioris. 2015. Berlin: De Gruyter.

CIRG   Pereira Menaut, Gerardo. 1991. *Corpus de inscricións romanas de Galicia. I. Provincia de A Coruña.* Santiago de Compostela: Consello da Cultura Galega.

Coll. Hisp.   [=*Collectio Hispana*] Martínez Díez, Gonzalo, and Félix Rodríguez, eds. 1966–2002. *La colección canónica Hispana,* 6 vol. Madrid: CSIC.

Cons. Caes.   [=*Consularia Caesaraugustana*] Cardelle de Hartmann, Carmen, and Roger Collins, eds. 2001. *Victoris Tunnunensis Chronicon: Cum reliquis ex consularibus Caesaraugustanis et Iohannis Biclarensis Chronicon,* Corpus Christianorum Series Latina, vol. 173A, 1–55. Turnhout: Brepols.

CTh.   [=*Codex Theodosianus*] Mommsen, Theodor, and Paulus M. Meyer. 1905. *Theodosiani Libri XVI: Cum constitutionibus Sirmondianis et leges novellae ad Theodosianum pertinentes.* Berlin: Weidmannsche Buchhandlung.

CV   [=*Concilios Visigodos*] Vives, José. 1963. *Concilios Visigóticos e Hispano-Romanos.* Barcelona: CSIC.

De Gub. Dei   [=Salvianus Massiliensis, *De gubernatione Dei*] Lagarrigue, George.
                   1975. *Salvien de Marseilles: Oevres. Tome 2. Du gouvernement de Dieu.*
                   Paris: Éditions du Cerf.
De vir. ill.   [=Eusebius Sophronius Hieronymus, *De viris illustribus*] Herding,
                   Wilhelm. 1879. *Hieronymi de viris illustribus liber.* Leipzig: Teubner.
Exp. Tot. Mun.   [=*Expositio Totius Mundi et Gentium*] Rougé, Jean. 1966. *Expositio
                   totius mundi et gentium.* Paris: Éditions du Cerf.
Formula   [=*Formula Vitae Honestae*] Barlow, Claude, ed. 1950. *Martini Episcopi
                   Bracarensis opera omnia*, Papers and Monographs of the American
                   Academy in Rome, vol. 12, 236–50. New Haven: Yale University
                   Press.
FW   [=*Formulae Wisigothicae*] Gil, Juan. 1972. *Miscellanea Wisigothica*,
                   70–112. Seville: Publicaciones de la Universidad de Sevilla.
HEp   *Hispania Epigraphica*
HW   [=Iulianus Toletanus, *Historia Wambae Regis*] Krusch, Bruno, and
                   Wilhelm Levison. 1910. *Passiones vitaque sanctorum aevi Merovingici*,
                   Monumenta Germaniae Historica: Scriptores Rerum Merovingicarum,
                   vol. 5, 501–35. Hanover: Impensis Bibliopolii Hahniani.
ICERV   Vives, José. 1969. *Inscripciones cristianas de la España Romana y Visigoda.*
                   Barcelona: CSIC.
Ioh. Bicl., Chron [=Iohannes Biclarensis, *Chronicon*] Cardelle de Hartmann, Carmen,
                   and Roger Collins. 2001. *Victoris Tunnunensis Chronicon: Cum reliquis
                   ex consularibus Caesaraugustanis et Iohannis Biclarensis Chronicon*,
                   Corpus Christianorum Series Latina, vol. 173A, 59–83. Turnhout, Belgium:
                   Brepols.
Isid. Hisp., Chron. [=Isidorus Hispalensis, *Chronica*] Martín, José Carlos. 2003. *Isidori
                   Hispalensis chronica*, Corpus Christianorum Series Latina, vol. 112.
                   Turnhout, Belgium: Brepols.
Isid. Hisp., HG   [=Isidorus Hispalensis, *Historia Gothorum*] Rodríguez Alonso,
                   Cristóbal. 1975. *Las historias de los Godos, Vándalos y Suevos de Isidoro
                   de Sevilla.* León, Spain: Centro de Estudios e Investigación "San
                   Isidoro."
Lib. Prec.   [=Faustinus et Marcellinus, *Libellus precum ad imperatores*] Canellis,
                   Aline. 2006. *Supplique aux empereurs: Libellus precum et lex Augusta.
                   Précédé de Faustin, confession de foi.* Paris: Éditions du Cerf.
LV   [=*Leges Visigothorum*] Zeumer, Karl. 1902. *Leges Visigothorum*,
                   Monumenta Germaniae Historica. Leges, vol. 1. Hanover: Impensis
                   Bibliopolii Hahniani.
Not. Dig.   [=*Notitia Dignitatum*] Neira Faleiro, Concepción. 2005. *La Notitia
                   Dignitatum: Nueva edición crítica y comentario histórico.* Madrid: CSIC.
Oros., Hist.   [=Paulus Orosius, *Historiae adversum paganos*] Zankemeister, Karl. 1889.
                   Pauli Orosii Historiarum adversum paganos libri VII. Leipzig: Teubner.
Pan. Lat.   [=*Panegyrici Latini*] Nixon, C. E. V., and Barbara Saylor Rodgers. 1994.
                   *In Praise of Later Roman Emperors: The Panegyrici Latini—Introduction,
                   Translation, and Historical Commentary with the Latin Text of R. A. B.
                   Mynors.* Berkeley: University of California Press.

PLRE	Jones, A. H. M., J. R. Martindale, and J. Morris. 1971–1992. *The Prosopography of the Later Roman Empire*. 3 vols. Cambridge: Cambridge University Press.
Proc., *Bell.*	[=Procopius, *De Bellis*] Haury, J., and G. Wirth. 1962–1963. *Procopii Caesariensis opera omnia*, vol. 1–2. Leipzig: Teubner.
PV	[=Pizarras Visigodas] Velázquez, Isabel. 2004. *Las pizarras visigodas (Entre el latín y su disgregación: La lengua hablada en Hispania, siglos VI–VIII)*. Burgos: Fundación Instituto Castellano Leonés de la Lengua.
Soz., *Hist. Ecc.*	[=Sozomenus, *Historia Ecclesiastica*] Hansen, Günther Christian. 2004. *Sozomenos: Historia ecclesiastica/kirchengeschichte*. Fontes Christiani, vol. 73. Turnhout: Brepols.
Strabo, *Geo.*	[=Strabo, *Geographica*] Aly, Wolfgang. 1972. *Strabonis geographica: Libri III–VI*, Antiquitas. Reihe 1. Abhandlungen zur alten Geschichte, vol. 19. Bonn: Rudolf Habelt Verlag.
Sulp. Sev., *Chron.*	[=Sulpicius Severus, *Chronica*] de Senneville-Grave, Ghislaine. 1999. *Sulpice Sévère: Chroniques*. Paris: Éditions du Cerf.
Sulp. Sev., *Dial.*	[=Sulpicius Severus, *Dialogi*] Fontaine, Jacques. 2006. *Gallus: Dialogues sur les "vertus" de Saint Martin*. Paris: Éditions du Cerf.
Sym., *Ep.*	[=Symmachus, *Epistulae*] Seeck, Otto. 1961. *Q. Aurelii Symmachi quaesupersunt*, Monumenta Germaniae Historica. Auctorum Antiquissimorum, vol. 6, 1–278. Berlin: Weidmannsche Buchhandlung.
Sym., *Or.*	[=Symmachus, *Orationes*] Seeck, Otto. 1961 *Q. Aurelii Symmachi quae supersunt*, Monumenta Germaniae Historica. Auctorum Antiquissimorum, vol. 6, 318–39. Berlin: Weidmannsche Buchhandlung.
Sym., *Rel.*	[=Symmachus, *Relationes*] Seeck, Otto. 1961. *Q. Aurelii Symmachi quae supersunt*, Monumenta Germaniae Historica. Auctorum Antiquissimorum, vol. 6, 279–317. Berlin: Weidmannsche Buchhandlung.
Them., *Or.*	[=Themistius, *Orationes*] Schenkl, H. 1971. *Themistii orationes quae supersunt*. 3 vols. Leipzig: Teubner.
Variae	[=Cassiodorus, *Variae*] Giardina, Andrea, Giovanni Alberto Cecconi, and Ignazio Tantillo. 2014. *Cassiodorus: Varie*. Rome: "L'Erma" di Bretschneider.
Virt. S. Mart.	[=Gregorii Turonensis, *De Virtutibus Sancti Martini*] Arndt, Wilhelm, and Bruno Krusch. 1885. *Gregorii Turonensis opera*, Monumenta Germaniae Historica. Scriptores Rerum Merovingicarum, vol. 1–2, 134–211. Hanover: Impensis Bibliopolii Hahniani.
Vita Fruct.	[=*Vita Fructuosi*] Díaz y Díaz, Manuel. 1974. *La vida de san Fructuoso de Braga: Estudio y edición crítica*. Braga: Diário do Minho.
VPE	Maya Sánchez, Antonio. 1992. *Vitas sanctorum patrum Emeretensium*, Corpus Christianorum Series Latina, vol. 116. Turnhout: Brepols.
VSE	[Braulio Caesaraugustanus, *Vita Sancti Emiliani*] Vázquez de Parga, Luis. 1947. *Sancti Braulionis Caesaraugustani episcopi Vita s. Emiliani*. Madrid: CSIC, Instituto Superior de Investigaciones Jerónimo Zurita.
Zos., *Hist. Nov.*	[=Zosimus, *Historia Nova*] Paschoud, François. 1971–1989. *Zosime: Histoire nouvelle*. 3 vols. Paris: Les Belles Lettres.

NOTES

INTRODUCTION

1. No ancient source conveys clear information on the exact boundaries of the province of Gallaecia. Based on the borders of the later ecclesiastical provinces, which were finally fixed at the peak of the Visigothic kingdom, historians have traditionally accepted that this province included the former *conventus* of Braga, Lugo, and Astorga. More likely, however, the late Roman province also included the middle and upper Duero Basin—that is, the ancient *conventus* Cluniensis. This interpretation is based on scattered references from fifth-century sources and not on the later, ecclesiastical organization. For this interpretation, and an analysis of the sources, see Díaz Martínez and Menéndez Bueyes 2005, 266–69, and Martin 2006, 14–17.

2. Richardson 1986, 5–7 et passim.

3. This follows Peregrine Horden and Nicholas Purcell's definition of connectivity as "the various ways in which microregions cohere, both internally and also one with another" (2000, 123).

4. Thonemann 2011, 203–41.

5. See, for instance, Naveiro López 1996, Fabião 2009 (cf. Carreras Monfort 1996), and Morillo, Fernández Ochoa, and Salido Domínguez 2016.

6. To remain consistent, I have chosen to use the Portuguese spelling of the Tagus River (Tejo) and the Spanish name of the Durius River (Duero) throughout the book.

7. Parodi Álvarez 2014, 187.

8. While it is not clear whether the Guadiana could be navigated up to Mérida, it was certainly navigable up to Mértola at least (Parodi Álvarez 2003, 53–54). In the case of the Tejo, ancient sources refer to the island of Amourol (Vila Nova da Barquinha, Santarém) as the limit for ships, while smaller vessels could navigate upstream (Parodi Álvarez 2014, 183). The Duero may have been navigable up to the present-day border between Portugal and Spain (Parodi Álvarez 2014, 186).

9. A synthesis of the Iberian road network can be found in Solana Sáinz and Sagredo San Eustaquio 2006.

10. On Atlantic navigation, see Wooding 1996, 6–21, and Cunliffe 2001, 64–108. On Mediterranean sea connectivity, see Horden and Purcell 2000, 133–43.

11. Shaw 2006.

12. Cunliffe 2001, 265–75.

13. The most recent introductions to late Roman Iberia are in Kulikowski 2004, 39–175, and Arce 2009.

14. For post-Roman Iberia (fifth to late sixth century), see Kulikowski 2004, 176–309; Arce 2007; and Díaz 2011.

15. A recent synthesis of Visigothic administration can be found in Valverde Castro 2000 and Martin 2003.

16. McCormick 1986, 297–327.

17. Stocking 2000.

18. For a discussion on Gothic *gens* and kingdoms, see Velázquez 2003.

19. Martin 2003, 321–70, and Wood 2012 are the best starting points on this question.

20. The most recent take on Visigothic military history is in Isla Frez 2010.

21. The best synthesis of Visigothic political history is in Collins 2004, 64–143.

22. Sánchez Albornoz 1971, 11–147. Cf. Sánchez Albornoz 1943.

23. Van Dam 1985, 50–53; Castellanos 2004.

24. García Moreno 1990; Fuentes Hinojo 2008, 316. Cf. Mathisen 1993 (Gaul).

25. I myself argued from a similar point of view in an earlier work (Fernández 2006).

26. Díaz and Valverde 2000.

27. Castellanos and Martín Viso 2005; Martín Viso 2013.

28. This strong–weak opposition has been summarized in Wickham 2005, 56.

29. For traditional approaches toward Iberian aristocracies, see Stroheker 1963 and Chastagnol 1965.

30. Bowes 2001, 2005, 2006, and 2008; Chavarría Arnau 2004, 2006, 2007a, and 2007b.

31. Díaz 2007; Martín Viso 2012.

32. Ripoll 1985, 1998, and 2010; Ripoll and Carrero 2009; Wood 2012; Koch 2012.

33. Curchin 2013–2014 and Curchin 2014.

34. For instance, see Martín Viso and Castellanos 2008. Outside of Western Iberia (and not necessarily focused on aristocracies), see Escribano Paño and Fatás Cabeza 2001.

35. Arce 2007.

36. Kulikowski 2004.

37. Chavarría Arnau 2007a.

38. Oepen 2012.

39. Reynolds 2010.

40. Ward-Perkins 2005; Heather 2010. See also Giardina 1999.

41. Vigil-Escalera Guirado 2015.

42. Scheidel 2013.

43. See, for instance, Poulantzas 1973.

44. Abrams 1988.

45. "[The state] is first and foremost an exercise in legitimation—and what is being legitimated is, we may assume, something which if seen directly and as itself would be illegitimate, an unacceptable domination" (Abrams 1988, 76).

46. Bourdieu 2012.

47. Cf. Tilly 1990.

48. Mann 1984.

49. Some important contributions in recent years are Brown 1992, Banaji 2001, Kelly 2004, Slootjes 2006, and Haldon 2012.

50. Grey 2011, 186–89.

51. Haldon 1993.

52. In late antique scholarship, historical definitions (definitions of a specific historical aristocratic group) tend to prevail over conceptual ones (what makes an aristocrat regardless of the historical period). A healthy exception to this tendency can be found in Wickham 2005, 153.

53. Bourdieu 1984, 480 et passim.

CHAPTER I. IN THE SHADOW OF EMPIRE: SETTLEMENT AND SOCIETY IN THE LATE ROMAN PERIOD

1. For a discussion of Hydatius's life, see Burgess 1993, 3–10.

2. For information on Egeria's trip, see Arce 1996. For monumental centers in Rome and Constantinople during late antiquity, see Bauer 1996. For Syrian villages, see Decker 2009, 33-45.

3. Curchin 1991.

4. For a good summary, see Richardson 1996, 127–210.

5. Edmondson 1992, 26–30.

6. See the collection of essays on recent archaeological research in Roman *fora* of Lusitania in Nogales Basarrate 2010.

7. For Mérida, see Mateos Cruz 2001. For Lemica, see Pérez Losada 2002, 214–27.

8. See Woolf 1998, 106-141, for different reasons behind "uneven" urbanism.

9. Keay 1988 still provides a good introduction. For the western half of the empire in general, see Laurence, Esmonde Cleary, and Sears 2011.

10. Kulikowski 2004, 17–38; Edmondson 2006, 272–73.

11. Kulikowski 2004, 39–64.

12. Together with the *vicarius Hispaniarum*, a short-lived office of *comes Hispaniarum* existed in the early fourth century, with overseeing functions (Chastagnol 1965, 271–73; Arce 2009, 72).

13. For governors, see Arce 1999, 73–78. For provinces, see Kulikowski 2004, 71–76. See also Palme 1999, who makes an argument for a less abrupt change in administrative practices between the early and the late empire.

14. Fernández Ochoa lists the following cities in the area with walls dating to the late third or early fourth century: Braga, Lugo, Astorga, Tiermes, Évora, Coimbra, Conimbriga, Chaves, Norba, Caurium, and Capara (1997, 249–65). Other centers with possible late third- and early fourth-century chronology for their walls are Tomar (Carvalho and Cheney 2007), Salamanca (Hernández Domínguez 2007, 197–98), and Mértola (Lopes 2003, 82–97; De Man 2011a, 226–29). Beja may have had Roman city walls under its medieval ones, although we need more excavations to prove this hypothesis (Lopes 2000, 127–38). Laurent Brassous casts serious doubts on the chronologies of these walls, some of which deserve careful consideration (2011, 278–86). For a case of an early fifth-century construction, see Uxama (García Merino 2007, 203–4). For another reassessment of the evidence of late Roman walls (limited to Lusitania), see De Man 2011a, who also casts doubt on a centralized program within a short chronological framework. See Corsi 2016, for Ammaia's walls.

15. This was the case in Lisbon (Gaspar and Gomes 2007, 693–94). Clunia maintained its early imperial walls (Abásolo Álvarez 1999, 91), but they may have been rebuilt during the late empire (Gillani 1995).

16. For a general synthesis (with somewhat different interpretations), see Liebeschuetz 2001, 82–85; Christie 2011, 91–111; and Esmonde Cleary 2013, 122–36.

17. For Italy, see Christie 2006, 319–56. For northern Gaul, see Esmonde Cleary 2013, 62–76. For Africa, see Sears 2007, 84–85.

18. For the *annona* route theory, see Fernández Ochoa and Morillo Cerdán 2005.

19. Dey 2010; Christie 2011, 102–5; Esmonde Cleary 2013, 122–26.

20. Fernández Ochoa 1997.

21. For the costs of wall construction, see Bachrach 2010. His estimate for the cost of construction of Bordeaux's walls reaches 35 million man-hours of labor. But note that the walls of Bordeaux (32.5 hectares) protected a larger city area than the average town in Western Iberia, which was closer, for instance, to the five hectares of Idanha-a-Velha's walled area.

22. *CTh.*, XV.1.34. See Christie 2006, 208–13, for a discussion of the use of *spolia* in late antique Italy and Gurt and Diarte Blasco 2011 for Hispania.

23. An interesting discussion of the problem is provided in De Man 2011a, 73–85.

24. Carreño Gascón and González Fernández 1999, 1179–81.

25. De Man 2006, 18–19, and 2011a, 188–89. Cf. Brassous 2011, 283, who raises doubts about the exact chronology of the wall.

26. Dey 2011, 111–22.

27. Esmonde Cleary 2003.

28. Curchin 2014, 295–97.

29. Dey 2011, 131.

30. On the question of occupied area and population levels, a good comparative case (Italy) and discussion can be found in Christie 2006, 249–63.

31. Alba Calzado 2007, 170–73.

32. For Lugo, see Carreño Gascón and González Fernández 1999, 1191–92. We have some evidence in this respect in Lisbon, where excavations near the cathedral revealed that an early imperial street was eliminated ir order to be replaced by an undefined structure (Amaro and de Matos 1996). Some houses in Lugo also follow the pattern of Mérida (Carreño Gascón and Gozález Fernández 1999, 1181). For the chronology of abandonment of Lisbon's public spaces, see Diogo and Trinidade 1999. For Uxama, see García Merino 2000, 181.

33. Dias 1999, 765. For the urban evolution of Tongobriga, see Dias 1997.

34. Vermeulen et al. 2012, 136.

35. For a survey of Iberian cities, see Diarte Blasco 2012.

36. For imperial cult complex, see Mateos Cruz 2006 and Pizzo 2006. For the Augustan colony, see Ayerbe Vélez, Barrientos Vera, and Palma García 2009, 807–15.

37. Ayerbe Vélez, Barrientos Vera, and Palma García 2009, 816–28.

38. Mateos Cruz, Pizzo, and Vázquez 2005, 251–53; Mateos Cruz 2006; Ayerbe Vélez, Barrientos Vera, and Palma García 2009, 828–31.

39. Correia 2010, 100–101.

40. Ponte 2010.

41. Iglesias Gil 2001–2002; Cepeda Ocampo, Iglesias Gil, and Ruiz Guitiérrez 2009.

42. For the theater, see Durán Cabello 2004, 118–28 and *CIIAE* 62 (= *HEp* 13, 111). For the circus, see *CIIAE* 63 (= *AE* 1975, 472).

43. Durán Cabello, 1998.

44. For information on Braga in general, see Martins and Delgado 1989–1990 and Panzram 2014, 459–60.

45. Alarcão 1994. For the possible chronology of the city's circus, see Sepúlveda et al. 2002.

46. *CIL* II.191; Reis 2004, 30.

47. *CTh.*, XVI.10.15. For the Iberian Peninsula in general, see Arce 2006a. Some excavations proved the abandonment of temples by the late fourth or early fifth century. For Mérida, see Mateos Cruz, Pizzo, and Vázquez 2005, 253–60 (temple at Calle Holguín, probably unoc-

cupied until the sixth century). Excavations of the *mithraeum* at Lugo did not detect destruction but mere abandonment after the mid-fourth century (Alvar, Gordon, and Rodríguez 2006). The temple of Santarém seems to have been in use during the late Roman period, although we do not know what it was used for (Arruda and Viegas 1999, 195–96).

48. For different possible "endings" of pagan temples in the Mediterranean world, see the collection of case studies in Lavan and Mulryan 2011.

49. For testimonies of an early Christian community in Mérida, León, and Astorga, see Teja 1990. The bishops of León, Faro, Mérida, and Évora attended the council of Elvira in the early fourth century (Council of Elvira, *Praef., Coll. Hisp.* IV, 239–41). For an introduction to early Christianity in Iberia, see García Moreno 2005.

50. Mateos Cruz 2000, 498–502.

51. The Christian building under Braga's cathedral dates from the fifth century or perhaps late fourth century but not earlier (Fontes, Lemos and Cruz 1997–1998, 140–41). For Astorga, see Burón Álvarez 2006, 308. For Idanha-a-Velha, see Sánchez Ramos and Morín de Pablos 2015, 409–10. For the uncertain identification of a late Roman church in Conimbriga, see De Man 2011b, 519.

52. For urban Christian buildings in the Iberian Peninsula, see Bowes 2005, 193–208, and the recent and thorough survey in Sánchez Ramos 2014.

53. For the cost of maintenance of public buildings, see Zuiderhoeck 2005, 168–74. For public baths, see Fagan 1999, 161–64.

54. For Astorga, see Burón Álvarez 2006, 306–7. For Lugo, see Carreño Gascón and González Fernández 1999, 1193–94. For Cauca, see Mañanes Pérez 2002, 160.

55. Pérez Losada 2002, 199–205.

56. Biers 1988, 31–43.

57. So far, the only cities that show the presence of public baths into the late Roman period in our region are Astorga, Braga, Clunia, Conimbriga, Lancia, Lisbon, León, Gijón, and Tongobriga. To this list, we can add Évora, Lugo, Tiermes, and Uxama, which possibly had public baths into the fourth century. Most of these sites present one or more signs of late Roman urban public interventions. Of course, more excavations can reverse this image, but their concentration in cities with other attested public works is remarkable (Fernández Ochoa and Zarzalejos Prieto 2001; Núñez Hernández 2008). See also Corsi and Vermeulen 2016, 69–85, for recent excavations in Ammaia.

58. Patterson 2006, 125–86.

59. Deschamps 2002.

60. Esmonde Cleary 2013, 75 (walls). For local elites and *munera*, see Chapter 2.

61. Melchor Gil 1994a and 1994b. See also Ceballos Hornero 2004, 179–295.

62. Cecconi 1994, 107–69; Le Roux 2014, 408–10. Honorific statues in Hispania show a similar trend, where emperors and, to a lesser extent, governors, are the only individuals with surviving inscriptions on statue bases (Witschel 2016, 72–75).

63. See note 42.

64. For Astorga, see *CIL* II.2635. For Mérida, see Hidalgo and Mendez Grande 2005.

65. For North Africa, see Sears 2007, 78–84. For a discussion of bathhouses in general, see Fagan 1999, 142–54.

66. Alba Calzado 2007, 168–73.

67. For Braga, see Martins and Delgado 1996, 124–25. Mosaics and private baths have been found in Lugo, all dating from the late Roman period (Carreño Gascón and González Fernández 1999, 1195–204). Although excavations in Astorga are still scanty, we know that an

aristocratic house near the forum was provided with baths by the early third century. Occupation continued at least into the fourth century, when mosaics were repaired using pieces of TSHT (Burón Álvarez 1999, 1051–53). For aristocratic houses in Uxama, see García Merino 2007, 211–12. For changes in Mértola during the late Roman period in general, see Lopes 2003, where aristocratic housing can be hinted at by the finding of mosaic floors. For Veleia, see Filloy, Eliseo Gil, and Iriarte Kortazar 1998, 466 (the evidence comes in this case from painted walls and mosaic floors). For Conimbriga, see Correia 2001.

68. Hernández Guerra and Sagredo San Eustaquio 1998, 124–27.

69. Polci 2003, 89–105.

70. For a general panorama of Gijón in the late Roman period, see Fernández Ochoa 1999. For the nearby territory, see Fernández Ochoa, Gil Sendino, and Orejas Saco del Valle 2004.

71. For similar developments in Italy, see Christie 2006, 214–23.

72. Díaz Álvarez and Garín García 1999a.

73. Edmondson 1992; Blanco González, López Sáez, and López Merino 2009, 277–79; Sánchez-Pardo 2010.

74. Maloney and Hale 1996, 280–84.

75. For late antique villas in the Iberian Peninsula, the main references are Chavarría Arnau 2005 and 2007a.

76. A thorough typological analysis is provided in Smith 1997.

77. The report of the excavations is provided in Alarcão, Étienne, and Mayet 1990. A more vivid and concise reconstruction of the architecture of seigneurial power can be found in Kulikowski 2004, 133–36.

78. For northern Gaul, see Van Ossel and Ouzoulias 2000. For Britain, see Dark 2004, 281–86.

79. For Mediterranean Iberia (and broader Iberian context), see Chavarría Arnau 2005. For southern Italy, see Sfameni 2006.

80. Balmelle 2001, 147–201.

81. Banaji 2001, 101–33.

82. Chavarría Arnau 2004.

83. Ellis 2000, 68–72.

84. Bowes 2010.

85. Scott 2004; Bowes 2006. See the cautionary remarks of Kim Bowes on the dangers of assuming a straightforward relationship between space and function in elite houses (Bowes 2010, 35–42).

86. For this type of elite culture, the best introduction is still to be found in Matthews 1975.

87. For Quinta das Longas, see Carvalho and Almeida 1999–2000. For Torre Águila, see López Quiroga and Rodríguez Martín 2000, 162–66.

88. For instance, Torre de Palma (Maloney and Hale 1996, 280–85) or Milreu (Teichner 2008, 114–23).

89. See, for instance, the the surveys of Capara (Cerrillo Martín de Cáceres et al. 1991).

90. See Gorges and Rodríguez Martín 2000 for the villas nearby Mérida on the road to Lisbon. Cordero Ruiz 2013 offers a catalogue of rural sites (particularly villas) as well as a thorough description of the road system in the territory of Mérida. The same distribution along the main roads is replicated in the cities of modern Extremadura, on the Vía de la Plata, with a possible intensification of rural settlement between the third and the fifth century (Alonso Sánchez et al. 1994). For settlement along the route between Lisbon and Braga, see Mantas

1999. Pessoa 2000 provides detailed information about the villa of Rabaçal and rural settlement in the area of Conimbriga. For villas in the area of Lisbon, see Silva 2000 (villa of Frielas) and Banha 1991–1992 (villa of Povos).

91. For a field survey in Alange, see Calero Carretero and Márquez Gabardino 1991, 585–90. For specific excavations, see Calero Carretero 1993.

92. Miguel Hernández and Benítez González 1993–1994. For the Leonese villas in general, see Regueras Grande 1996. A similar case, but in the central parts of the northern plateau, was the villa of Picón de Castrillo (Ampudia), in the southern part of the province of Palencia. This early imperial site underwent reforms around the late third century and a last expansion (the most important one, including baths) by the end of the fourth century (Balado Pachón and Martínez García 2004). For the eastern part of the plateau and the territory of Uxama in particular, see García Merino 2007, 230–33. The Zamora and Salamanca regions followed similar chronological patterns, although with a less intense presence of monumentalized villas (for Zamora, see Regueras Grande 1996; for Salamanca, see Ariño Gil 2006 and Ariño Gil et al. 2015).

93. Regueras Grande and Del Olmo 1998. The settlement pattern along the Carrión River, where La Olmeda is located, illustrates the dense rural settlement dominated by villas and the agglomerated rural settlement, La Morterona. Field surveys in the province of Palencia illustrate the coexistence of large, monumental aristocratic mansions with sites of less but sizable importance. See Sayas Abengochea 1990, 686–87, and Nozal Calvo 1995.

94. Palol and Cortes 1974. For the territory of La Olmeda, see Nozal Calvo 1995.

95. Nozal Calvo, Cortes, and Abásolo Álvarez 2000.

96. García Merino and Sánchez Simón 2004, 418–20.

97. For an overview of the region, see Blanco González, López Sáez, and López Merino 2009, 279–81.

98. For the importance of the northern road system, see Arce 1990, 37–38.

99. A synthesis of recent theories is provided in Kaiser 2015, 243–45.

100. *Not.Dig. Occ.* XLII, 25–32. For an introduction to the sources on the late Roman army in Iberia, see Kulikowski 2004, 76–82.

101. Solana Sáinz and Sagredo San Eustaquio 1998. The corpus of inscriptions is in Rodríguez Colmenero, Ferrer Sierra, and Álvarez Asorey 2004 (cf. *CIL* XVII.1).

102. Millett 2001.

103. Carlsson-Brandt 2011.

104. Martins and Delgado 1989–1990, 30–32.

105. For Dume, see Fontes 1995. For Toralla, see Hidalgo Cuñarro 1994.

106. Fernández Ochoa, Gil Sendino, and Orejas del Saco Valle 2004, 198–208.

107. The classic treatment of the subject is in Burnham and Wacher 1990. See also Arthur 2004. For the Iberian context, see I Toledo, 5 (*Coll. Hisp.* IV, 330).

108. Teichner 2008, 243–50. Cf. Noguera Celdrán and Antolinos Marín 2009, 207–10 (Cipreses, Murcia, in Mediterranean Iberia).

109. Abásolo Álvarez, Cortes, and Pérez Rodríguez-Aragón 1997; Chavarría Arnau 2012; Vigil-Escalera Guirado 2015, 187–88 et passim.

110. Moreda Blanco et al. 2010–2011.

111. Requejo Pagés 2007.

112. Fanjul Peraza and Menéndez Bueyes 2004, 46–70.

113. For Viladonga in general, in the context of late Roman settlement types, see Arias Vilas 1996. For cattle raising in that site, see Fernández Rodríguez 2002; for the material culture of the settlement, see Llana Rodríguez and Varela Arias 1999.

114. Sánchez Pardo 2012, 33–34.

115. Teichner 2008, 61–91.

116. Mulvin 2002, 23.

117. Alba Calzado 2007, 172–73.

118. Heijmans 2006, 48.

CHAPTER 2. AN UNPROVINCIAL ARISTOCRACY:
ARISTOCRATIC IDENTITY IN A RENEWED EMPIRE

1. On Ammianus in general, see Barnes 1998 and Kelly 2008.

2. Barnes 1998, 132–42; Kelly 2008, 280–81.

3. Amm. Mar., *Res Gestae,* XVI.8–9; Barnes 1998, 179–80.

4. For Ammianus and *nobilitas*, see Salzman 2001, 381–82.

5. On the senatorial aristocracy, see Jones 1964, 523–62; Barnish 1988; Chastagnol 1992, 233–344; Heather 1998; and Salzman 2002. Also see Weisweiler 2010 for an innovative take on the Roman senatorial aristocracy. On decurions, see Jones 1964, 724–57; Lepelley 1979, 197–242; and Laniado 2002.

6. For a discussion of the evolution of bishops' privileges, see Rapp 2005, 236–60.

7. For the beginning of this process and the merging of senatorial and equestrian careers, see Dillon 2015, 45–53.

8. For the development of a distinct Constantinopolitan senatorial order, see Chastagnol 1992, 259–65.

9. Matthews 1975, 101–21; Ebbeler and Sogno 2007, 237–38.

10. Garbarino 1988, 73–183.

11. Salzman 2002, 72.

12. Garbarino 1998, 363–91.

13. Weisweiler 2012. Cf. Chastagnol 1992, 291.

14. For the theoretical inheritability of senatorial status but its noninheritability in practice, see Hopkins and Burton 1983.

15. For Fl. Eucherius and court politics, see Matthews 1975, 76–77 and 94–95.

16. *PLRE,* 288; Jones 1964, 333 and 427–37.

17. McLynn 2005, 95–96. But see Canto 2006, where the author rejects the idea of Cauca as the birthplace of the Theodosian family.

18. Matthews 1975, 94.

19. McLynn 2005, 102. Cf. Skinner 2013, 31–32.

20. A similar civil career is attested in the case of another potential Spaniard, Flavius Sallustius, although we do not know his exact place of origin. Among other positions, he was vicar of the *Hispaniae*, praetorian prefect of Gaul, and reached the consulate in 363 (*PLRE,* 797–98).

21. *PLRE,* 834.

22. *PLRE,* 835; *De vir. ill.,* 111; Chastagnol 1965, 272–73; Arce 1999, 76. For the inscription, see Chapter 1, note 42.

23. *PLRE,* 370–71; Garbarino 1988, 87–97; Sogno 2006, 25–28; Curchin 2010.

24. Sym., *Or.* 8.

25. Statistical information for the late empire is scanty. In addition to Mérida and Évora, Baetica (and especially Córdoba) and northeastern Iberia may have continued as the breadbasket of senatorial families (Le Roux 1982; Castillo García 1982; Étienne 1982; Gabrielli 1995–1996).

26. Bravo 1996; Arce 2008, 12–13. Cf. Chastagnol 1965 and Matthews 1975, 107–13.

27. Chastagnol 1992, 266.

28. This is based on Themistius's likely exaggerated assertion that he had increased the number of members of the Constantinopolitan senate from three hundred to two thousand during the reign of Constantius II (Them., *Or.* 34.13). See also Heather (1998, 190), who estimates around 3000 positions that could have led to senatorial status.

29. Lepelley 1979, 253–55; Liebeschuetz 2001, 105 et passim. Cf. Cecconi 2006, 44–50.

30. Edmondson 2006, 272–78.

31. Nicols 1988.

32. Garnsey 1970, 242–45.

33. For late antique *curiales*, see Jones 1964, 737–57.

34. Bransbourg 2008; Hostein 2012, 167–70.

35. *CTh.*, XII.6.20.

36. Lepelley 1979, 199–201.

37. Grey 2011, 183–85.

38. Lepelley 1979, 257–69; Laniado 2002, 7. Cf. Skinner 2013 for the eastern Roman Empire.

39. Andreu Pintado 1999, 56–61.

40. *CTh.*, XII.1.151. For *gesta municipalia*, see Lepelley 1979, 223–24.

41. For flamines, see Conc. Elib. 2–4 (*Coll. Hisp.* IV, 242–43). For *duoviri*, see Conc. Elib., 56 (*Coll. Hisp.* IV, 259–60); Kulikowski 2004, 39–42. Cf. I Toledo 8 (*Coll. Hisp.* IV, 331–32). See also Lepelley 1979, 150–63.

42. *AE* 1921, 6–9; Rabanal Alonso and García Martínez 2001, 365–68. This document has been dated to the years between 227 and 310, with a more probable chronology between 267 and 276 (Fernández Ochoa, Morillo Cerdán, and Gil Sendino 2012).

43. *Chron.*, 40. Cf. *CTh.*, XII.6.20. For the *exactor* in the late empire, see Jones 1964, 456–57 and 727–29.

44. For the Latin West, see Lepelley 1979, 201–5. For the Greek East, see Laniado 2002, 201–11.

45. Modii l(ex) iuxta sacram iussio[n]em ddd(ominorum) nnn(ostrorum) Valentiniani Valent(i)s et Gratiani invictissimorum | principum iubente Mario Artemio v(iro) c(larissimo) ag(ente) vic(ariam) p(raefecturam) cur(antibus) Potamio et Quentiano principalibus (*CIRG* I, 87 = *AE* 1915, 75). See also Chastagnol 1965, 276; Arce 2009, 262–63.

46. This transformation is explained in Borg and Witschel 2001.

47. For the *munera* in general, see Lepelley 1979, 206–13.

48. Lemcke 2016, 61–74.

49. Barrientos Vera 2011, 332–33.

50. Lepelley 1979, 298–318.

51. Cf. Cecconi 1994, 147–51.

52. Garnsey 1970, 244.

53. Tax collecting was a compulsory service (*munus*) according to laws from 365 and 386 (*CTh.*, XII.6.6 and XII.6.20). Another law from 364 (*CTh.*, XII.6.7) established that these *susceptores* could not be members of the curial order but had to possess the appropriate "reputation and property" (*moribus quam facultatibus*) to perform this task.

54. Curchin 2014, 284–86.

55. Lepelley 1979, 256–70.

56. Chastagnol 1992, 271–76.

57. Matthews 1975, 93; Amm. Mar. *Res Gestae*, XXIX.5.

58. Chastagnol 1992, 358–61.

59. For Hispania, see Kulikowski 2004, 45–47; Grey 2011, 200–201.

60. Grey 2011, 183–84.

61. See also Curchin 2014, 290–92, on the possible manipulation of tax measures in favor of collection agents.

62. Cf. *CTh.*, XII.6.21.

63. For the role of petitions in late antiquity, see Brown 1992, 7–34.

64. Kelly 2004, 138–85; Humfress 2009, 381–85.

65. Sulp. Sev., *Chron.*, II.47.2. Local magistrates (*seculares iudices*), possibly in Iberia, helped them obtain an imperial rescript from Gratian against Priscillianist bishops.

66. Sulp. Sev., *Chron.*, II.48.2: lobbying ("bribing," *corrupto*) Macedonius, *magister officiorum* in Milan; II.49:1: Volventius governor (*proconsul*) of Lusitania. *PLRE*, 526 and 975.

67. Per libidinem et potentia paucorum cuncta ibi venalia erant (Sulp. Sev., *Chron.*, II.49.1). *PLRE*, 404.

68. However, Neil McLynn argues that the episode shows the impotence of Gratian's court to solve controversies of this type (McLynn 1994, 149–51).

69. Sulp. Sev., *Chron.*, II.49.1–51.5

70. However, Sulpicius's hostility moved toward the anti-Priscillianist faction in other works (cf. Sulp. Sev., *Dial.*, III.11–13).

71. Kulikowski 2004, 48–49.

72. *Pan. Lat.* II.9.3.

73. Barbara Rodgers and C. E. V. Nixon (1994, 459, n. 34) believe that Pacatus may have been briefed on Theodosius's life in Iberia based on his own words before he describes Theodosius's "retreat" (Audio etiam imperator, et credo . . . , *Pan. Lat.* II.9.4).

74. For the different forms of patronage in late antiquity, see Krause 1987.

75. The most thorough reconstruction of the events can be found in Escribano Paño 2000 and Arce 2007, 36–47.

76. Oros., *Hist.*, VII.40.5.

77. Zos., *Hist. Nov.*, V.43 and VI.1; Soz. *Hist. Ecc.*, IX.11.4 (suggenēs).

78. Lenski 2009, 151–58.

79. The legitimacy of their actions may have been questioned. Hence did Orosius, a firm supporter of the Theodosian family, take pains to argue the authority of their intervention (Oros., *Hist.*, VII.40.5–6). See Curchin 2013–2014, 130–31, who argues that both young men were of senatorial rank.

80. For instance, Sulp. Sev., *Chron.*, II.46.3. See also Burrus 1995, 79–101 and Sanchez 2009, 29–38.

81. Liebeschuetz 2001, 104–36; Laniado 2002, 131–223. For the (admittedly scanty) evidence from fourth-century Hispania, see Curchin 2014, 282–84.

82. Weisweiler 2012. See also Weisweiler 2015a, where a similar argument is made for the senatorial aristocracy empirewide.

83. For land concentration, see Chavarría Arnau 2004. For senatorial identity, see Chavarría Arnau 2005, 540–43; Sfameni 2006, 182–84.

84. Ward-Perkins 1998, 373–82.

85. Sivan 1993, 49–66.

86. Skinner 2013, 37–43.

87. For a hypothesis on the relatively small number of theaters in Western Iberia, see Brassous 2015, 276–77.

88. Sodini 2003.

89. Palol 1977, 303–5.

90. Kim Bowes has led this historiographical renewal. See Bowes 2008, 158–60 et passim; 2010, 61–99; and 2013.

91. Bowes 2005, 208–18; Chavarría Arnau 2007a, 120–24.

92. Serra Ráfols 1949; Oepen 2012, 168–75.

93. Bowes 2006, 83.

94. See Sfameni 2014, 77–97, for a discussion of the social implications of mausolea and temples in western villas.

95. Bowes 2006, 85–86.

96. Bowes 2006, 87–88; Esmonde Cleary 2013, 241.

97. García Entero 2005, 741.

98. The most comprehensive work on Iberian bathhouses (both early and late Roman) is in García Entero 2005. See also Reis 2004 (for Lusitania).

99. Nozal Calvo, Cortes, and Abásolo Álvarez 2000. See García Entero 2006, 100–108, for villa bathhouses in general.

100. Correia and Reis 2000, 276–77; García Entero 2005, 566–70.

101. See, for instance, Balmelle 2001, 190–201 (Aquitaine).

102. An example is found at the villa of La Cocosa (Badajoz) (García Entero 2006, 104–5).

103. García Entero 2010, 66–67.

104. Teichner 2008, 181–93.

105. Fernández Ochoa and Gil Sendino 2008, 440–48.

106. Nogales Basarrate, Carvalho, and Almeida 2004.

107. Regueras Grande 2011–2012.

108. Regueras Grande 2010.

109. Álvarez Martínez 1976, 451–56.

110. López Monteagudo 2010; Panzram 2002, 293–97. See Ceballos Hornero 2004, 426–51 for a broader Iberian context.

111. Blázquez 1993, 18–19.

112. Morand 1994; Álvarez Martínez 2006–2007, 19–21. For Aquitanian villas, see Balmelle 2001, 238–301.

113. For mythological motifs in villas of the region, see La Olmeda, see Cortes 2008. For Noheda, see Valero Tevar 2013. For Torre de Palma, see Lancha and André 2000, 143–280. For the theme of Achilles on Skyros in second- to fourth-century elite houses in the Mediterranean (mosaics and wall paintings), see Delbarre, Fuchs, and Paratte 2008.

114. Nogales Basarrate, Carvalho, and Almeida 2004, 143–44.

115. Neira Jiménez 2007; Cordero Ruiz 2013, 284–88. Cf. Blázquez 1997, 17–18. See also Stirling 2007, for a discussion of local, Iberian trends in late antique villa statuary.

116. Balmelle 2001, 238–325. See also Esmonde Cleary 2016 for Britain.

117. Esmonde Cleary 2013, 238–39. See cautionary remarks in Bowes 2010, 39–42.

118. Ellis 1997.

119. Polci 2003, 80–89.

120. Teichner 2008, 176–81.

121. Alba Calzado 2007, 171–73.

122. Fernández Ochoa and Gil Sendino 2008, 440–44.

123. Esmonde Cleary 2013, 206. However, Bowes 2010, 51–52, raises doubts against the idea of trickling-down imperial majesty.

124. Bowes 2010, 54–60.

125. See a synthesis in Esmonde Cleary 2013, 136–40 (urban houses) and 245–63 (rural villas).

126. Amm. Mar. *Res Gestae*, XXVIII.4; *De Gub. Dei*, IV.4–6.

127. For the "gray area," see Barnish 1988, 122–23.

CHAPTER 3. ECONOMIC STRATEGIES IN A RENEWED EMPIRE:
ARISTOCRATIC ECONOMIC UNITS IN THE LATE ROMAN PERIOD

1. *CIL* VI.1690 (=*AE* 1976.15). For Proculus's religious sympathies, see also Sym., *Ep.* 1.2.4. For his career in general, see Weisweiler 2012, 337–41.

2. This position in the career of Valerius Proculus has been highlighted by Javier Arce (2009, 231–36).

3. Jones 1964, 454–55.

4. Cf. Sym., *Rel.* 9.7, 18, 35, and 37.

5. Tereso, Ramil Rego, and Almeida da Silva 2013, 2853–54.

6. Lowe 2009, 8–86.

7. Hopkins 1980.

8. Domergue 1990, 288–307; Edmondson 1987, 25–87; Lowe 2009, 102–9.

9. Hirt 2010, 119–25. See also Edmondson 1987, 37–39, who also argues for a less direct state intervention in the case of silver and copper mines.

10. Orejas Saco del Valle 1996, 116–53; Fernández Ochoa 2006, 281–85.

11. Edmondson 1987, 67–70.

12. Edmondson 1989, 93–97.

13. Remesal Rodríguez 1986; Étienne and Mayet 2004; Reynolds 2010, 24–25.

14. Carreras Monfort and Williams 2003, 68.

15. *CTh.*, XIII.5.4 and XIII.5.8. See also Cañizar Palacios 2009–2010.

16. Reynolds 2010, 74–84.

17. Edmondson 1989, 88–91.

18. For containers, see Remesal Rodríguez 1991. For production facilities, see Peña Cervantes 2010, 188–90.

19. Two succinct introductions to the late Roman tax system appear in Grey 2011, 178–97, and Bransbourg 2015.

20. Jones 1964, 396–97. See also the doubts raised in Carrié 1994, 42–43.

21. See Fernández Ochoa and Morillo Cerdán 2005, 334 (in kind), and Bowes 2013, 206–13 (in coin).

22. On the importance of imperial salaries, see Banaji 2001, 116 et passim. Doubts on the increase of senatorial wealth have been raised in Weisweiler 2015b.

23. See Jones 1964, 396–401, who argues that the bulk of imperial official incomes came from extortion rather than salaries. Cf. Kelly 2004, 138–85.

24. *Lib. Prec.*, 32 and 42.

25. Cf. Lepelley 1979, 319–20.

26. As an introduction to the archaeological evidence, see Lagóstena Barrios 2001 and Teichner 2008 (though focused on a few cases in southern Lusitania, it is one of the most detailed and thorough analyses available).

27. This may be illustrated by the factory of the Ilha do Pessegueiro, halfway between Lisbon and the Algarvian coast, which during the late empire specialized in fish products. The

early imperial site had a more commercial orientation that is completely lost to us, at least with regard to long-distance commerce. During the late empire, by the fourth century, the center of Ilha do Pessegueiro turned into an almost exclusively productive center, with parallel investments in buildings and renovations (Silva and Soares 1997). For the same process in other factories, see Lagóstena Barrios 2001, 319–22.

28. Étienne, Makaroun, and Mayet 1994, 82–93.

29. Edmondson 1987, 128–29, 131–34.

30. Étienne, Makaroun, and Mayet 1994 (a synthesized version in Étienne and Mayet 2006).

31. For several production facilities at Cerro da Vila, see Teichner 2008, 368–402.

32. For northwestern Iberia, see Lagóstena Barrios 2001 and Ramil González 2003 (Bares). For Algarve, see Fabião 1992–1993, and Lagósterna Barrios 2001, 321–22.

33. See Rosenstein 2008, 18–24 (who also downplays the impact of agricultural wealth in the amassing of senatorial fortunes in Italy during the Republic).

34. Vera 1999; Wickham 2005, 470–73.

35. For *actores* and *villici* in earlier Roman sources, see Carlsen 1995.

36. Chavarría Arnau 2004.

37. Banaji 2001, 134–70; Sarris 2006, 181–93.

38. Carrié 2012, 26–30.

39. This is a phenomenon attested to in other parts of the late Roman world (for Syria, see Decker 2009, 44–48; for Carthage's hinterland, see Rossiter 2007, 382–387).

40. Dossey 2010, 92–93; Weisweiler 2011, 352–56.

41. Wickham 2005, 442–65; Decker 2009, 33–44.

42. Wickham 2005, 466–71; Chavarría Arnau 2007a, 53–55; Vera 2012, 120–22.

43. Harper 2008, 92.

44. This was also the case of the territory of Salamanca, where cereal growing dominated over large-scale husbandry (Ariño Gil, Riera i Mora, and Rodríguez Hernández 2002, 296) or Castro Ventosa, where cereal and chestnut tree dominate the late Roman landscape (López Merino, López Sáez et al. 2008). See also Castelo Ruano, López Sáez et al. 2010–2011, 213.

45. For cereals in antiquity, see Sallares 2007, 31–34.

46. Chavarría Arnau 2007a, 80. For *fundi* and tax collection, see note 96.

47. For instance, pollen analyses show olive oil cultivation in the northern slopes of the Sistema Central, at Sierra de Gredos in the province of Ávila (López Sáez et al. 2009, 21–22). Some villas of the northern meseta had presses that can be related to oil production, such as the villa of Villaverde de Medina in Valladolid, where surface materials include late Roman pottery and various millstones (Mangas 1980). However, these sites still lack the proper excavations, which would allow us to determine the exact nature of this production.

48. Tereso, Ramil Rego, and Almeida da Silva 2013, 2854.

49. Teichner 2003, 112.

50. Alarcão, Étienne, and Mayet 1990, 236–37.

51. Valdeomillos Rodríguez et al. 1996.

52. Lowe 2009, 32–33. Cf. Étienne and Mayet 2000, 15–20.

53. For Lusitanian production during antiquity, see Carvalho 1999. For northwestern Iberia, see Morais 1997–1998. The latter work suggests increasing local production of wine after the third century, although based on scant evidence.

54. Carvalho 1999, 362–64.

55. Rodríguez Martín and Gorges 1999. For La Sevillana, see Aguilar Sáenz 1991, 451. For São Cucufate, see Alarcão, Étienne, and Mayet 1990, 236–37. For Pozo de la Cañada, see Heras Mora and Gilotte 2008, 53–54.

56. Teichner 2006, 208–9.

57. García Merino and Sánchez Simón 2004.

58. Ariño Gil 2006, 326–27.

59. Martín Chamoso 2006, 44.

60. García Guinea 1990, 28.

61. Gómez-Pantoja 2001. For Lusitania, see Sáez Fernández 1993. For an introduction to the *mesta*, see García Martín 1990.

62. López Sáez et al. 2009.

63. Strabo, *Geo.*, III.3.7; Morais 1997–1998.

64. Soto Arias, Fernández Rodríguez, and Menéndez Llorente 1999, 1162–64. For Lugo, see Altuna and Mariezkurrena 1996. A pattern similar to A Proba can be found in Santomé, Ourense, a *castrum* reoccupied during the late Roman period (Fernández Rodríguez and Rodríguez González 1999).

65. Fernández Rodríguez, López Pérez, and Prado Fernández 1999, 69–70.

66. Coruscatione villae exuste <et> greges ovium concremati (*Chron.*, 213).

67. Mañanes Pérez 2002, 231–40. Yet, tellingly, game animals represent almost 60 percent of animal remains.

68. Pérez Losada et al. 1992, 74.

69. Regueras Grande 1996, 102.

70. Carneiro 2010, 242–44.

71. For pottery, see Miguel Hernández and Benéitez González 1993–1994, 119–21. For textiles, see Aguilar Sáenz 1991, 273 (villa of Monroy), and Pessoa and Rodrigo 2005, 136–38 (villa of Rabaçal).

72. Pro demesne, see Sarris 2004; contra, see Vera 2012. Cf. Wickham 2005, 272–80, who accepts some demesnelike land management but without continuity into the manorial economy of the Middle Ages.

73. In this respect, see the cases of the meseta villas in García Merino 2008, 428–29.

74. Gorges and Rico 1999. For one specific case for which we can assert a late Roman date (Correiro Mor, Elvas, Portugal), see Gorges and Rodríguez Martín 1999. See also Sillières 1995, with a field survey of Vila de Frades, near Beja, where the author also detected new investments in irrigation after the second century, and Quintela and De Mascarenhas 2006, for Portugal in general. For some cases of water management in the northern meseta associated with residential villas (although of uncertain use), see García Merino 2008, 429. See also the recent survey by Juan Carlos Castillo Barranco (2015), although limited to the Spanish territory.

75. A good introduction to grain storage in the Iberian Peninsula villas can be found in Salido Domínguez 2008. For Lusitania, see Carneiro 2010, 239–41. See also the pertinent chapters in Arce and Goffaux 2011.

76. For Monroy, see Aguilar Sáenz 1991, 273–74. For Veranes, see Fernández Ochoa and Morillo Cerdán 2002, 388–89. For Bares, see Ramil González 2003, 200.

77. Benéitez González and Miguel Hernández 1993–1994, 123 (Navatejera). See also Chavarría Arnau 2012.

78. Alarcão, Étienne, and Mayet 1990, 243–44.

79. Rodríguez Martín 1988.

80. See Martín González 2009, 24–28, although the results of these emergency excavations are still provisional.

81. Hickey 2007; Grey 2011, 198–202.

82. Wickham 2005, 265–80. See Dahí Elena 2007, for a late Roman numeral slate from the villa of San Pelayo (Salamanca), which suggests accounting practices in association with central facilities.

83. Pérez Losada 1995, 172.

84. See the overview in Sánchez Pardo 2010, 141–44. For radiocarbon analysis, see Jordá Pardo et al. 2009.

85. See Peña Cervantes 2010 for continuities in the tradition of infrastructural investments.

86. Horden and Purcell 2000, 201–4; Grey 2011, 61–62. Also note Grey's ampler definition of risk management, including social strategies in addition to economic ones (63–90).

87. Hernández Guerra 2001, 159–60 (num. 186); Arce 2009, 236–37.

88. Wickham 2005, 708–10; Grey 2011, 178–97.

89. Debaccantibus per Hispanias barbaris et seuiente nihilominus pestilentiae malo opes et conditam in urbibus substantiam tyrannicus exactor diripit et milites exauriunt (*Chron.*, 40).

90. For parallels on tax collection and apocalyptic discourse, see Robinson 2000, 48–49.

91. *CTh.*, XIII.1.3. See Shaw 1981, 53–64, on the relationship among rural markets, peasant production, and taxation in North Africa.

92. During the late fourth and early fifth centuries, Baetican oil amphorae were found in the western Mediterranean, especially in Tarraconensis, southern Gaul, and Rome. See Reynolds 2005, 384–87, and 2010, 33–36. For northwestern Africa (Mauritania Tingitana), see Kulikowski 2004, 71–74.

93. Cf. *Not.Dig. Occ.* VII.118–34.

94. Fernández Ochoa, Gil Sendino, and Orejas del Saco Valle 2004, 208–16.

95. *CTh.*, XI.22.4; Mirković 1996; Sarris 2006, 150–54; Grey 2011, 198–206.

96. Sarris 2004, 290–91.

97. Durliat 1990, 81–82.

98. Conc. Elib., 19 (*Coll. Hisp.* IV, 248).

99. Spania terra lata et maxima et dives . . . in omnibus negotiis <pollens>, quorum ex parte dicemus: oleum enim et liquamen et vestem variam et lardum et iumenta mittens, omni mundo sufficiens (*Exp. Tot. Mun.*, 59).

100. Crawford and Reynolds 1979, 185 (35.1.17); Arnaud 2007.

101. Boulay 2016.

102. See the comparative cases of southern Gaul (Durand and Leveau 2004, 208) and Aquitaine (Balmelle 2001, 62).

103. Étienne and Mayet 2000, 21–58. See also the various chapters collected by Javier Andreu Pintado (2012) in a synthesis of *cupae* in different Iberian regions.

104. Calderón Fraile 2000, 363–64.

105. Fabião 1998, 189–92.

106. In the case of Braga, the contrast is with post-Roman, eastern wine amphorae. During the late Roman period, wine "imports" are absent (Morais 2000). Wine amphorae from extraregional origins are found in the first- and second-century strata of the villa of Povos. Yet late Roman amphorae are exclusively fish related (Banha 1991–1992).

107. See Reynolds 2005, 398–400.

108. Hitchner 2002, 72.

109. Remesal Rodríguez 1991; González Cesteros 2010.

110. Calderón Fraile 2000, 365.

111. Reynolds 2005, 383–87.

112. Ibid., 391–93. See also the case studies collected in Pinto, Almeida, and Martin 2016, 139–460.

113. See note 99. On Iberian horses, see the letters of Symmachus requesting horses for the games that would celebrate his sons' praetorship, especially *Ep.* 4.60, 4.63, 5.82, 5.83, and 9.21. See also *CTh.*, XV.10.1. There is a synthesis in Arce 1982.

114. Peña 2007, 35–38.

115. Studies on TSHT still treat the work of Françoise Mayet (1984) and José López Rodríguez (1985) as the main references. Critiques of this work and debates about its typology and classification have continued since then, and the field is in great need of a new synthesis. Juan Tovar 1998 remains the standard classification and historical analysis of TSHT. More recently, however, Vigil-Escalera Guirado 2015 has challenged some of the established ideas about fifth-century production. For TSHT kilns and their links to urban centers, see Pérez Rodríguez-Aragón and Domínguez Bolaños 2005. See Paz Peralta 2008, with bibliography.

116. Juan Tovar 1998, 548–58.

117. Paz Peralta 1991, 47–50.

118. For Asturias, see Zarzalejos Prieto 2005, 171–72. The exception in the area seems to be Gijón, which partially follows the pan-Mediterranean world of ARS (see Fernández Ochoa, García Díaz, and Uscatescu Barrón 1992).

119. For Braga, see Morais 2005, 128–29. For Zaragoza, see Paz Peralta 1991.

120. Dahí Elena 2010, 224–25.

121. In Astorga, TSHT wares are attested to in a residential mansion next to the Augustan *forum* (Burón Álvarez 1999, 1053) as well as in the excavations in the walls (García Marcos, Morillo Cerdán, and Campomanes 1997, 520–24). For Iria Flavia, see López Pérez, Álvarez González, and López González 1999, 248–49. For other examples of northwestern Iberia, see Menéndez Llorente 2000, 71–84 (Valdeorras, Ourense). Even in sites with evidence of ARS and TSHT, such as the villa of O Cantón Grande, the former only becomes dominant over the latter in the fifth century, and even then, the number of fragments seems to be relatively modest in comparison to other sigillatas (López Pérez and Vázquez Collazo 2007, 97–101). For Lugo, see Alcorta Irastorza 2005, 200. For Castro Ventosa, see Díaz Álvarez and Garín García 1999b, 79–85. For Almenara, see Mañanes Pérez 1992. For La Olmeda, see Nozal, Cortes, and Abásolo Álvarez 2000, 314.

122. Menéndez Llorente 2000, 71–84.

123. See a discussion on land transportation cost in Adams 2007, 11–14.

124. The classic introduction and categorization of ARS are in Hayes 1972, 13–299, and 1980, 484–523. Two different types of ARS wares reached the peninsula in late antiquity: ARS C and D. The chronology of the first overlaps with the late Roman period (mid-third century to mid-fifth century), whereas ARS D was produced between the early fourth through the seventh centuries (Carandini 1983, 150–51).

125. For the commercial character of this network, see Carandini 1983. Contra, arguing for a structuring role of state-based (tax) transportation but without necessarily denying commercial exchanges, see Wickham 1988, 190–93.

126. Pioneer synthesis works in this field are Simon Keay's study of amphorae in Catalonia (1984) and Paul Reynolds's work on the Vinalopó valley (1993).

127. Parker 1992, n. 1100.

128. Panella 1986, 437–46.

129. Quaresma 1999.

130. Viegas 2006.

131. For Conimbriga, see De Man 2006, 108–15. For Porto, see Guimarães and Teixeira Pinto 2000, 500–501.

132. ARS wares are the main late Roman fine ware in Lusitanian villas even in those cases in which a considerable number of TSHT wares appear in excavations. See Carneiro and Sepúlveda 2004 for an analysis of a handful of sites in Alentejo.

133. For amphora evidence, see Diogo and Paixão 2001, 120–21 (naturally, Lusitanian amphorae are overwhelmingly present in this site owing to the large complex of fish factories, but African amphorae appear in significant numbers). ARS wares remain the only late Roman fine ware in the site (Fonseca 2004).

134. Zarzalejos Prieto 2005.

135. For São Cucufate, see Alarcão, Étienne, and Mayet 1990, 248–55. For Quinta das Longas, see Almeida and Carvalho 2005, 316–17.

136. García-Hoz Rosales et al. 1991, 396.

137. Carneiro and Sepúlveda 2004, 444.

138. For table wares, see Almeida and Carvalho 2005. For amphorae, see Almeida and Carvalho 1998.

139. Bost 1994.

140. Decker 2009, 233–37.

141. Sane ad uictum sibi conquirendum aut filium aut libertum aut mercennarium aut amicum aut quemlibet mittant (Conc. Elib., 19, *Coll. Hisp.* IV, 248).

142. For commercial and state transportation, see Adams 2007, 159–253. For the North African "consumer revolution," see Dossey 2010, 62–97.

CHAPTER 4. ADAPTING TO A NEW WORLD: POST-ROMAN
SETTLEMENT IN WESTERN IBERIA

1. For the inscription, see Chapter 5, 166.

2. *VPE*, IV.3.18–20 (remarked on in Isla Frez 2007, 12–13).

3. See the essays collected in Olmo Enciso 2008.

4. There are a few exceptions to this pattern in the peninsula, especially in Mediterranean Iberia. Tarragona might be a good example of post-450 continuity in use of late Roman ceremonial buildings, but certainly not later than the early sixth century (Macias Solé 2008, 298–99).

5. For a survey of different types of reuse of public spaces in late antique Iberian cities, see Gurt 2000–2001.

6. See Chapter 1, note 32. The bathhouse of Gijón may have had a similar fate (Fernández Ochoa and Zarzalejos Prieto 2001, 25).

7. Mateos Cruz, Pizzo, and Pliego Vázquez 2005.

8. Núñez Hernández 2008, 173–75.

9. For Conimbriga, see De Man 2006, 76–81. For Clunia, see Núñez Hernández 2008, 172. For Tiermes, see Dohijo 2007.

10. Cantino Wataghin 1999; I Braga 18 (*CV,* 75).

11. This was probably the case in Conimbriga (De Man 2011b, 520).

12. Lemos, Leite, and Cunha 2007, 335–37. For post-Roman walls in general, see Gutiérrez González 2014, 199–200.

13. Vigil-Escalera Guirado and Tejerizo García 2014.

14. The first excavations in the area, and the source for most of the later research, can be found in García Guinea, Iglesias Gil, and Caloca 1973. For an update of more recent scholarship on Monte Cildá, see Iglesias Gil and Ruiz Gutiérrez 2007.

15. Gonzalo González 2007. For hilltops in the area, see Martín Viso 2006a. For similar cases in the northern plateau, see Lecanda Esteban 2000 and Lecanda Estaban and Palomino 2001 (Tedeja). For analysis of specific cases with an updated bibliography, see the essays collected in Catalán, Fuentes, and Sastre 2014 and Quirós Castillo and Tejado Sebastián 2012.

16. Caballero Arribas and Peñas Pedrero 2012, 220–22.

17. Domínguez Bolaños and Nuño González 1997; Nuño González and Domínguez Bolaños 2014.

18. Sánchez Pardo 2012, 34–35.

19. Tejado Sebastián 2013.

20. Tejado Sebastián 2011.

21. For a synthesis of excavations, see Olmo Enciso 2007, 183–85.

22. The signatories at the Third Council of Toledo (589) included the bishops of Mérida, Braga, Beja, Lisbon, Egara, Dume, Porto, Tui, Viseu, Lamego, Iria, Salamanca, Lugo, Segovia, Astorga, and Cauria (*Coll. Hisp.* V, 139–48).

23. In Conimbriga, the "paleo-Christian" basilica discovered in the *domus Tancinus* has an unknown, yet post-Roman, chronology (De Man 2006, 74–75; De Man 2005). For questions of its chronology, see De Man 2011b, 519, and Correia, De Man, and Reis 2011. For Viseu, see Pedro and Vaz 1995. For Mértola, see Macias 1995. For Uxama, see García Merino 2000, 190–93. For Idanha-a-Velha, see Sánchez Ramos and Morín de Pablos 2015. For Mérida, Braga, and Astorga, see Chapter 1, notes 50 and 51.

24. For Lugo, see López Quiroga and Lovelle 1999, 1396–97. For Cauca, see Blanco García 1998, 383. For Lisbon, see Alarcão 1994, 64.

25. Sánchez Ramos and Morín de Pablos 2015.

26. For Santa Eulalia, see Mateos Cruz 1999. See also Mateos Cruz and Alba Calzado 2000. Possible identification of urban churches can be found in Mateos Cruz 1999, 192–93.

27. Macias 1995.

28. Fuentes Hinojo 2006, 288.

29. For Italy, see Christie 2006, 206–7. For Africa, see Leone 2007, 198–208, and Sears 2007, 100–106. For Gaul, see Gauthier 1999 and Guyon 2006. See also Dey 2015, who argues for considerable continuity in ceremonial "armature" (gates, porticoed streets, etc).

30. Lavan 2003.

31. *VPE,* V.5.

32. Real 2000, 27–28. Fontes 2015, 400–02.

33. The Suevic king Rechila may have resided in Mérida between his conquest of the city in 439 and his death in that city in 448. Rechila could have used the city to launch his attacks on southern Iberia in 441, when the Suevic kingdom reached its peak in terms of territorial expansion (*Chron.*, 111, 115, and 129). For Porto, see *Chron.*, 190.

34. For Visigothic royal cities, see Ripoll 2000.

35. Isid. Hisp., *HG* 46.

36. Gillet 2003, 36–77.

37. Smith 2005, 198–213. See also Hardt 1998, 276–280.

38. This has been detected in excavations in Mérida (Alba Calzado 2007, 177–78). A similar case of a multifamily house with a central patio occupied in the sixth century has recently been excavated in Cauca (Pérez González and Reyes Hernando 2007, 169–70).

39. Pérez González, Illarregui Gómez, and Arribas Lobo 2015, 246.

40. Caballero Arribas and Peña Pedrero 2012, 22226.

41. Mateos Cruz, Pizzo, and Pliego Vázquez 2005, 260–61.

42. Lewit 2003, 264–67; Arce, Chavarría Arnau, and Ripoll 2007, 322–26.

43. *Chron.*, 225.

44. *VPE*, V.10.37–39.

45. For North Africa, see Leone 2007, 134–48, although there are more exceptions to a marked, abrupt break (but exceptions nonetheless). For Italy, see Christie 2006, 202–63, with similar general trends in the fifth and early sixth centuries, although the weight of the Church and royal and imperial capitals altered some of these patterns in specific instances. For Spain in general (especially Mediterranean Iberia), see Kulikowski 2004, 289–98. For southern Gaul, see Loseby 1996, 52–67 (Arles) and Riess 2013, 110–23 (Narbonne).

46. Mateos Cruz 2007.

47. Kulikowski 2004, 303–9. See also Martin 2003, 32–40 (including the seventh century).

48. *Chron.*, 179.

49. Martin 2003, 48–51.

50. Theudericus Emeritam depredari moliens beatae Eulaliae martyris terretur ostentis (*Chron.*, 175). Cf. *Chron.*, 80.

51. *VPE*, V.8.14–29.

52. This process was much better documented in Gaul owing to the abundance of sources. Brown 2003, 106–10; Beaujard 2000, 117–41.

53. Tejado Sebastián 2013.

54. See Utrero Agudo and Moreno Martín 2015 (most of the evidence, however, dates from the late sixth and seventh centuries).

55. *VPE*, IV.2.57–76.

56. Brown 2012.

57. Chavarría Arnau 2007a, 96–116 et passim. For problems of abandonment in the Roman West, see Ripoll and Arce 2000.

58. Some notable exceptions are the villas of Bares (Ramil González 2003), Noville (Pérez Losada 1992), and possibly Milreu, which may have been occupied as residential units into the Islamic period despite a few transformations in the peristyle villa (Teichner 2006, 213–14; and 2008, 123).

59. See Isla Frez 2001, 12–15. It has been suggested that the *castella* mentioned in the sources, especially Hydatius and Isidore, makes reference to villas rather than fortified towns (Arce 2006b, 9–12), although there is not conclusive evidence to prove this point (cf. Isla Frez 2001, 10–12). For the origins of the medieval *villa*, see Mínguez 1998.

60. Mañanes Pérez 1992; García Merino and Sánchez Simón 2004, 181.

61. Jimeno Martínez, Gómez Santa Cruz, and Argente Oliver 1988–1989.

62. Chavarría Arnau 2007a, 126–28. Still earlier examples may have existed in the meseta, such as the Villa de Prado in Valladolid (Sánchez Simón 1998, 726). However, Alexandra Chavarría Arnau has found problems with the dating of the abandonment (attributed to the early fourth century), which may suggest a later (post-Roman) process of nonelite occupation (Chavarría Arnau 2007a, 222). Another post-Roman reuse for productive purposes may be the site of La Armuña (Salamanca), (Ariño et al. 2015).

63. Heras Mora and Gilotte 2008. A similar evolution occurred in some of the Roman villas of Alcoutim, where most of the late Roman villas continued being occupied into the post-Roman period, although only a few of them had religious buildings dating from the fifth century onward (Catarino 2005–2006, 120–24). For Cerro da Vila, see Teichner 2008, 314, and Matos 1994, 524.

64. Nozal Calvo 1995, 317; Chavarría Arnau 2007a, 218.

65. Gómez Sobrino, González Santiso, and Martínez Tamuxe 1980.

66. See the discussion in Vigil-Escalera Guirado 2015.

67. Teichner 2008, 250–68.

68. *HW* 3.

69. There are a few examples of post-450 villa occupation in a "traditional way" (that is, as aristocratic Roman-style houses). One of them might be Torre de Palma (Maloney and Hale 1996; Maloney 1999–2000).

70. For Bares, see Ramil González 2003. For Noville, see Pérez Losada et al. 1992. In general, continuous occupation seems to have been the norm in the whole microregion of Nedos (Sánchez Pardo 2006, 27–30).

71. For modern Galicia, see Rodríguez Resino 2005, 173–77. For northern Portugal (between the Minho and Duero Rivers), see López Quiroga 2004, 264–66, although the association between burials and rural churches will only be confirmed with further excavations in specific sites. Continuity in settlement was also the norm in areas with less monumental villas, such as the region of Alto Pavia (Beira Alta), between the northern Lusitanian cities of Lamego and Viseu, where a settlement pattern based on rural farms survived into the seventh century (Vieira 2005–2006, 261–65).

72. Arguments on the end of the villa related to changing housing tastes can be found in Lewit 2004 and 2005. In the Iberian context, this change in tastes has been associated with the end, so to speak, of senatorial aristocracy (Chavarría Arnau 2004, 89–90).

73. For the arguments on poverty as a driving force behind settlement change, see Ward-Perkins 2005, 104–10. See also Wickham 2005, 255.

74. Fundamental work on post-Roman villages in the Iberian Peninsula in Vigil-Escalera Guirado 2000, Quirós Castillo and Vigil-Escalera Guirado 2006, and Vigil-Escalera Guirado 2007 and 2015. See also the essays collected in Quirós Castillo 2009.

75. Vigil-Escalera Guirado 2000 (for house typology); Quirós Castillo and Vigil-Escalera Guirado 2006, 92–93; Vigil-Escalera Guirado 2007, 266–67.

76. Quirós Castillo and Vigil-Escalera Guirado 2006, 91.

77. Larrén et al. 2003, 284–90.

78. Ballesteros Arias and Blanco Rotea 2009.

79. Ariño Gil, Barbero, and Díaz 2004–2005. Cf. Ariño Gil and Rodríguez Hernández 1997, for the territory of Salamanca in general.

80. Gutiérrez González 1996, 65–68.

81. Calleja Martínez 2001.

82. A possible exception is Cuarto de las Hoyas in Salamanca, in which we find a series of small buildings with stone foundations and farmyards (Storch de Gracia y Asensio 1998).

83. For Pelambre, see Pérez Rodríguez-Aragon and González Fernández 2009. For Vega de Duero, see Bellido Blanco 1997. For farms, see Vigil-Escalera Guirado 2007, 258–64.

84. Martín Viso et al. (forthcoming).

85. Vigil-Escalero Guirado 2000, 228–35.

86. For internal development, see Martín Viso 2012, 49. For external development, see Chavarría Arnau 2013, 153–54.

87. For peasant autonomy, see Quirós Castillo and Vigil-Escalera Guirado 2006, 106–7, and, more recently, Vigil-Escalera Guirado 2015. More emphasis on landowners with large properties can be found in Iñaki Martín Viso 2012, 49–50 (although the author sees villages as peasant initiatives in newly cultivated areas).

88. See Grey 2011, 148–77, which presents a multilayered analysis of the social impulses beyond peasant solidarity vis-à-vis landowners.

89. An introduction to rural settlement in Merovingian Gaul can be found in Périn 2002. For the question of village and estate, see Wickham 2005, 393–406. This latter work presents two models of village organization, one under the aegis of the aristocratic landowners (Île de France) and another one organized "from the bottom" as a protection against the same aristocracy (the middle Rhineland).

90. See Hamerow 2002, 87, for northwestern Europe.

91. Arbeiter 2003; Ripoll and Chavarría Arnau 2005.

92. For a short presentation of the basilica and scholarship on the site, see Oepen 2012, 141–48.

93. For the most updated list of post-Roman (and Visigothic) rural churches, see Oepen 2012 (although it only includes sites with previous villa occupation). See Utrero Agudo 2010 for issues of rural church chronology (either with or without previous villa occupation) in northern Iberia.

94. Maciel 1993; Maciel 1996; Oepen 2012, 110–16.

95. Oepen 2012, 146–47.

96. Lopes and Alfenim 1994, 494–95.

97. Alfenim and Lopes 1995; Oepen 2012, 126–32.

98. Wolfram 2011, 274–81.

99. The basilica of Marialba, near León, was perhaps originated in a *martyrium* of the fourth century, which underwent different reforms during the fifth and sixth centuries. By the early seventh century, the building had a baptistery (Martínez Peñín 2011; Oepen 2012, 398–407).

100. García Merino 2000, 186–87.

101. Lecanda Esteban 2000.

102. The best introduction to Christian architecture in Galicia is in Sánchez Pardo 2012 (although this study does not include other areas of northwestern Iberia).

103. II Braga 5 (*CV*, 83).

104. Christianity is archaeologically invisible in this region with the possible exception of certain caves, which have been associated with ascetic movements (Azkárate 1988, 115–498). However, it has been pointed out that economic rather than religious reasons lay behind this type of occupation (Castellanos and Martín Viso 2005, 18).

105. For Spanish historiography, see Torres López 1928 and Martínez Díez 1959 (with different assessments of proprietary rights over these churches). The most updated and extensive survey of this phenomenon in the post-Roman West is in Wood 2006.

106. For the very slow process of parish formation in the peninsula, see Ripoll and Velázquez 1999, 111–21.

107. Canon 3 of the Council of Lérida makes reference to laypersons donating basilicas under the disguise of monastic foundations so as to avoid placing these churches under episcopal authority. The council met in 546 (*Coll. Hisp.* IV, 300–301).

108. Wood 2006, 18–25 et passim.

109. For parallels in Gaul, see Brown 2015, 171–74.

110. For instance, IV Toledo 33 (*Coll. Hisp.* V, 220–21). Cf. III Toledo 19 (*Coll. Hisp.* V, 127).

111. For the question of property and episcopal vs. lay jurisdictions, see Wood 2006, 18–25.

112. Martin 2003, 321–70.

113. Fernández 2016b, 69. Cf. *Chron.*, 228. See Kock 2014 for the flexible boundaries between Nicene and Arian identities.

114. See Kreiner 2014, 189–229, for Merovingian Gaul.

115. Fernández 2016b.

116. García Moreno 1987. Javier Arce suggests continuity of the road system into the early Islamic period (Arce 1993, 178). See Dohijo 2011, 395–98, for the case of Soria.

CHAPTER 5. CRAFTING FRAGMENTED STATEHOOD: ARISTOCRATIC IDENTITY IN THE POST-ROMAN WORLD

1. Drinkwater 1998, 271-87. For the events in the peninsula, two interesting reconstructions appear in Arce 2007, 31–67, and in Díaz 2011, 46–55.

2. *Chron.*, 41.

3. For different interpretations of the division of lands in Iberia and the problems related to the sources, see Arce 2007, 67–72; Díaz 2011, 55–63; and Modéran 2014, 80–84.

4. King 1972, 183–84; Martin 2003, 105–6.

5. *Chron.*, 60.

6. *Chron.*, 66. Indeed, when the Vandals were defeated in Gallaecia, Hydatius said that they fled to the more distant Baetica rather than to Lusitania.

7. Significantly, Castinus fled to Tarragona and not to Mérida (*Chron.*, 69).

8. *Chron.*, 80. We do not know which parts of Lusitania suffered the presence of these armies, although it certainly included the area of Mérida (Qui [Heremigarius] aud procul de Emerita, quam cum sanctae martyris Eulaliae iniuria spreuerat, maledictis per Gaisericum caesis ex his quos secum habebat).

9. *Chron.*, 91 (for Gallaecia) and 106 (for Baetica).

10. *Chron.*, 111.

11. Rechila died in the city in 448 (*Chron.*, 128).

12. Censurius comes, qui legatus missus fuerat ad Sueuos, residens Martyli obsessus a Rechila in pace se tradidit (*Chron.*, 113).

13. Ad Sueuos Mansuetus comes Hispaniarum et Fronto similiter comes legati pro pace mittuntur et optinent conditiones iniunctas (*Chron.*, 147).

14. *Chron.*, 106, 115, 126, and 161.

15. *Chron.*, 175, 188, 201, 225, 237, and 240.

16. *Chron.*, 240.

17. Pliego Vázquez 2009, 124–25 (with the exceptions of Talavera de la Reina and Lisbon). See also Collins 1980 for the prominent role of Mérida (which was eventually eclipsed by Toledo, however) and Panzram 2010.

18. *ICERV* 363; Díaz y Díaz 1983, 51. Cf. Velázquez 2008, who is in favor of a seventh-century dating for the inscription.

19. Solberat antiquas moles ruinosa vetustas. | Lapsum et senio ruptum pendebat opus. | Perdiderat usum suspensa via p(er) amnem. | Et liberum pontis casus negabat iter. | Nunc tempore

potentis Getarum Ervigii regis, | Quo deditas sibi precepit excoli terras, | Studuit magnanimus factis extendere n(o)m(e)n, | Veterum et titulis addit Salla suum. | Nam postquam eximiis nobabit moenib(us) urbem, | Hoc magis miraculum patrare non destitit. | Construxit arcos, penitus fundabit in undis | Et mirum auctoris imitans vicit opus. Nec non et patrie tantum cr(e)are munimen | Su(m)mi sacerdotis Zenonis suasit amor. | Urbs Augusta felix mansura p(er) s(e)c(u)la longa | Nobate studio ducis et pontificis. era DXXI. See also Fernández 2016a, 114–15, for questions related to the document translation.

20. Thomas and Witschel 1992.

21. I have developed these arguments in greater detail in Fernández 2016a.

22. A discussion of the title in later sources appears in Martin 2003, 167–75.

23. Salla is usually identified as the emissary that Theoderic sent to the Suevic king Remismund in 466 (*Chron.*, 233).

24. Martin 2003, 161–65.

25. *CE* 322 García Moreno 1974, 8–12; Dumézil 2008, 84–89.

26. Panzram 2014; Heinzelmann 1976; Brown 2003, 106–15.

27. *LV*, XII.1.2.

28. Theudericus Emeritam depredari moliens beatae Eulaliae martyris terretur ostentis (*Chron.*, 175).

29. Sanctorum basilicae effractae; altaria sublata atque confracta; uirgines dei exim quidem abductae, sed integritate seruata; clerus usque ad nuditatem pudoris exutus (*Chron.*, 167).

30. *Chron.*, 170 and 174.

31. *Chron.*, 80.

32. *Chron.*, 179.

33. For bishops and competing urban leadership in late antique cities, see Brown 1992, 71–117.

34. For the eastern Empire, see Whittow 1990; Laniado 2002, 131–223. For the post-Roman west, see Loseby 1998, 245–49 and Barbier 2014, 70–99. (Gaul); Liebeschuetz 2001, 124–36; Schmidt-Hofner 2014.

35. In the Byzantine Empire, where government by notables was a formal institution, bishops probably did not become members of these assemblies until the reign of Anastasius. See Laniado 2006. A *novella* of Majorian from 458 (*Nov. Maj.*, 3) does not include bishops and clergy within the civic assembly in charge of electing the *defensor*, but only the *curiales* (*municipes*), *honorati*, and the people (*plebs*).

36. On civic government in the *Breviary*, see Curchin 2014, 286–87.

37. *Brev. Al.*, II.1.8, Interpretatio (defensores aut assertores pacis). For seventh-century *defensores*, see *LV* II.1.25. See also *Brev. Al.*, I.10 and VIII.2.1.

38. *LV*, XII.1.2.

39. For the defensorate in the post-Roman West, see Schmidt-Hofner 2014.

40. *LV*, V.4.19.

41. *LV*, XII.2.13 (in polipticis publicis); *CTh.*, XI.26.2 (Cf. *Brev. Al.*, XI.7).

42. See Chapter 2, note 40. For *gesta municipalia* in the post-Roman world, see Brown 2012.

43. *VPE*, IV.2.15.

44. Thompson 1969, 115–16.

45. *VSE*, 33. Castellanos 1998a, 37–52.

46. *VPE*, V.5.20–106.

47. A discussion of these arguments appears in Martin 2008a, 325–28.

48. Paterno tra(h)ens lineam Getarum (*ICERV* 86).

49. Quosdam Gotorum nobiles genere opibusque perquam ditissimos, e quibus etiam nonnulli in quibusdam ciuitatibus comites a rege fuerant constituti (*VPE*, V.10.1).

50. Claudium uirum clarissimum, ducem Emeritensis ciuitatis . . . Claudius nobili genere hortus Romanis fuit parentibus progenitus (*VPE*, V.10.6–7).

51. See Sivan 1998 for the evolution of intermarriage between Goths and Romans. See also Mathisen 1993, 134–35.

52. Koch 2012, 375–404.

53. Buchberger 2015. Cf. Liebeschuetz 2013. See also Martin 2008b.

54. For Vandal Africa, see Conant 2012.

55. Patzold 2014.

56. Arce 2007, 130–31. Cf. Díaz 2011 for a more skeptical approach toward the numbers.

57. *Chron.*, 41: Calliciam Vandali occupant et Suaeui sitam in extremitate Oceani maris occidua. The most persuasive interpretation of this passage points toward a Vandal settlement in the northern plateau (Tranoy 1974, 39–42). For a different interpretation, see López Quiroga and Lovelle 1995–1996, where it is argued that the Suevi received the territory centered in Braga, whereas the Vandals' territory was centered in Lugo.

58. Sueui . . . per plebem quae castella tutiora retinebat acta suorum partim caede, partim captiuitate, pacem quam ruperant familiarum que tenebantur redhibitione restaurant (*Chron.*, 81).

59. For the "end of the kingdom," see *Chron.*, 168 (regnum destructum et finitum est Sueuorum).

60. III Toledo, 2 (*Coll. Hisp.* V, 110).

61. For instance, see *Chron.*, 81, 86, and 91.

62. *Chron.*, 81.

63. Sueui cum parte plebes Calleciae cui aduersabantur pacis iura confirmant (*Chron.*, 105).

64. *Chron.*, 129.

65. Theudorico rege cum exercitu ad Bracaram extremam ciuitatem Galleciae pertendente . . . Romanorum magna agitur captiuitas captiuorum (*Chron.*, 167).

66. Sueui in partes diuisi pacem ambiunt Galleciorum . . . Solito more perfidiae Lusitaniam depraedatur (*Chron.*, 181). Solita perfidia, again, in *Chron.*, 183.

67. *Chron.*, 191.

68. *Chron.*, 196; Kulikowski 2004, 199.

69. *Chron.*, 243.

70. *Chron.*, 194. Pablo Díaz suggests that this *rector* was a *defensor civitatis*-like figure (Díaz 2011, 90). See also Arce 2007, 195–96.

71. In conuentus parte Bracarensis latrocinantum depredatio perpetratur (*Chron.*, 172).

72. *Chron.*, 164, 123, and 189.

73. For the Aregensi as an independent polity, see Collins 2004, 54.

74. Ioh. Bicl., *Chron.*, 35.

75. Martín Viso 2008.

76. *Chron.*, 245.

77. Ando 2000, 93–94; Gillett 2003.

78. *Chron.*, 86 and 88.

79. Nam si firmissimum hoc brebilegium usque nunc retinent civitates, ut nullo modo intra ambitus murorum cuiuslibet defuncti corpus humetur, quanto magis hoc venerabilium martyrum debet reverentia obtinere (I Braga 18) (*CV*, 75).

80. While there have been attempts to connect material funerary culture with Suevic (and other) ethnic origins in earlier moments of barbarian settlements, the evidence is rather scanty. See Barroso Cabrera, López Quiroga, and Morín de Pablos 2006, 214–15, and Heras Mora and Olmedo Gragera 2015.

81. Rodríguez Resino 2003. For dress codes and Roman-barbarian military culture, see von Rummel 2007, 97–196. For the elusive Suevic ethnic identity, see Díaz 2015.

82. Leovigildus rex in Gallaecia Suevorum fines conturbat et a rege Mirone per legatos rogatus pacem eis pro parvo tempore tribuit (Ioh. Bicl., *Chron.*, 39). But note that fines can also mean "boundaries."

83. For a recent summary of the different possible locations, see Ariño Gil and Díaz 2014, 187, n. 30.

84. Ioh. Bicl., *Chron.*, 27.

85. The classical formulation of this thesis is in Barbero and Vigil 1974, 33–51.

86. David 1947, 31–44.

87. *Chron.*, 180 and 190.

88. On Martin and Dume, see Díaz 2011, 231–34.

89. A recent analysis appears in Díaz 2011, 191–95.

90. Sánchez Pardo 2012, 259–61.

91. II Braga, 5 (*CV*, 83).

92. *Chron.*, 448; Díaz 2011, 219–30.

93. Conant 2012, 180–86.

94. *Chron.*, 219 and 222.

95. *Chron.*, 228.

96. I Braga, Praef. (*CV*, 65–67).

97. In nomine domini perfectum est templum hunc per Marsipalla deo uota sub die XIII kalendas Apriles era DLXXIII regnante serenissimo Veremundu rege (reconstruction by Ferreiro 1997, 264; cf. *ICERV* 355 and 510).

98. Ferreiro 1997.

99. *Virt. S. Mart.* I.11; Ferreiro 1995. For Christian buildings in the area of Braga, see Fontes 2015.

100. *Formula*, I.

101. Time prius Deum et ama Deum . . . Amabis enim Deum, si illum in hoc imitaberis, ut velis omnibus prodesse, nulli nocere et tunc te iustum virum appellabunt omnes, sequentur, venerabuntur et diligent (*Formula*, V, trans. Barlow 1969, modified). Cf. *LV*, I.1.5.

102. His barbaris quasi in pretium victoriae primum praedandi in Palentinis campis licentia data, dehinc supra dicti montis claustrorumque eius cura permissa est remota rusticanorum fideli et utili custodia (Oros., *Hist.*, VII.40.8).

103. *Chron.*, 41.

104. *Chron.*, 60.

105. *Chron.*, 63 and 66.

106. See note 58.

107. *Chron.*, 91.

108. *Chron.*, 117 and 120.

109. *Chron.*, 132–34.

110. For Manichaeans, see *Chron.*, 122, 125, and 127. For natural prodigies, see *Chron.*, 118, 128, 141, 143, and 151. For Rechiarius's expedition, see *Chron.*, 129.

111. But see Juan José Larrea's remarks on the "fierce Basques" arguing that complete independence may not have been the case in the area (Larrea 1998, 134–59).

112. *HW*, 10.

113. Isidore, *Chron.*, 61–62. For the Suevic campaign, Ioh. Bicl., *Chron.*, 21.

114. Díaz and Menéndez Bueyes 2005.

115. For the Suevic-Visigothic frontier, see Ariño Gil and Díaz 2014.

116. See Arce 2011, 133–45 (contra Barbero and Vigil 1974, who argued for a formal frontier between the Visigothic kingdom and a supposedly independent Basque people).

117. Even in northern Burgos, it is not clear whether the "invaders" mentioned by John of Biclarum were a recent presence or a well-established, independent community (Ioh. Bicl., *Chron.*, 32).

118. For the general context of the letter, see Martin 2006.

119. Necesse nobis erit domini nostri exinde auribus intimare, pariter et filio nostro Ergani suggerere, et huiusmodi ausum praecepta culminis eius uel districtio iudicis non sine uuestro detrimento seuerissime uindicabunt (II Toledo, *Ad Toribium, Coll. Hisp.* IV, 365–66).

120. Cum . . . adhuc floreres in saeculo (II Toledo, *Ad Toribium, Coll. Hisp.* IV, 363).

121. The earliest attested bishop in Salamanca (Leutrius) is from the late sixth century (III Toledo, *Edictum regis, Coll. Hisp.* V, 144). Cauca may have also maintained a municipal status (II Toledo, *Ad Toribium, Coll. Hisp.* IV, 365).

122. For Palencia as head of a territory, see *Chron.*, 179. The above-mentioned Toribius might have been a former civic-military leader or a retired royal officer who became a monk and a Christian leader of the town.

123. See note 45.

124. Dunn 1997, 147.

125. Martín Viso 1999.

126. Proc., *Bell.* V.12.50–51.

127. I follow Javier Arce's interpretation of this body as a personal guard rather than a private army (Arce 2011, 105–6.)

128. Cf. Rio 2008.

129. García Moreno 1974, 77–86.

130. Caballero Arribas and Peñas Pedrero 2012, 226–31.

131. Cf. Sarris 2006, 162–75, for the porous boundaries between public and private armies.

132. Vigil-Escalera Guirado 2015, 210–13. Cf. Martín Viso 2014, 260.

133. Ripoll 1985, 1998, and 2010.

134. *Cons. Caes.*, 71a and 75a.

135. Koch 2006; Arce 2011, 38–39 (who pushes the date of settlements to the second third of the sixth century); Martín Viso 2012, 36–37.

136. Ripoll 1985; Ripoll 1993–1994.

137. Ripoll 2010.

138. Kulikowski 2001, however, admits the possibility in the case of the meseta cemeteries. Cf. Chavarría Arnau 2013, 152–53.

139. Arce 2011, 42–43.

140. Von Rummel 2013, 393.

141. Cf. Tejerizo García 2011.

142. See the stimulating discussion in Esmonde Cleary 2013, 364–76.

143. *Chron.*, 122 (cf. *Chron.*, 125, 127, and 130).

144. *VSE*, 24 and 29; Castellanos 1998a, 39–43.

145. Narrat ille [i.e., Aemilian] quod uiderat: sclera eorum [i.e., of the "senators"], caedes, furta, incesta, uiolentias, caeteraque uitia increpat . . . quumque omnes reuerenter auditum praeberent (*VSE*, 33).

146. For charismatic authority, see Hillgarth 1980, 34–45, Martin 2003, 99–105, and Díaz 2013.

147. *VPE*, III.36–58.

148. Innes 2000, 165–72.

CHAPTER 6. PRESERVING WEALTH IN A CHANGING WORLD: POST-ROMAN
ARISTOCRATIC ECONOMIC STRATEGIES

1. Gregum suorum requireret rationes (*Vita Fruct.*, II).

2. Vigil and Barbero 1970.

3. Martin 2003, 178–79.

4. Martín Viso 2013, 78–79.

5. The bibliography on this debate is vast, and the controversy does not seem to be settled. Basic references are Goffart 1980; Barnish 1986; Durliat 1990, 97–110; Wood 1998; Wickham 1984 and 2005, 80–124; and Halsall 2007, 422–42.

6. *Chron.*, 41.

7. See the discussion in Díaz 2011, 58–62.

8. Subuersis memorata plagarum crassatione Hispaniae prouinciis barbari ad pacem ineundam domino miserante conuersi, sorte ad inhabitandum sibi prouinciarum diuidunt regiones (*Chron.*, 41).

9. Díaz 2011, 59–61.

10. See Díaz 2011, 159–62, who, in my opinion, has offered the most thoughtful explanation for this possibility.

11. For tax, see Goffart 1980, 103–26. For land, see Wickham 2005, 84–87. See also Halsall 2007, 436–42, who is open to the idea of an earlier payment in taxes and a later (especially post-439) distribution of public and seized land.

12. For instance, see *LV*, X.1.8, on the enforcement of Roman and Gothic portions of divided land. See Goffart 1980, 105–6, who raises doubts about the direct incorporation of these earlier laws in the later Visigothic legislation without emendation. For the main laws on land division between Romans and Goths, see *CE* 276 and 277; *LV*, X.1.8, 9, 15, and 16; *LV*, X.2.1; and *LV*, X.3.5. All of the legislation in the Visigothic Code are *antiquae*, which indicates that they were issued before the reign of Reccared.

13. See the vague comments in Hydatius's *Chronicle* on the peace between Theoderic and Majorian, which may have established the overall framework for Gothic influence in the peninsula in 459 (*Chron.*, 192). For possible retaliations against Romans who sided with the Suevi, see *Chron.*, 179 and 240.

14. Cf. Innes 2006, 50–51.

15. For seventh-century reform legislation, see *LV*, IX.2.8 (Wamba) and IX.2.9 (Erwig).

16. Isla Frez 2010, 45–88.

17. A summary of the "declining thesis" of taxation appears in Wickham 2005, 93–100 (although it is centered in the post-Leovigild period).

18. *LV*, IX.2.6.

19. Curiales . . . vel privati, qui caballos ponere vel in arca publica functionem exolvere consueti sunt (*LV*, V.4.19).

20. Cf. *CTh*., XI.4.1, a law that, in principle, demands a similar procedure as *LV*, V.4.19. However, in the first case, the problem seems to have been that former owners were required to pay taxes on lands they no longer owned because the transaction had not been incorporated into the tax registers (*censuales paginae*). In the second case, the issue was more likely to have been the interruption of payments by the new owners.

21. Bjornlie 2014.

22. See Pliego Vázquez 2009, 199–213, which shows the steady decline of the gold content in coinage from the early seventh century, with a small bump in the central decades of that century. The correlation between coinage and taxation levels is argued in Hendy 1988 (although, as the author argues, the Visigoths maintained a remarkably high level of gold content in their coins in comparison to other so-called barbarian kingdoms).

23. XVI Toledo, *Tomus* (*CV*, 485).

24. *Variae*, V.39.

25. Martín Viso 2013, 73–74.

26. García Moreno 1971 and 1974, 21–65. For *numerarii* in the late empire, see Palme 1999, 110–11.

27. *LV*, XII.1.2.

28. XVI Toledo, *Lex edita* (*CV*, 517–18).

29. Fernández 2006.

30. Olmo Enciso 1998, 113–15. See also Velázquez and Ripoll 2000, 538–44, and Olmo Enciso 2007.

31. Proc., *Bell.*, V.12.54.

32. *Variae*, V.35 and V.39.

33. See Pliego Vázquez 2009, the most thorough and updated synthesis of Visigothic monetary history. See also Cabral and Metcalf 1997 and Díaz 2004.

34. Hendy 1988, 49–59; Martín Viso 2008.

35. This is a surprisingly understudied phenomenon. See Retamero 1999, 271–79, and Metcalf 1999, 205–6.

36. Clear examples are *PV*, 5, 10, 34, 45, 46, 47, 48, 52, 93, 95, 124, 125, 139, and 141.

37. *PV*, 20.

38. *PV*, 45–48. Iñaki Martín Viso has suggested that these lands may have been fiscal units (2013, 80).

39. For textiles, see *PV*, 49. For cheese, see *PV*, 11.

40. Díaz and Martín Viso 2011.

41. For estate accounts, see Velázquez 2004, 85–101; Wickham 2005, 223–26. For taxation, see Martín Viso 2006b, 283–90.

42. For instance, *PV*, 2, mentions taxes on the movement of animals (pedagium).

43. [. . .] s(estaria) VI | [. . .]s et Simplicius mod(ium) I | [. . .]+sus Maseti s(e)s(taria) IV | [. . .]+s dedi licias mod(ium) I | [. . .]s et Sigerius et Iustina mod(ium) I | [. . .] Precurasor mod(ios) III | [. . .]deo mod(ios) III | [. . .]uit Ioannis in angarias mod(ios) LX | [. . .]ota XII ‖ [. . .] [[om ad oc]] | [. . .]n+etum adicie p(er) Sigerius ad mod(ios?) a Lebaia | semertura

mod(io)s XVI, tritico mod(io)s [. . .] | Flascino mod(ios) II, Flaine s(estaria) VI cum a[…] | suas conlibertas Flaina s(estarium) I, Maxima s(estaria) IIII | Manno mod(ium) I, Procula s(estaria) III, Bonus et Flamnus | et Nonnus maior et Patricius mod(ium) I | exprendit Ioannis ad kaballos mod(ios) | XXXIII, Masetius mod(ios) II | ad Bodenecas mod(ios) III. For a full commentary on the text, see Velázquez 2004, 131–41.

44. *LV*, XII.1.2; Mitchell 1976; Goffart 1982, 7; Martín Viso 2013, 79.

45. *LV*, V.4.19. Cf. *Brev. Al.*, VIII.2.1. See also Lemcke 2016, 128.

46. Martín Viso 2013, 80.

47. Iubemus ut nullis indictionibus, exactionibus, operibus vel angariis . . . vilicus [pro sua utilitate] populus adgravare [praesumat] (*LV*, XII.1.2). García Moreno 1974, 33–34.

48. *VPE*, III.10.37–40: Qui [i.e., Leovigild] quamlibet esset Arrianus, tamen ut se eius precibus Domino commendaret, eidem uiro auctoritate conscripta de quodam precipuo loco fisci dixerit, ut alimenta aut indumenta exinde cum suis fratribus haberet. The "food and clothing" referred to in this passage must have been rents. A similar formula is found in canon XVI of II Braga (an "eastern canon") about the revenues of the church's properties administered by the bishop: "Si tamen ipse [i.e., the bishop] aut qui cum eo sunt fratres indiguerint aliquid ut necessitatem ut nullomodo patiantur secundum sanctum apostolum dicentem: Victu et tegumento his contenti sumus" (*CV*, 90–91).

49. *LV*, XII.1.2.

50. López Sáez et al. 2003, 148–49.

51. But the chronology here is wider, between the fifth and the ninth century. See Rodríguez González and Durany Castrillo 1998, 49–56.

52. López Sáez et al. 2009, 22–23.

53. Ariño Gil, Riera i Mora, and Rodríguez Hernández 2002, 296–97.

54. Martín Viso et al. (forthcoming).

55. Valdeomillos Rodríguez et al. 1996.

56. For hilltop occupation, see Fernández Mier 1999, 121–87. For walnut and chestnut tree cultivation, see López Merino, López Sáez et al. 2009.

57. Wickham 2005, 280–301.

58. Vigil-Escalera Guirado 2015, 158–60.

59. Castellanos 1998b.

60. Bonnassie 1991, 71–74; García Moreno 2001.

61. Hec ergo loca, cum edificiis, terris, vineis, oleis, ortis, pratis, pascuis, aquis aquarumue ductibus, aditibus accessibus, colonis vel servis atque omni iure suo peculio. (Fortacín Piedrafrita 1983, 60).

62. Monnellum vero ingenuum esse decernimus; colonicam quam tenet in locum gestaui ei ei (*sic*) concedimus (Fortacín Piedrafrita 1983, 64).

63. Decimas vero praestationis vel exenia, ut colonis est consuetudo, annua inlatione me promitto persolvere (*FW*, 36).

64. As in *LV*, V.4.13, where it is established that a slave can sell his own *peculium*, including animals. See also *LV*, X.1.7, a law that regulates the division of goods from a slave family whose members belong to different masters implicitly recognizes the reality of slaves possessing lands. See also García Moreno 2001, 208–9.

65. King 1972, 170–77.

66. *LV*, V.7.17; King 1972, 180–81.

67. *FW*, 32. Pablo Díaz has correctly called attention to the fact that there is no mention of servile status or slavery in general, although the tone of the formula stressed total submission

to the *dominus* as expressed in the later part of the *formula*: Et ideo memoratum statum meum ex hodierna die habeas, teneas, et posideas, iure dominioque tuo in perpetuum vindices ac dedendas, vel quicquid in meam vel de meam personam facere vilueris directa tibe erit per omnia vel certa potestas (Díaz 2007).

68. Cf. Banaji 2009, 73 et passim.

69. Díaz 2007.

70. Miguel Hernández and Benéitez González 1993–1994, 117–21.

71. Caballero Arribas and Peñas Pedrero 2012, 225.

72. *PV*, 54 (consignemus Simplicio, id est, VI sesq[uannes , , ,] cum agnus su'u's det scroua una, uacca una, Matratium q<u>am pariat in corte domni sui Valentini).

73. For *curtis* and villa, see Halsall 2006, 217–18.

74. *Vit. Fruct.*, 2. Against this interpretation, see Vigil and Barbero 1970, 78–82, according to whom the father of the future saint was collecting taxes as a *dux*.

75. *PV*, 53.

76. Carvalho 1999, 376–77.

77. Rodríguez Martín and Gorges 1999, 426.

78. Teichner 2006, 216.

79. For Milreu, see Teichner 2003, 112. For La Cocosa, see Cerrillo Martín de Cáceres 1983.

80. [Domno] Paulo Fasutinus saluto tuam/[—]em et rogo te domne ut comodo consu/[etum] facere est p(er) te ipsut oliba illa collige,/[cur?]a ut ipsos mancipios in iura{re}mento/[coger]e debeas ut tibi fraudem non fa/[cian]t illas cupas collige calas/[d]e cortices et sigilla de tuo anulo et vide/[il]las tegolas cas astritas sunt de fibula quo/[m]odo ego ipsas demisi (*PV*, 103).

81. Ramil González 2008.

82. Lagóstena Barrios 2001, 332.

83. Pérez Losada, Fernández Fernández, and Vieito Covela 2008, 502–3.

84. Vigil-Escalera Guirado 2007, 265–66. In terms of production, the post-Roman period was one of "invisible" production of oil and wine in the sense that we know these items continued being produced but no centralized facility for their production is dated after the sixth century (Peña Cervantes 2005–2006, 108).

85. Ariño Gil, Barbero, and Díaz 2004–2005.

86. *PV*, 95.

87. Bellido Blanco 1997; Blanco González, López Sáez, and López Merino 2009, 281–83. See also Bellido Blanco 1997, 307–9, for silos in a (very likely) village or farm in Villabáñez, Valladolid.

88. Sánchez Pardo and Rodríguez Resino 2009.

89. Vigil-Escalera Guirado 2013 shows that some villages had significant storage capacities, though not necessarily on a large scale.

90. Martín Viso et al. (forthcoming).

91. Ariño Gil 2006, 329–30.

92. Tejerizo 2012, 185–86.

93. Storch de Gracia y Asensio 1998, 146–51.

94. Ariño Gil and Díaz 2003.

95. *VPE*, IV.3. See Arce 2002, 209–12, who casts doubts on the veracity of the episode.

96. See, for instance, Dahí Elena 2012.

97. The turn of the sixth century remains the standard interpretation (Paz Peralta 1991, 230–31), but an earlier chronology has recently been suggested by Alfonso Vigil-Escalera Guirado (2015, 153–54).

98. Íñigo Erdozain and Martínez González 2002 (the chronology of the site is, however, established on the basis of similarities between ceramic forms found at the site and Paz Peralta's classification). See Martínez González 2005.

99. An introduction is provided in Rigoir, Rigoir, and Meffre 1973.

100. Uscatescu, Fernández Ochoa, and García Díaz 1994; Iglesias Gil 1994, 63–80. For El Cañal de Las Hoyas, see Ariño Gil 2006, 330.

101. Viegas 2013, 274.

102. Wooding 1996, 56–59.

103. For Braga, see Morais 2000. For Lisbon, see Diogo and Trinidade 1999, 85–86. For Gijón, see Zarzalejos Prieto 2005, 172–73.

104. As demonstrated in Sousa 2001, most of the eastern fine wares are found in areas with direct access to urban commercial nodes, such as Lisbon and the Tejo estuary.

105. However, it has been argued that the findings in Iberia only represent a minimum amount of this commercial network when compared with the findings in Britain (Wooding 1996, 41–42).

106. Reynolds 2005, 423–26.

107. Reynolds 2010, 92–93.

108. *PV*, 75 (from Diego Álvaro), recording payments in kind and coin (*tremisses*), although it is not clear whether this slate records rent payments or tax payments.

109. Marot 2000–2001.

110. *VPE*, V.3.

111. *VPE*, V.3. For different wares as containers for transportations, see Peña 2007, 197–200.

112. For kilns and production techniques in the plateau and northwestern Iberia, see Juan Tovar 2016.

113. The fundamental reference for post-Roman ceramics still is Luis Juan Tovar and Juan Blanco Garcia's study (1997) of the ceramics from the province of Segovia, which has correctly changed the focus from decoration and forms to production techniques as parameters of classification. Another attempt at classification can be found in Larrén et al. 2003. The most recent synthesis and classification is in Juan Tovar 2012.

114. Alba Calzado and Feijoo Martínez 2004, 486–89.

115. This tradition was characterized by the lack of uniformity and considerable regional variations (Juan Tovar and Blanco García 1997, 205–10; Manzano Moreno 2003, 549–51).

116. Almeida and Carvalho 2005.

117. Juan Tovar 2013.

118. Zarzalejos Prieto 2005, 174.

119. For instance, in Mérida (Alba Calzado and Feijoo Martínez 2004, 494 et passim).

120. Gaspar 2003.

121. De Man 2004 and 2006, 146–50.

122. Centeno Cea, Palomino Lázaro, and Negredo García 2016.

123. Juan Tovar and García Blanco 1997, 202–4. One must keep in mind that the production centers of these ceramics have not been found as yet, and, therefore, there is a possibility that

these common wares were produced in different microregions rather than in a single locality and distributed to other areas.

124. Lecanda Esteban 2003, 305 (Santa Mará de Mijangos) and 308–9 (Santa María de los Reyes Godos).

125. One example is provided by the so-called imitations of DSP found in the Cantabrian Basin and some specific spots of the northern meseta (Uscatescu, Fernández Ochoa, and García Díaz 1994, 216–23; see also the comments about classification of these wares in Juan Tovar and Blanco García 1997, 199–200).

126. Larrén et al. 2003, 291–304.

127. As in Conimbriga (De Man 2006, 137–42) or Mérida (Alba Calzado and Feijoo Martínez 2004, 486–89).

BIBLIOGRAPHY

Abásolo Álvarez, José Antonio. 1999. "La ciudad romana en la meseta norte durante la antigüedad tardía." In *Complutum y las ciudades hispanas en la antigüedad tardía*, ed. Luis García Moreno and Sebastián Rascón Marqués, 87–100. Alcalá de Henares: Universidad de Alcalá.

Abásolo Álvarez, José Antonio, Javier Cortes, and Fernando Pérez Rodríguez-Aragón. 1997. *La necrópolis norte de La Olmeda (Pedrosa de la Vega, Palencia)*. Palencia: Diputación Provincial de Palencia.

Abrams, Philip. 1988. "Notes on the Difficulty of Studying the State (1977)." *Journal of Historical Sociology* 1(1): 58–89.

Adams, Colin. 2007. *Land Transport in Roman Egypt: A Study of Economics and Administration in a Roman Province*. Oxford: Oxford University Press.

Aguilar Sáenz, Antonio. 1991. "Excavaciones arqueológicas en la villa romana de 'La Sevillana.'" *Extremadura Arqueológica* 2: 445–56.

Alarcão, Jorge. 1994. "Lisboa romana e visigótica." In *Lisboa Subterrânea*, 58–63. Lisbon: Electa.

Alarcão, Jorge, Robert Étienne, and François Mayet. 1990. *Les villas romaines de São Cucufate (Portugal)*. Paris: Boccard.

Alba Calzado, Miguel. 2007. "Diacronía de la vivienda señorial en Emerita (Lusitania, Hispania): desde las *domus* altoimperiales y tardoantiguas a las residencias palaciales omeyas (s. I–IX)." In *Archeologia e società tra tardo antico e alto medioevo*, ed. Gian Pietro Brogiolo and Alexandra Chavarría Arnau, 163–92. Mantua: SAP.

Alba Calzado, Miguel, and Santiago Feijoo Martínez. 2004. "Pautas evolutivas de la cerámica común de Mérida en épocas visigoda y emiral." In *Cerámicas tardorromanas y altomedievales en la Península Ibérica: Ruptura y continuidad*, ed. Luis Caballero Zoreda, Pedro Mateos Cruz, and Manuel Retuerce Velasco, 483–504. Madrid: CSIC.

Alcorta Irastorza, Enrique. 2005. "*Lucus Augusti* como centro de producción y consumo cerámico." In *Unidad y diversidad en el arco atlántico en época romana*, ed. Carmen Fernández Ochoa and Paloma García Díaz, 191–202. Oxford: Archaeopress.

Alfenim, Rafael, and Maria Conceição Lopes. 1995. "A basílica paleocristã/visigótica do Monte da Cegonha." In *IV Reunió d'arqueologia cristiana hispànica*, 389–99. Barcelona: Institut d'Estudis Catalans.

Almeida, Maria José de, and Antonio Carvalho. 1998. "Ânforas da villa romana da Quinta das Longas (S. Vicente e Ventosa, Elvas)." *Revista Portuguesa de Arqueologia* 1(3): 137–63.

———. 2005. "Villa romana da Quintas das Longas (Elvas, Portugal): A lixeira baixo-imperial." *Revista Portuguesa de Arqueologia* 8(1): 299–368.

Alonso Sánchez, Ángela, Enrique Cerrillo Martín de Cáceres, and José María Fernández Corrales. 1994. "Tres ejemplos de poblamiento rural romano en torno a ciudades de la Vía de la Plata: *Augusta Emerita*, *Norba Caesarina* y *Capara*." In *Les campagnes de Lusitanie romaine: Occupation du sol et habitats*, ed. Jean-Gérard Gorges, 67–87. Madrid: Casa de Velázquez.

Altuna, Jesús, and Koro Mariezkurrena. 1996. "Estudio arqueológico de los restos óseos hallados en las excavaciones romanas de Lugo." In *Lucus Augusti. I. El amanecer de una ciudad*, ed. Antonio Rodríguez Colmenero, 55–106. A Coruña: Fundación Pedro Barrié de la Maza.

Alvar, Jaime, Richard Gordon, and Celso Rodríguez. 2006. "The Mithraeum at Lugo (*Lucus Augusti*) and Its Connection with *Legio VII Gemina*." *Journal of Roman Archaeology* 19: 267–77.

Álvarez Martínez, José María. 1976. "La villa romana de 'El Hinojal' en la dehesa de 'La Tiendas' (Mérida)." *Noticiario Arqueológico Español: Arqueología* 4: 433–88.

————. 2006–2007. "Aspectos de las élites emeritenes en el bajo imperio a través de los programas iconográficos." *Anas* 19–20: 11–29.

Amaro, Clementino, and José Luís de Matos. 1996. "Trabalhos arqueológicos no claustro da Sé de Lisboa: Notícia preliminar." In *Ocupação romana dos estuários do Tejo e do Sado*, ed. Graça Filipe and Jorge Manuel Cordeiro Raposo, 215–24. Lisbon: Dom Quixote.

Ando, Clifford. 2000. *Imperial Ideology and Provincial Loyalty in the Roman Empire*. Berkeley: University of California Press.

Andreu Pintado, Javier. 1999. "Munificencia pública en la provincia Lvsitania: Una síntesis de su desarrollo entre los siglos I y IV d.C." *Conimbriga* 38: 31–64.

————, ed. 2012. *Las cvupae hispanas: Orígen/difusión/uso/tipología*. Uncastillo: Fundación Uncastillo.

Arbeiter, Achim. 2003. "Los edificios de culto cristiano: Escenario de la liturgia." In *Repertorio de arquitectura cristiana en Extremadura: Época tardoantigua y altomedieval*, ed. Pedro Mateos Cruz and Luis Caballero Zoreda, 177–230. Mérida: Instituto de Arqueología de Mérida.

Arce, Agustín. 1996. *Itinerario de la virgen Egeria (381–384)*. 2nd ed. Madrid: Biblioteca de Autores Cristianos.

Arce, Javier. 1982. "Los caballos de Símmaco." *Faventia* 4(1): 35–44.

————. 1990. "El *cursus publicus* en la Hispania tardorromana." In *Simposio sobre la red viaria en la Hispania romana*, 35–40. Zaragoza: Institución Fernando el Católico.

————. 1993. "La ciudad en la España tardorromana: ¿Continuidad o discontinuidad?" In *Ciudad y comunidad cívica en Hispania: Siglos II y III d.C.*, 178–84. Madrid: Casa de Velázquez.

————. 1999. "Los gobernadores de la *dioecesis hispaniarum* (ss. IV–V D.C.) y la continuidad de las estructuras administrativas romanas en la Península Ibérica." *Antiquité Tardive* 7: 73–83.

————. 2002. *Mérida Tardorromana, 300–580 d.C.* Mérida, Spain: Museo Nacional de Arte Romano.

————. 2006a. "*Fana, templa, delubra destrui praecipimus*: El final de los templos de la Hispania romana." *Archivo Español de Arqueología* 79: 115–24.

————. 2006b. "*Villae* en el paisaje rural de Hispania romana durante la antigüedad tardía." In *Villas tardoantiguas en el Mediterráneo occidental*, ed. Alexandra Chavarría, Javier Arce, and Gian Pietro Brogiolo, 9–15. Madrid: CSIC.

————. 2007. *Bárbaros y romanos en Hispania, 400–507 A.D.* 2nd ed. Madrid: Marcial Pons.

————. 2008. "La Hispania de Teodosio: 379–395 AD." *Antiquité Tardive* 16: 9–18.

————. 2009. *El último siglo de la España romana (248–409)*. 2nd ed. Madrid: Alianza.

————. 2011. *Esperando a los Árabes: Los Visigodos en Hispania (507–711)*. Madrid: Marcial Pons.

Arce, Javier, Alexandra Chavarría Arnau, and Gisela Ripoll. 2007. "The Urban *Domus* in Late Antique Hispania: Examples from Emerita, Barcino and Complutum." In *Houses in Late Antiquity: From Palaces to Shops*, ed. Luke Lavan, Lale Özgenel, and Alexander Sarantis, 305–36. Leiden: Brill.

Arce, Javier, and Bertrand Goffaux, eds. 2011. *Horrea d'Hispanie et de la Méditerranée romaine: Collection de la Casa de Velázquez*. Madrid: Casa de Velázquez.

Arias Vilas, Felipe. 1996. "Poblamiento rural: La fase tardía de la cultura castreña." In *Los finisterres atlánticos en la antigüedad: Época prerromana y romana*, ed. Carmen Fernández Ochoa, 181–88. Madrid.

Ariño Gil, Enrique. 2006. "Modelos de poblamiento rural en la provincia de Salamanca (España) entre la antigüedad y la alta edad media." *Zephyrus* 59: 317–37.

Ariño Gil, Enrique, Lorenzo Barbero, and Pablo Díaz. 2004–2005. "El yacimiento agrícola en El Cuquero y el modelo de poblamiento en época visigoda en el valle del río Alagón (Salamanca, España)." *Lancia* 6: 205–31.

Ariño Gil, Enrique, Sarah Dahí Elena, Ekhine García García, Jesús Liz, Jesús Rodríguez, María Reyes de Soto, and Robert Tamba. 2015. "Intensive Survey in the Territory of Salamanca: Aerial Photography, Geophysical Prospecting and Archaeological Sampling." *Journal of Roman Archaeology* 28: 283–301.

Ariño Gil, Enrique, and Pablo Díaz. 2003. "Poblamiento y organización del espacio. La tarraconense pirenaica en el siglo VI." *Antiquité Tardive* 11, 223–37.

———. 2014. "La frontera suevo-visigoda: Ensayo de lectura de un territorio en disputa." In *Las fortificaciones de la tarodantigüedad: Élites y articulación del territorio (siglos V–VIII d.C.)*, ed. Raúl Catalán, Patricia Fuentes, and José Carlos Sastre, 179–90. Madrid: La Ergástula.

Ariño Gil, Enrique, Santiago Riera i Mora, and José Rodríguez Hernández. 2002. "De Roma al medioevo: Estructuras de hábitat y evolución del paisaje vegetal en el territorio de Salamanca." *Zephyrus* 55: 283–309.

Ariño Gil, Enrique, and José Rodríguez Hernández. 1997. "El poblamiento romano y visigodo en el territorio de Salamanca: Datos de una prospección intensiva." *Zephyrus* 50: 225–45.

Arnaud, Pascal. 2007. "Diocletian's Prices Edict: The Prices of Seaborne Transport and the Average Duration of Maritime Travel." *Journal of Roman Archaeology* 20: 321–36.

Arruda, Ana Margarida, and Catarina Viegas. 1999. "The Roman Temple of *Scallabis* (Santarém, Portugal)." *Journal of Iberian Archaeology* 1, 185–224.

Arthur, Paul. 2004. "From Vicus to Village: Italian Landscapes, AD 400–1000." In *Landscapes of Change: Rural Evolutions in Late Antiquity and the Early Middle Ages*, ed. Neil Christie, 103–34. Aldershot: Ashgate.

Ayerbe Vélez, Rocío, Teresa Barrientos Vera, and Félix Palma García. 2009. "Los complejos forenses de *Augusta Emerita*." In *El foro de Augusta Emerita: Génesis de sus recintos monumentales*, ed. Rocío Ayerbe Vélez, Teresa Barrientos Vera, and Félix Palma García, 667–832. Madrid: CSIC.

Azkárate Garai-Olaun, Agostin. 1988. *Arqueología cristiana de la antigüedad tardía en Álava, Guipúzcoa y Viscaya*. Vitoria-Gasteiz: Diputación Foral de Álava.

Bachrach, Bernard. 2010. "The Fortification of Gaul and the Economy of the Third and Fourth Centuries." *Journal of Late Antiquity* 3(1): 38–64.

Balado Pachón, Arturo and Ana Belén Martínez García. 2004. "Resultado de las intervenciones arqueológicas de 2001 y 2002 en la villa romana de Picón de Castrillo (Ampudia, Palencia)." *Sautuola* 10, 187–202.

Ballesteros Arias, Paula, and Rebeca Blanco Rotea. 2009. "Aldeas y espacios agrarios altomedievales en Galicia." In *The Archaeology of Early Medieval Villages in Europe*, ed. Juan Antonio Quirós Castillo, 115–35. Bilbao: Universidad del País Vasco.

Balmelle, Catherine. 2001. *Les demeures aristocratiques d'Aquitaine: Société et culture de l'antiquité tardive dans le sud-ouest de la Gaule.* Bordeaux: Ausonius.

Banaji, Jairus. 2001. *Agrarian Change in Late Antiquity: Gold, Labour, and Aristocratic Dominance.* Oxford: Oxford University Press.

———. 2009. "Aristocracies, Peasantries and the Framing of the Early Middle Ages." *Journal of Agrarian Change* 9(1): 59–91.

Banha, Carlos Manuel dos Santos. 1991–1992. "As ânforas da villa romana de Povos." *Boletim Cultural CIRA* 5: 50–78.

Barbero, Abilio, and Marcelo Vigil. 1974. *Sobre los orígenes sociales de la Reconquista.* Barcelona: Ariel.

Barbier, Josiane. 2014. *Archives oubliées du haut Moyen Âge. Les gesta municipalia en Gaule franque (VIe-IXe siècle).* Paris: Honoré Champion Éditeur.

Barlow, Claude. 1969. *Iberian Fathers, Volume I: Martin of Braga, Paschasius of Dumium, Leander of Seville.* Washington, DC: Catholic University of America Press.

Barnes, Timothy. 1998. *Ammianus Marcellinus and the Representation of Historical Reality.* Ithaca: Cornell University Press.

Barnish, S. J. B. 1986. "Taxation, Land and Barbarian Settlement in the Western Empire." *Papers of the British School at Rome* 54: 170–95.

———. 1988. "Transformation and Survival in the Western Senatorial Aristocracy, c. A.D. 400–700." *Papers of the British School at Rome* 56: 120–55.

Barrientos Vera, Teresa. 2011. "Arquitectura termal de Mérida: Un siglo de hallazgos." In *Actas Congreso Internacional 1910–2010: El Yacimiento Emeritense*, ed. José María Álvarez Martínez and Pedro Mateos Cruz, 327–44. Mérida: Ayuntamiento de Mérida.

Barroso Cabrera, Rafael, Jorge López Quiroga, and Jorge Morín de Pablos. 2006. "Mundo funerario y presencia 'germánica' en 'Hispania.'" In *Gallia e Hispania en el contexto de la presencia 'germánica' (ss. V–VII): Balance y perspectivas*, ed. Jorge López Quiroga, Artemio Martínez Tejera, and Jorge Morín de Pablos, 213–24. Oxford: John and Erica Hedges.

Bauer, Franz Alto. 1996. *Stadt, Platz und Denkmal in der Spätantike: Untersuchungen zur Ausstattung des öffentlichen Raums in den spätantiken Städten Rom, Konstantinopel und Ephesos.* Mainz: Philipp von Zabern.

Beaujard, Brigitte. 2000. *Le culte des saints en Gaule: Les premiers temps—D'Hilaire de Poitiers à la fin du VIe siècle.* Paris: Éditions du Cerf.

Bellido Blanco, Antonio. 1997. "La ocupación de época visigoda en Vega de Duero (Villabáñez, Valladolid)." *Archivo Español de Arqueología* 70: 307–16.

Benéitez González, Carmen and Fernando Miguel Hernández. 1993–94. "Relectura arqueológica de la villa romana de Navatejera (León)." *Numantia* 6: 103–26.

Biers, William, ed. 1988. *Mirobriga: Investigations at an Iron Age and Roman Site in Southern Portugal by the University of Missouri–Columbia, 1981–1986.* Oxford: BAR.

Bjornlie, Shane. 2014. "Law, Ethnicity and Taxes in Ostrogothic Italy: A Case for Continuity, Adaptation and Departure." *Early Medieval Europe* 22(2): 138–70.

Blanco García, Juan Francisco. 1998. "Aproximación a la *Cauca* del bajo imperio." In *Congreso Internacional la Hispania de Teodosio*, ed. Ramón Teja and Cesáreo Pérez, 2:377–93. Segovia: Universidad SEK.

Blanco González, Antonio, José Antonio López Sáez, and Lourdes López Merino. 2009. "Ocupación y uso del territorio en el sector centromeridional de la cuenca del Duero entre la antigüedad y la alta edad media (siglos I–XI D.C.)." *Archivo Español de Arqueología* 82: 275–300.

Blázquez, José María. 1993. *Mosaicos romanos de España*. Madrid: Cátedra.

———. 1997. "Las elites de la Hispania romana en el bajo imperio." *Antiquitas* 22: 7–19.

Bonnassie, Pierre. 1991. *From Slavery to Feudalism in South-Western Europe*. Trans. Jean Birrell. Cambridge: Cambridge University Press.

Borg, Barbara, and Christian Witschel. 2001. "Veränderungen im Repräsentationsverhalten der römischen Eliten während des 3. Jhs. n. Chr." In *Inschriftliche Denkmäler als Medien der Selbstdarstellung in der römischen Welt*, ed. Géza Alföldy and Silvio Panciera, 47–120. Stuttgart: Franz Steiner.

Bost, Jean-Pierre. 1994. "Villa y circulación monetaria: Hipótesis de trabajo." In *Les campagnes de Lusitaine romaine*, ed. Jean-Gérard Gorges, 219–25. Madrid: Casa de Velázquez.

Boulay, Thibaut. 2016. "Vineyard Ownership: A *Habitus* of Power? The Roots of Land Tenure and the Culture of Wine-Making Among a New Political Class, from Constantine to Julian." *Journal of Late Antiquity* 9(2): 415–35.

Bourdieu, Pierre. 1984. *Distinction: A Social Critique of the Judgement of Taste*. Cambridge, MA: Harvard University Press.

———. 2012. *Sur l'état*. Paris: Raisons d'Agir/Éditions du Seuil.

Bowes, Kim. 2001. "'*Nec sedere in villam*': Villa-Churches, Rural Piety, and the Priscillianist Controversy." In *Urban Centers and Rural Contexts in Late Antiquity*, ed. Thomas Burns and John Eadie, 323–48. East Lansing: Michigan State University Press.

———. 2005. "'Une coterie espagnole pieuse': Christian Archaeology and Christian Communities in Fourth- and Fifth-Century Hispania." In *Hispania in Late Antiquity: Current Perspectives*, ed. Kim Bowes and Michael Kulikowski, 189–258. Leiden: Brill.

———. 2006. "Building Sacred Landscapes: Villa and Cult." In *Villas tardoantiguas en el Mediterráneo occidental*, ed. Alexandra Chavarría Arnau, Javier Arce, and Gian Pietro Brogiolo, 73–95. Madrid: CSIC.

———. 2008. *Private Worship, Public Values, and Religious Change in Late Antiquity*. Cambridge: Cambridge University Press.

———. 2010. *Houses and Society in the Later Roman Empire*. London: Duckworth.

———. 2013. "Villas, Taxes and Trade in Fourth Century Hispania." In *Local Economies? Production and Exchange of Inland Regions in Late Antiquity*, ed. Luke Lavan, 191–226. Leiden: Brill.

Bransbourg, Gilles. 2008. "Fiscalité impériale et finances municipales au IVe siècle." *Antiquité Tardive* 16: 255–96.

———. 2015. "The Later Roman Empire." In *Fiscal Regimes and the Political Economy of Premodern States*, ed. Andrew Monson and Walter Scheidel, 258–81. Cambridge: Cambridge University Press.

Brassous, Laurent. 2011. "Les enceintes urbaines tardives de la péninsule ibérique." In *L'Empire romain en mutation: Répercussions sur les villes romaines dans la deuxième moitié du 3e siècle*, ed. Regula Schtzmann and Stefanie Martin-Kilcher, 275–99. Montagnac: Éditions Monique Mergoil.

———. 2015. "Les édifices de spectacles d'Hispanie entre les IIe et IVe siècles." In *Urbanisme civique en temps de crise: Les espaces publics d'Hispanie et de l'occident romain entre le IIe et le IVe siècle*, ed. Laurent Brassous and Alejandro Quevedo, 273–88. Madrid: Casa de Velázquez.

Bravo, Gonzalo. 1996. "Prosopographia theodosiana (I): En torno al llamado 'clan hispano.'" *Gerión* 14: 381–98.

Brown, Peter. 1992. *Power and Persuasion in Late Antiquity: Towards a Christian Empire.* Madison: University of Wisconsin Press.

———. 2003. *The Rise of Western Christendom*, 2nd ed. Malden: Blackwell.

———. 2012. *Through the Eye of a Needle: Wealth, the Fall of Rome, and the Making of Christianity in the West, 350–550 AD.* Princeton: Princeton University Press.

———. 2015. *The Ransom of the Soul: Afterlife and Wealth in Early Western Christianity.* Cambridge, MA: Harvard University Press.

Brown, Warren. 2012. "On the *Gesta Municipalia* and the Public Validation of Documents in Frankish Europe." *Speculum* 87(2): 345–75.

Buchberger, Erica. 2015. "The Growth of Gothic Identity in Visigothic Spain: The Evidence of Textual Sources." In *Identidad y etnicidad en Hispania: Propuestas teóricas y cultura material en los siglos V–VIII*, ed. Juan Antonio Quirós Castillo and Santiago Castellanos, 87–100. Bilbao, Spain: Universidad del País Vasco.

Burgess, Richard. 1993. *The Chronicle of Hydatius and the Consularia Constantinopolitana.* Oxford: Oxford University Press.

Burnham, Barry, and John Wacher. 1990. *The Small Towns of Roman Britain.* Berkeley: University of Calfornia Press.

Burón Álvarez, Milagros. 1999. "Una gran *domus* en las proximidades del foro de Asturica Augusta: La casa del pavimento de *opus signinum*." In *Los orígenes de la ciudad en el noroeste hispánico*, ed. Antonio Rodríguez Colmenero, 2:1,039–56. Lugo: Diputación Provincial de Lugo.

———. 2006. "El trazado urbano de "Asturica Augusta": Génesis y evolución." In *Nuevos elementos de ingeniería romana: III Congreso de las obras públicas romanas*, ed. Isaac Moreno Gallo, 289–312. Valladolid: Junta de Castilla y León, Consejería de Cultura y Turismo.

Burrus, Virginia. 1995. *The Making of a Heretic: Gender, Authority, and the Priscillianist Controversy.* Berkeley: University of California Press.

Caballero Arribas, Jesús, and David Peñas Pedrero. 2012. "Un *castrum* de época visigoda en el valle Amblés: La Cabeza de Navasangil (Solosancho, Ávila)." In *Los castillos altomedievales en el noroeste de la Península Ibérica*, ed. Juan Antonio Quirós Castillo and José María Tejado Sebastián, 213–38. Bilbao: Universidad del País Vasco.

Cabral, J. M. Peixoto, and David M. Metcalf. 1997. *A moeda sueva.* Porto: Sociedade Portuguesa de Numismática.

Calderón Fraile, María Nieves. 2000. "Sobre ánforas romanas halladas en Mérida." *Mérida: Excavaciones Arqueológicas* 6: 361–70.

Calleja Martínez, María Victoria. 2001. "El poblamiento de época visigoda en el sureste de la provincia de Valladolid." In *V Congreso de arqueología medieval española*, 1:125–30. Valladolid: Consejería de Educación y Cultura.

Cañizar Palacios, José Luis. 2009–2010. "Los *navicularii Hispaniarum* en el contexto de la documentación legislativa tardoantigua." *Hispania Antiqua* 33–34: 295–310.

Cantino Wataghin, Gisella. 1999. "The Ideology of Urban Burials." In *The Idea and Ideal of the Town Between Late Antiquity and the Early Middle Ages*, ed. Gian Pietro Brogiolo and Bryan Ward-Perkins, 147–80. Leiden: Brill.

Canto, Alicia María. 2006. "Sobre el origen bético de Teodosio I el Grande, y su improbable nacimiento en 'Cauca' de 'Gallaecia.'" *Latomus* 65(2): 388–421.

Carandini, Andrea. 1983. "Pottery and the African Economy." In *Trade in the Ancient Economy*, ed. Peter Garnsey, 145–62. London: Chatto & Windus.

Carlsen, Jesper. 1995. *Vilici and Roman Estate Managers Until AD 284.* Rome: L'Erma di Bretschneider.

Carlsson-Brandt, Erik. 2011. "El poblamiento rural en la Galicia romana: Un ejemplo, las villae— metodología y problemática en su estudio." *Estrat Crític: Revista d'Arqueologia* 5(1): 156–67.

Carneiro, André. 2010. "Em *pars* incerta: Estruturas e dependencias agrícolas nas *villae* da Lusitânia." *Conimbriga* 49: 225–50.

Carneiro, André, and Eurico Sepúlveda. 2004. "*Terra sigillata* hispânica tardia do concelho de Fronteira: Exemplares recolhidos entre 1999 e 2003." *Revista Portuguesa de Arquelogia* 7(2): 435–58.

Carreño Gascón, María, and E. González Fernández. 1999. "La capital del extremo noroeste hispánico: *Lucus Augusti* y su tejido urbano a la luz de las últimas intervenciones arqueológicas." In *Los orígenes de la ciudad en el noroeste hispánico*, ed. Antonio Rodríguez Colmenero, 2:1,171–208. Lugo: Diputación Provincial de Lugo.

Carreras Monfort, César. 1996. "El comercio de *Asturia* a través de las ánforas." In *Los finisterres atlánticos en la Antigüedad: Época prerromana y romana*, ed. Carmen Fernández Ochoa, 205–10. Gijón: Ayuntamiento de Gijón.

Carreras Monfort, César, and David Williams. 2003. "Spanish Olive Oil Trade in Late Roman Britain: Dressel 23 Amphorae from Winchester." *Journal of Roman Pottery Studies* 10: 64–68.

Carrié, Jean-Michel. 1994. "Dioclétien et la fiscalité." *Antiquité Tardive* 2: 33–64.

———. 2012. "Nommer les structures rurales entre fin de l'Antiquité et Haut Moyen Âge: Le répertoire lexical gréco-latin et ses avatars modernes (1re partie)." *Antiquité Tardive* 20: 25–46.

Carvalho, António. 1999. "Evidências arqueológicas da produção de vinho nas villae romanas do território português: Grainhas de uva, alfaias vitícolas e lagares de vinho." In *Économie et territoire en Lusitanie romaine*, ed. Jean-Gérard Gorges and Germán Rodríguez Martín, 361–90. Madrid: Casa de Velázquez.

Carvalho, Antonio, and Maria José de Almeida. 1999–2000. "A villa romana da Quinta das Longas (S. Vicente e Ventosa, Elvas): Uma década de trabalhos arqueológicos (1991–2000)." *A Cidade* 13–14: 13–37.

Carvalho, Pedro Sobral de, and António Cheney. 2007. "A muralha romana de Viseu: A descoberta arqueologica." In *Murallas de ciudades romanas en el occidente del imperio: Lucus Augusti como paradigma*, ed. Antonio Rodríguez Colmenero and Isabel Rodà de Llanza, 729–45. Lugo: Diputación Provincial de Lugo.

Castellanos, Santiago. 1998a. *Poder social, aristocracias y hombre santo en la Hispania Visigoda: La Vita Aemiliani de Braulio de Zaragoza*. Logroño: Universidad de La Rioja.

———. 1998b. "Terminología textual y relaciones de dependencia en la sociedad hispanovisigoda: En torno a la ausencia de coloni en las Leges Visigothorum." *Gerión* 16: 451–60.

———. 2004. *La hagiografía visigoda: Dominio social y proyección cultural*. Logroño: Fundación San Millán de la Cogolla.

Castellanos, Santiago, and Iñaki Martín Viso. 2005. "The Local Articulation of Central Power in the North of the Iberian Peninsula (500–1000)." *Early Medieval Europe* 13(1): 1–42.

Castelo Ruano, Raquel, José Antonio López Sáez, Ana María López Pérez, Leonor Peña Chocarro, Corina Liesau, Mónica Ruiz Alonso, Lourdes López Merino, Sebastián Pérez Díaz, Rosario García Giménez, José Luis Gómez, and Gregorio Manglano. 2010–2011. "Una aproximación interdisciplinar a las actividades agropecuarias y cinegéticas de un asentamiento rural lusitano. El Saucedo (Talavera la Nueva, Toledo)." *Boletín de la Asociación Española de Amigos de la Arqueología* 46: 205–34.

Castillo Barranco, Juan Carlos. 2015. *Las presas romanas en España*. Oxford: BAR.

Castillo García, Carmen. 1982. "Los senadores béticos: Relaciones familiares y sociales." In *Atti del Colloquio internazionale AIEGL su epigrafia e ordine senatorio, Roma, 14–20 maggio 1*, 465–519. Rome: Edizioni di Storia e Letteratura.

Catalán, Raúl, Patricia Fuentes, and José Carlos Sastre, eds. 2014. *Fortificaciones en la tardoantigüedad: Élites y articulación del territorio (siglos V–VIII d.C.)*. Madrid: Ediciones de La Ergástula.

Catarino, Helena. 2005–2006. "Formas de ocupação rural em Alcoutim (séculos V–X)." *Cuadernos de Prehistoria y Arqueología de la Universidad Autónoma de Madrid* 31–32: 117–36.

Ceballos Hornero, Alberto. 2004. *Los espectáculos en la Hispania romana: La documentación epigráfica*. Mérida: Museo Nacional de Arte Romano.

Cecconi, Giovanni Alberto. 1994. *Governo imperiale e élites dirigenti nell'Italia tardoantica: Problemi di storia politico-amministrativa (270–476 d.C)*. Como: Edizioni New Press.

———. 2006. "Honorati, possessores, curiales: Competenze istituzionali e gerarchie di rango nella città tardoantica." In *Le trasformazioni delle élites in età tardoantica*, ed. Rita Lizzi Testa, 41–64. Rome: "L'Erma" di Bretschneider.

Centeno Cea, Inés, Ángel Palomino Lázaro, and María Negredo García. 2016. "Transición y continuidad Época Romana-Alta Edad Media en el sur de Palencia: Los contextos cerámicos de la 2.a mitad del s. V de Soto de Cerrato." In *La cerámica de la alta edad media en el cuadrante noroeste de la Península Ibérica (siglos V–X)*, ed. Alfonso Vigil-Escalera Guirado and Juan Antonio Quirós Castillo, 255–77. Bilbao: Universidad del País Vasco.

Cepeda Ocampo, Juan José, José Manuel Iglesias Gil, and Alicia Ruiz Gutiérrez. 2009. "El foro romano de *Ivliobriga* (Cantabria): Nuevas investigaciones arqueológicas." *Archivo Español de Arqueología* 82: 97–114.

Cerrillo Martín de Cáceres, Enrique. 1983. "La villa de 'La Cocosa' y su área territorial: Análisis de un asentamiento rural romano." In *VI Congreso de Estudios Extremeños*, 87–101. Madrid: Ministerio de Cultura.

Cerrillo Martín de Cáceres, Enrique, Gregorio Herrera, Juana Molano Brías, Manuel Alvarado Gonzalo, Jesús Castillo Castillo, and Miguel Hernández López. 1991. "Intervenciones arqueológicas en la antigua ciudad romana de Cápara (Cáparra, Cáceres)." *Extremadura Arqueológica* 2, 373–77.

Chastagnol, André. 1965. "Les espagnols dans l'aristocratie gouvernementale à l'époque de Théodose." In *Les empereurs romains d'Espagne*, 269–92. Paris: Éditions du Centre National de la Recherche Scientifique.

———. 1992. *Le Sénat romain à l'époque impériale: Recherches sur la composition de l'Assemblée et le statut de ses membres*. Paris: Les Belles Lettres.

Chavarría Arnau, Alexandra. 2004. "Interpreting the Transformation of Late Roman Villas: The Case of Hispania." In *Landscapes of Change: Rural Evolutions in Late Antiquity and the Early Middle Ages*, ed. Neil Christie, 67–102. Aldershot: Ashgate.

———. 2005. "Villas in Hispania During the Fourth and Fifth Centuries." In *Hispania in Late Antiquity: Current Perspectives*, ed. Kim Bowes and Michael Kulikowski, 519–52. Leiden: Brill.

———. 2006. "Aristocracias tardoantiguas y cristianización del territorio (siglos IV–V): ¿Otro mito historiográfico?" *Rivista di Archeologia Cristiana* 82: 201–30.

———. 2007a. *El final de las villae en Hispania (siglos IV–VII D.C.)*. Turnhout, Belgium: Brepols.

———. 2007b. "*Splendida sepulcra ut posteri audiant*: Aristocrazie, mausolei e chiese funerarie nelle campagne tardoantiche." In *Archeologia e società tra tardoantico e alto medioevo*, ed. Gian Pietro Brogiolo and Alexandra Chavarría Arnau, 127–46. Mantua: SAP.

———. 2012. "Reflexiones sobre los cementerios tardoantiguos de la villa de La Olmeda." In *In Durii regione romanitas: Estudios sobre la Romanización del Valle del Duero en homenaje a Javier Cortes Álvarez de Miranda*, ed. Carmelo Fernández Ibáñez and Ramón Bohigas Roldán, 147–54. Palencia/Santander: Diputación de Palencia/Instituto Sautuola de Prehistoria y Arqueología.

———. 2013. "¿Castillos en el aire? Paradigmas interpretativos 'de moda' en la arqueología medieval española." In *De Mahoma a Carlomagno: Los primeros tiempos (siglos VII–IX)*, 131–66. Pamplona: Gobierno de Navarra.

Christie, Neil. 2006. *From Constantine to Charlemagne: An Archaeology of Italy, AD 300–800.* Burlington: Ashgate.

———. 2011. *The Fall of the Western Roman Empire: An Archaeological and Historical Perspective.* New York: Bloomsbury Academic.

Collins, Roger. 1980. "Mérida and Toledo: 550–585." In *Visigothic Spain: New Approaches*, ed. Edward James, 189–219. Oxford: Oxford University Press.

———. 2004. *Visigothic Spain, 409–711.* Malden: Blackwell.

Conant, Jonathan. 2012. *Staying Roman: Conquest and Identity in Africa and the Mediterranean, 439–700.* Cambridge: Cambridge University Press.

Cordero Ruiz, Tomás. 2013. *El territorio emeritense durante la antigüedad tardía (siglos IV–VIII): Génesis y evolución del mundo rural lusitano.* Mérida, Spain: CSIC, Instituto de Arqueología.

Correia, Virgilio Hipólito. 2001. "Conimbriga, casa atribuída a Cantaber. Trabalhos arqueológicos 1995–1998." *Conimbriga* 40: 83–140.

———. 2010. "O forum de Conimbriga e a evolução do centro urbano." In *Ciudad y foro en Lusitania Romana*, ed. Trinidad Nogales Basarrate, 89–105. Mérida: Museo Nacional de Arte Romano.

Correia, Virgílio Hipólito, and Jorge Alarcão. 2008. "Conimbriga: Um ensaio de topografia histórica." *Conimbriga* 47: 31–46.

Correia, Virgílio Hipólito, Adriaan De Man, and Maria Pilar Reis. 2011. "A propósito de uma obra recente sobre o período tardo-antigo e medieval em Conímbriga." *Conimbriga* 50: 127–46.

Correia, Virgílio Hipólito, and Maria Pilar Reis. 2000. "As termas de Conimbriga: Tipologías arquitectónicas e integraçao urbana." In *Termas romanas en el occidente del imperio*, ed. Carmen Fernández Ochoa and Virginia García Entero, 271–80. Gijón: Ayuntamiento de Gijón.

Corsi, Cristina. 2016. "Comparative Research, Interpretation and Volumetric Reconstruction." In *Ammaia II. The Excavation Contexts 1994–2011*, ed. Cristina Corsi, 145–8. Ghent: Academia Press.

Corsi, Cristina, and Frank Vermeulen. 2016. "The New Excavations (2008–2011)." In *Ammaia II. The Excavation Contexts 1994–2011*, ed. Cristina Corsi, 69–85. Ghent: Academia Press.

Cortes, Javier. 2008. *Mosaicos en la villa romana La Olmeda.* Palencia: Diputación de Palencia.

Crawford, Michael, and Joyce Reynolds. 1979. "The Aezani Copy of the Prices Edict." *Zeitschrift für Papyrologie und Epigraphik* 34: 163–210.

Cunliffe, Barry. 2001. *Facing the Ocean: The Atlantic and Its Peoples, 8000 BC–AD 1500.* Oxford: Oxford University Press.

Curchin, Leonard. 1991. *Roman Spain: Conquest and Assimilation.* London: Routledge.

———. 2010. "The Last Lusitanian Senator." *Conimbriga* 49: 87–96.

———. 2013–2014. "Senator or Curialis? Some Debatable *Nobiles* in Late Antique Hispania." *Hispania Antiqua* 37–38: 129–35.

————. 2014. "The Role of Civic Leaders in Late Antique Hispania." *Studia Historica: Historia Antigua* 32: 281–304.

Dahí Elena, Sarah. 2007. "Un contexto cerámico de la Antigüedad tardía: el yacimiento de San Pelayo (Aldealengua, Salamanca). Nuevos datos sobre la cronología de las pizarras visigodas." *Pyrenae* 38(1): 79–104.

————. 2010. "Vidrios de los siglos IV–V d.C. procedentes del yacimiento de la Viña de la Iglesia (Sotoserrano, Salamanca)." *Zephyrus* 66: 219–26.

————. 2012. *Contextos cerámicos de la Antigüedad Tardía y Alta Edad Media (siglos IV–VIII d.C.) en los asentamientos rurales de la Lusitania Septentrional (Provincia de Salamanca, España)*. Oxford: Archaeopress.

Dark, Ken. 2004. "The Late Antique Landscape of Britain, AD 300–700." In *Landscapes of Change: Rural Evolutions in Late Antiquity and the Early Middle Ages*, ed. Neil Christie, 279–99. Aldershot: Ashgate.

David, Pierre. 1947. *Études historiques sur la Galice et le Portugal*. Lisbon: Portugália.

De Man, Adriaan. 2004. "Algumas considerações em torno da cerâmica comun tardia conimbrigense." *Revista Portuguesa de Arqueologia* 7(2): 459–71.

————. 2005. "Sobre a cristianização de um forum." *Al-Madan* 13: VI.1–4.

————. 2006. *Conimbriga: Do baixo império à idade media*. Lisbon: Sílabo.

————. 2011a. *Defensas urbanas tardias da Lusitânia*. Mérida: Museo Nacional de Arte Romano.

————. 2011b. "Recent Archaeological Research on Late and Post-Roman Conimbriga." *Madrider Mitteilungen* 52: 514–27.

Decker, Michael. 2009. *Tilling the Hateful Earth: Agricultural Production and Trade in the Late Antique East*. Oxford: Oxford University Press.

Delbarre, Sophie, Michel Fuchs, and Claude-Alain Paratte. 2008. "Achilles on Skyros: Crossing over Architecture, Mosaic, and Wall Painting." In *IV. Uluslararası Türkiye mozaik korpusu sempozyum bildirileri "Geçmişten günümüze mozaik köprüsü"*, ed. Mustafa Şahin, 35–42. Bursa: Uludağ Üniversitesi Mozaik Araştırmaları Merkezi Yayınları Serisi.

Deschamps, Lucienne. 2002. "*L'amoenitas* de la vie à Bordeaux dans la première moitié du Ve siècle d'après Paulin de Pella." *Caesarodunum* 35–36: 449–59.

Dey, Hendrik. 2010. "Art, Ceremony, and City Walls: The Aesthetics of Imperial Resurgence in the Late Roman West." *Journal of Late Antiquity* 3(1): 3–37.

————. 2011. *The Aurelian Wall and the Refashioning of Imperial Rome, AD 271–855*. Cambridge: Cambridge University Press.

————. 2015. *The Afterlife of the Roman City. Architecture and Ceremony in Late Antiquity and the Early Middle Ages*. Cambridge: Cambridge University Press.

Diarte Blasco, Pilar. 2012. *La configuración urbana de la Hispania tardoantigua: Transformaciones y pervivencias de los espacios públicos romanos, s. III–VI d. C.* Oxford: Archaeopress.

Dias, Lino Augusto Tavares. 1997. *Tongobriga*. Lisbon: Instituto Português do Património Arquitectónico.

————. 1999. "Tongobriga." In *Los orígenes de la ciudad en el noroeste hispánico*, ed. Antonio Rodríguez Colmenero, 2:751–78. Lugo: Diputación Provincial.

Díaz Álvarez, Inés, and Alberto Garín García. 1999a. "Bergidum." In *Los orígenes de la ciudad en el noroeste hispánico*, ed. Antonio Rodríguez Colmenero, 2:1125–52. Lugo: Diputación Provincial de Lugo.

————. 1999b. "Estudios de los materiales arqueológicos de Castro Ventosa." *Estudios Bercianos* 25: 74–95.

Díaz, Pablo. 2004. "Acuñación monetaria y organización administrativa en la Gallaecia tardoantigua." *Zephyrus* 57: 367–75.

———. 2007. "Sumisión voluntaria: Estatus degradado e indiferencia de estatus en la Hispania visigoda." *Studia Historica: Historia Antigua* 25: 507–24.

———. 2011. *El reino suevo (411–585)*. Madrid: AKAL.

———. 2013. "Valerio del Bierzo: La equívoca marginalidad de un asceta tardoantiguo." In *Marginados sociales y religiosos en la Hispania tardorromana y visigoda*, ed. Raúl González Salinero, 293–315. Madrid: Signifer Libros.

———. 2015. "Los bárbaros y la península ibérica. El caso de los suevos en su contexto; a vueltas con la identidad." In *Identidad y etnicidad en Hispania: Propuestas teóricas y cultural material en los siglos V–VIII*, ed. Juan Antonio Quirós Castillo and Santiago Castellanos, 53–65. Bilbao: Universidad del País Vasco.

Díaz, Pablo, and Iñaki Martín Viso. 2011. "Una contabilidad esquiva: Las pizarras numerales visigodas y el caso de El Cortinal de San Juan (Salvatierra de Tormes, España)." In *Between Taxation and Rent: Fiscal Problems from Late Antiquity to Early Middle Ages*, ed. Pablo Díaz and Iñaki Martín Viso, 221–50. Bari: Edipuglia.

Díaz, Pablo, and Luis Menéndez Bueyes. 2005. "The Cantabrian Basin in the Fourth and Fifth Centuries: From Imperial Province to Periphery." In *Hispania in Late Antiquity: Current Perspectives*, ed. Kim Bowes and Michael Kulikowski, 265–97. Leiden: Brill.

Díaz, Pablo, and María del Rosario Valverde. 2000. "The Theoretical Strength and Practical Weakness of the Visigothic Monarchy of Toledo." In *Rituals of Power: From Late Antiquity to the Early Middle Ages*, ed. Frans Theuws and Janet Nelson, 59–93. Leiden: Brill.

Díaz y Díaz, Manuel. 1983. *Códices visigóticos en la monarquía leonesa*. León: Centro de Estudios e Investigaciones "San Isidoro."

Dillon, John Noël. 2015. "The Inflation of Rank and Privilege: Regulating Precedence in the Fourth Century AD." In *Contested Monarchy: Integrating the Roman Empire in the Fourth Century AD*, ed. Johannes Wienand, 42–66. Oxford: Oxford University Press.

Diogo, Antonio Manuel Dias, and Antonio Manuel Cavaleiro Paixão. 2001. "Ânforas de escavações no povoado industrial romano de Tróia, Setúbal." *Revista Portuguesa de Arqueologia* 4(1): 117–40.

Diogo, Antonio Manuel Dias, and Laura Trinidade. 1999. "Ânforas e sigillatas tardias (claras, focenses e cipriotas) provenientes das escavações de 1966/67 do teatro romano de Lisboa." *Revista Portuguesa de Arqueologia* 2(2): 83–95.

Dohijo, Eusebio. 2007. "La necrópolis hispanovisigoda del área foral de Termes." *Pyrenae* 38(1): 129–62.

———. 2011. *La Antigüedad Tardía en el alto valle del Duero*. Oxford: Archaeopress.

Domergue, Claude. 1990. *Les mines de la péninsule ibérique dans l'Antiquité romaine*. Rome: École Française de Rome.

Domínguez Bolaños, Alonso, and Jaime Nuño González. 1997. "Reflexiones sobre los sistemas defensivos tardoantiguos en la meseta norte: A propósito de la muralla de *El Cristo de San Esteban*, Muelas del Pan (Zamora)." In *Congreso Internacional la Hispania de Teodosio*, ed. Ramón Teja and Cesáreo Pérez, 2: 435–49. Segovia: Universidad SEK.

Dossey, Lesley. 2010. *Peasant and Empire in Christian North Africa*. Berkeley: University of California Press.

Drinkwater, John. 1998. "The Usurpers Constantine III (407–411) and Jovinus (411–413)." *Britannia* 29: 269–98.

Dumézil, Bruno. 2008. "Le compte et l'administration de la cité dans del Bréviaire d'Alaric." In *Le Bréviaire d'Alaric. Aux origins du Code civil*, ed. Michel Rouche and Bruno Dumézil, 73–90. Paris: Presses de l'Université Paris-Sorbonne.

Dunn, Archibald. 1997. "Stages in the Transition from the Late Antique to the Middle Byzantine Urban Centre in S. Macedonia and S. Thrace." In *Aphierōma ston N.G.L. Hammond*, 137–60. Thessaloniki: Hetaireia Makedonikōn Spoudōn.

Durán Cabello, Rosalía-María. 1998. *La última etapa del teatro romano de Mérida (la uersura oriental y los sellos laterticios)*. Mérida: Museo Nacional de Arte Romano.

———. 2004. *El teatro y el anfiteatro de Augusta Emérita: Contribución al conocimiento histórico de la capital de Lusitania*. Oxford: Archaeopress.

Durand, Aline, and Philippe Leveau. 2004. "Farming in Mediterranean France and Rural Settlement in the Late Roman and Early Medieval Periods: The Contribution from Archaeology and Environmental Sciences in the Last Twenty Years (1980–2000)." In *The Making of Feudal Agricultures?* ed. Miquel Barceló and François Sigaut, 177–253. Leiden: Brill.

Durliat, Jean. 1990. *Les finances publiques de Dioclétien aux carolingiens*. Sigmaringen: Jan Thorbecke.

Ebbeler, Jennifer, and Cristiana Sogno. 2007. "Religious Identity and the Politics of Patronage: Symmachus and Augustine." *Historia* 56(2): 230–42.

Edmondson, Jonathan. 1987. *Two Industries in Roman Lusitania: Mining and Garum Production*. Oxford: BAR.

———. 1989. "Mining in the Later Roman Empire and Beyond: Continuity or Disruption?" *Journal of Roman Studies* 79: 84–102.

———. 1992. "Creating a Provincial Landscape: Roman Imperialism and Rural Change in Lusitania." *Studia Historica: Historia Antigua* 10: 13–30.

———. 2006. "Cities and Urban Life in the Western Provinces of the Roman Empire 30 BCE–250 CE." In *A Companion to the Roman Empire*, ed. David Potter, 250–80. Malden, MA: Blackwell.

Ellis, Simon. 1997. "Late-Antique Dining: Architecture, Furnishing, and Behavior." *Journal of Roman Archaeology* 22: 41–51.

———. 2000. *Roman Housing*. London: Duckworth.

Escribano Paño, María Victoria. 2000. "Usurpación y defensa de las Hispanias: Dídimo y Veriniano (408)." *Gerión* 18: 509–34.

Escribano Paño, María Victoria, and Guillermo Fatás Cabeza, ed. 2001. *La antigüedad tardía en Aragón (284–714)*. Zaragoza: Caja de Ahorros de la Inmaculada de Aragón.

Esmonde Cleary, Simon. 2003. "Civil Defences in the West Under the High Empire." In *The Archaeology of Roman Towns: Studies in Honour of John S. Wacher*, ed. Pete Wilson, 73–85. Oxford: Oxbow.

———. 2013. *The Roman West, AD 200–500: An Archaeological Study*. Cambridge. U.K.: Cambridge University Press.

———. 2016. "The Villas of Late Roman Britan and the Vocabulary of Aristocratic Power and Culture in the West." In *Libera Curiositas: Mélanges d'histoire romaine et d'antiquité tardive offerts à Jean-Michel Carrié*, ed. Christel Freu, Sylvain Janniard, and Arthur Ripoll, 333–346. Turnhout: Brepols.

Étienne, Robert. 1982. "Sénateurs originaires de la province de Lusitanie." In *Atti del Colloquio internazionale AIEGL su epigrafia e ordine senatorio, Roma, 14–20 maggio 1*, 521–29. Rome: Edizioni di Storia e Letteratura.

Étienne, Robert, Yasmine Makaroun, and François Mayet. 1994. *Un grand complexe industriel à Tróia (Portugal)*. Paris: Diffusion E. de Boccard.

Étienne, Robert, and François Mayet. 2000. *Le vin hispanique*. Paris: Éditions de Boccard.

———. 2004. *L'huile hispanique*. Paris: Éditions de Boccard.

———. 2006. "La place de Tróia dans l'industrie romaine des salaisons de poisson." In *Itineraria Hispanica: Recueil d'articles de Robert Étienne*, ed. François Mayet, 561–72. Bordeaux: Ausonius.

Fabião, Carlos. 1992–1993. "Garum na Lusitania rural? Alguns comentários sobre o povoamento romano do Algarve." *Studia Historica: Historia Antigua* 10–11: 227–52.

———. 1998. "O vinho na Lusitânia: Reflexões em torno de um problema arqueológico." *Revista Portuguesa de Arqueologia* 1(1): 169–98.

———. 2009. "A dimensão atlântica da Lusitânia: Periferia ou charneira no Império Romano?" In *Lusitânia romana: entre o mito e a realidade—Actas da VI Mesa-Redonda Internacional sobre a Lusitânia Romana*, ed. Jean-Gérard Gorges, José d'Encarnação, Trinidad Nogales Basarrate, and António Carvalho, 53–74. Cascais: Câmara Municipal de Cascais.

Fagan, Garrett. 1999. *Bathing in Public in the Roman World*. Ann Arbor: University of Michigan Press.

Fanjul Peraza, Alfonso, and Luis Menéndez Bueyes. 2004. *El complejo castreño de los astures transmontanos: El poblamiento de la cuenca central de Asturias*. Salamanca, Spain: Universidad de Salamanca.

Fernández, Damián. 2006. "What Is the *De fisco Barcinonensi* About?" *Antiquité Tardive* 14: 217–24.

———. 2016a. "Persuading the Powerful in Post-Roman Iberia: King Euric, Local Powers, and the Formation of a State Paradigm." In *Motions of Late Antiquity: Essays in Religion, Politics and Society in Honor of Peter Brown*, ed. Jamie Kreiner and Helmut Reimiz, 107–28. Turnhout: Brepols.

———. 2016b. "Property, Social Status, and Church Building in Visigothic Iberia." *Journal of Late Antiquity* 9(2): 512–41.

Fernández Mier, Margarita. 1999. *Génesis del territorio en la edad media: Arqueología del paisaje y evolución histórica en la montaña asturiana—el valle del río Pigüeña*. Oviedo: Universidad de Oviedo.

Fernández Ochoa, Carmen. 1997. *La muralla romana de Gijón*. Madrid: Electa España.

———. 1999. "La ciudad romana de Gijón: Orígenes y dinámica histórica." In *Los orígenes de la ciudad en el noroeste hispánico*, ed. Antonio Rodríguez Colmenero, 2:1109–24. Lugo: Diputación Provincial de Lugo.

———. 2006. "Los castros y el inicio de la romanización en Asturias: Historiografía y debate." *Zephyrus* 59: 275–88.

Fernández Ochoa, Carmen, Paloma García Díaz, and Alexandra Uscatescu Barrón. 1992. "Gijón en el período tardoantiguo: Cerámicas importadas de las excavaciones de Cimadevilla." *Archivo Español de Archeología* 65: 105–49.

Fernández Ochoa, Carmen, and Fernando Gil Sendino. 2008. "La villa romana de Veranes (Gijón, Asturias) y otras villas de la vertiente septentrional de la cordillera Cantábrica." In *Las villae tardorromanas en el occidente del imperio: Arquitectura y function*, ed. Carmen Fernández Ochoa, Virginia García Entero, and Fernando Gil Sendino, 435–79. Gijón: Ediciones Trea.

Fernández Ochoa, Carmen, Fernando Gil Sendino, and Almudena Orejas Saco del Valle. 2004. "La villa romana de Veranes: El complejo rural tardorromano y propuesta de estudio del territorio." *Archivo Español de Archeología* 77: 197–219.

Fernández Ochoa, Carmen, and Ángel Morillo Cerdán. 2002. "La configuración del territorio en la Asturia transmontana." In *Cursos sobre el patrimonio histórico*, ed. José Manuel Iglesias, 381–400. Santander: Universidad de Cantabria.

———. 2005. "Walls and the Urban Landscape of Late Roman Spain: Defense and Imperial Strategy." In *Hispania in Late Antiquity: Current Perspectives*, ed. Kim Bowes and Michael Kulikowski, 299–361. Leiden: Brill.

Fernández Ochoa, Carmen, Ángel Morillo Cerdán, and Fernando Gil Sendino. 2012. "El *Itinerario de Barro*: Cuestiones de autenticidad y lectura." *Zephyrus* 70: 151–79.

Fernández Ochoa, Carmen, and Mar Zarzalejos Prieto. 2001. "Las termas públicas de las ciudades hispanas del Bajo Imperio." In *Hispania en la antigüedad tardía, ocio y espectáculos*, ed. Luis García Moreno and Sebastián Rascón Marqués, 19–35. Alcalá de Henares: Fundación Colegio del Rey.

Fernández Rodríguez, Carlos. 2002. "Análisis de los restos faunísticos recuperados en el Castro de Viladonga (Castro de Rei, Lugo)." *CROA: Boletín da Asociación de Amigos do Museo do Castro de Viladonga* 12: 7–14.

Fernández Rodríguez, Carlos, Catalina López Pérez, and Otilia Prado Fernández. 1999. "Resultados de las intervención arqueológica (Segunda Fase–1997) en el asentamiento romano de El Fresno–San Román de Bembibre." *Estudios Bercianos* 25: 63–73.

Fernández Rodríguez, Carlos, and Xulio Rodríguez González. 1999. "Análisis de los restos faunísticos del conjunto arqueológico de Santomé (Ourense)." *Boletín Auriense* 29: 23–38.

Ferreiro, Alberto. 1995. "Braga and Tours: Some Observations on Gregory's *De virtutibus sancti Martini* (1.11)." *Journal of Early Christian Studies* 3(2): 195–210.

———. 1997. "Veremundu R(eg)e: Revisiting an Inscription from San Salvador de Vairão (Portugal)." *Zeitschrift für Papyrologie und Epigraphik* 116: 263–72.

Filloy Nieva, Idoia, Eliseo Gil, and Aitor Iriarte Kortazar. 1998. "El territorio alavés en el bajo imperio." In *Congreso Internacional la Hispania de Teodosio*, ed. Ramón Teja and Cesáreo Pérez, 2:465–75. Segovia: Universidad SEK.

Fonseca, Cristóvão Pimentel. 2004. "A *terra sigillata* do fundeadouro de Tróia." *Revista Portuguesa de Arqueologia* 7(1): 421–49.

Fontes, Luis Fernando de Oliveira. 1995. "A igreja sueva de Dume (Braga)." In *IV Reunió d'arqueologia cristiana hispànica*, 415–27. Barcelona: Institut d'Estudies Catalans.

———. Fontes, Luis. 2015. "Powers, territories, and architecture in North-West Portugal: An Approach to the Christian Landscapes of Braga Between the Fifth and Eleventh Centuries." In *Churches and Social Power in Early Medieval Europe: Integrating Archaeological and Historical Approaches*, ed. José Sánchez Pardo, and Michael Shapland, 387–417. Turnhout: Brepols.

Fontes, Luis Fernando de Oliveira, Francisco Sande Lemos, and Mário da Cruz. 1997–98. "'Mais velho' que a Sé de Braga. Intervenção arqueológica na catedral bracarense: Notícia preliminar." *Cadernos de Arqueologia* 14–15, 137–64.

Fortacín Piedrafita, Javier. 1983. "La donación del diácono Vicente al monasterio de Asán y su posterior testamento como Obispo de Huesca en el siglo VI: Precisiones críticas para la fijación del texto." *Cuadernos de Historia Jerónimo Zurita* 47–48: 7–70.

Fuentes Hinojo, Pablo. 2006. "Sociedad urbana, cristianización y cambios topográficos en la Hispania tardorromana y visigoda (siglos IV–VI)." *Studia Historica: Historia Antigua* 24: 257–89.

———. 2008. "Patrocinio eclesiástico, rituales de poder e historia urbana en la Hispania tardoantigua (siglos IV al VI)." *Studia Historica: Historia Antigua* 26: 315–44.

Gabrielli, Chantal. 1995–1996. "L'aristocrazia senatoria ispanica, nel corso del III e del IV secolo d.C., dall'avvento di Settimio Severo alla morte di Teodosio (193 d.C.–395 d.C.)." *Studia Historica: Historia Antigua* 13–14: 331–78.

Garbarino, Paolo. 1988. *Ricerche sulla procedura di ammissione al senato nel tardo Impero Romano*. Milan: A. Giuffrè Editore.

García Entero, Virginia. 2005. *Los balnea domésticos, ámbito rural y urbano en la Hispania romana*. Madrid: CSIC.

———. 2006. "Los *balnea* de las *villae* tardoantiguas en Hispania." In *Villas tardoantiguas en el Mediterráneo occidental*, ed. Alexandra Chavarría Arnau, Javier Arce, and Gian Pietro Brogiolo, 97–111. Madrid: CSIC.

———. 2010. "La élite hispanoromana en la antigüedad tardía a través de las trasformaciones de los espacios domésticos: Las termas." In *Momentos y espacios de cambio: La sociedad hispanorromana en la antigüedad tardía*, ed. Pilar Fernández Uriel, 59–74. Zaragoza: Libros Pórtico.

García Guinea, Miguel Ángel. 1990. *La villa romana de Quintanilla de la Cueza, Palencia: Guía de las excavaciones*. Palencia: Diputación de Palencia.

García Guinea, Miguel Ángel, José Manuel Iglesias Gil, and P. Caloca. 1973. *Excavaciones de Monte Cildá, Olleros de Pisuerga, (Palencia): Campañas de 1966 a 1969*. Madrid: Servicio Nacional de Excavaciones Arqueológicas.

García-Hoz Rosales, María Concepción, Manuel Alvarado Gonzalo, Jesús Castillo Castillo, Miguel Hernández López, and Juana Molano Brías. 1991. "La villa romana del 'Olivar del Centeno' (Millanes de la Mata, Cáceres)." *Extremadura Arqueológica* 2: 387–402.

García Marcos, Victorino, Ángel Morillo Cerdán, and Emilio Campomanes. 1997. "Nuevos planteamientos sobre la cronología del recinto defensivo de *Asturica Augusta* (Astorga, León)." In *Congreso Internacional la Hispania de Teodosio*, ed. Ramón Teja and Cesáreo Pérez, 2:515–31. Segovia: Universidad SEK.

García Martín, Pedro. 1990. *La mesta*. Madrid: Historia 16.

García Merino, Carmen. 2000. "Las raíces históricas de la sede episcopal oxomense: Aproximación a la etapa tardoantigua de Uxama." In *I Semana de estudios históricos de la diócesis de Osma-Soria*, ed. Teófilo Portillo Capilla, 1:179–96. Soria: Diputación de Soria.

———. 2007. "Crecimiento urbano, abastecimiento de agua y territorio en *Uxama Argaela*." In *Villes et territoires dans le bassin du Douro à l'époque romaine*, ed. Milagros Navarro Caballero and Juan José Palao Vicente, 203–35. Bordeaux: Ausonius.

———. 2008. "Almenara de Adaja y las villas de la submeseta norte." In *Las villae tardorromanas en el occidente del imperio: Arquitectura y function*, ed. Carmen Fernández Ochoa, Virginia García Entero, and Gil Sendino, 411–34. Gijón: Ediciones Trea.

García Merino, Carmen, and Margarita Sánchez Simón. 2004. "De nuevo acerca de la villa romana de Almenara de Adaja (Valladolid): Excavaciones de 1998 a 2002." *Archivo Español de Arqueología* 77: 177–95.

García Moreno, Luis. 1971. "Algunos aspectos fiscales de la Península Ibérica durante el siglo VI." *Hispania Antiqua* 1: 233–56.

———. 1974. "Estudios sobre la organización administrativa del reino visigodo de Toledo." *Anuario de Historia del Derecho Español* 44: 5–155.

———. 1987. "La arqueología y la historia militar visigoda en la Península Ibérica." In *Arqueología medieval española: II Congreso, Madrid 19–24 Enero 1987*, 2:331–36. Madrid: Dirección General del Patrimonio.

———. 1990. "Élites e Iglesia hispanas en la transición del imperio romano al reino visigodo." In *La conversión de Roma: Cristianismo y paganismo*, ed. José Candau Morón, 223–58. Madrid: Ediciones Clásicas.

———. 2001. "From *coloni* to *servi*: A History of the Peasantry in Visigothic Spain." *Klio* 83(1): 198–212.

———. 2005. "El cristianismo en las Españas: Los orígenes." In *El Concilio de Elvira y su tiempo*, ed. Manuel Sotomayor Muro and José Fernández Ubiña, 169–93. Granada: Universidad de Granada.

Garnsey, Peter. 1970. *Social Status and Legal Privilege in the Roman Empire*. Oxford: Clarendon.

Gaspar, Alexandra. 2003. "Cerâmicas cinzentas da antiguidade tardia e alto-medievais de Braga e Dume." In *Cerámicas tardorromanas y altomedievales de la Península Ibérica*, ed. Luis Caballero Zoreda, Pedro Mateos Cruz, and Manuel Retuerce, 455–81. Madrid: CSIC.

Gaspar, Maria Alexandra, and Ana Gomes. 2007. "As muralhas de Olisipo: O troço junto ao Tejo." In *Murallas de ciudades romanas en el occidente del Imperio: Lucus Augusti como paradigma*, ed. Antonio Rodríguez Colmenero and Isabel Rodà de Llanza, 687–97. Lugo: Museo Provincial de Lugo.

Gauthier, Nancy. 1999. "La topographie chrétienne entre idéologie et pragmatisme." In *The Idea and Ideal of the Town Between Late Antiquity and the Early Middle Ages*, ed. Gian Pietro Brogiolo and Bryan Ward-Perkins, 195–209. Leiden: Brill.

Giardina, Andrea. 1999. "Esplosione di tardoantico." *Studi Storici* 40(1): 157–80.

Gillani, Giacomo. 1995. "Algunas breves consideraciones sobre las murallas de la *Colonia Clunia Sulpicia*." *Boletín del Seminario de Estudios de Arte y Arqueología: BSAA* 61: 119–24.

Gillett, Andrew. 2003. *Envoys and Political Communication in the Late Antique West, 411–533*. Cambridge: Cambridge University Press.

Goffart, Walter. 1980. *Barbarians and Romans, A.D. 418–584: The Techniques of Accommodation*. Princeton: Princeton University Press.

———. 1982. "Old and New in Merovingian Taxation." *Past and Present* 96: 3–21.

Gómez-Pantoja, Joaquín. 2001. "*Pastio agrestis*: Pastoralismo en Hispania Romana." In *Los rebaños de Gerión: Pastores y trashumancia en Iberia antigua y medieval*, ed. Joaquín Gómez-Pantoja, 177–213. Madrid: Casa de Velázquez.

Gómez Sobrino, Jesús, Aquilino González Santiso, and Xoán Martínez Tamuxe. 1980. "La villa romana y necrópolis germánica de Currás-Tomiño." *Tuy, Museo y Archivo Histórico Diocesano* 3: 321–38.

González Cesteros, Horacio. 2010. "La llegada de ánforas hispanas a Germania durante los últimos siglos de la dominación romana: Una cuestión para el futuro." *Cuadernos de Prehistoria y Arqueología de la Universidad Autónoma de Madrid* 36: 107–29.

Gonzalo González, José María. 2007. *El Cerro del Castillo, Bernardos (Segovia): Un yacimiento arqueológico singular en la provincia de Segovia durante la Antigüedad Tardía*. Segovia: Ayuntamiento de la Villa de Bernardos.

Gorges, Jean-Gérard, and Christian Rico. 1999. "Barrages ruraux d'époque romaine en moyenne vallée du Guadiana." In *Économie et territoire en Lusitanie romaine*, ed. Jean-Gérard Gorges and F. Germán Rodríguez Martín, 157–95. Madrid: Casa de Velázquez.

Gorges, Jean-Gérard, and Francisco Germán Rodríguez Martín. 1999. "Un exemple de grande hydraulique rurale dans l'Espagne du Bas-Empire: La villa romaine de 'Correio Mor' (Elvas, Portugal)." In *Économie et territoire en Lusitanie romaine*, ed. Jean-Gérard Gorges and Francisco Germán Rodríguez Martín, 227–40. Madrid: Casa de Velázquez.

———. 2000. "Voies romaines, propriétés et propriétaires à l'ouest de Mérida: Problèmes d'occupation du sol en moyenne vallée du Guadiana sous le Haut-Empire." In *Sociedad y cultura en Lusitania romana*, ed. Jean-Gérard Gorges and Trinidad Nogales Basarrate, 101–53. Mérida: Editora Regional de Extremadura.

Grey, Cam. 2011. *Constructing Communities in the Late Roman Countryside.* Cambridge: Cambridge University Press.

Guimarães, Gonçalves, and Carla Teixeira Pinto. 2000. "Cerâmica arqueológica de Gaia: Análise de elementos de uma sequência de longa duração." In *III Congresso de Arqueologia Peninsular*, 1:451–510. Porto: ADECAP.

Gurt i Esparraguera, Josep. 2000–2001. "Transformaciones en el tejido urbano de las ciudades hispanas durante la antigüedad tardía: Dinámicas urbanas." *Zephyrus* 53–54: 443–71.

Gurt i Esparraguera, Josep, and Pilar Diarte Blasco. 2011. "*Spolia et Hispania*: Alcuni esempi peninsulari." *Hortus Artium Medievalium* 17: 7–22.

Gutiérrez González, José. 1996. "El páramo leonés: Entre al antigüedad y la alta edad media." *Studia Historica: Historia Medieval* 14: 47–96.

———. 2014. "Fortificaciones tardoantiguas y visigodas en el Norte Peninsular (ss. V–VIII)." In *Las fortificaciones en la tardoantigüedad: Élites y articulación del territorio (siglos V–VIII d.C.)*, ed. Raúl Catalán, Patricia Fuentes, and José Carlos Sastre, 191–214. Madrid: Ediciones de La Ergástula.

Guyon, Jean. 2006. "La topographie chrétienne des villes de la Gaule." In *Die Stadt in der Spätantike: Niedergang oder Wandel?* ed. Jens-Uwe Krause and Christian Witschel, 105–28. Stuttgart: Franz Steiner.

Haldon, John. 1993. *The State and the Tributary Mode of Production.* London: Verso.

———. 2012. "Comparative State Formation: The Later Roman Empire in the Wider World." In *The Oxford Handbook of Late Antiquity*, ed. Scott Fitzgerald Johnson, 1111–47. Oxford: Oxford University Press.

Halsall, Guy. 2006. "Villas, Territories and Communities in Merovingian Northern Gaul." In *People and Space in the Middle Ages, 300–1300*, ed. Wendy Davies, Guy Halsall, and Andrew Reynolds, 209–31. Turnhout: Brepols.

———. 2007. *Barbarian Migrations and the Roman West, 376–568.* Cambridge: Cambridge University Press.

Hamerow, Helena. 2002. *Early Medieval Settlements: The Archaeology of Rural Communities in Northwest Europe, 400–900.* Oxford: Oxford University Press.

Hardt, Matthias. 1998. "Royal Treasures and Representation in the Early Middle Ages." In *Strategies of Distinction. The Construction of Ethnic Communities, 300–800*, ed. Walter Pohl and Helmut Reimitz, 255–80. Leiden: Brill.

Harper, Kyle. 2008. "The Greek Census Inscriptions of Late Antiquity." *Journal of Roman Studies* 98: 83–119.

Hayes, John. 1972. *Late Roman Pottery.* London: British School at Rome.

———. 1980. *A Supplement to Late Roman Pottery.* London: British School at Rome.

Heather, Peter. 1998. "Senators and Senates." In *The Cambridge Ancient History.* Vol. 13, *The Late Empire, A.D. 337–425*, ed. Averil Cameron and Peter Garnsey, 184–210. Cambridge: Cambridge University Press.

———. 2010. *Empires and Barbarians: The Fall of Rome and the Birth of Europe.* Oxford: Oxford University Press.

Heijmans, Marc. 2006. "Les habitations urbaines en Gaule méridionale durant l'Antiquité tardive." *Gallia* 63: 47–57.

Heinzelmann, Martin. 1976. *Bischofsherrschaft in Gallien: Zur Kontinuität römischer Führungsschichten vom 4. Bis zum 7. Jahrhundert—soziale, prosopographische und bildungsgeschichtliche Aspekte.* Zürich: Artemis.

Hendy, Michael. 1988. "From Public to Private: The Western Barbarian Coinages as a Mirror of the Disintegration of Late Roman State Structures." *Viator* 19: 29–78.

Heras Mora, Francisco, and Sophie Gilotte. 2008. "Primer balance de las actuaciones arqueológicas en el Pozo de la Cañada (2002–2005): Transformación y continuidad en el campo emeritense (ss. I–IX d.C.)." *Arqueología y Territorio Medieval* 15: 51–72.

Heras Mora, Francisco, and Ana Olmedo Gragera. 2015. "Identidad y contexto en la necrópolis tardorromana de Mérida." In *Identidad y etnicidad en Hispania: Propuestas teóricas y cultura material en los siglos V–VIII,* ed. Juan Antonio Quirós Castillo and Santiago Castellanos, 275–90. Bilbao: Universidad del País Vasco.

Hernández Domínguez, Irene. 2007. "Salmantica en época imperial: Un estado de la cuestión." In *Villes et territoires dans le bassin du Douro à l'époque romaine,* ed. Milagros Navarro Caballero, María Ángeles Magallón Botaya, and Juan José Palao Vicente, 195–202. Bordeaux: Ausonius.

Hernández Guerra, Liborio. 2001. *Epigrafía de época romana de la provincia de Salamanca.* Valladolid: Universidad de Valladolid.

Hernández Guerra, Liborio, and Luis Sagredo San Eustaquio. 1998. *La romanización del territorio de la actual provincia de Palencia.* Palencia: Universidad de Valladolid, Diputación de Valencia.

Hickey, Todd. 2007. "Aristocratic Landholding and the Economy of Byzantine Egypt." In *Egypt in the Byzantine World, 300–700,* ed. Roger Bagnall, 288–308. Cambridge: Cambridge University Press.

Hidalgo Cuñarro, José Manuel. 1994. "La villa romana de Toralla." In *La ciutat en el món romà,* 2:206–7. Tarragona: CSIC and Institut d'Estudis Catalans.

Hidalgo Martín, Luis, and Guadalupe Méndez Grande. 2005. "*Octavius Clarus,* un nuevo *Vicarius Hispaniarum* en *Augusta Emerita.*" *Mérida: Excavaciones Arqueológicas* 8: 547–64.

Hillgarth, Jocelyn. 1980. "Popular Religion in Visigothic Spain." In *Visigothic Spain: New Approaches,* ed. Edward James, 3–60. Oxford: Oxford University Press.

Hirt, Alfred Michael. 2010. *Imperial Mines and Quarries in the Roman World: Organizational Aspects, 27 BC–AD 235.* Oxford: Oxford University Press.

Hitchner, Robert. 2002. "Olive Oil Production and the Roman Economy: The Case for Intensive Growth in the Roman Empire." In *The Ancient Economy,* ed. Walter Scheidel and Sitta von Reden, 71–83. New York: Routledge.

Hopkins, Keith. 1980. "Taxes and Trade in the Roman Empire (200 B.C.–A.D. 400)." *Journal of Roman Studies* 70: 101–25.

Hopkins, Keith, and Graham Burton. 1983. "Ambition and Withdrawal: The Senatorial Aristocracy Under the Emperors." In *Death and Renewal,* 120–99. Cambridge: Cambridge University Press.

Horden, Peregrine, and Nicholas Purcell. 2000. *The Corrupting Sea: A Study of Mediterranean History.* Malden: Blackwell.

Hostein, Antony. 2012. *La cité et l'empereur: Les Éduens dans l'Empire romain d'après les Panégyriques latins.* Paris: Publications de la Sorbonne.

Humfress, Caroline. 2009. "Law in Practice." In *A Companion to Late Antiquity,* ed. Philip Rousseau, 377–91. Malden: Wiley-Blackwell.

Iglesias Gil, José Manuel. 1994. *Intercambio de bienes en el Cantábrico oriental en el alto imperio romano.* Santander: Universidad de Cantabria.

———. 2001–2002. "Contexto histórico y vida cotidiana en la ciudad romana de *Iuliobriga* (Cantabria)." *Aquitania* 18: 261–78.

Iglesias Gil, José Manuel, and Alicia Ruiz Gutiérrez. 2007. "La muralla tardoantigua de Monte Cildá (Aguilar de Campoo, Palencia)." In *Murallas de ciudades romanas en el occidente del Imperio: Lucus Augusti como paradigma*, ed. Antonio Rodríguez Colmenero and Isabel Rodà de Llanza, 449–66. Lugo: Museo Provincial de Lugo.

Íñigo Erdozain, Lidia, and María Milagros Martínez González. 2002. "Nuevo alfar de *terra sigillata* hispánica tardía en el valle medio del Najerilla." *Iberia* 5: 217–74.

Innes, Matthew. 2000. *State and Society in the Early Middle Ages: The Middle-Rhine Valley, 400–1000.* Cambridge: Cambridge University Press.

———. 2006. "Land, Freedom and the Making of the Medieval West." *Transactions of the Royal Historical Society* 16: 39–74.

Isla Frez, Amancio. 2001. "*Villa, villula, castellum*: Problemas de terminología rural en época visigoda." *Arqueología y Territorio Medieval* 8: 9–19.

———. 2007. "El lugar de habitación de las aristocracias en época visigoda, siglos VI–VIII." *Arqueología y Territorio Medieval* 14: 9–19.

———. 2010. *Ejército, sociedad y política en la Península Ibérica entre los siglos VII y XI.* Madrid: CSIC.

Jimeno Martínez, Alfredo, Julio Gómez Santa Cruz, and José Luis Argente Oliver. 1988–1989. "La 'Villa' de San Pedro de Valdanzo (Soria)." *Zephyrus* 41–42: 419–54.

Jones, A. H. M. 1964. *The Later Roman Empire, 284–602: A Social, Economic, and Administrative Survey.* Norman: University of Oklahoma Press.

Jordá Pardo, Jesús Francisco, Josefa Rey Castiñeira, Israel Picón Plata, Emilio Abad Vidal, and Carlos Marín Suárez. 2009. "Radiocarbon and Chronology of the Iron Age Hillforts of Northwestern Iberia." In *Interpretierte Eisenzeiten: Fallstudien, Methoden, Theorie— Tagungsbeiträge der 3 Linzer Gespräche zur interpretativen Eisenzeitarchäologie*, ed. Raimund Karl and Jutta Leskovar, 81–98. Linz: Oberösterreichischen Landesmuseum.

Juan Tovar, Luis. 1998. "Las industrias cerámicas hispanas en el Bajo Imperio: Hacia una sistematización de la Sigillata Hispánica Tardía." In *Congreso Internacional la Hispania de Teodosio*, ed. Ramón Teja and Cesáreo Pérez, 2:543–68. Segovia: SEK.

———. 2012. "Las cerámicas imitación de *sigillata* (CIS) en la meseta norte durante el siglo V: Nuevos testimonios y precisiones cronológicas." In *In Durii regione romanitas: Estudios sobre la Romanización del Valle del Duero en homenaje a Javier Cortes Álvarez de Miranda*, ed. Carmelo Fernández Ibáñez and Ramón Bohigas Roldán, 365–72. Palencia/Santander: Diputación de Palencia/Instituto Sautuola de Prehistoria y Arqueología.

———. 2013. "La vajilla de cerámica hispánica tardía gris y naranja en 'Asturica Augusta' (Astorga, León): Conjunto C." *Ex Officina Hispana: Cuadernos de la SECAH* 1: 217–55.

———. 2016. "Talleres y hornos cerámicos tardoantiguos y altomedievales en el noroeste peninsular: Estructuras y tecnologías." In *La cerámica de la alta edad media en el cuadrante noroeste de la Península Ibérica (siglos V–X)*, ed. Alfonso Vigil-Escalera Guirado and Juan Antonio Quirós Castillo, 339–62. Bilbao: Universidad del País Vasco.

Juan Tovar, Luis, and Juan Blanco García. 1997. "Cerámica común tardorromana, imitación de sigillata, en la provincia de Segovia." *Archivo Español de Arqueología* 70: 171–219.

Kaiser, Anna Maria. 2015. "Egyptian Units and the Reliability of the *Notitia Dignitatum, Pars Orientis*." *Historia* 64(2): 243–61.

Keay, Simon. 1984. *Late Roman Amphorae in the Western Mediterranean: A Typology and Economic Study—the Catalan Evidence.* 2 vols. Oxford: B.A.R.

————. 1988. *Roman Spain*. Berkeley: University of California Press.

Kelly, Christopher. 2004. *Ruling the Later Roman Empire*. Cambridge, MA: Belknap.

Kelly, Gavin. 2008. *Ammianus Marcellinus: The Allusive Historian*. Cambridge: Cambridge University Press.

King, Paul D. 1972. *Law and Society in the Visigothic Kingdom*. Cambridge: Cambridge University Press.

Koch, Manuel. 2006. "*Gothi intra Hispanias sedes acceperunt*. Consideraciones sobre la supuesta inmigración visigoda en la Península Ibérica." *Pyrenae* 37(2): 83–104.

————. 2012. *Etnische Identität im Entstehungsprozess des spanischen Westgotenreiches*. Berlin: Walter de Gruyter.

————. 2014. "Arianism and Ethnic Identity in Sixth-Century Visigothic Spain." In *Arianism: Roman Heresy and Barbarian Creed*, ed. Guido Berndt and Roland Steinacher, 257–270. Burlington: Ashgate.

Krause, Jens-Uwe. 1987. *Spätantike Patronatsformen im Westen des römischen Reiches*. Munich: C. H. Beck.

Kreiner, Jamie. 2014. *The Social Life of Hagiography in the Merovingian Kingdom*. Cambridge: Cambridge University Press.

Kulikowski, Michael. 2001. "Review of *Toreutica de la Betica (Siglos VI y VII D.C.)* by Gisela Ripoll." *Medieval Review* 01.05.05. http://scholarworks.iu.edu/journals/index.php/tmr /article/view/15064/21182.

————. 2004. *Late Roman Spain and Its Cities*. Baltimore: John Hopkins University Press.

Lagóstena Barrios, Lázaro. 2001. *La produción de salsas y conservas de pescado en la Hispania Romana (II a.C.–VI-d.C)*. Barcelona: Universitat de Barcelona.

Lancha, Janine, Pierre André, and Fátima Abraços, eds. 2000. *La villa de Torre de Palma*. Lisbon: Instituto Português de Museus.

Laniado, Avshalom. 2002. *Recherches sur les notables municipaux dans l'Empire Protobyzantin*. Paris: Association des Amis du Centre d'Histoire et Civilisation de Byzance.

————. 2006. "Le christianisme et l'évolution des institutions municipales du Bas-Empire: L'example du *defensor civitatis*." In *Die Stadt in der Spätantike: Niedergang oder Wandel?* ed. Jens-Uwe Krause and Christian Witschel, 319–34. Stuttgart: Franz Steiner.

Larrea, Juan José. 1998. *La Navarre du IVe au XIIe siècle: Peuplement et société*. Brussels: De Boeck.

Larrén, Hortensia, Juan Francisco Blanco, Olatz Villanueva, Jesús Caballero, Alonso Domínguez, Jaime Nuño, Francisco Javier Sanz, Gregorio Marcos, Miguel Ángel Martín, and Jesús Misiego. 2003. "Ensayo de sistematización de la cerámica tardoantigua en la cuenca del Duero." In *Cerámicas tardorromanas y altomedievales en la Península Ibérica: Ruptura y continuidad*, ed. Luis Caballero Zoreda, Pedro Mateos Cruz, and Manuel Retuerce, 273–306. Madrid: CSIC.

Laurence, Ray, Simon Esmonde Cleary, and Gareth Sears. 2011. *The City in the Roman West, c. 250 BCE–c. AD 250*. Cambridge: Cambridge University Press.

Lavan, Luke. 2003. "The Political Topography of the Late Antique City: Activity Spaces in Practice." In *Theory and Practice in Late Antique Archeology*, ed. Luke Lavan and William Bowden, 314–37. Leiden: Brill.

Lavan, Luke, and Michael Mulryan. 2011. *The Archaeology of Late Antique "Paganism."* Leiden: Brill.

Le Roux, Patrick. 1982. "Les sénateurs originaires de la province d'Hispania citerior en Haut-Empire romain." In *Atti del Colloquio internazionale AIEGL su epigrafia e ordine senatorio, Roma, 14–20 maggio 1981*, 439–64. Rome: Edizioni di Storia e Letteratura.

————. 2014. *Espagnes romaines: L'empire dans ses provinces—scripta varia II*. Rennes: Presses Universitaires de Rennes.

Lecanda Esteban, José Ángel. 2000. "Mijanjos: La aportación de la epigrafía y el análisis arqueológico al conocimiento de la transición a la alta edad media en Castilla." In *Visigodos y Omeyas: Un debate entre la antigüedad tardía y la alta edad media*, ed. Luis Caballero Zoreda and Pedro Mateos Cruz, 181–206. Madrid: CSIC.

————. 2003. "Cerámica tardorromana, visigoda y altomedieval en el alto valle del Ebro." *Sautuola* 9: 301–14.

Lecanda Esteban, José Ángel, and Ángel Luis Palomino. 2001. "Dos modelos de ocupación del territorio en época visigoda en la provincia de Burgos." In *V Congreso de Arqueología Medieval Española*, 1:37–48. Valladolid: Junta de Castilla y León.

Lemcke, Lukas. 2016. *Imperial Transportation and Communication from the Third to the Late Fourth Century: The Golden Age of the* cursus publicus. Brussels: Latomus.

Lemos, Francisco Sande, José Manuel de Freitas Leite, and Armandino Cunha. 2007. "A muralha romana (baixo império) de *Bracara Augusta*." In *Murallas de ciudades romanas en el occidente del Imperio: Lucus Augusti como paradigma*, ed. Antonio Rodríguez Colmenero and Isabel Rodà de Llanza, 329–41. Lugo: Museo Provincial de Lugo.

Lenski, Noel. 2009. "Schiavi armati e formazione di eserciti privati nel mondo tardoantico." In *Ordine e sovversione nel mondo greco e romano*, ed. Gianpaolo Urso, 145–75. Pisa, Italy: ETS.

Leone, Anna. 2007. *Changing Townscapes in North Africa from Late Antiquity to the Arab Conquest*. Bari: Edipuglia.

Lepelley, Claude. 1979. *Les cités de l'Afrique Romaine au Bas-Empire*. Paris: Études Augustiniennes.

Lewit, Tamara. 2003. "'Vanishing Villas': What Happened to Élite Rural Habitation in the West in the 5th–6th C.?" *Journal of Roman Archaeology* 16: 260–74.

————. 2004. *Villas, Farms and the Late Roman Rural Economy, Third to Fifth Centuries AD*. Oxford: Archaeopress.

————. 2005. "Bones in the Bathhouse: Re-evaluating the Notion of 'Squatter Occupation' in 5th–7th Century Villas." In *Dopo la fine delle ville: Le campagne dal VI al IX secolo*, ed. Gian Pietro Brogiolo, Alexandra Chavarría Arnau, and Marco Valenti, 251–62. Mantua: Società Archeologica.

Liebeschuetz, J. H. W. G. 2001. *Decline and Fall of the Roman City*. Oxford: Oxford University Press.

Liebeschuetz, J.H.W.G. 2013. "Goths and Romans in the *Leges Visigothorum*." In *Integration in Rome and in the Roman World. Proceedings of the Tenth Workshop of the International Network Impact of Empire (Lille, June 23–25, 2011)*, ed. G. Kleijn and Stéphane Benoist, 89–104. Leiden: Brill.

Llana Rodríguez, José César, and Elena Varela Arias. 1999. "Una aproximación a las actividades realizadas en la zona oriental del barrio norte del Castro de Viladonga." *CROA: Boletín da Asociación de Amigos do Museo do Castro de Viladonga* 9: 14–29.

Lopes, Maria da Conceição. 2000. *A cidade romana de Beja: Percursos e debates em torno de Pax Iulia*. Doctoral dissertation, Universidade de Coimbra, Coimbra, Portugal.

Lopes, Maria da Conceição and Rafael Alfenim. 1994. "A villa romana do Monte da Cegonha." In *Arqueolgía en el entorno del Bajo Guadiana*, ed. Juan Manuel Campos Carrasco, Juan Pérez Macías, and Francisco Gómez, 485–502. Huelva: Universidad de Huelva.

Lopes, Virgílio. 2003. *Mértola na antiguidade tardia: A topografia histórica da cidade e do seu território nos alvores do cristianismo*. Mértola: Campo Arqueológico de Mértola.

López Merino, Lourdes, José Antonio López Sáez, Daniel Abel Schaad, Francisco Sánchez Palencia and Guillermo-Sven Reher Díez. 2008. "Dinámica antrópica en El Bierzo (León) desde época romana: studio palinológico de Castro Ventosa." *Polen* 18: 25–36.

López Merino, Lourdes, José Antonio López Sáez, Francisco Javier Sánchez-Palencia, Guillermo-Sven Reher Díez, and Sebastián Pérez Díaz. 2009. "Antropización de los paisajes de Asturias y León en época romana." *Cuadernos de la Sociedad Española de Ciencias Forestales* 30: 93–99.

López Monteagudo, Guadalupe. 2010. "Nuevos mosaicos emeritenses con inscripciones." In *Doctrina a magistro discipulis tradita: Estudios en homenaje al Prof. Dr. D. Luis García Iglesias*, ed. Adolfo Domínguez Monedero and Gloria Mora, 235–60. Madrid: Ediciones UAM.

López Pérez, Catalina, Yolanda Álvarez González, and Luis Francisco López González. 1999. "Evidencias materiales de la actividad comercial romana en Iria Flavia (Padrón, A Coruña): Las sigillatas." *Gallaecia* 18: 239–64.

López Pérez, María Catalina, and Santiago Vázquez Collazo. 2007. "La mesa y la villa romana de O Cantón Grande (A Coruña): Aproximación al yacimiento a través de la *terra sigillata*." *Gallaecia* 26: 85–108.

López Quiroga, Jorge. 2004. *El final de la antigüedad en la Gallaecia: La transformación de las estructuras de poblamiento entre Miño y Duero (siglos V al X)*. Coruña: Fundación Pedro Barrié de la Maza.

López Quiroga, Jorge, and Mónica Lovelle. 1995–96. "De los vándalos a los suevos en Galicia: Una visión crítica sobre su instalación y organización territorial en el noroeste de la Península Ibérica en el siglo V." *Studia Historica: Historia Antigua* 13–14: 421–36.

———. 1999. "La topografía funeraria 'urbana' en el noroeste de la península ibérica (s. IV–XI)." In *Los orígenes de la ciudad en el noroeste hispánico*, ed. Antonio Rodríguez Colmenero, 1395–409. Lugo: Diputación Provincial de Lugo.

López Quiroga, Jorge, and F. Germán Rodríguez Martín. 2000. "El 'final' de las *villae* en Hispania I: La transformación de las *pars urbana* de las *villae* durante la antigüedad tardía." *Portugalia* 21–22: 137–90.

López Rodriguez, José. 1985. *Terra sigillata hispánica tardía decorada a molde de la Península Ibérica*. Salamanca: Universidad de Salamanca.

López Sáez, José Antonio, Lourdes López Merino, Francisca Alba Sánchez, and Sebastián Pérez Díez. 2009. "Contribución paleoambiental al estudio de la trashumancia en el sector abulense de la Sierra de Gredos." *Hispania* 69(231): 9–38.

López Sáez, José Antonio, César Oubiña Parcero, Elena Lima Oliveira, Pilar López García, Felipe Criado Boado, Rosario Macías Rosado, Antonio Martínez Cortizas, and Susana Franco Maside. 2003. "Paleopaisajes concretos: Polen, suelos y arqueología del yacimiento de As Pontes (Abadín, Lugo)." *Trabajos de Prehistoria* 60(1): 139–51.

Loseby, Simon. 1996. "Arles in Late Antiquity: Gallula Roma Arelas and Urbs Genesii." In *Towns in Transition: Urban Evolution in Late Antiquity and the Early Middle Ages*, ed. Neil Christie and Simon Loseby, 45–69. Aldershot: Scholar Press.

———. 1998. "Gregory's Cities: Urban Functions in Sixth-Century Gaul." In *Franks and Alamanni in the Merovingian Period: An Ethnographic Perspective*, ed. Ian Wood, 239–84. Rochester, U.K.: Boydell.

Lowe, Benedict. 2009. *Roman Iberia: Economy, Society and Culture*. London: Duckworth.

Macias, Santiago. 1995. "A basílica paleocristã de Mértola." In *IV Reunió d'arqueologia cristiana hispànica*, 277–96. Barcelona: Institut d'Estudis Catalans.

Macias Solé, Josep María. 2008. "*Tarracona* visigoda: ¿Una ciudad en declive?" *Zona Arqueológica* 9: 293–301.

Maciel, Manuel Justino. 1993. "Reescavações na villa romana do Montinho das Laranjeiras (Alcoutim)." *Arqueologia Medieval* 2: 33–38.

———. 1996. *Antiguidade tardia e paleocristianismo em Portugal.* Lisbon: Sociedade Industrial Gráfica Telles da Silva.

Maloney, Stephanie. 1999–2000. "As escavações da Universidade de Louisville na villa de Torre de Palma, Portugal, 1983–2000: Alguns resultados preliminares." *A Cidade* 13–14: 105–20.

Maloney, Stephanie, and John Hale. 1996. "The Villa of Torre de Palma (Alto Alentejo)." *Journal of Roman Archaeology* 9: 275–94.

Mangas, Julio. 1980. "Villa romana en Villaverde de Medina (Medina del Campo, Valladolid)." *Memorias de Historia Antigua* 4: 213–20.

Mann, Michael. 1984. "The Autonomous Power of the State: Its Origins, Mechanisms and Results." *European Journal of Sociology* 25(2): 185–213.

Manzano Moreno, Eduardo. 2003. "La cerámica de los siglos oscuros." In *Cerámicas tardorromanas y altomedievales en la Península Ibérica*, ed. Luis Caballero Zoreda, Pedro Mateos Cruz, and Manuel Retuerce, 541–57. Madrid: CSIC.

Mañanes Pérez, Tomás. 1992. *La villa romana de Almenara-Puras (Valladolid).* Valladolid: Diputación Provincial de Valladolid.

———. 2002. *Arqueología del área central de la cuenca del río Duero: De Simancas a Coca.* Valladolid: Diputación Provincial de Valladolid.

Marot, Teresa. 2000–2001. "La Península Ibérica en los siglos V–VI: Consideraciones sobre la provisión, circulación y usos monetarios." *Pyrenae* 31–32: 133–60.

Martin, Céline. 2003. *La géographie du pouvoir dans l'Espagne visigothique.* Villeneuve d'Ascq: Presses Universitaires du Septentrion.

———. 2006. "Montanus et les schismatiques: La reprise en main d'une périphérie hispanique au début du VIe siècle." *Médiévales* 51: 9–20.

———. 2008a. "Hiérarchie et service dans le monde wisigothique: La militia des laïcs." In *Hiérarchie et stratification sociale dans l'Occident médiéval (400–1000)*, ed. François Bougard, Dominique Iogna-Prat, and Régine Le Jan, 325–41. Turnhout: Brepols.

———. 2008b. "La notion de gens dans la péninsule ibérique des VIe–VIIe siècles: quelques interpretations." In *Identité et ethnicité: concepts, débats historiographiques, exemples, IIIe–XIIe siècle*, ed. Véronique Gazeau, Pierre Bauduin, and Yves Modéran, 75–89. Caen: Publications du CRAHM.

Martín Chamoso, María Concepción. 2006. "Nuevos hallazgos en la villa romana Sahelices El Chico (Salamanca)." *Revista de Arqueología* 27: 40–47.

Martín González, Saúl. 2009. "La villa romana de Miralrío: Aproximación a un nuevo centro productivo en el Valle del Guadiana entre Alange y Mérida (Badajoz)." *Revista de Estudios Extremeños* 65(1): 11–38.

Martín Viso, Iñaki. 1999. "Organización episcopal y poder entre la antigüedad tardía y el medioevo (siglos V–XI): Las sedes de Calahorra, Oca y Osma." *Iberia* 2: 151–90.

———. 2006a. "Central Places and the Territorial Organization of Communities: The Occupation of Hilltop Sites in Early Medieval Northern Castile." In *People and Space in the Middle Ages, 300–1300*, ed. Wendy Davies, Guy Halsall, and Andrew Reynolds, 167–85. Turnhout: Brepols.

———. 2006b. "Tributación y escenarios locales en el centro de la península ibérica: Algunas hipótesis a partir del análisis de las pizarras 'visigodas.'" *Antiquité Tardive* 14: 263–90.

———. 2008. "*Tremisses y potentes* en el nordeste de Lusitania (siglos VI–VII)." *Mélanges de la Casa de Velázquez* 38(1): 175–200.

———. 2012. "Un mundo en transformación: Los espacios rurales en la Hispania post-romana (siglos V–VII)." In *Visigodos y Omeyas: El territorio*, ed. Luis Caballero Zoreda, Pedro Mateos Cruz, and Tomas Cordero Ruiz, 31–63. Madrid: CSIC.

———. 2013. "Prácticas locales de la fiscalidad en el reino visigodo de Toledo." In *Lo que vino de Oriente: Horizontes, praxis y dimensión material de los sistemas de dominación fiscal en Al-Andalus (ss. VII–IX)*, ed. Xavier Ballestín and Ernesto Pastor, 72–85. Oxford: Archaeopress.

———. 2014. "*Castella* y elites en el suroeste de la meseta del Duero postromana." In *Las fortificaciones en la tardoantigüedad: Élites y articulación del territorio (siglos V–VIII d.C.)*, ed. Raúl Catalán, Patricia Fuentes, and José Carlos Sastre, 247–74. Madrid: La Ergástula.

Martín Viso, Iñaki, and Santiago Castellanos, ed. 2008. *De Roma a los bárbaros: Poder central y horizontes locales en la cuenca del Duero*. León: Universidad de León.

Martín Viso, Iñaki, Rubén Rubio Díez, José Antonio López Sáez, Mónica Ruiz Alonso, and Sebastián Pérez Díaz. (forthcoming). "La formación de un nuevo paisaje en el centro de la Península Ibérica en el periodo postromano: El yacimiento de La Genestosa (Casillas de Flores, Salamanca)." *Archivo Español de Arqueología* 90.

Martínez Díez, Gonzalo. 1959. *El patrimonio eclesiástico en la España visigoda*. Santander: Universidad Pontificia de Comillas.

Martínez González, María Milagros. 2005. "La producción de terra sigillata hispánica tardía en el área riojana: Valorización arqueológica de los datos disponibles." *Iberia* 8: 113–34.

Martínez Peñín, Raquel. 2011. "Los orígenes de la iglesia cristiana: Marialba de la Ribera in suburbio Legionense—fuentes documentales y datos arqueológicos." In *Iglesia y ciudad: Espacio y poder (siglos VIII–XIII)*, 103–36. Oviedo: Universidad de Oviedo.

Martins, Manuela, and Manuela Delgado. 1989–1990. "História e arqueologia de uma cidade en devir: Bracara Augusta." *Cadernos de Arqueologia* 6–7: 11–38.

———. 1996. "Bracara Augusta: Uma cidade na periferia do Império." In *Los finisterres atlánticos en la antigüedad: Época prerromana y romana*, ed. Carmen Fernández Ochoa, 121–27. Gijón: Electa.

Mateos Cruz, Pedro. 1999. *La basílica de santa Eulalia de Mérida. Arqueología y urbanismo*. Madrid: CSIC - Consorcio de la Ciudad Monumental de Mérida.

———. 2000. "*Augusta Emerita*, de capital de la *diocesis Hispaniarum* a sede temporal visigoda." In *Sedes Regiae (ann. 400–800)*, ed. Gisela Ripoll and Josep Gurt, 491–520. Barcelona: Reial Acadèmia de Bones Lletres.

———. 2001. "*Augusta Emerita*: La investigación arqueológica en una ciudad de época romana." *Archivo Español de Arqueología* 74: 183–208.

———. 2006. "El culto imperial en el llamado 'foro provincial' de *Augusta Emerita*." In *El "foro provincial" de Augusta Emerita: Un conjunto monumental de culto imperial*, ed. Pedro Mateos Cruz, 315–54. Madrid: CSIC.

———. 2007. "Die Anfänge der Christianisierung in den Städten Hispaniens." In *Städte im Wandel: Bauliche Inszenierung und literarische Stilisierung lokaler Eliten auf der Iberischen Halbinsel*, ed. Sabine Panzram, 237–63. Hamburg: LIT.

Mateos Cruz, Pedro, and Miguel Alba Calzado. 2000. "De *Emerita Augusta* a Marida." In *Visigodos y Omeyas: Un debate entre la antigüedad tardía y la alta edad media*, ed. Luis Caballero Zoreda and Pedro Mateos Cruz, 141–168. Mérida: CSIC.

Mateos Cruz, Pedro, Antonio Pizzo, and Ruth Pliego Vázquez. 2005. "Un tesoro de tremises visigodos hallado en el llamado 'foro provincial' de *Augusta Emerita*." *Archivo Español de Arqueología* 78: 251–70.

Mathisen, Ralph. 1993. *Roman Aristocrats in Barbarian Gaul: Strategies for Survival in an Age of Transition*. Austin: University of Texas Press.

Matos, José Luís de. 1994. "Cerro da Vila." In *Arqueología en el entorno del Bajo Guadiana*, ed. Juan Manuel Campos Carrasco, Juan Pérez Macías, and Francisco Gómez, 521–26. Huelva, Spain: Universidad de Huelva.

Matthews, John. 1975. *Western Aristocracies and Imperial Court, A.D. 364–425*. Oxford: Clarendon.

Mayet, François. 1984. *Les céramiques sigillées hispaniques*. Paris: Difussion de Boccard.

McCormick, Michael. 1986. *Eternal Victory: Triumphal Rulership in Late Antiquity, Byzantium, and the Early Medieval West*. Cambridge: Cambridge University Press.

McLynn, Neil. 1994. *Ambrose of Milan: Church and Court in a Christian Capital*. Berkeley: University of California Press.

———. 2005. "'Genere Hispanus': Theodosius, Spain and Nicene Orthodoxy." In *Hispania in Late Antiquity: Current Perspectives*, ed. Kim Bowes and Michael Kulikowski, 77–120. Leiden: Brill.

Melchor Gil, Enrique. 1994a. "Summae Honorariae y donaciones ob honorem en la Hispania romana." *Habis* 25: 193–212.

———. 1994b. "Consideraciones acerca del origen, motivación y evolución de las conductas evergéticas en Hispania romana." *Studia Historica: Historia Antigua* 12: 61–82.

Menéndez Llorente, Adriángela. 2000. *La comarca de Valdeorras en época romana: La cerámica sigillata*. Ourense, Spain: Peymar Artes Gráficas.

Metcalf, David. 1999. "Visigothic Monetary History: The Facts, What Facts?" In *The Visigoths: Studies in Culture and Society*, ed. Alberto Ferreiro, 201–17. Leiden: Brill.

Miguel Hernández, Fernando, and Carmen Benéitez González. 1993–1994. "Relectura arqueológica de la villa romana de Navatajera (León)." *Numantia* 6: 103–26.

Millett, Martin. 2001. "Roman Interaction in North-western Iberia." *Oxford Journal of Archaeology* 20(2): 157–70.

Mínguez, José María. 1998. "Continuidad y ruptura en los orígenes de la sociedad astruleonesa: De la villa a la comunidad campesina." *Studia Historica: Historia Medieval* 16: 89–127.

Mirković, Miroslava. 1996. "Autopragia and the Village Aphrodito." *Zeitschrift der Savigny-Stiftung für Rechtsgeschichte: Romanistische Abteilung* 113(1): 346–57.

Mitchell, Stephen. 1976. "Requisitioned Transport in the Roman Empire: A New Inscription from Pisidia." *Journal of Roman Studies* 66: 106–31.

Modéran, Yves. 2014. *Les Vandales et l'Empire romain*. Arles: Éditions Errance.

Morais, Rui. 1997–1998. "Sobre a hegemonia do vinho e a escassez do aceite no Noroeste Peninsular nos inícios da romanização." *Cadernos de Arqueologia* 14–15: 175–82.

———. 2000. "De *oppidum* a *dives Bracara*: O comércio da cidade através das ânforas." *Arqueologia* 26: 71–87.

———. 2005. "Produção e comércio de cerâmicas em *Bracara Augusta*." In *Unidad y diversidad en el arco atlántico en época romana*, ed. Carmen Fernández Ochoa and Paloma García Díaz, 125–38. Oxford: Archaeopress.

Morand, Isabelle. 1994. *Idéologie, culture et spiritualité chez les propriétaires ruraux de l'Hispanie romaine*. Paris: De Boccard.

Moreda Blanco, Francisco Javier, Santiago Vilar Labarta, Rosalía Serrano Noriega, and Raúl Carral Fernández. 2010–2011. "La necrópolis tardorromana de villa de 'El Vergel' (San Pedro del Arroyo, Ávila)." *Oppidum* 6–7: 141–84.

Morillo, Ángel, Carmen Fernández Ochoa, and Javier Salido Domínguez. 2016. "Hispania and the Atlantic Route in Roman Times: New Approaches to Ports and Trade." *Oxford Journal of Archaeology* 35(3): 267–84.

Mulvin, Lynda. 2002. *Late Roman Villas in the Danube-Balkan Region*. Oxford: Archaeopress.

Naveiro López, Juan. 1996. "Registro cerámico e intercambios en el Noroeste en la época romana." In *Los finisterres atlánticos en la Antigüedad: Época prerromana y romana*, ed. Carmen Fernández Ochoa, 201–4. Gijón: Ayuntamiento de Gijón.

Neira Jiménez, María Luz. 2007. "Aproximación a la ideología de las elites en Hispania durante la antigüedad tardía: A propósito de los mosaicos figurados de *domus* y *villae*." *Anales de Arqueología Cordobesa* 18: 263–90.

Nicols, John. 1988. "On the Standard Size of the Ordo Decurionum." *Zeitschrift der Savigny-Stiftung für Rechtsgeschichte: Romanistische Abteilung* 105(1): 712–19.

Nixon, C. E. V., and Barbara Saylor Rodgers. 1994. *In Praise of Later Roman Emperors: The Panegyrici Latini—Introduction, Translation, and Historical Commentary with the Latin Text of R. A. B. Mynors*. Berkeley: University of California Press.

Nogales Basarrate, Trinidad, ed. 2010. *Ciudad y foro en Lusitania romana*. Mérida: Museo Nacional de Arte Romano.

Nogales Basarrate, Trinidad, António Carvalho, and María José Almeida. 2004. "El programa decorativo de la Quinta das Longas (Elvas, Portugal): Un modelo excepcional de las *uillae* de la Lusitania." In *Actas de la IV reunión sobre escultura romana en Hispania*, ed. Trinidad Nogales Basarrate and Luis Jorge Rodrigues Gonçalves, 103–56. Madrid: Ministerio de Cultura.

Noguera Celdrán, José Miguel, and Juan Antonio Antolinos Marín. 2009. "Áreas productivas y zonas de servicio de la villa romana de Los Cipreses (Jumilla, Murcia)." *Archivo Español de Arqueología* 82: 191–220.

Nozal Calvo, Miguel. 1995. "El yacimiento de La Olmeda: La villa y el territorio." In *Actas del III Congreso de Historia de Palencia*, ed. María Valentina Calleja González, 315–40. Palencia: Diputación Provincial de Palencia.

Nozal Calvo, Miguel, Javier Cortes, and José Antonio Abásolo Álvarez. 2000. "Intervenciones arqueológicas en los baños de la villa de La Olmeda (Pedrosa de la Vega, Palencia)." In *Termas romanas en el occidente del imperio: II Coloquio Internacional de Arqueología en Gijón—Gijón 1999*, ed. Carmen Fernández Ochoa and Virginia García Entero, 311–18. Gijón: Ayuntamiento de Gijón.

Núñez Hernández, Sara Isabel. 2008. "Conjuntos termales públicos en ciudades romanas de la cuenca del Duero." *Zephyrus* 62: 163–93.

Nuño González, Jaime, and Alonso Domínguez Bolaños. 2014. "La muralla tardoantigua de Muelas del Pan (Zamora): Una construcción de urgencia en un tiempo convulso." In *Las fortificaciones en la tardoantigüedad: Élites y articulación del territorio (siglos V–VIII d.C.)*, ed. Raúl Catalán, Patricia Fuentes, and José Carlos Sastre, 297–329. Madrid: La Ergástula.

Oepen, Alexis. 2012. *Villa und christlicher Kult auf der Iberischen Halbinsel in Spätantike und Westgotenzeit*. Wiesbaden: Reichert.

Olmo Enciso, Lauro. 1998. "Consideraciones sobre la ciudad en época visigoda." *Arqueología y territorio medieval* 5: 109–18.

———. 2007. "The Royal Foundation of *Recópolis* and the Urban Renewal in Iberia During the Second Half of the Sixth Century." In *Post-Roman Towns, Trade and Settlement in Europe and Byzantium*, ed. Joachim Henning, 1:181–96. Berlin: Walter de Gruyter.

———, ed. 2008. *Zona Arqueológica 9: Recópolis y la ciudad en la época visigoda*.

Orejas Saco del Valle, Almudena. 1996. *Estructura social y territorio: El impacto romano en la cuenca noroccidental del Duero*. Madrid: CSIC.

Palme, Bernhard. 1999. "Die Officia der Statthalter in der Spätantike: Forschungsstand und Perspektiven." *Antiquité Tardive* 7: 85–133.

Palol, Pedro de. 1977. "Romanos en la meseta: El Bajo Imperio y la aristocracia agrícola." In *Segovia y la arqueología romana*, 297–308. Barcelona: Universidad de Barcelona and Caja de Ahorros y Monte de Piedad de Segovia.

Panella, Clementina. 1986. "Le merci: Produzioni, itinerari e destini." In *Societá romana e impero tardoantico*, ed. Andrea Giardina, 3:431–59. Bari: Laterza.

Panzram, Sabine. 2002. *Stadtbild und Elite: Tarraco, Corduba und Augusta Emerita zwischen Republik und Spätantike*. Stuttgart: Franz Steiner.

———. 2010. "Mérida contra Toledo, Eulalia contra Leocadia: Listados 'fasificados' de obispos como medio de autrepresentación municipal." In *Espacios urbanos en el Occidente Mediterráneo (S. VI–VIII): Congreso Internacional Toledo 2009*, ed. Alfonso García, Ricardo Izquierdo, Lauro Olmo Enciso, and Diego Peris, 123–30. Toledo: Toletum Visigodo.

———. 2014. "Die Iberische Halbinsel um 500 n. Chr.–Herrschaft 'am Ende der Welt': Eine Geschichte in neun Städten." In *Chlodwigs Welt: Organisation von Herrschaft um 500*, ed. Mischa Meier and Steffen Patzold, 449–86. Stuttgart: Franz Steiner.

Parker, Anthony. 1992. *Ancient Shipwrecks of the Mediterranean and the Roman Provinces*. Oxford: Tempus Reparatum.

Parodi Álvarez, Manuel. 2003. "Notas sobre la economía del Anas: Apuntes sobre la navegación antigua." In *Puertos fluviales antiguos: Ciudad, desarrollo e infraestructuras*, ed. Guillermo Pascual Berlanga and José Pérez Ballester, 49–58. Valencia: Universitat de València.

———. 2014. "Los ríos occidentales de la Hispania romana en las fuentes clásicas: Una aproximación." *Onoba* 2: 179–89.

Patterson, John. 2006. *Landscapes and Cities: Rural Settlement and Civic Transformation in Early Imperial Italy*. Oxford: Oxford University Press.

Patzold, Steffen. 2014. "Bischöfe, soziale Herkunft und die Organisation lokaler Herrschaft um 500." In *Chlodwigs Welt: Organisation von Herrschaft um 500*, ed. Mischa Meier and Steffen Patzold, 523–43. Stuttgart: Franz Steiner.

Paz Peralta, Juan Ángel. 1991. *Cerámica de mesa romana de los siglos III al VI d. C. en la provincia de Zaragoza*. Zaragoza: Institución Fernando el Católico.

———. 2008. "Las producciones de terra sigillata hispánica intermedia y tardía." In *Cerámicas hispanorromanas: Un estado de la cuestión*, ed. Darío Bernal Casasola and Albert Ribera i Lacomba, 497–540. Cádiz: Universidad de Cádiz.

Pedro, Ivone, and João Luis Inês Vaz. 1995. "Basílica e necrópole altomedievais de Viseu." In *IV Reunió d'arqueologia cristiana hispànica*, 343–52. Barcelona: Institut d'Estudis Catalans.

Peña Cervantes, Yolanda. 2005–2006. "Producción de vino y aceite en los asentamientos rurales de *Hispania* durante la antigüedad tardía (s. IV–VII d.C.)." *Cuadernos de Prehistoria y Arqueología de la Universidad Autónoma de Madrid* 31–32: 103–16.

———. 2010. *Torcularia: La producción de vino y aceite en Hispania*. Tarragona: Institut Català d'Arqueologia Clàssica.

Peña, J. Theodore. 2007. *Roman Pottery in the Archaeological Record*. Cambridge: Cambridge University Press.

Pérez González, Cesáreo, Emilio Illarregui Gómez, and Pablo Arribas Lobo. 2015. "Tiermes en los siglos II–IV: Evolución del poblamiento y del urbanismo de una ciudad de la cuenca del Duero." In *Urbanisme civique en temps de crise: Les espaces publics d'Hispanie et de l'occident romain entre le IIe et le IVe siècle*, ed. Laurent Brassous and Alejandro Quevedo, 237–51. Madrid: Casa de Velázquez.

Pérez González, Cesáreo, and Olivia Reyes Hernando. 2007. "Coca, la antigua 'Cauca.'" In *Villes et territoires dans le bassin du Douro á l'époque romaine: Actes de la table-ronde internationale (Bordeaux, Septembre 2004)*, ed. Milagros Navarro Caballero, Juan José Palao Vicente, and María Ángeles Magallón Botaya, 149–70. Bordeaux: Ausonius.

Pérez Losada, Fermín. 1992. "Estudo do material arqueolóxico da villa romana de Noville (Mugardos, A Coruña)." *Minius* 1: 57–88.

———. 1995. "Arqueoloxia e arte no mundo rural: Habitat e arquitectura das villae gallaicoromanas." In *Arqueoloxía e arte na Galicia prehistórica e romana: Lectura arqueolóxica dos aspectos artísticos da cultura material galega desde a prehistoria ata a Romanización*, ed. Fermín Pérez Losada and Ladislao Castro Pérez, 165–88. A Coruña: Edicións do Museu Arqueolóxico e Histórico de A Coruña.

———. 2002. *Entre a cidade e a aldea: Estudio arqueohistórico dos "aglomerados secundarios" romanos en Galicia*. A Coruña: Museo Arqueolóxico e Histórico Castelo de San Antón.

Pérez Losada, Fermín, Adolfo Fernández Fernández, and Santiago Vieito Covela. 2008. "Toralla y las villas marítimas de la Gallaecia atlántica. Emplazamiento, arquitectura y función." In *Las villae tardorromanas en el occidente del imperio: Arquitectura y función—IV Coloquio Internacional de Arqueología en Gijón*, ed. Carmen Fernández Ochoa, Virginia García Entero, and Fernando Gil Sendino, 481–506. Gijón: Editiones Trea.

Pérez Losada, Fermín, Juan Naveiro López, Francisco Doval Galán, Ladislao Castro Pérez, José Vázquez Varela, and Carlos Fernández Rodríguez. 1992. "Estudio do material arqueolóxico procedente da villa romana de Noville." *Minus* 1: 57–88.

Pérez Rodríguez-Aragón, Fernando, and Alonso Domínguez Bolaños. 2005. "*Terra Sigillata Hispánica Tardía* del alfar de San Antón, en Lerma (Burgos)." *Boletín del Seminario de Estudios de Arte y Arqueología* 71: 275–98.

Pérez Rodríguez-Aragón, Fernando, and María Luz González Fernández. 2009. "El material cerámico de la antigüedad tardía en 'El Pelambre.'" In *El Pelambre: Villaornate, León— el horizonte Cogotas I de la Edad de Bronce y el periodo tardoantiguo en el valle medio del Esla*, ed. María Luz González Fernández, 321–40. Madrid: Grupo Tragsa.

Périn, Patrick. 2002. "Settlement and Cemeteries in Merovingian Gaul." In *The world of Gregory of Tours*, ed. Kathleen Mitchel and Ian Wood, 67–98. Leiden: Brill

Pessoa, Miguel. 2000. *Villa romana de Rabaçal: Um centro na periferia?* Master's thesis, Universidade de Coimbra, Coimbra.

Pessoa, Miguel, and Lino Rodrigo. 2005. *Catalogue: Museum Roman Villa of Rabaçal*. Penela: Câmara Municipal de Penela.

Pinto, Inês Vaz, Rui Roberto de Almeida, and Archer Martin, ed. 2016. *Lusitanian Amphorae: Production and Distribution*. Oxford: Archaeopress.

Pizzo, Antonio. 2006. "El 'arco de Trajano,' puerta de acceso al conjunto monumental: Análisis histórico, arquitectónico y arqueológico." In *El "foro provincial" de Augusta Emerita: Un conjunto monumental de culto imperial*, ed. Pedro Mateos Cruz, 207–49. Madrid: CSIC.

Pliego Vázquez, Ruth. 2009. *La moneda visigoda*. Seville: Universidad de Sevilla, Secretariado de Publicaciones.

Polci, Barbara. 2003. "Some Aspects of the Transformation of the Roman *Domus* Between Late Antiquity and the Early Middle Ages." In *Theory and Practice in Late Antique Archaeology*, ed. Luke Lavan and William Bowden, 79–109. Leiden: Brill.

Ponte, Maria de la Salete da. 2010. "O *Forum* de *Seilium/Sellium* (Tomar)." In *Ciudad y foro en Lusitania Romana*, ed. Trinidad Nogales Basarrate, 325–32. Mérida: Museo Nacional de Arte Romano.

Poulantzas, Nicos. 1973. *Political Power and Social Classes*. London: NLB.

Quaresma, José Carlos. 1999. "*Terra sigillata* africana, hispânica, foceense tardia e cerâmica africana de cozinha de *Mirobriga* (Santiago do Cacém)." *Conimbriga* 38: 137–200.

Quintela, António and José Manuel de Mascarenhas. 2006. "Barrages romains du Portugal. Types et fonctions." *Mélanges de la Casa de Velázquez* 36(2): 17–38.

Quirós Castillo, Juan Antonio, ed. 2009. *The Archaeology of Early Medieval Villages in Europe*. Bilbao: Universidad del País Vasco.

Quirós Castillo, Juan Antonio, and José María Tejado Sebastián, eds. 2012. *Los castillos altomedievales en el noroeste de la Península Ibérica*. Bilbao: Universidad del País Vasco.

Quirós Castillo, Juan Antonio, and Alfonso Vigil-Escalera Guirado. 2006. "Networks of Peasant Villages Between Toledo and *Velegia Alabense*, Northwestern Spain (V–Xth Centuries)." *Archeologia Medievale* 33: 79–128.

Rabanal Alonso, Manuel Abilio, and Sonia María García Martínez. 2001. *Epigrafía romana de la provincia de León: Revisión y actualización*. León: Universidad de León.

Ramil González, Emilio. 2003. "Villa romana de Bares: Excavación arqueolóxica no xacemento Eirexa-Vella de Bares–Concello de Mañón (A Coruña)—Campaña 1997." *Brigantium* 14: 185–224.

———. 2008. "Villa romana e poboado medieval de Area (Viveiro, Lugo)." *Férvedes* 5: 487–92.

Rapp, Claudia. 2005. *Holy Bishops in Late Antiquity: The Nature of Christian Leadership in an Age of Transition*. Berkeley: University of California Press.

Real, Manuel Luis. 2000. "Portugal: Cultura visigoda e cultura moçárabe." In *Visigodos y Omeyas: Un debate entre la Antigüedad tardía y la Alta Edad Media*, ed. Luis Caballero Zoreda, 21–75. Madrid: CSIC.

Regueras Grande, Fernando. 1996. "Villas romanas leonesas: Una ordenación." In *ArqueoLeón: Historia de León a través de la arqueología*, 91–106. León: Instituto Leonés de Cultura.

———. 2010. "Mosaicos de la villa astur-romana de Camarzana de Tera (Zamora)." *Espacio, Tiempo y Forma, Serie II, Historia Antigua* 23: 477–525.

———. 2011–2012. "Escultura en las villae romanas del Duero: Síntesis e inventario." *Brigecio* 21–22: 23–47.

Regueras Grande, Fernando, and Julio Del Olmo. 1998. "La villa de los Casares (Armuña, Segovia): Propuestas de lectura." In *Congreso internacional la Hispania de Teodosio*, ed. Ramón Teja and Cesáreo Pérez, 2:675–86. Segovia: Universidad SEK.

Reis, Maria Pilar. 2004. *Las termas y balnea romanos de Lusitania*. Madrid: Museo Nacional de Arte Romano.

Remesal Rodríguez, José. 1986. *La annona militaris y la exportación de aceite bético a Germania*. Madrid: Universidad Complutense.

———. 1991. "El aceite bético durante el bajo imperio." *Antigüedad y Cristianismo* 8: 355–62.

Requejo Pagés, Otilia. 2007. "Hallazgos romanos en la zona central de Asturias: Necrópolis de Paredes y Hornos de Cayés." In *Astures y romanos: Nuevas perspectivas*, ed. Juan Fernández-Tresguerres, 95–131. Oviedo: Real Instituto de Estudios Asturianos.

Retamero, Félix. 1999. "As Coins Go Home: Towns, Merchants, Bishops and Kings in Visigothic Hispania." In *The Visigoths from the Migration Period to the Seventh Century: An Ethnographic Perspective*, ed. Peter Heather, 271–305. Woodbridge: Boydell.

Reynolds, Paul. 1993. *Settlement and Pottery in the Vinalopó Valley (Alicante, Spain), A.D. 400–700.* Oxford: Tempus Reparatum.

———. 2005. "Hispania in the Late Roman Mediterranean: Ceramics and Trade." In *Hispania in Late Antiquity: Current Perspectives,* ed. Kim Bowes and Michael Kulikowski, 369–486. Leiden: Brill.

———. 2010. *Hispania and the Roman Mediterranean, AD 100–700.* London: Duckworth.

Richardson, John. 1986. *Hispaniae: Spain and the Development of Roman Imperialism, 218–82 BC.* Cambridge: Cambridge University Press.

———. 1996. *The Romans in Spain.* Oxford: Blackwell.

Riess, Frank. 2013. *Narbonne and Its Territory in Late Antiquity: From the Visigoths to the Arabs.* Burlington: Ashgate.

Rigoir, Jacqueline, Yves Rigoir, and Jean-François Meffre. 1973. "Les dérivées des sigilées paléochrétiennes du groupe atlantique." *Gallia* 31: 207–63.

Rio, Alice. 2008. "High and Low: Ties of Dependence in the Frankish Kingdom." *Transactions of the Royal Historical Society* 18: 43–68.

Ripoll, Gisela. 1985. *La necrópolis visigoda de El Carpio del Tajo (Toledo).* Madrid: Ministerio de Cultura.

———. 1993–1994. "La necrópolis visigoda de El Carpio de Tajo: Una nueva lectura a partir de la topocronología y los adornos personales." *Butlletí de la Reial Acadèmia Catalana de Belles Arts de Sant Jordi* 7–8: 187–250.

———. 1998. *Toréutica de la Bética (siglos VI y VII D.C.).* Barcelona: Reial Acadèmia de Bones Lletres.

———. 2000. "*Sedes regiae* en la Hispania de la antigüedad tardía." In *Sedes regiae, ann. 400–800,* ed. Gisela Ripoll and Josep Gurt i Esparraguera, 371–402. Barcelona: Reial Acadèmia de Bones Lletres.

———. 2010. "The Archaeological Characterization of the Visigothic Kingdom of Toledo: The Question of the Visigothic Cemeteries." In *Völker, Reiche und Namen im frühen Mittelalter,* ed. Matthias Becher and Stefanie Dick, 161–79. Munich: Wilhelm Fink.

Ripoll, Gisela, and Javier Arce. 2000. "The Transformations and End of Roman *Villae* in the West (Fourth–Seventh Centuries): Problems and Perspectives." In *Towns and Their Territories Between Antiquity and the Early Middle Ages,* ed. Gian Pietro Brogiolo, Nancy Gauthier, and Neil Christie, 63–114. Leiden: Brill.

Ripoll, Gisela, and Alexandrea Chavarría Arnau. 2005. "El altar en Hispania. Siglos IV-X." *Hortus Artium Medievalium* 11: 29–48.

Ripoll, Gisela, and Isabel Velázquez. 1999. "Origen y desarrollo de las *parrochiae* en la *Hispania* de la antigüedad tardía." In *Alle origini della parrocchia rurale (IV–VIII sec.),* 101–65. Vatican City: Pontificio Istituto di Archeologia Cristiana.

Robinson, Chase. 2000. *Empire and Elites After the Muslim Conquest: The Transformation of Northern Mesopotamia.* Cambridge: Cambridge University Press.

Rodríguez Colmenero, Antonio, Santiago Ferrer Sierra, and Rubén Álvarez Asorey. 2004. *Miliarios e outras inscricións viarias romanas do noroeste hispánico (conventos bracarense, lucense e asturicense).* Santiago de Compostela: Consello da Cultura Galega.

Rodríguez González, María de Carmen, and Mercedes Durany Castrillo. 1998. "Ocupación y organización del espacio en el Bierzo Bajo entre los siglos V al X." *Studia Historica: Historia Medieval* 18: 45–87.

Rodríguez Martín, Francisco. 1988. "Prensas y lagares en la villa romana de Torre Águila." In *X Jornadas de viticultura y enología de Tierra de Barros*, 223–42. Mérida: Consejería de Agricultura y Comercio de la Junta de Extremadura.

Rodríguez Martín, Germán, and Jean-Gérard Gorges. 1999. "Prensas de aceite y de vino en una villa romana de la cuenca media del Guadiana (Torre Águila, Barbaño, Badajoz)." In *Économie et territoire en Lusitanie romaine*, ed. Jean-Gérard Gorges and Germán Rodríguez Martín, 403–26. Madrid: Casa de Velázquez.

Rodríguez Resino, Álvaro. 2003. "Aproximación á caracterización arqueolóxica da presencia xermánica na *Gallaecia* (s. V–VIII): Os axuares funerarios." *Gallaecia* 22: 281–96.

———. 2005. *Do Imperio Romano á Alta Ideade Media: Arqueoloxía da tadoantigüidade en Galicia (séculos V–VIII)*. Noia: Toxosoutos.

Rosenstein, Nathan. 2008. "Aristocrats and Agriculture in the Middle and Late Republic." *Journal of Roman Studies* 98: 1–26.

Rossiter, Jeremy. 2007. "Domus and Villa: Late Antique Housing in Carthage and Its Territory." In *Housing in Late Antiquity. From Palaces to Shops,* ed. Luke Lavan, Lale Özgenel, and Alexander Sarantis, 367–392. Leiden: Brill.

Sáez Fernández, Pedro. 1993. "La ganadería extremeña en la antigüedad." In *Trashumancia y cultura pastoril en Extremadura*, ed. Salvador Rodríguez Becerra, 37–49. Mérida: Asamblea de Extremadura.

Salido Domínguez, Javier. 2008. "Los sistemas de almacenamiento y conservación de grano en las *villae* hispanorromanas." In *Las villae tardorromanas en el occidente del imperio: Arquitectura y función—IV Coloquio Internacional de Arqueología en Gijón*, ed. Carmen Fernández Ochoa, Virginia García Entero, and Fernando Gil Sendino, 693–706. Gijón: Editiones Trea.

Sallares, Robert. 2007. "Ecology." In *The Cambridge Economic History of the Greco-Roman World*, ed. Walter Scheidel, Ian Morris, and Richard Saller, 15–37. Cambridge: Cambridge University Press.

Salzman, Michele. 2001. "Competing Claims to 'Nobilitas' in the Western Empire of the Fourth and Fifth Centuries." *Journal of Early Christian Studies* 9(3): 359–85.

———. 2002. *The Making of a Christian Aristocracy: Social and Religious Change in the Western Roman Empire*. Cambridge, MA: Harvard University Press.

Sanchez, Sylvain Jean Gabriel. 2009. *Priscillien, un chrétien non conformist: Doctrine et pratique du Priscillianisme du IVe au VIe siècle*. Paris: Beauchesne.

Sánchez Albornoz, Claudio. 1943. *Ruina y extinción del municipio romano en España e instituciones que le reemplazan*. Buenos Aires: Facultad de Filosofía y Letras.

———. 1971. *Estudios visigodos*. Rome: Instituto Storico Italiano per il Medio Evo.

Sánchez Pardo, José Carlos. 2006. "Análisis espacial de un territorio altomedieval: Nendos (A Coruña)." *Arqueología y Territorio Medieval* 13(1): 4–48.

———. 2010. "Castros y aldeas galaicorromanas: Sobre la evolución y transformación del poblamiento indígena en la Galicia romana." *Zephyrus* 65: 129–48.

———. 2012. "Los contextos de fundación de las iglesias tardoantiguas en Galicia (ss. V–VIII): Substratos arqueológicos, distribución y significados." *Antiqué Tardive* 20: 255–73.

Sánchez Pardo, José Carlos, and Álvaro Rodríguez Resino. 2009. "Poblamiento rural altomedieval en Galicia: Balance y perspectivas de trabajo." In *The Archaeology of Early Medieval Villages in Europe*, ed. Juan Antonio Quirós Castillo, 137–48. Bilbao: Universidad del País Vasco.

Sánchez Ramos, Isabel. 2014. *Topografía cristiana de las ciudades hispanas durante la antigüedad tardía*. Oxford: Archaeopress.

Sánchez Ramos, Isabel, and Jorge Morín de Pablos. 2015. "Nueva lectura arqueológica del conjunto episcopal de Egitania (Idanha-a-Velha, Portugal)." *Madrider Mitteilungen* 55: 398–428.

Sánchez Simón, Margarita. 1998. "Villa de Prado (Valladolid): Consideraciones sobre la planta y cronología." In *Congreso Internacional la Hispania de Teodosio*, ed. Ramón Teja y Cesáreo Pérez, 2:713–27. Segovia: Universidad SEK.

Sarris, Peter. 2004. "The Origins of the Manorial Economy: New Insights from Late Antiquity." *English Historical Review* 119: 279–311.

———. 2006. *Economy and Society in the Age of Justinian*. Cambridge: Cambridge University Press.

Sayas Abengochea, Juan José. 1990. "El territorio palentino durante el bajo imperio." In *Actas del II Congreso de Historia de Palencia*, 1:655–91. Palencia: Diputación Provincial de Palencia.

Scheidel, Walter. 2013. "Studying the State." In *The Oxford Handbook of the State in the Ancient Near East and Mediterranean*, ed. Peter Bang and Water Scheidel, 5–57. Oxford: Oxford University Press.

Schmidt-Hofner, Sebastian. 2014. "Der *defensor civitatis* und die Entstehung des Notabelnregiments in den spätrömischen Städten." In *Chlodwigs Welt: Organisation von Herrchaft um 500*, ed. Mischa Meier and Steffen Patzold, 487–522. Stuttgart: Franz Steiner.

Scott, Sarah. 2004. "Elites, Exhibitionism and the Society of the Late Roman Villa." In *Landscapes of Change: Rural Evolution in Late Antiquity and the Early Middle Ages*, ed. Neil Christie, 39–65. Aldershot, U.K.: Ashgate.

Sears, Gareth. 2007. *Late Roman African Urbanism: Continuity and Transformation in the City*. Oxford: Archaeopress.

Sepúlveda, Eurico, Ana Vale, Victor Sousa, Victor Santos, and Natalina Guerreiro. 2002. "A cronologia do circo de *Olisipo*: A *terra sigillata*." *Revista Portuguesa de Arqueologia* 5(2): 245–75.

Serra Ráfols, José de C. 1949. "La capilla funeraria de la dehesa de 'La Cocosa.'" *Revista de Estudios Extremeños* 5: 105–16.

Sfameni, Carla. 2006. *Ville residenziali nell'Italia tardoantica*. Bari: Edipuglia.

———. 2014. *Residenze e culti in età tardoantica*. Rome: Scienze e Lettere.

Shaw, Brent. 1981. "Rural Markets in North Africa and the Political Economy of the Roman Empire." *Antiquités Africaines* 17: 37–83.

———. 2006. *At the Edge of the Corrupting Sea: A Lecture Delivered at New College, Oxford, on 9th May 2005*. Oxford: University of Oxford.

Sillières, Pierre. 1995. "Approche d'un espace rural antique: L'example de Vila de Frades en Lusitanie Méridionale." In *Du latifundium au latifondo: Un héritage de Rome, une création médiévale ou moderne?* 21–29. Paris: Diffusion de Boccard.

Silva, Ana Raquel Mendes da. 2000. "A villa romana de Frielas." *O Arqueólogo Português* 18: 71–84.

Silva, Carlos Tavares, and Joaquina Soares. 1997. "A Ilha do Pessegueiro na época romana." In *Portugal romano: A exploração dos recursos naturais*, ed. Adília Alarcão, 62–64. Lisbon: Museu Nacional de Arqueologia.

Sivan, Hagith. 1993. *Ausonius of Bordeaux: Genesis of a Gallic Aristocracy*. London: Routledge.

———. 1998. "The Appropriation of Roman Law in Barbarian Hands: 'Roman-Barbarian' Marriage in Visigothic Gaul and Spain." In *Strategies of Distinction: The Construction of Ethnic Communities, 300–800*, ed. Walter Pohl and Helmut Reimitz, 198–203. Leiden: Brill.

Skinner, Alexander. 2013. "Political Mobility in the Later Roman Empire." *Past and Present* 218: 17–53.

Slootjes, Daniëlle. 2006. *The Governor and His Subjects in the Later Roman Empire*. Leiden: Brill.

Smith, Julia. 2005. *Europe After Rome: A New Cultural History, 500–1000*. Oxford: Oxford University Press.

Smith, J. T. 1997. *Roman Villas: A Study in Social Structure*. New York: Routledge.

Sodini, Jean-Pierre. 2003. "Archaeology and Late Antique Social Structures." In *Theory and Practice in Late Antique Archaeology*, ed. Luke Lavan and William Bowden, 25–56. Leiden: Brill.

Sogno, Cristiana. 2006. *Q. Aurelius Symmachus: A Political Biography*. Ann Arbor: University of Michigan Press.

Solana Sáinz, José María, and Luis Sagredo San Eustaquio. 1998. "La política edilicia viaria imperial en la Hispania del s. IV d.C." In *Congreso Internacional la Hispania de Teodosio*, ed. Ramón Teja and Cesáreo Pérez González, 255–74. Segovia: Universidad SEK.

———. 2006. *La red viaria romana en Hispania: Siglos I–IV d. C.* Valladolid: Universidad de Valladolid.

Soto Arias, Purificación, Carlos Fernández Rodríguez, and Adriángela Menéndez Llorente. 1999. "Cronología y funcionalidad del núcleo habitacional secundario de *A Proba de Valdeorras*." In *Los orígenes de la ciudad en el noroeste hispánico*, ed. Antonio Rodríguez Colmenero, 2:1153–70. Lugo: Diputación Provincial de Lugo.

Sousa, Élvio Melim de. 2001. "Contributos para o estudo da cerâmica foceense tardia ('late Roman C ware') no municipium Olisiponense." *Conimbriga* 40: 199–224.

Stirling, Lea. 2007. "Statuary Collecting and Display in the Late Antique Villas of Gaul and Spain: A Comparative Study." In *Statuen in der Spätantike*, ed. Franz Alto Bauer and Christian Witschel, 307–321. Wiesbaden: Reichert.

Stocking, Rachel. 2000. *Bishops, Councils, and Consensus in the Visigothic Kingdom, 589–633*. Ann Arbor: University of Michigan Press.

Storch de Gracia y Asensio, José. 1998. "Avance de las primeras actividades arqueológicas en los hispano-visigodos de la Dehesa del Canal (Pelayos, Salamanca)." *Arqueología, Paleontología y Etnografía* 4: 141–60.

Stroheker, Karl. 1963. "Spanische Senatoren der spätrömischen und westgotischen Zeit." *Madrider Mitteilungen* 4: 107–32.

Teichner, Felix. 2003. "Resultados preliminares das últimas escavaçoes na pars rústica noroeste da villa romana de Milreu." *XELB: Revista de Arqueologia, Arte, Etnologia e História* 4: 103–14.

———. 2006. "De lo romano a lo árabe: La transición del sur de la provincia de Lusitania a Al-Gharb al-Andalus." In *Villas tardoantiguas en el Mediterráneo occidental*, ed. Alexandra Chavarría, Javier Arce, and Gian Pietro Brogiolo, 207–20. Madrid: CSIC.

———. 2008. *Zwischen Land und Meer: Architektur und Wirtschaftsweise ländlicher Siedlungsplätze im Süden der römischen Provinz Lusitanien (Portugal)*. Mérida: Museo Nacional de Arte Romano.

Teja, Ramón. 1990. "La Carta 67 de S. Cipriano a las comunidades cristianas de León-Astorga y Mérida: Algunos problemas y soluciones." *Antigüedad y Cristianismo* 7: 115–124.

Tejado Sebastián, José María. 2011. "Castros militares altomedievales en el alto valle del Iregua (La Rioja, España): Una realidad 'poco común.'" *Archeologia Medievale* 38: 137–81.

———. 2013. "Comparación entre los espacios del valle del Ebro y la meseta: La Rioja y Burgos en la antigüedad tardía." In *Fortificaciones en la tardoantigüedad: Élites y articulación del territorio (siglos V–VIII d.C)*, ed. Raúl Catalán, Patricia Fuentes, and José Carlos Sastre, 95–120. Madrid: La Ergástula.

Tejerizo García, Carlos. 2011. "Ethnicity in Early Middle Age Cemeteries: The Case of the 'Visigothic' Burials." *Arqueología y Territorio Medieval* 18: 29–43.

————. 2012. "Early medieval household archaeology in Northwest Iberia (6th–11th centuries)." *Arqueología de la Arquitectura* 9: 181–94.

Tereso, João Pedro, Pablo Ramil Rego, and Rubim Almeida da Silva. 2013. "Roman Agriculture in the *Conventus Bracaraugustanus* (NW Iberia)." *Journal of Archaeological Science* 40: 2848–58.

Thomas, Edmund, and Christian Witschel. 1992. "Constructing Reconstruction: Claim and Reality of Roman Rebuilding Inscriptions from the Latin West." *Papers of the British School at Rome* 60: 135–77.

Thompson, Edward A. 1969. *The Goths in Spain*. Oxford: Oxford University Press.

Thonemann, Peter. 2011. *The Maeander Valley: A Historical Geography from Antiquity to Byzantium*. Cambridge: Cambridge University Press.

Tilly, Charles. 1990. *Coercion, Capital, and European States, AD 990–1992*. Malden: Blackwell.

Torres López, Manuel. 1928. "El origen del sistema de 'iglesias propias.'" *Anuario de Historia del Derecho Español* 5: 83–217.

Tranoy, Alain. 1974. *Hydace, Cronique: Tome II—Commentaire et index*. Paris: Éditions du Cerf.

Uscatescu, Alexandra, Carmen Fernández Ochoa, and Paloma García Díaz. 1994. "Producciones atlánticas de *terra sigillata* gálica tardía en la costa cantábrica de Hispania." *Cuadernos de Prehistoria y Arqueología de la Universidad Autónoma de Madrid* 21: 183–234.

Utrero Agudo, María Ángeles, and Francisco Moreno Martín. 2015. "Euergetism Among the Bishops of Hispania Between the Sixth and Seventh Centuries: A Dialogue Between Archaeological and Documentary Sources." *Journal of Early Christian Studies* 23(1): 97–131.

Utrero Agudo, María de los Ángeles. 2010. "Late-Antique and Early Medieval Hispanic Churches and the Archaeology of Architecture: Revisions and Reinterpretation of Constructions, Chronologies and Contexts." *Medieval Archaeology* 54: 1–33.

Valdeomillos Rodríguez, Ana, Tomás Martín-Arroyo, Miriam Dorado Valiño, and Blanca Ruiz Zapata. 1996. "Estudio polínico de los sedimentos del embalse romano de Proserpina." In *Estudios Palinológicos*, ed. Blanca Ruiz Zapata, 125–30. Alcalá de Henares: Universidad de Alcalá.

Valero Tévar, Miguel Ángel. 2013. "The Late-Antique Villa at Noheda (Villar de Domingo García) Near Cuenca and Its Mosaics." *Journal of Roman Archaeology* 26: 307–30.

Valverde Castro, María del Rosario. 2000. *Ideología, simbolismo y ejercicio del poder real en la monarquía visigoda: Un proceso de cambio*. Salamanca: Ediciones Universidad de Salamanca.

Van Dam, Raymond. 1985. *Leadership and Community in Late Antique Gaul*. Berkeley: University of California Press.

Van Ossel, Paul, and Pierre Ouzoulias. 2000. "Rural Settlement Economy in Northern Gaul in the Late Empire: An Overview and Assessment." *Journal of Roman Archaeology* 13: 133–60.

Velázquez, Isabel. 2003. "*Pro patriae gentisque Gothorum statu*." In *Regna and Gentes: The Relationship Between Late Antique and Early Medieval Peoples and Kingdoms in the Transformation of the Roman World*, ed. Hans-Wener Goetz, Jamut Jarnut, and Walter Pohl, 161–217. Leiden: Brill.

————. 2004. *Las pizarras visigodas (Entre el latín y su disgregación: La lengua hablada en Hispania, siglos VI–VIII)*. Burgos: Fundación Instituto Castellano Leonés de la Lengua.

————. 2008. "El puente de Mérida: Algo más que un problema de traducción." *Pyrenae* 39(2): 127–35.

Velázquez, Isabel, and Gisela Ripoll. 2000. "*Toletum*, la construcction de una *urbs regia*." In *Sedes Regiae (ann. 400–800)*, ed. Gisela Ripoll and Josep Gurt i Esparraguera, 521–78. Barcelona: Reial Acadèmia de Bones Lletres.

Vera, Domenico. 1999. "Massa fundorum: Forme della grande proprietà e poteri della città in Italia fra Costantino e Gregorio Magno." *Mélanges de l'Ecole française de Rome: Antiquité* 111(2): 991–1025.

———. 2012. "Questioni di storia agraria tardoromana: schiavi, coloni, *villae*." *Antiquité Tardive* 20: 115–22.

Vermeulen, Frank, Cristina Corsi, and Morgan De Dapper. 2012. "Surveying the Townscape of Roman Ammaia in Portugal: An Integrated Geoarchaeological Investigation of the Forum Area." *Geoarchaeology* 27(2): 123–39.

Viegas, Catarina. 2006. *A cidade romana de Balsa (Torre de Ares–Tavira): (I) A terra sigillata*. Tavira: Instituto Português de Museus, Município de Tavira.

———. 2013. "Red in West: Consumption Patterns of Gallo-Roman Sigillata in Southwest Lusitania." In *Seeing Red: New Economic and Social Perspectives on Terra Sigillata*, ed. Michael Fulford and Emma Durham, 258–77. London: School of Advanced Study, University of London.

Vieira, Marina Afonso. 2005–2006. "Formas de povoamento rural na região do Alto Pavia (séculos V–X)." *Cuadernos de Prehistoria y Arqueología de la Universidad Autónoma de Madrid* 31–32: 259–79.

Vigil, Marcelo, and Abilio Barbero. 1970. "Algunos aspectos de la feudalización del reino visigodo en relación a su organización financiera y militar." *Moneda y Crédito* 112: 71–91.

Vigil-Escalera Guirado, Alfonso. 2000. "Cabañas de época visigoda: Evidencias arqueológicas del sur de Madrid—tipología, elementos de datación y discusión." *Archivo Español de Arqueología* 73: 223–52.

———. 2007. "Granjas y aldeas altomedievales al norte de Toledo (450–800 D.C.)." *Archivo Español de Arqueología* 80: 239–84.

———. 2013. "Ver el silo medio lleno o medio vacío: La estructura arqueológica en su contexto." In *Horrea, Barns and Silos: Storage and Incomes in Early Medieval Europe*, ed. Alfonso Vigil-Escalera Guirado, Giovanna Bianchi, and Juan Antonio Quirós Castillo, 127–44. Bilbao: Universidad del País Vasco.

———. 2015. *Los primeros paisajes altomedievales en el interior de Hispania: Registros campesinos del siglo quinto d.C.* Bilbao: Universidad del País Vasco.

Vigil-Escalera Guirado, Alfonso, and Carlos Tejerizo García. 2014. "Asentamientos fortificados altomedievales en la meseta: Algunas distorsiones historiográficas." In *Las fortificaciones en la tardoantigüedad: Élites y articulación del territorio (siglos V–VIII d.C.)*, ed. Raúl Catalán, Patricia Fuentes, and José Carlos Sastre, 229–45. Madrid: Ediciones de La Ergástula.

von Rummel, Philipp. 2007. *Habitus barbarus: Kleidung und Repräsentation spätantiker Eliten im 4. und 5. Jahrhundert.* Berlin: Walter de Gruyter.

———. 2013. "The Fading Power of Images: Romans, Barbarians, and the Uses of a Dichotomy in Early Medieval Archaeology." In *Post-Roman Transitions: Christian and Barbarian Identities in the Early Medieval West*, ed. Walter Pohl and Gerda Heydemann, 365–406. Turnhout: Brepols.

Ward-Perkins, Bryan. 1998. "The Cities." In *The Cambridge Ancient History*. Vol. 13, *The Late Empire, A.D. 337–425*, ed. Averil Cameron and Peter Garnsey, 371–410. Cambridge: Cambridge University Press.

———. 2005. *The Fall of Rome and the End of Civilization*. Oxford: Oxford University Press.

Weisweiler, John. 2010. *State Aristocracy: Resident Senators and Absent Emperors in Late-Antique Rome, c. 320–400*. Doctoral dissertation, Cambridge University, Cambridge.

———. 2011. "The Price of Integration: State and Élite in Symmachus Correspondence." In *Der wiederkehrende Leviathan: Staatlichkeit und Staatswerdung in Spätantike und früher Neuzeit*, ed. Peter Eich, Sebastian Schmidt-Hofner, and Christian Wieland, 343–73. Heidelberg: Universitätsverlag Winter.

———. 2012. "From Equality to Asymmetry: Honorific Statues, Imperial Power, and Senatorial Identity in Late-Antique Rome." *Journal of Roman Archaeology* 25: 320–50.

———. 2015a. "Domesticating the Senatorial Elite: Universal Monarchy and Transregional Aristocracy in the Fourth Century AD." In *Contested Monarchy: Integrating the Roman Empire in the Fourth Century AD*, ed. Johannes Wienand, 17–41. Oxford: Oxford University Press.

———. 2015b. "Capital in the Fourth Century: Aristocratic Power, Inequality and the State in the Roman Empire." Paper delivered at the conference "Capital Before Capitalism? Wealth, Inequality, and State in the Ancient World." Buenos Aires, August 6–7.

Whittow, Mark. 1990. "Ruling the Late Roman and Early Byzantine City: A Continuous History." *Past and Present* 129: 3–29.

Wickham, Chris. 1984. "The Other Transition: From the Ancient World to Feudalism." *Past and Present* 103: 3–36.

———. 1988. "Marx, Sherlock Holmes, and Late Roman Commerce." *Journal of Roman Studies* 78: 183–93.

———. 2005. *Framing the Early Middle Ages*. Oxford: Oxford University Press.

Witschel, Christian. 2016. "Hispania, Gallia, and Raetia." In *The Last Statues of Antiquity*, ed. R.R.R. Smith and Bryan Ward-Perkins, 69–79. Oxford: Oxford University Press.

Wolfram, Mélanie. 2011. *Uma síntese sobre a cristanização do mundo rural no sul da Lusitania: Arqueologia, Arquitectura, Epigrafia*. Doctoral dissertation, Universidade de Lisboa, Lisbon.

Wood, Ian. 1998. "The Barbarian Invasions and First Settlements." In *The Cambridge Ancient History*. Vol. 13, *The Late Empire, A.D. 337–425*, ed. Averil Cameron and Peter Garnsey, 516–37. Cambridge: Cambridge University Press.

Wood, Jamie. 2012. *The Politics of Identity in Visigothic Spain: Religion and Power in the Histories of Isidore of Seville*. Leiden: Brill.

Wood, Susan. 2006. *The Proprietary Church in the Medieval West*. Oxford: Oxford University Press.

Wooding, Jonathan. 1996. *Communication and Commerce Along the Western Sealanes, AD 400–800*. Oxford: Tempvs Reparatvm.

Woolf, Greg. 1998. *Becoming Roman: The Origins of Provincial Civilization in Gaul*. Cambridge: Cambridge University Press.

Zarzalejos Prieto, María del Mar. 2005. "Comercio y distribución de cerámicas romanas en Asturias." In *Unidad y diversidad en el arco Atlántico en época romana*, ed. Carmen Fernández Ochoa and Paloma García Díaz, 163–89. Oxford: Archaeopress.

Zuiderhoek, Arjan. 2005. "The Icing on the Cake. Benefactors, Economics, and Public Building in Roman Asia Minor." In *Patterns in the Economy of Roman Asia Minor*, ed. Stephen Mitchell and Constantina Katsari, 167–86. Swansea: Classical Press of Wales.

INDEX

ACKNOWLEDGMENTS

The present book first took shape at Princeton University over a decade ago. Many years of research lie behind these pages, and, contrary to what is unfortunately a growing belief in certain circles, research in the humanities demands as much institutional and financial support as in other areas of knowledge. Thus, I would first like to acknowledge the institutions that provided me with vital funding for the research behind this book: the Group of the Study of Late Antiquity (Princeton University), the Institute for Research in the Humanities (University of Wisconsin, Madison), the Institute for the Study of the Ancient World (New York University), the Luso-American Foundation, and Northern Illinois University. I would like to thank especially the Northern Illinois University History Department; the Princeton Institute for International and Regional Studies and the Program in the Ancient World, Princeton University; and the Whiting Foundation. To all of them, I am grateful for their belief in my project and more generally for their conviction that the humanities remain important fields of human endeavor.

Parts of this book were presented and refined at different academic institutions, including Cambridge University, Institute for the Study of the Ancient World–New York University, Northern Illinois University, Princeton University, the University of Chicago, and the University of Wisconsin, Madison, where they benefited enormously from discussions with colleagues. I would like to particularly thank the wonderful cohort of visiting scholars with whom I shared my year at the Institute for the Study in the Ancient World and my equally exceptional fellow Solmsen Fellows at the Institute for Research in the Humanities. I have also been very fortunate in having excellent colleagues in Northern Illinois University's History Department, who have encouraged me for many years.

I want to express my gratitude to those colleagues who read parts of this book and offered insightful feedback: Greg Aldrete, Clifford Ando, Shane Bjornlie, Giles Bransbourg, Frank Clover, Santiago Curci, Janet Downie, John Haldon, Céline Martin, Richard Payne, Gisela Ripoll, and John Weisweiler.

Kim Bowes, Helmut Reimitz, and Brent Shaw provided me with abundant comments and suggestions that helped me frame this book at an early stage. I similarly benefited from the invaluable suggestions of Leonard Curchin and Jonathan Edmondson. I have also been inspired by personal conversations and correspondence with Scott De Brestian, Adriaan De Man, Santiago Castellanos, Valerie Garver, Anna Kaiser, Noel Lenski, Molly Lester, Ariel López, Iñaki Martín Viso, Francisco Moreno Martín, Richard Payne, Marie Roux, Brian Sandberg, Jack Tannous, José María Tejado, and John Weisweiler.

Sonia García López and José Ignacio Padilla helped me locate bibliographical material and offered their support and friendship during my numerous trips to Spain. Mariano Tellechea accompanied me on visits to several of the sites mentioned in this book, often under the blazing sun of Iberian summers. Molly Lester did a wonderful job helping me with the final edits to the manuscript. The Ancient World Mapping Services provided the maps for this volume, working sometimes under the pressure of tight deadlines. I am very grateful to all of my colleagues who supplied and authorized the use of their images.

I would like to express special thanks to two people. Clifford Ando demonstrated keen interest in my project from its very beginnings. His constant backing throughout the often arduous process of finishing my book manuscript and his generous encouragement of my research provided vital motivation. And I cannot sufficiently express my gratitude to Peter Brown, who has provided steadfast support to my research throughout the years. He has fostered, taught, and inspired me in ways too numerous to list. His intellectual and personal generosity are constant reminders of what academic life should be. To him I owe the subtitle of the Introduction, after he described an early version of the book, in one of his characteristic flights of precise poetry, as "the story of an invisible class in a silent land."

My family and friends have been an inestimable presence throughout the past few years of writing, even when they were hundreds or thousands of kilometers away. My daughter Iris was born while I was writing some of the following chapters and reminded me, when I most needed it, that there were more important things than late antique Iberian aristocrats. My partner in life, Delphine, read every single word of this book and offered priceless suggestions and comments. She forced me to examine the relationship between arcane late antique topics and our contemporary world, pointing to the relevance of my work at times I could not see it. Above all, I felt her constant and loving presence during those challenging moments of writing when I was, as it were, invisible and silent.